East–West Relations in the 1990s
The Naval Dimension

Studies in Contemporary Maritime Policy and Strategy
Edited by Professor Geoffrey Till, Royal Naval College,
Greenwich

East–West Relations in the 1990s

The Naval Dimension

Edited by John Pay and Geoffrey Till

Pinter Publishers, London

© John Pay, Geoffrey Till and Contributors, 1990

First published in Great Britain in 1990 by
Pinter Publishers Limited
25 Floral Street, London WC2E 9DS

British Library Cataloguing in Publication Data

A CIP catalogue record for this book is available from the British Library
ISBN 0 86187 0379

Typeset by Selectmove, London
Printed and bound in Great Britain by Biddles Ltd.

Contents

Part III: The European Dimension

List of Figures and Tables

FIGURES

TABLES

List of contributors

A.D. Baker is the Editor of *Combat Fleets of the World* and contributing editor to the USNI *Proceedings*. He is the author of numerous articles on current naval policy.

Christopher N. Donnelly is the Director of the Soviet Studies Research Centre, Royal Military Academy Sandhurst. His most recent book is *Red Banner* (London: Jane's, 1988).

Admiral Sir James Eberle became Director of the Royal Institute of International Affairs in January 1984 and is Chairman of the Editorial Advisory Board of *Naval Forces*.

Jonathan Eyal is the Assistant Director (Studies) at the Royal United Services Institute, London. He has written widely on Soviet and East European Affairs, his most recent book being, *Warsaw Pact Military Expenditure* (London: Jane's, 1988).

Peter Frank is Senior Lecturer in Soviet Government and Politics in the Department of Government at the University of Essex. In addition to numerous articles on contemporary Soviet politics, he co-authored, *The Soviet Communist Party* (London: Allen & Unwin, 1987).

Lawrence Freedman is Professor and Head of the Department of War Studies at King's College London. Amongst his many books are, *Britain and the Falklands War* (London: Basil Blackwell, 1988).

Norman Friedman is an independent consultant and author of a large number of books and articles on naval affairs, most recently, *The U.S. Maritime Strategy* (London: Jane's, 1989).

Eric Grove is Naval Research Director for the Foundation for International Security. He has written widely on all aspects of naval policy, his most recent book being, *The Future of Sea Power* (London: Croom Helm, 1990).

Rear-Admiral J.R. Hill is Under Treasurer of the Middle Temple, London and the author of a number of books including, *Arms Control at Sea* (London: Routledge, 1989).

John Jordan is a freelance naval consultant, and author of many articles on current naval policy.

Lawrence S. Kaplan is the Director of the Lyman L. Lemnitzer Center for NATO Studies, Kent State University, Kent, Ohio. Among his most recent books is *NATO and the United States: An enduring alliance* (1988).

Edward A. Kolodziej is Research Professor of Political Science and Director, Project on European Arms Control and Security at the University of Illinois at Urbana-Champaign. His most recent book is *Making and Marketing Arms: The French experience and its implications for the international system* (Princeton University Press, 1987).

Vice-Admiral Sir Ian McGeoch, an ex-Flag Officer Submarines, was formerly the Editor of the *Naval Review*.

Vice-Admiral Metcalf retired from active naval service in the US Navy in November 1987. He is the author of a number of articles on current issues of maritime strategy.

William Park is a Principal Lecturer in the Department of History and International Affairs at the RN College Greenwich. His most recent book is *The Defence of the West* (Hemel Hempstead: Harvester Wheatsheaf, 1986).

John Pay is a Senior Lecturer in the Department of History at the RN College Greenwich and has produced a doctorate and several articles on US naval policy.

Phillip A. Petersen is currently in the Policy Support Programs Staff in the Office of the Deputy Under Secretary of Defense for Policy. His publications have appeared in a wide range of books and journals.

Bryan Ranft was formerly Professor of History at the RN College Greenwich and Senior Research Fellow at the Department of War Studies, King's College London. He has written widely on maritime issues and co-authored, *The Sea in Soviet Strategy* (London: Macmillan, 1989).

Cdr J.J.A.A. van Rooyen, Royal Netherlands Navy, is currently serving in the Naval Staff Plans/Policy of the Minstry of Defence in The Hague.

Geoffrey Till is the Professor of the Department of History and International Affairs at the RN College Greenwich. Among his books is the co-authored, *The Sea in Soviet Strategy* (London: Macmillan, 1989).

Robert G. Weinland is an independent naval analyst and author of numerous articles, most especially on aspects of Soviet naval power.

Phil Williams is now a member of the Department of Politics at the University of Pittsburg. His most recent publication is *Nuclear Weapons in Europe in the 1990s* (London: Chatham House, 1989).

List of abbreviations

AAAM	Advanced air-to-air missile
AAW	Anti-air warfare
ABM	Anti-ballistic missile
ACM	Advanced course missile
AIWS	Advanced interdiction weapon system (Stand-off bomb)
ALCM	Air-launched cruise missile
AMRAAM	Advanced medium range air-to-air missile
ASAT	Anti-satellite weapons
ASCM	Anti-ship cruise missile
ASM	Air-to-surface missile
ASRAM	Advanced short range air-to-air missile
ASROC	Anti-submarine rocket
ATB	Advanced technology bomber
ASTOR	Anti-submarine torpedo
ASUW	Anti-surface warfare
ASW	Anti-submarine warfare
ATA	Advanced technology aircraft
ATACMS	Advanced tactical missile system
ATF	Advanced tact fighter
ATGW	Anti tank guided weapon
AWACS	Airborne warning and control system
AWST	*Aviation Week and Space Technology*
BMD	Ballistic missile defence
C^{3}I	Command, control, communications and intelligence
CAPTOR	Encapsulated torpedo
CBM	Confidence building measure
CCD	Conference of the Committee on Disarmament
CD	Conference on Disarmament
CDE	Conference on Confidence and Security Building and Disarmament in Europe (Stockholm Conference)
CEP	Circular error probable
CFE	(negotiation on) Conventional (Armed) Forces in Europe
CG	Guided missile cruiser
CIA	Central Intelligence Agency
CIC	Combat Information Centre
CINCEASTLANT	Commander-in-Chief Eastern Atlantic (NATO)
CINCHAN	Commander-in-Chief Channel (NATO)

CM	Cruise missile
CNO	Chief of Naval Operations (US)
CNS	Chiefs of Naval Staff (NATO)
CO	Commanding officer
COMNAVBALTAP	Commander Naval Forces, Baltic Approaches (NATO)
COMNAVSOUTH	Commander Naval Forces South (NATO)
CSBM	Confidence and security building measure
CSCE	Conference on Security and Co-operation in Europe
CV	Aircraft carrier
CVBG	Aircraft-carrier (aviation) battle group
CVN	Nuclear propelled aircraft carrier
DDG	Guided missile destroyers
DOD	Department of Defense (US)
DPC	Defence Planning Committee (NATO)
EC	European Community
ECM	Electronic counter measures
EEZ	Exclusive economic zone
ENDC	Eighteen-Nation Disarmament Committee
FEBA	Forward edge of the battle area
FFG	Guided missile frigate
FOFA	Follow-on forces attack
FRAS	Free rocket anti-submarine
FROD	Functionally related observable difference
GDR	German Democratic Republic
GIUK	Greenland–Iceland–United Kingdom (Gap)
GLCM	Ground-launched cruise missile
GNP	Gross National Product
ICBM	Intercontinental ballistic missile
INF	Intermediate nuclear forces
IRBM	Intermediate range ballistic missile
JCS	Joint Chiefs of Staff (US)
JDW	*Jane's Defence Weekly* (journal)
JSTARS	Joint surveillance and target acquisition radar system
LRCCM	Long range conventional cruise missile
MBFR	Mutual balanced force reductions
MCM	Mine counter measures
MIRV	Multiple independently targetable re-entry vehicle
MLRS	Multiple launch rocket system
MOD	Modification
MPA	Maritime patrol aircraft
MPS	Multiple protective structure – basing mode for MX
MX	A long-range, in service US ICBM
NATO	North Atlantic Treaty Organization
NCA	National Command Authority
NCS	National Security Council
NCND	Neither confirm nor deny
NSNW	Non-strategic nuclear weapon
NST	Nuclear and Space Talks

OPCON	Operational control
PAL	Permissive action link
PDMA	Prevention of Dangerous Military Activities (Agreement)
POMCUS	Prepositioned overseas material configured in unit sets
PVO	Soviet Air Defence Command
R&D	Research and development
RDF	Rapid Deployment Force
SAC	Strategic Air Command
SACEUR	Supreme Allied Commander Europe
SADARM	Seek and destroy armor
SALT	Strategic Arms Limitation Talks
SAM	Surface-to-air missile
SCN	Ship construction naval
SDI	Strategic Defence Initiative
SIOP	Single Integrated Operational Plan
SLBM	Submarine-launched ballistic missile
SLCM	Sea-launched cruise missile
SLEP	Service Lift Extension Program
SLOC	Sea line(s) of communication
SNA	Soviet naval aviation
SNF	Short range nuclear forces
SOSUS	Sound Surveillance System (US)
SOSS	Soviet Ocean Surveillance System
SRINF	Short range intermediate nuclear forces
SSBN	Nuclear-powered ballistic missile (strategic) submarine
SSGN	Guided missile armed nuclear-propelled submarine
SSK	Diesel-propelled submarine
SSM	Surface-to-surface missile
SSN	Nuclear-powered attack submarine
START	Strategic Arms Reduction Talks
SUBROC	Submarine rocket
TNF	Theatre nuclear forces
UNCLOS	United Nations Convention on the Law of the Sea
URG	Underway replenishment group
USN	US Navy
VLS	Vertical launch system
V/STOL	Vertical/short take-off and landing
WTO	Warsaw Treaty Organization

1 Introduction

1989 was a remarkable year. It was significant for many things, among them the fortieth anniversary of the foundation of NATO and the seventy-fifth anniversary of the foundation of the Royal Naval Staff College at the Royal Naval College Greenwich. To commemorate both of these events it was decided to hold a large international conference at Greenwich to look forward to the naval future. It is hard to think of a more suitable or historic location in which to discuss some large maritime theme, and so we decided to address the issue of East–West relations in the 1990s, focusing particularly on their naval dimension.

Assessing the nature and significance of the future maritime balance is no easy task, especially given the current rate of change in Eastern Europe. But even if we were living through more normal times, the problem for naval planners is compounded by an unavoidable mismatch between the quality of help available from the foreign policy community in outlining its future programme and requirements and the long lead time associated with the procurement of weapon systems and general force planning. As far as navies are concerned, Admiral Sir James Eberle some years ago put the matter very well:

In my country it is said that in the military sphere, the Ministry of Defence is dealing with horizons for developing equipment of between 5 and 15 years. That is the long term. The short term is perhaps not more than 5 years. Now in the Foreign Office in Whitehall, their short-term time-scale is what is happening today; and their long time-scale is what is happening tomorrow! So I think we must recognise this very clear difference in time horizon.

When we come to look to what sort of ships or what sort of equipment we need to develop we have to look long periods ahead; and we first turn to our political authorities and say 'Please, I now want to know what sort of world we are going to have in 10 to 15 years time. And unless you give me an answer, I cannot decide what sort of forces we need.' We are asking, I am afraid, an impossible question. In political terms I don't believe we shall get the sort of answers we are looking for and I don't believe we should expect them. . . . What is certain about the future is that we don't know what it is going to be.

This constant failure to get coherent long-term political direction encourages the military planner to produce unspecific and general-purpose forces:

What then are we to do? I believe that we have to look much more to planning force structures to provide for our political authorities the maximum number of military options. So that we have a big 'piano' on which we try to provide as many keys as possible so that political authorities can press them to make the tune which they require.[1]

This problem may be particularly acute for sailors for two reasons. First, their major weapon systems have often to last even longer than their army and airforce equivalents. The naval constructors of the New York Navy Yard would have been surprised rather than amazed to learn that the ship they laid down as the *Iowa* in June 1940 would still be a major asset of the US Navy 50 years later, because this is only an extreme example of the norm. In the Royal Navy, the life of a destroyer is expected to be 22 years and of a frigate 20–8 years. The US Navy's destroyers and frigates are likewise expected to last some 30 years, its carriers 45, its nuclear-propelled submarines 30.

Secondly, sea power is, much more often than not, a dependent variable, the form and success of which are crucially influenced by the details of scenario in which it operates. Also, arguably, bluewater navies need to be able to cope with a far wider range of possible war and peacetime scenarios than their army and air force counterparts. Moreover, their own experience tells them that they frequently end up doing things they had neither expected nor trained for. In the Second World War, for instance, navies on all sides only really discovered their functions when the fighting started. The British, for example, found themselves heavily engaged in oceanic ASW operations and in amphibious warfare, for neither of which had they prepared in peacetime. Once again, in 1982, the Royal Navy, then above all a navy dedicated to ASW tasks in the NATO area, had rapidly to develop the capacity for amphibious operations on the other side of the world. For both these reasons, sailors resist being tied down to one scenario lest it unsuit them for another and prefer to rely instead on the inherent flexibility of seapower to provide the necessary options.

The sailor's instinctive aversion to the specific, his preference for what Robert Komer calls 'parametric planning', and his almost mystical faith in the capacity of a first-rate balanced fleet to cope with virtually anything, can be distinctly irritating to the unsympathetic.[2]

This necessary woolliness, moreover, makes sailors vulnerable in financial regimes where payment (or the allocation of resources) is by observable and measurable result whether actual or anticipated. Sceptics sometimes argue that navies ought to concentrate more on improving the quality of their prophecy rather than on trying to develop the flexibility that allows them to cope with its failures. The sailors' reluctance to articulate the functions of seapower is sometimes interpreted as a tacit admission that it has none, or fewer than it did.

The second problem to be faced in attempting to look at the future naval balance derives from the fact that, in comparing East and West, we are comparing chalk and cheese so far as the maritime dimension is concerned. One of the clearest declarations that NATO Europe is a fundamentally maritime place comes, rather unexpectedly, in the midst of the 1983 Defence White Paper of the Federal Republic of Germany:

NATO is an alliance of maritime orientation, much more so than seen in the Central European perspective. It is an alliance spanning the North Atlantic. Its leading power, the United States, is both an Atlantic and a Pacific power. Owing to the situation of the North American continent between two oceans, the weight and prestige of the United States depend on its determination and ability to bridge oceans and to protect its overseas allies.

This implies an essential geostrategic disadvantage for the West: Western Europe is separated from the strategic reserves of NATO's leading power, the United States by some 6,000 kilometres of Atlantic Ocean.

But European NATO territory as such has also a strongly maritime orientation. West Europe is a heavily broken peninsula-like appendix to the Eurasian land mass, bordering on maritime areas in the North, West and South. In this general topography, numerous individual countries in turn are of peninsular character. In fact, almost all the European NATO countries border on seas, some of them having coastlines of considerable length. A number of these countries are by tradition sea powers operating and recognised as such worldwide.[3]

It follows from all this that Western Europe has certain obvious and irreducible maritime requirements which must be met if it is to prevail against threats to its security. The most fundamental of these is that the seas which wash its shores must not be controlled by a hostile power for if they were it would be far more difficult for Western Europe to defend itself against all forms of sea-based attack and to use the sea as a means of transporting soldiers and equipment to wherever they are needed. If Europe were ever to become a peninsula stuck out into a hostile sea, it would not survive.

In peacetime as well, the simple facts of geography mean Western prosperity depends on the sea, for it is by sea that Western Europe trades with the world, and international trade is much more important to its economic health than is the case for most other countries, the United States and the Soviet Union included. 'In peace and war alike', the White Paper concludes, 'Western Europe has to rely on external and overseas energy and natural resources and intact sea lines of communication',[4] and this is held to apply especially to the Federal Republic itself.

While none of this is very new, the extent to which Western Europe depends on the sea is often forgotten. Although exact figures are hard to come by, well over half, measured by weight, of the trade of nearly all West European countries is carried by sea; in many cases, such as Britain, Portugal, Greece and the Netherlands, the proportion is far higher. Moreover, in some key types of trade, such as crude oil for example, the seaborne percentage is very high indeed. Europe's well-known dependence on vital strategic materials like cobalt, chromium, manganese and so forth is also a dependence on the medium by which it is principally conveyed. More generally, European countries conduct some 45 per cent of world seaborne trade and 27 per cent of all the world's trade passes through European ports.

Navalists often overlook the fact that sea dependence, as all this illustrates, is not usually a matter of choice and is as much a source of weakness as it is of strength since a resourceful adversary would doubtless seek to exploit the vulnerabilities dependency creates.

Although in the era of President Gorbachev, the Soviet Union looks a good deal less threatening to Western Europe than it once did, it would be imprudent entirely to dismiss the need to take due precautions. Such an assumption having been made, one of the most striking changes of the past two decades or so has been the emergence of the Soviet Union as a first-class maritime power.

This is especially significant because, in the past, geography has been a considerable disadvantage to Russian navalists. It has always been difficult for Russian sailors even to reach the sea, and such success as they have had in this has usually been more the product of the efforts of their army colleagues than their own. The sheer size and position of the Soviet Union has also made most places it might want to reach accessible by land, and this clearly reduces incentives to construct the capacity to do so by water. Finally, the Soviet Union is one of the few powers in the world with what is still basically an autarchic economy and which can find virtually all the minerals it needs from within its own borders. Seapower is, therefore, a good deal less 'natural' for the Soviet Union than it is for Western Europe, and this, no doubt, helps explain why the Soviet Navy is so often portrayed in the same light as the High Sea Fleet before the First World War – something which is 'unfair, underhand and damned unRussian'.

This is not to say that the Soviet Union has no legitimate maritime requirements because, of course, it has. But even if Admiral Amelko is right to stress the 'markedly defensive functions of the Soviet Navy',[5] these functions require the Soviet Union to control precisely the same seas which Western Europe needs for its strategic survival. This is largely a function of geographic proximity. While it may be entirely understandable for the Soviet Union to seek to push its forward defensive frontier into and beyond the Greenland–Iceland–United Kingdom (GIUK) gap – so as best to be able to defend its territory and naval assets from attack – this action, in itself, threatens the security of countries behind wherever the Soviet Navy seeks to draw the line, and most of Western Europe could easily fall into this category.

In some ways, the situation is analogous to what it was before the First World War. In order to feel safe, Britain then needed to control the seas of northern Europe but, though entirely understandable, this aspiration was bound to increase Germany's sense of vulnerability, especially when relations between the two countries were bad. Although it may matter only in times of tension, the fact that Western Europe and the Soviet Union are potentially antagonistic at sea in this way means that West Europeans will need to take the implications of the growth of Soviet seapower very seriously.

Before the Soviet Union was a first-class sea power, Western sailors could rely on an impressive margin of overall superiority that would make it possible for them to cater for nearly all contingencies, and which reduced their incentives to worry about priorities and the sequence of anticipated operations. But now, since the Soviet Union is in a much better position to interfere with what the West might seek to do at sea, Western navies have to make choices. Admiral Lee Baggett, then the US Navy's Director of Naval Warfare made just this point in 1982 when arguing before Congress for a 600-ship navy:

It [a 600-ship navy] would enable us to more closely meet the commitments we have without having to worry, as we do now, about trade-offs. Will we deploy carrier battle groups to the Indian Ocean first, or will we pose a threat to the Soviet homeland in the Northern Pacific first? Will we deploy carrier battle groups to the North Atlantic or will we worry about the Mediterranean first?[6]

Making such choices sensibly, and preparing for their consequences requires an overall view of the role of seapower in the defence of Western Europe. The rise of the Soviet Navy has done two things. It has changed the general strategic situation and it has concentrated naval minds on the need to think about such matters as 'prioritization in sequential operations', to borrow one of Admiral Baggett's less felicitous phrases.

This was also the inspiration for the US Navy's 'Maritime Strategy' which first appeared in public in January 1986.[7] Since then this strategy has been the focus of considerable interest and some criticism.[8] The philosophy behind the strategy and its operational implications are dealt with at length later in this book but it is worth bearing some of the criticisms in mind as well. These have been most trenchantly expressed by Robert Komer. In his view the Maritime Strategy represents too big a shift in strategy towards the sea:

My deep concern is that the United States might be drifting in practice toward an unbalanced maritime strategy and posture at the expense of other equally pressing needs, and that this will not only undermine our alliances but will lead to disaster in case of a major non-nuclear war.[9]

In Komer's view, the stress on the US Navy characteristic of the Reagan Administration led to its getting the lion's share of the defence budget and this had seriously imperilled the United States' capacity to counter Soviet threats to Western security. The problem as he saw it in 1984 was that there had been a fundamental shift in the military balance such that, 'the USSR's capacity to attack conventionally in the NATO, China/Japan/Korea or Persian Gulf theater has grown more rapidly than have Western defensive capabilities. In the crucial European theater NATO has at best "only a delayed tripwire" defence.' Soviet air and sea forces notwithstanding, this was an essentially air/land threat.

Even if all Soviet home and overseas naval bases were put out of action, and Soviet naval and merchant vessels swept from the high seas, this would not suffice to prevent Moscow from seizing or dominating the rimlands of Eurasia, including the two industrial agglomerations of Europe and Japan, and cutting off their economic lifeblood – Middle East oil.[10]

Simply by projecting its air/land power outwards, the Soviet Union could engulf all the resources of the Eurasian landmass and so dominate the world. Moreover, as a landpower, the Soviet Union is largely impervious to Western maritime attack and so, 'A predominantly maritime strategy would offer little hope of being able to prevent a decisive shift in the balance of power against the United States and any remaining allies.'[11] Worse, the ultimately vain attempt to make the Soviet Union significantly vulnerable to sea power threatens to absorb so many defence resources that it would fundamentally undermine the effectiveness of the ground and air forces of the alliance, and thereby make the situation even worse than it was before.

This would also be the effect of the American unilateralism that so clearly underlies the Maritime Strategy. Whether it consciously means to or not, argues Komer, the US Navy seeks to reduce the United States' dependence on possibly unreliable allies and to enhance its capacity for independent action in support of national interests. Thus Admiral Stansfield Turner in 1984:

We then come to the defense of Western Europe. Here our posture is more precarious: the balance of conventional forces in the European theater continues to tilt against us. However, this imbalance cannot be corrected by the United States; it can only be done in conjunction with our European allies. Until they make a greater effort in manpower and resources in their own defense, it would be foolish for us to step up our military contribution. Hence, I view this as a low priority for the time being.[12]

But, says Komer, the naval unilateralism that so permeates such views as these is ultimately self-defeating because the United States needs its allies for economic and strategic reasons and a strategy that weakens the West's capacity for coalition warfare will doom it to defeat. Instead Komer advocates a strategy which focuses on the central struggle for control of land and urges that the size and shape of the US and other navies be tailored so that it best supports the ground and air forces of the Western alliance in this endeavour. How well the Maritime Strategy survives this kind of operational, political and strategic criticism will be crucial to the US Navy's prospects and, therefore, to the future of the naval balance between East and West.

The nature of that balance is also much affected by the fact that it involves comparison between two quite different phenomena: the United States is a maritime power; the Soviet Union is a landpower with a large navy. Although, as we have seen, being maritime means having unique kinds and degrees of vulnerability, the navies of maritime powers are usually reasonably assured of their position in the scheme of things, even in an era of budgetary constraint.

The Soviet Navy, though, faces a more uncertain future. Under President Gorbachev's strategic concept of Defensive Sufficiency, all the Soviet services are likely to enter an era of constraint, and it is hardly likely that the Soviet Navy will be exempted from this process. Here the debate is about how far this restraint will go and what form it will take.

But the East–West balance at sea is not merely a function of the navies of the superpowers, but of those of the Europeans as well. Here too we face a decade in which there will certainly be economic and demographic constraints. On the one hand, the West Europeans may face a less menacing future; on the other they may find themselves less assured of maritime support from the other side of the Atlantic.

The burden of this book, therefore, will be to deal with the problems and prospects of the world's major navies as we move into a new decade. Geography is a good base to the discussion. A glance at a map shows that there is a good deal of sea, that it is nearly all connected and mostly surrounded by land either closely or distantly. This means that events in the seas around the coasts of Western Europe will be heavily influenced by developments in other parts of what the Russians call the World Ocean and, even more so, by developments ashore. Navies, therefore, operate in, and are much constrained by, an international environment which largely determines what they do and what they do it with. In this volume we will consider the changing strategic environment and seek to explore where it will take the world's major navies.

But it is also important to remember the claims that sailors make. They do not portray themselves as passive victims of circumstance, but as actors on the world scene. Their policies and activities have an influence on the outcome of events; were this not so, then navies would indeed become wasting assets. In short, the connections between the strategic environment and the evolution of naval power are a two-way process. Navies still seem to matter and so will the relationship between them in the coming decade.

In this book we have addressed a number of issues. In the first section we will consider the foreign and defence policies of the superpowers. First, there is the question of the development and influence of the political and strategic context. The pace of events in Eastern Europe is so commanding that in this book we will begin with the Soviet Union. International politics over the past few years, and especially since Gorbachev's United Nations speech of 7 December 1988, has been dominated by speculation about the motives and the effects of the Gorbachev revolution. In the first chapter we will address the issue of President Gorbachev's prospects and in Chapters 4 and 5 the kind of threat, if any, his country could pose the West in the 1990s.

In less dramatic times, the trend of events in the United States would have commanded equal attention. The shape of US foreign, economic and strategic policy in the next few years looks more uncertain than it has at any other time since 1945. This too we will consider, in Chapters 6 and 7.

Having addressed these general environmental issues, we will deal in the second section of this book with the strategic concepts currently animating the two superpower navies. In both cases we will then take a closer look at their problems, prospects and programmes for the future. We will round this section off by analysing in Chapters 14 and 15 the extent to which it is reasonable to hope that arms control processes will effect a major transformation of the security relationship between East and West in the 1990s – especially at sea.

In the third section of the book, we will tackle the third and final theme by exploring how all of this might affect NATO and European security in the 1990s. Will this crisis be like all the others which have in the past seemed likely to lead to the dismantling of the alliance but which in the event did not? Or, this time, are radical changes really and finally at hand? Finally, we will attempt to see how these superpower issues will affect Europe and the navies of Europe.

As we have already remarked, the chapters in this book are the product of the conference we held at Greenwich in February 1989. But of course events through the rest of that year have been quite startling and have carried the world a good deal further than most of us would have foreseen at the time. As editors we were faced with something of a dilemma. One option was to present the papers, the commentaries and our report of the reactions to them as they were at the time and as a kind of historic record frozen in the past. Another option would have been to rewrite everything along the lines of what would have been said had we all known then what we all know now. Needless to say, perhaps, we have instead attempted a compromise between the two. In the main what follows in this book is a record of what was said at the time; it seems to us that our contributors largely got it right. However, where it seemed necessary to us to incorporate later material because it allowed us to carry the argument on one stage further, then we have done so. In most cases it will be obvious where we have succumbed to this temptation. Our experience in putting this book together suggests that this technique will become increasingly common if the pace of events on the world scene remains as fast as it was in the last half of 1989.

It should not be assumed that the Editors, the Royal Naval College Greenwich, the Ministry of Defence or any other body or persons, necessarily agree with all or any of the ideas expressed in the book. Contributors are responsible for the ideas expressed in their own sections only. We would like to thank them all for their performance during the Conference and for their patience and good humour since.

The Conference was co-hosted by the Royal Naval Staff College and the Department of History and International Affairs at the RN College Greenwich. We very much appreciate the support and enthusiasm of Commodore Jeremy Blackham, then Commodore of the RNSC, at every stage of this project. The whole thing was also made possible by the bureaucratic skills and general persuasiveness of Captain Gordon Wilson, Head of Defence Studies (RN) to whom we were, and remain, very grateful. The administrative burden of the Conference was borne, in the main, by Commander Sam Prather, US Navy and his doughty team. Commander Prather is now commanding a new US Navy frigate in the Pacific, an altogether simpler task.

But as in the case of all conference books, the amount of typing and secretarial work required before, during and after the event was prodigious. We would like to acknowledge with real gratitude the help of Kathy Mason and John Gwyther of the Department of History and International Affairs and of Jean Whitta and the Typing Pool at the Royal Naval College Greenwich. Finally we would like to thank our departmental colleagues and our families for putting up with us during the whole enterprise.

John Pay,
Geoffrey Till,
Department of History and International Affairs,
Royal Naval College,
Greenwich

NOTES AND REFERENCES

1. In J.H. Veldman and F.T. Olivier, *West-European Navies and the Future* (Den Helder: R. Neth Naval College, 1980), pp. 134–5.
2. Robert Komer, *Maritime Strategy or Coalition Defense?* (Cambridge, Mass.: Abt Books, 1984).
3. Defence White Paper of the Federal Republic of Germany (Bonn: 1983), p. 40.
4. Ibid.
5. Admiral N.N. Amelko, article in *Narodna Armiya*, 14 June 1983 and 'The Soviet Fleet: Offensive or defensive?', *Naval Forces*, no. IV: 1984.
6. Admiral Lee Baggett, testimony before House Armed Services Committee, Seapower Subcommittee, Hearings for FY 1983, March 1982, p. 66.
7. See the special supplement to the *Proceedings* of the USNI, January 1986. For a full treatment of the strategy see Norman Friedman, *The US Maritime Strategy* (London: Tri-Service Press, 1988).
8. See Komer, op. cit., and John Mearsheimer, 'A strategic misstep', *International Security*, Fall 1986.
9. Komer, op cit., p. xvii.
10. Ibid., pp. 14, 67.
11. Ibid., p. 67.
12. Stansfield Turner, 'A strategy for the 90s' *New York Times Magazine*, 6 May 1984.

Part I

Foreign and Defence Policy of the Superpowers

2 Internal constraints on Soviet security policy
Peter Frank

The appointment of Mikhail Gorbachev as General Secretary of the Communist Party of the Soviet Union (CPSU) in March 1985 and his emergence as a statesman of world stature have presented a disturbing challenge to the West. Accustomed to dealing with hidebound, ailing Soviet leaderships, Western politicians are now having to cope with a man who is relatively youthful, imaginative, determined, intelligent and extremely adept at exploiting the mass media.

Mrs Thatcher, the British prime minister, was the first Western leader to recognise that Mr Gorbachev was of a different ilk to his predecessors. Now, every contender for nomination to run for the US presidency goes out of his way to suggest that it is he who is best able to match Gorbachev's skills in managing the superpower relationship. Too often, however, the challenge posed by Gorbachev is characterized in terms of his personal attributes. These are considerable; but excessive concentration upon them tends to divert attention away from even more important questions. Why, for example, was it necessary to engage in 'new political thinking'? What are the reasons for *perestroika*; what is its goal; and, by when is that goal to be attained? Does Gorbachev's persistent claim that the new political thinking arises out of domestic considerations mark a radical departure in Soviet foreign policy, or is it merely a device to enable the Soviet Union to resolve its internal problems before resuming its traditional foreign policy? And, lastly, what precisely *is* the relationship between Soviet domestic and foreign policy?

By the early 1980s, the USSR had degenerated into a state of incipient crisis. The decline in the growth rate was such that the economy was approaching stagnation. The scientific and technological gap between Western industrialized states and the USSR was widening. Society was in the grip of inertia.

Although in themselves extremely serious, these negative features were the symptoms of a malaise, and not its cause: the real threat to social and political stability derived not primarily from economic factors; it lay, rather, in the realm of morality. The USSR had become a society in which speculation and corruption were widespread, where lying and deceit were commonplace, and from which compassion had virtually disappeared. Crime was increasing alarmingly, including organized crime. Alcoholism and drunkenness had reached epidemic proportions, which in turn contributed to an uncommonly high divorce rate, attendant family breakdown, rising infant mortality and, alone among developed nations, declining life expectancy. Decaying social services, an acute housing problem and general environmental degradation made matters worse. Confidence in the Communist Party had eroded to an alarming degree; and, most worrying of all, a gripping sense of social injustice was spreading among the masses. By late 1984, with Chernenko still in office, Gorbachev was guardedly, yet publicly, voicing concern about the risk of political instability if order were not quickly restored.[1]

The extreme gravity of the crisis demanded an urgent remedy. Immediately upon his appointment as General Secretary, Gorbachev launched a campaign to accelerate (*uskoryat'*) scientific and technological innovation and thus, it was hoped, stimulate economic growth. However, it soon became clear that rapid acceleration would not occur unless a multitude of other problems was tackled; and it was out of this realization that there grew the idea of a thoroughgoing restructuring (*perestroika*) of all aspects of Soviet life – social, political, moral, economic.

The main components of *perestroika* are by now well known. Acceleration requires a release of resourcefulness, innovativeness and initiative – qualities that will flourish only in a political environment in which *glasnost'* (openness) and *demokratizatsiya* are guaranteed. In addition, radical economic reform is necessary in order to overcome the negative effects of a system that has outlived its capacity to meet society's increasingly complex needs. The intention is to achieve the highest world levels of social productivity in the shortest possible time.

It is a goal that is beguilingly simple to express. Yet, given the huge discrepancies in productivity between the USSR and other advanced industrial countries, the magnitude of the task is immense. It also raises the question of the time-scale involved: what is meant by 'the shortest possible time'? On this point, Gorbachev is not explicit; but the answer, initially, appeared to be, by the year 2000. Why 2000? In that year – a convenient symbolic watershed – Gorbachev will have been in office for fifteen years and will be approaching the age of 70. Much more significantly, 2000 is the year that marks the culmination of a rolling programme of three five-year plans.

This brief analysis of recent political developments is relatively uncontroversial. But once an attempt is made to draw inferences from it and to speculate about future Soviet behaviour, opinion divides sharply.

One view is hostile to Gorbachev's innovations. In broad terms, it accepts the foregoing analysis, but argues that the 'new political thinking' does not represent a fundamental change in Soviet long-term goals, claiming instead that it is a ploy to lull the West into a false sense of security while the USSR solves its internal crisis and gathers strength before once more reverting to its customary, belligerent, expansionist patterns of behaviour. Such a view was argued vigorously and cogently by Lord Chalfont in *The Times*:[2]

In the deceptive glow from the artificial lights of summitry, the West ought to contemplate a sombre proposition. If Gorbachev fails, he will be succeeded by a leadership which will ruthlessly exploit any weakness in the West which his diplomacy has opened up. If he succeeds we shall be faced with an adversary whose basic foreign policy remains substantially unchanged, who will be better placed to pursue that foreign policy by the threat of armed force and who will be immeasurably more effective and self-confident.

Another view suggests a quite different outcome. It claims that the 'new political thinking' represents a genuine, permanent change of attitude. If *perestroika* succeeds, the argument goes, material affluence in the USSR will lead to a growing sense of contentment and well-being among the population which in turn will be reflected in the rising self-confidence of the political leadership which, as it rids itself of its long-standing inferiority complex, will be disinclined to put social and political stability at risk by re-engaging in an arms race or by behaving adventuristically in international relations.

There is also a third variant, very close to the second, which might be described as the 'sceptically optimistic' view, according to which *perestroika* will lead to limited domestic improvement, sufficient to secure political stability, and enough to narrow the scientific-technological gap somewhat; but that the gap will remain sufficiently wide as to act as a restraint upon any temptation to behave aggressively in the conduct of international relations.

What is so striking about these two diametrically opposite views is that, although each projects a fundamentally different outcome, both derive from the same empirical premise. In other words, each forecast stems not from a different set of 'facts', but, rather, from differing hopes, prejudices or perceptions of Soviet ideology and political behaviour. Moreover, as well as sharing a common empirical basis, both views hold two assumptions in common. The first is that *perestroika*, as defined by Gorbachev, will be successful; and the second is that Gorbachev will remain in office for at least as long as is necessary to ensure that *perestroika* becomes irreversible. Obviously, to a considerable degree, these assumptions are interdependent.

Four years into a fifteen-year programme is not a good vantage-point from which to assess the fortunes of *perestroika*, much less at a moment when Gorbachev seems to be meeting stiff resistance from deeply entrenched bureaucratic interests and is also having to cope with potentially destabilising unrest among several of the non-Russian nationalities of the USSR. What can be said, however, is that, since coming to office Gorbachev has succeeded in fashioning a Politburo that shares his perception of the nature and gravity of the crisis, and which also endorses the proposed remedy, *perestroika*. But where the consensus risks breaking down is over the issues of the pace of reconstruction and the degree to which *glasnost'* and *demokratizatsiya* should be encouraged. Also, although the Politburo and Secretariat are in broad agreement with the General Secretary's programme, the much larger Central Committee appears to be much less enthusiastic about it.

In the short term, progress may be measured according to the degree of personnel change, improvements in social services, and the fluctuating fortunes of those in the media who are trying to extend further the boundaries of revelation and debate. In the end, however, the success or failure of *perestroika* will be judged according to whether or not it manages to attain its overall objective, namely, to move from stagnation to at least economic parity with the West by 2000 – now only eleven years hence.

The goal of closing the West–East productivity gap by the year 2000 depends upon each of the three five-year plans between now and the end of the century being fulfilled, with the success of each year's plan being contingent upon the success of the previous year's plan, so that, cumulatively, the fulfilment of each five-year plan is conditional upon the fulfilment of the plan that went before it. In other words, these are not three discrete, free-standing plans; but, rather, a single, interdependent, rolling programme.

According to this scheme, the current twelfth five-year plan (1986–90) will prepare the ground for rapid economic growth. Then, having by 1990 broken away from the force of inertia, the thirteenth five-year plan (1991–5) must achieve a qualitative breakthrough leading to further acceleration in the rate of economic growth. On this basis, it is envisaged that the fourteenth five-year plan (1996–2000) will be characterised by very rapid growth leading to a qualitative transformation of the economy and thus, by the year 2000, the attainment of the highest world level of social productivity.

It is impossible to imagine the realization of this ambitious project unless there is a major reallocation of resources – human, financial, production facilities, raw materials – from the military sector of the economy to the civilian. Likewise, it is difficult to see how there could be such a shift so long as the old-style, Soviet political thinking prevails. Hence the advent of the 'new political thinking' (*novoe politicheskoe myshlenie*), which is founded on the premises that countries of differing economic and social systems have differing *legitimate* interests; that the world – and, therefore, the states in it – are interdependent; that nuclear war is inconceivable (the principal agreement to emerge from the Geneva Summit); and that the superpowers should aim for 'sufficiency' in defence. The corollary to the new thinking is disarmament.

It is at this juncture that the linkage between Soviet domestic considerations and foreign policy becomes explicit; for a juxtaposition of the timetable of rolling five-year plans and the proposals set out in Gorbachev's statement of 15 January 1986[3] reveals a precise congruence between the two. That this perfect chronological parallelism is not merely coincidental is evidenced by the fact that the staged disarmament programme is phased in such a way that, if implemented, the release of resources from the military sector would correspond to the needs of the civilian sector as the pace of economic development quickened.

It is this linkage that underpins Gorbachev's proposals of January 1986. As he says in the preamble to his statement: 'The entire effort of the CPSU is directed towards guaranteeing the further improvement of the life of the Soviet people'; and, 'A breakthrough for the better is needed in the international arena'. Then, as with the five-year plans, the specific proposals that follow build up into a rolling programme of multi-staged (*mnogoetapno*), phased disarmament. Moreover, each stage of disarmament matches a five-year-plan period exactly, so that the first phase coincides with the first five-year plan; the second, like the second five-year plan, begins 'no later than' 1990; while the third phase, beginning in 1995 and culminating in complete, universal, nuclear disarmament, comes to fruition at the same time as the third five-year plan at the end of the century (see Table 2:1).

Gorbachev's statement of 15 January 1986 calling for universal nuclear disarmament by the year 2000 was received with incredulity in the West. Lord Chalfont called it 'foolish chatter'; Mrs Thatcher insisted that the nuclear bomb cannot be disinvented; Western peace movements paid the proposals relatively scant attention. It seemed that the USSR had committed itself to two extravagant, probably unrealizable objectives: complete nuclear disarmament and the attainment of the highest world level of social productivity, both by the year 2000. Why?

It is uncharacteristic of Gorbachev to leave himself hostage to fortune by defining goals and setting timetables that are impossible to fulfil. So, a possible explanation is that his disarmament proposals are merely opportunistic and designed to leave him with the initiative – the 'high ground' – in the superpower relationship by placing the West in the position of having constantly to behave reactively to a systematic, clearly defined and – however improbable – coherent programme. But if that is the explanation, then it is not without risk for him, too: failure to attain the goals set out so incrementally and precisely could be used by his opponents to embarrass and impede him.

On the other hand, the possibility should not be excluded that Gorbachev is in earnest about the twin goals that he has set for the Soviet Union. There is ample evidence to suggest that he views himself as a man of destiny, a visionary – Lenin's disciple whose task it is to save the USSR from self-destruction and restore it, and thus world socialism, to the forefront of history. It is tempting to dismiss these ambitions as vanity or self-delusion. Yet Gorbachev's actual behaviour belies any such assertion.

None of this is meant to imply that Gorbachev should simply be taken at his word and that the West should give away positions that for forty years have constituted the cornerstone of NATO alliance policies. But if the West is itself serious about the desirability of drastic reductions in nuclear arsenals, then it should have a strategy of its own to match the Soviet programme that is so clearly signposted in the five-year plans and in the January 1986 statement.

Already, Gorbachev is building on the foundation provided by his January 1986 statement and has credited the INF treaty to it. Speaking to the Soviet people on television shortly after his return to Moscow from the Washington Summit (*Pravda*, 15 December 1987), he said: 'The philosophical-political basis of this preparation [for the summit] were the decisions of the XXVII Congress of our party and the programme for a nuclear-free world set out on 15 January 1986.' Then, having outlined the course of the negotiations, he added:

TABLE 2:1   The congruence of Soviet economic and disarmament programmes

Domestic programme	Disarmament programme
1986 (–1990) 12th Five-Year Plan	*Stage 1: 1986 (to 1990–3)*
Enhancing growth rates and efficiency by means of scientific-technological progress (Ryzhkov).	USSR and USA to halve number of nuclear weapons capable of reaching each other's territory, with the number of launchers remaining not to exceed 6,000.
	No arms in space.
	Duration of Stage 1: five to eight years (i.e. 1986 to 1990–3).
1991 (–1995) 13th Five-Year Plan	*Stage 2: 1990 (to 1995–7)*
	Note: Stage 2 must begin by not later than 1990.
Qualitative breakthrough leading to further acceleration of growth.	Other nuclear powers must freeze their nuclear arsenals and agree not to station their weapons on the territory of other states.
	Complete the 50 per cent reduction of Soviet and US arsenals agreed under Stage 1.
	Embark upon 'next radical step': liquidation by all nuclear powers of tactical nuclear weapons (i.e. with a radius of up to 1,000 km.
	The Soviet–US agreement concluded under Stage 1 not to take arms into space to be extended to other advanced industrial countries.
	Cessation of nuclear testing.
	Ban on non-nuclear weapons based on new physical principles.
	Duration of Stage 2: five to seven years (i.e. 1990 to 1995–7).
1996 (–2000) 14th Five-Year Plan	*Stage 3: 1995 (to end of 1999)*
	Note: Stage 3 must begin by not later than 1995.
Very rapid growth; qualitative transformation of the economy; attainment of the highest world level of social productivity.	All remaining nuclear weapons to be liquidated, so that 'by the end of 1999 no nuclear weapon will remain on Earth' (Gorbachev).

The chief result of the visit to Washington is, of course, the signing of the Agreement to abolish two classes of nuclear missile. This is the first step towards a practicable elimination of the nuclear arsenal. Only yesterday this seemed to many to be utopia. Today it is becoming a fact.

The same point was emphasised by USSR Deputy Minister of Foreign Affairs V. Petrovskii who, on the second anniversary of Gorbachev's statement, claimed that:

The reaching of the Soviet–US accord on intermediate- and shorter-range missiles, *which signifies the implementation – ahead of time – of two points mentioned in the Statement of 15 January 1986*, means that international relations have reached a new stage . . . and marks the beginning of the practical implementation of the Programme for ridding mankind of nuclear weapons by the year 2000.[4]

The West's response to the INF treaty has been ambivalent. While welcoming the abolition of two classes of nuclear missile, and 'while seeking security and stability at lower levels of armaments', NATO has declared itself to be 'determined to sustain the requisite efforts to ensure the continued viability, credibility and effectiveness of [its] conventional and nuclear forces'.[5] Paradoxically, from Gorbachev's point of view, progress on disarmament appears to have made the NATO alliance *more* resolved to strengthen its nuclear defences than it was before. That being so, is it possible to reconcile the USSR's total nuclear disarmament position and NATO's reliance upon deterrence?

Perhaps it is. NATO now sees the main threat to its security not only in the Soviet Union's nuclear capacity, but also in the Warsaw Pact's superiority in conventional forces. In fact, Western anxieties about conventional forces appear to increase in proportion to reductions in the size of nuclear arsenals, so that 'the establishment of a stable and secure level of conventional forces, by the elimination of disparities in the whole of Europe' has become a principal strand of NATO policy. This stance may turn out to be in surprisingly close accord with Gorbachev's priorities and thus provide the basis for a convergence of the self-interest of both sides.

Nuclear weapons are *relatively* cheap to produce; there are only modest economies to be made in the short to medium term by getting rid of them. Any substantial savings can come only from major reductions in conventional forces and weaponry. On the one hand, the West seeks reductions in conventional forces for reasons of security; on the other, the Soviet Union needs reductions in order to divert resources from the military to the civilian sector of the economy: as Petrovskii put it, 'To us, disarmament is both the main line to security and the way to release funds for development purposes.'

Despite the instrumental economic reasons for the USSR's desire to reduce present military levels, from the Western alliance's perspective, universal nuclear disarmament, despite Gorbachev's protestations, still seems to be either a public relations ploy or a utopian goal. However, ratification of the INF treaty plus future major reductions in conventional forces and weapons in Europe (particularly if such cuts were asymmetrical) together with movement towards a halving of strategic arsenals would be progress on a scale unimaginable at the beginning of the 1980s.

As well as Western mistrust of the USSR's motives, there was another problem, too. A major flaw in Gorbachev's January 1986 proposal was that it made no provision for guaranteeing regional or world security against nuclear blackmail. With the number of countries possessing nuclear weapons – or having the capability to produce them – increasing all the time, how realistic was it to expect the United States, Britain, France and China (not to mention the USSR itself) to get rid of the very means of deterrence which, they would argue, have ensured their safety since the end of the Second World War? How, for instance, could a nuclear peace be ensured between, say, Iran and Iraq, should one or the other acquire a nuclear capability? What restraints would there be upon unstable mavericks such as Colonel Gadaffi? What if one side cheated?

There is only one plausible answer to these dilemmas consistent with the spirit of the January 1986 declaration, and that is that a supranational body should exercise supervision on a world-wide scale. Once that point is accepted, it follows that the Soviet Union could hardly propose the creation of a new supranational body when one existed already – the United Nations. The problem was that, in the past, the USSR had exploited the UN for its own self-serving needs. It was time to turn over a new leaf.

After what appeared to be a lull – probably while a new position was being formulated – a remarkable transformation in Soviet attitudes towards the United Nations began to manifest itself. Long-standing arrears were paid, including backdated contributions to UN peace-keeping operations. There was a new emphasis upon the utility of the Security Council, particularly with respect to its potential role as monitor and verifier of arms control agreements; while at the same time the importance of international law became a consistent theme in Soviet pronouncements.

The culmination of this new emphasis in Soviet diplomacy came on 7 December 1988 when, at the United Nations headquarters in New York, President Gorbachev addressed the General Assembly with a speech that was hailed by sympathisers and critics alike as being of considerable significance for the disarmament process. Yet, apart from the specification of the proposed unilateral arms reductions, there was very little in Gorbachev's UN speech that had not been pre-figured in an article by him published in September 1987 to mark the opening of the forty-second session of the General Assembly entitled 'Realities and guarantees for a secure world'.

Proof of the linkage between the January 1986 initiative and the new attitude towards the role of the United Nations came early in 1989. While Gorbachev himself noted that the final document of the follow-up meeting of the Conference on Security and Co-operation in Europe (CSCE) had been agreed in Vienna 'exactly three years after we published our forward-looking programme for creating a nuclear-free world and eliminating all kinds of weapons of mass destruction by the year 2000' – a 'meaningful' coincidence, as he put it – other authoritative Soviet commentators were describing Gorbachev's United Nations speech as being 'a further development, deepening and realization of the ideas set out in the [January 1986] Declaration'. Indeed, those ideas had constituted 'an important component of that speech, which should be regarded as the platform for further activities by the USSR in the realm of the humanization and democratization of international relations'.[6]

In the meantime, in contrast to Gorbachev's striking successes in the realm of international politics (particularly with respect to influencing Western public opinions), the Soviet domestic situation was proving to be stubbornly resistant to change. If before Gorbachev came to office in March 1985 food, goods and services were scarce and of poor quality, at least they were cheap. By early 1989 food, goods and services were in even shorter supply, still of poor quality, yet had increased sharply in price. To make matters worse, ahead lay the alarming prospect of retail price reform, a measure that will undoubtedly raise prices (and public discontent) still further.

Nor has fate treated Gorbachev kindly. The effect of the decline in the world-market price of oil (the USSR's main hard-currency-earning export), the unanticipated loss of revenue as a consequence of the ill-judged anti-alcohol campaign, Chernobyl, the material and moral costs of the war in Afghanistan, the Armenian earthquake – followed closely in the New Year by the earthquake in Tadzhikistan – all have combined to set back the Soviet Union's economic recovery and to aggravate the low morale of the population at large. Little wonder, then, that a Central Committee official close to Gorbachev (Nikolai Shishlin) should admit that he 'regretfully allows that the timetable outlined in the Declaration by Mikhail Gorbachev [on 15 January 1986] may not be followed closely and its fulfilment may be dragged out'.[7]

As January 1989 drew to a close it appeared that the timetable set out in January 1986 was still somewhat ahead of schedule, although temporarily at a standstill while the transition from the Reagan Administration to Bush's was effected in Washington. But the economic goals of *perestroika* were as far away from being achieved as ever, with most of Soviet society's attention being focused on the process of political reform. Intra-Party bureaucratic opposition to Gorbachev seemed to be asserting itself more confidently, even to the extent that doubts were being raised as to whether or not Gorbachev could survive politically.[8]

That Gorbachev might be deposed or that, while remaining in office, his programme might be blocked by his political opponents is a possiblity that cannot be discounted. If he were to be dropped, it is extremely unlikely that he would be succeeded by someone more reform-minded than himself (otherwise, what would be the point of getting rid of him in the first place?). On the other hand, a successor drawn from the traditionalist wing of the Soviet leadership would be unlikely to adopt policies more congenial to the West's interests than those at present being pursued by Gorbachev. Again, any compromise replacement (Ryzhkov, for example) would owe his position more to the traditionalist wing than to the reformists, so the same argument would apply. In other words, the thrust of the present analysis is that, with whatever reservations from the West's point of view, Gorbachev's continued tenure is to be preferred. Whether or not it is possible for the West to facilitate that outcome; and – if it is possible – whether or not it should do so, are political questions. It is, therefore, the politicians who must provide the answers.

Linkages between foreign and domestic policy in the Soviet Union
Jonathan Eyal

Simply to observe that there is a link between internal policies and external policies is neither very helpful nor very original, unless it serves a particular purpose. In this case, however, it does. If we are able to see the limits and the aims of Soviet foreign policy through the prism of internal imperatives, then we can dispose of the seemingly never-ending question: 'Is Gorbachev sincere about what he is doing and can we possibly trust him?'. The question should not be that at all. The question should be instead: 'Is it in his interest and does it coincide with ours?'. If we put the issue like that, then, of course, we have a much more helpful framework for debate all around. For us this is really the importance of internal developments in the Soviet Union.

As far as opportunism is concerned we must not expect the Soviet Union to give up its involvement in the Third World for nothing. We must expect the Soviet Union to exact the maximum price that it can, even if it wants to dispose of particular assets. Indeed, if we look at the disengagement from Afghanistan, it was preceded by a very heavy offensive in January 1988, just before the serious negotiations had started. Angola was preceded by exactly the same heavy offensive and the same thing has happened in Kampuchea. It seems that the aim was to probe Western interest up to the limit, and, then, the moment that was achieved, sit down at the negotiating table and get a deal. Now we must not blame the Soviet Union for that. Such a policy is neither duplicitous, nor does it show bad faith. It is simply the way countries work and we should expect Gorbachev to defend his country's interests. So I would try not to get involved in the whole argument of 'Is he trying to lull the West into a sense of false security?'. The answer to that question is no, if we remember the frailty of the system and his own vulnerability in the Soviet Union. The same sort of arguments were heard during the first period of incipient detente in the late 1960s and early 1970s under a very different kind of person in the Kremlin.

Now, does the Soviet Union want to create 'a quiet world'? If a quiet world means a world with a particular set of international relations that answers the internal and external needs of that country, then that is what the Soviet Union wants.

Another, perhaps crucial, point is the fact that we are not entirely certain that the Soviet leadership is actually aware of the problems that it faces. The sharp veering between having a great interest in internal political affairs, and then a quick move to foreign affairs and then a rush back to economic affairs and then another move to foreign affairs before returning once more to a phase of great concentration on economic affairs, indicates a sort of finger-in-the-dyke approach. This approach very much suggests that, as problems mount, the leadership's attention is turned to damage limitation, rather than to seeking radical solutions. Much more alarmingly, it is often also clear that, as they unravel one package, Soviet leaders are surprised to discover that there are three or four time bombs ticking away inside which need to be defused.

The question of how to increase productivity is a good example of this and it was the first issue raised. It quickly became obvious that there were no indices for productivity. Then they realized that these indices for productivity could only be achieved if there was a real price structure. But a real price structure meant real prices and real prices meant ultimately the abolition of subsidies and an enormous increase in prices. Even that was not enough because, if you talk about greater trade exchanges with the West, you have to talk about convertibility of the currency and then you suddenly discover that you have a 100 billion rouble-deficit in the national account, purely fictional of course, because you can simply keep on printing money. Now all these things have come up one after another and the main problem was the lack of data, the lack of information. The Soviet Union assumed that the secrecy was fooling us. In fact, it was fooling them and Gorbachev was quite explicit about that at the Central Committee as early as January 1987.

This has great significance for his plan to divert resources from the military sector to the civilian economy, for two reasons. First, because, according to all the plans I have seen and to all the indications about what they call 'conversion' in the Soviet Union now – conversion from the military sector to the civilian sector – assumes that the capital currently invested in the military sector would have the same productivity in the civilian sector. It would not. The reason it has a higher productivity in the military sector is because the military sector actually has a customer, which is the top brass, who demand good quality and who do not care about the price. The civilian economy still does not, and is unlikely to have, such a customer, even if the market was much more open than it is now, simply because Soviet citizens have piled up enormous savings, and any growth in the supply of consumer goods would disappear in seconds. Any such supply would just be soaked up by enormous savings of worthless roubles, or at least at the moment worthless roubles. There is a second problem. The Soviet leadership simply does not know how much it spends on its military. It is rather paradoxical that the people we were accusing in the West, for so many years, of inflating the threat posed by Soviet danger, by inventing a defence expenditure of 15–17 per cent of GNP, are exactly the people that are being called upon by the Soviet Union to help them analyse the size of their defence expenditures. The techniques used by the CIA in gauging GNP, and production levels, are actually used by the Soviet Union today. So, regardless of what the figures show at the moment, and regardless of what the pronouncements are, when it comes down to actual practicalities, we have a long way to go.

The real tragedy for the Soviet Union was of course the wrong priorities taken at the beginning, with absence of knowledge of the real facts. Take the nationalities issue, for instance. Encouragement was given to the Balts to go ahead and experiment with the economy because they were the more developed republics of the Soviet Union, only to find out very quickly that what they wanted was actually their own national status. The wholesale dismissal of bureaucrats in the Central Asian republics was another example. It was part of the great fight against corruption, but the leadership did not realise that in the Asian republics of the Soviet Union corruption actually had a purpose. It was the glue that bound the empire together. It was the part of the social contract between Brezhnev and the local Party leaders, who run the republics like fiefdoms.

There is a contradiction between some of Gorbachev's internal aims, and there is not necessarily a link between some of his foreign aims, and indeed achievements, and the internal political scene. I would point to one particular concept, that of the Common European Home, which I think shows a very clear linkage between economic, political and military imperatives. It is probably the realization that, unlike what Brezhnev said and thought, probably for many years, the number of the neutrals in Europe is not likely to grow but rather to decline. The Soviet Union has realized that neutrality of the sort we have today is probably doomed. It also realises that Western Europe has a community of political interests and economic interests, and one day will also have the third part of the triad which is military interests. This explains Gorbachev's attempt to negotiate with the European Community and to try to steer it towards economic rather than military interests. This is why he does not want to alarm the West or Western Europe, nor even to remove the American pillar. All this also serves the main economic purpose of getting enhanced contacts between East and West.

One area where the Soviet Union has shown itself to be surprisingly quiet in contrast to its foreign policy towards the West was, of course, Eastern Europe. There was a great deal of quiet, and a great deal of expectation and a great deal of praying that nothing would blow up. We have seen the easiest part of the Soviet policy towards Eastern Europe. I think hard choices from now on will not be avoided; they can not. It seems to me that the one-party state in Hungary is slipping away very fast and the Soviet Union will have to decide sooner or later whether it wants to accept that or not. The same is true in the Polish case and as to the case of Czechoslovakia or Romania, your guess is as good as mine.[9] But all this has very important implications for the Soviet Union and is a clear case of foreign policy impacting on the internal situation because, if the reforms in Hungary are going to lead to the abolition of the one-party state, and indeed the disappearance of the Communist Party – which is what it looks like at the moment – and if developments continue at the pace which we have experienced over the past year, then that would create many problems for the Soviet leadership and would frighten a lot of people in Moscow. Furthermore, if the Soviet leadership decides to make a stand and makes a botched job out of it, rather as they did in 1956, then of course very hard questions are going to be asked in Moscow, and indeed in the West.

What can the West do? What should it do after analysing the internal situation in the Soviet Union? First of all, unrestrained, uncontrolled loans to the Soviet Union in order to perk up internal consumption are not the answer; the Soviets are convinced of that themselves. While the use of foreign currency in enterprises has been decentralized, the loan-making powers have actually been centralized simply because the Soviet Union has realised that if it borrows at the moment it would probably invest the money very badly, rather like Hungary, Poland and Romania did in the 1960s and 1970s, and would probably end up with a very high debt and not a few white elephants. So that is certainly not a solution. What might be provided as an interim solution instead is the realization in the West that a lot of the reforms and a lot of the pace depends on Gorbachev, on the man himself and on his survival. Perhaps we should seek other ways of helping him to survive? Above all we should remember that history is littered with empires that went down, knowing that they would go down, but unable to do anything about it because any other choice seemed too awful at that time.

NOTES AND REFERENCES

1.   This point is discussed in Peter Frank, 'Gorbachev's dilemma: social justice or political instability?', *The World Today*, vol. 42, no. 6 June 1986, pp. 93–5.
2.   *The Times*, 17 December 1987, p. 16.
3.   *Pravda*, 16 January 1986.
4.   *Soviet News*, 20 January 1988, p. 28 (emphasis added).
5.   NATO Declaration, 3 March 1988.
6.   Lt-Gen. K.F. Mikhailov, first deputy head of the Department of Arms Reduction and Disarmament of the USSR Ministry of Foreign Affairs, in *Krasnaya Zvezda*, 17 January 1989.
7.   *Moscow News*, no 3, 15 January 1989, p. 3.
8.   Academician Sakharov, as reported in *The Times*, 26 January 1989.
9.   This statement was made in February 1989!

3   The future of the Soviet Union: further discussion

Any discussion of the wider environment for navies in the closing decade of the twentieth century and beyond has to face the riddle and paradox presented by the Soviet Union under Mikhail Gorbachev. The years since 1985 have already seen political changes and arms control stances that seemed impossible five years before. So rapid has been the speed of change, and so great its scope, that Western navies now find themselves in an environment where past, easy, images of the Soviet threat look inappropriate alongside the image of a youthful, popular Soviet leader bearing gifts of peace. Developing a realistic, sustainable, view of the threat in a more ambiguous situation is one of the more difficult problems facing Western governments and publics alike. Getting the Soviet Union in the proper focus, however, is more than a matter of finding a more appropriate metaphor than the Afghanistan-invading bear. The dangers of misperceiving change in the Soviet Union and making mistaken responses to that change are clear. Understanding the Soviet Union has probably never been so important, or, perhaps, so difficult.

The task is difficult not least because it is similar to the problem of unwrapping a rather large Russian doll. Problems entwine at varying levels of analysis. At one level we can assess change in Soviet force structures and attempt to read change in foreign and defence policy from this. At another, changes in declaratory defence policy can be compared with changes in capabilities. Beyond this, however, we move firmly into the area of intentions rather than capabilities and a whole stream of issues open up that demand our attention. Does Soviet policy since 1985 really reflect a change of objectives or one of tactics? Do changing policies reflect systemic change in the Soviet Union (or, indeed, in the international system) or is change the product of one man: Mikhail Gorbachev? In so far as the character of Gorbachev is important, how are we to explain a leader who willingly seems to have taken on a task that many might consider impossible? How deep are the problems that promote change? Are they such as to determine that any Soviet leader would have to make inroads into Soviet defence budgets? What are the links between defence and the economy? What are the chances for economic success? If Gorbachev fails who might succeed him? What constitutes failure? What policies might a successor follow? All of these questions seem essential if we are to answer the twin questions of what threats and what opportunities Gorbachev's Soviet Union offers the West and what threats might or might not materialize in the relative future.

GREENWICH CONFERENCE DISCUSSION

The first two speakers articulated issues that, at the Conference, and subsequently, led to a lively discussion between sovietologists, strategists, arms control specialists and Western naval analysts. There was general agreement that understanding the nature of Gorbachev's reforms and, indeed, the economic, technological and moral crisis which brought Gorbachev to office was crucial to any understanding of Soviet defence policy.

Several key issues emerged. The importance of understanding the crisis backdrop to *perestroika* – a major feature of Peter Frank's presentation – was reiterated. The situation that Gorbachev inherited, with a stagnating economy, growing debt, concealed inflation and growing queues would have been bad enough if it had not been complemented by a social, moral(e) and political crisis. The point was made that one of the key features of the 1917 Revolutions was a terrible sense of social injustice as people saw physical shortages of goods exacerbated by manifestly unfair distribution of what there was. The Party, with its closed shops, corruption and nepotism, may have looked like emulating by 1985 the system it had overthrown in 1917. Appreciation of this by some of the more astute members of the Party may have been a major feature in building a power base for Gorbachev's rise. Even without this, the need to meet tangible domestic and external challenges was pressing by 1985. With crime, antisocial behaviour, sickness, alchoholism and corruption increasing and initiative and productivity falling, the Soviet Union was clearly heading for a bleak future if it could not arrest the decline. If we add to this the long-term effects on the Soviet Union's status and power of a falling growth rate – both in absolute terms and more so relative to key competitors like Europe, Japan, China and the United States – the necessity of reversing the trend seems imperative.

If there was, and is, consensus among external experts on the bleak picture that produced Gorbachev, there was, and is, also a consensus that the task he had assumed was an enormous one. Continuing revelations of the slowness of Soviet growth, the size of the budgetary deficit and the rate of Soviet inflation all seem to support the view that we were observing an administration that came to power in the Soviet Union with a clear feeling that reform was needed after decades of stagnation only to find, as they thought through what should be done, that the situation was even worse than they believed.

Admiration for Gorbachev's bravery in confronting such a task was not, however, matched by optimism about his chances for success. In economic terms, there has, as yet, been no substantial improvement in Soviet growth rates, whilst deficits and inflation had risen since 1985. Luck had not been on Gorbachev's side with Chernobyl, earthquakes and pipeline explosions, but the deeper reasons for pessimism were more deep rooted in fundamental questions about the nature of the Soviet political system and Russian culture.

The first problem was a doubt about how far reform could go. Western, and many Soviet, analysts of the Soviet economy have continually underlined the incompatibility of key features of the Soviet economy like central control, planning and party power with economically desirable facets like efficiency, initiative, incentives and consumer demand. The need to move from extensive to intensive growth, where attention focuses more and more on how efficiently increasingly scarce resources can be used, lies at the heart of the Soviet economic crisis. Higher growth can only be obtained by working harder and by making informed local decisions about how to produce at the least cost. Working harder requires incentives and incentives require some response from other factories to produce what people are prepared to work harder for. The logic is clear, but so always have been the implications for Soviet political life. If the Party is the vanguard of the proletariat and its decisions are always right – guided as they are by party debate and Marx's scientific laws – the right of the Party to control the economy and political life is clear. If, on the other hand, economic decisions are taken by plant managers reacting to consumer demand, the role of the Party is far less obvious. Indeed, if choice became a universal part of everyday life, how long would it be before fundamental questions were asked about the lack of political choice and the role of a party machine that no longer was seen to be doing everything?

Gorbachev's position on this problem was seen as an ambiguous one. The logic of changing the political superstructure as a necessary precondition of economic success has been accepted. Elections, increasing use of public opinion as a lever against entrenched party positions and more open public debate are all important signs of movement. *Glasnost* as a companion of *perestroika* seems intended to help produce ideas and a more favourable political environment. Just how far change will be allowed to go remains unclear. Peter Frank made the telling observation that the language of change needs to be carefully listened to. Words mean what they say and seem to have been picked to avoid saying something different. Gorbachev has, therefore, spoken about democratization, *Glasnost'* and pluralism of opinion but has not talked about democracy, freedom of speech or political pluralism. There might be more democracy, more openness and a wider range of opinion, but there will not be a democracy where there is freedom of speech and political opinions are matched by the right to compete for power between different political parties. Gorbachev might have new ideas but he still seemed, throughout 1989, to believe in the merits of both the Party and socialism. On the key question of the role of the Party, it was noted at the Conference that, on every issue up to early 1989 when its leading role was threatened, the Party had been supported by Gorbachev against those calling for more radical reform.

The second major problem identified was the related question of the nature of Soviet society and the interrelated nature of the problems it poses to the current Soviet leadership. If initiative and decentralized decision-making are required, they cannot necessarily be produced overnight in a society which has long sought to control them. Nor can social problems be wished away. Alchoholism may be a problem, but prohibition predictably seems to have only produced a shortage of sugar as illicit stills assume the role of state ones. Revenue lost from alcohol sales in the legal economy of course increases government spending deficits at the same time as it boosts the black market. Other problems with markets, transport and incentives seem intractable. Even bumper harvests can do little good in an economy that still has a third-world distribution system to get the food from field to kitchen. Transport is an interesting example of the limitations posed on any reform programme by the realities of Soviet organization, geography and climate. No amount of exhortation is likely to make the food flow from where it grows to where it is needed. Nor is the food likely to overflow the shelves whilst the question of incentives remains unsolved. The basis for productivity must lie in incentives – seventy years of exhorting New Soviet Man to work for the collective good have had only limited success. Money incentives are, however, little use until there are actually goods in the shops to buy. The chicken and egg situation seems unavoidable – more effort is required to produce more goods to buy but the effort must precede the reward, perhaps by years. With empty shelves in the shops, the dilemma of economic reform is startlingly bare. Success in a real sense breeds success here and Mr Gorbachev seems to have little impact so far. The wave of strikes in the Soviet mining industry in 1989 indicated clearly that workers were more interested in having merchandise to buy than money to count whilst standing in queues for the unobtainable. Yet the problem remains that better living standards have to serve as the motivation for *perestroika* at the same time as they can only result from *perestroika*. The possibility looms that the people will not work harder today, and accept the instability of increased efficiency and unemployment, merely in the hope of future improvement.

This economic and political crisis seems directly tied to developments in Soviet foreign and defence policy under Gorbachev.[1] The 14 per cent cut in the defence budget promised by 1991 looks to be directly related to the need to try to stimulate growth by moving resources from defence (and particularly defence procurement) to capital investment. On the negative side of the equation, a situation where Soviet defence budgets continued to grow at 3–4 per cent per annum when GNP grew at 2 per cent must have looked alarmingly unsustainable to any leadership that considered the economic consequences of an ever increasing percentage of GNP going to Soviet defences. Defence expenditure also must feature high in Gorbachev's analysis of his economic woes. It represents the only possible source of new resources to be moved towards *perestroika* at the same time as the burden of the present, let alone increasing, future, defence efforts represented a major part of the problem. It seems probable, therefore, that any new leadership convinced of the need for reform, and cognizant of the concept of cost-effectiveness, would have asked significant questions of, and make major changes in, Soviet foreign and defence policy. *Perestroika* might be necessary to provide funds and technology for future Soviet military security, but security tomorrow inevitably required less expenditure on security today.

Three problems were stressed for any assessment of the impact of all this on Soviet defence policy. The first is the technical one of what confidence either Western commentators, or the Soviets themselves, can have in Soviet statistics. It may be that the Soviets themselves have not yet emerged from the shadow of a command economy where accounting may bear more relationship to Monopoly money than actual costs. If so, the relationship between economic need and defence budget cut may not be as exact as it appears. It might also be the case that a 14 or a 19 per cent cut may mean something else in a system where it is acknowledged that the concept of cost is itself a developing concept.

More important, however, are the questions of just what has changed in foreign and defence policy and what Gorbachev's goals actually are. There was agreement at the Conference that Soviet foreign policy interests were now being evaluated through a less ideological prism – one more attuned to the logic of cost and benefit. However, there seemed no firm idea of what sort of role Gorbachev envisaged. If the aim of *perestroika* was to maintain the Soviet Union's position as a superpower, we would find ourselves dealing with a different Soviet Union than if *perestroika* was just an attempt to maintain a more limited existence as a major state. Just how important is superpower status to the new Soviet leadership? Equally, what does security now require? What are the priorities? A whole range of questions await answers here, ranging from the degree of control the Soviet Union still desires over Eastern Europe, through its aims for West Germany, to narrower defence issues about the relative roles of offensive forces, homeland defence and nuclear deterrents. The last question seems particularly interesting as it is possible to envisage a Soviet defence budget where homeland defence retains its priority whilst conventional offensive capability is allowed to decline and reliance is placed on smaller numbers of nuclear weapons. This is what Khrushchev did, but it is not clear if Gorbachev's reforms have retained the traditional interest in defending the motherland from all potential forms of attack.

Behind this, however, lies an even more basic question about Gorbachev's vision. Peter Frank's chapter shows clearly the linkage in timescale between Gorbachev's economic plans and the timetable for nuclear disarmament offered in 1986. This, however, raises the key question of just what sort of man Gorbachev is. The idea of a leader who could call for universal nuclear disarmament in fifteen years encouraged doubts about his sincerity in some quarters. If he did not, were we really dealing with a Soviet leader with new aims or just one with greater sophistication in his bid to divide the West? If, as a majority felt, he did mean what he said – and seemed to have made economic success dependent on arms control success – what were we to make of this? There seems to be an inherent incompatibility in Gorbachev's realisation that the command economy should give way to a more pluralistic, efficient, economic system and his belief that even the most difficult political and economic changes can be orchestrated to the timetables of five-year plans. Did this mean we were dealing with a leader who did not appreciate the political impossibility of meeting such precise schedules in an international climate dominated by multiple decision-making centres and the impossibility of verifying complete nuclear disarmament? On the other hand, did it signify that we were dealing with a true revolutionary leader, a man with a vision and the determination, like Lenin, to ensure it was enacted? Indeed, given the problems facing the Soviet Union, just what sort of man could come to the fore in 1985 and what sort of man would accept such an imposing mission?

The general conclusion of the Conference and, indeed, one shared by most Western analysts, was that chances for success in terms of substantial increases in economic growth rates were very limited. It was also clear that the attempt at reform was creating its own problems. The scale of recent industrial, ethnic and political unrest, however, ought to be seen as a symptom of the underlying malaise rather than Gorbachev's attempts at improving the situation. Gorbachev's surgery might cause some bleeding but the alternative was slow and increasingly painful death by systemic disease. Blaming the doctor for the side-effects of the treatment did not seem particularly sensible when the alternative was to sit back and do nothing and watch the patient sink lower into his decline.

THE CENTRAL PROBLEM – THE PARTY?

The Party, however, has done more than fail to control the religious, political, social and ethnic values of the citizenry. It itself seems to be a major feature behind the decline. Attempts to revitalize it, to make it responsive to popular pressure and open to needed reform and to distinguish between the progressive party and obstructive bureaucrats, all seem limited, partly cosmetic, gestures. Gorbachev's parliament may meet many of the demands for a voice which the Chinese gerontocracy prefered to massacre, but the role of the Party in Soviet society remains a problem. It might be possible to develop the legislature as a pressure-valve, even a talking shop, while real power continued to lie with the Party. Parliaments elsewhere exist with little influence on the executive or economic power. The Soviet Communist Party, however, faces the problem that Soviet citizens may demand real power for their legislature. The Soviet Communist Party has the misfortune to be both more engaged and less successful than many ruling elites. Its power and its responsibility for failure are both plain to see. It may not be possible to palm the public off with a powerless parliament. Telling the public that parliament is important may well spawn the expectation that it should be. Political demands may also fall out of the barrel of economic reforms. If economic decisions are to be made by markets, consumers, foreigners and managers what becomes of the leading role of the Party? If people are free to make choices in the economic sphere how long before they demand political choice? Similarly, if glasnost allows a flow of ideas, how can the Party claim a monopoly on truth and power? If the Party is resented because it has authority, such resentment can only grow as it is blamed for failure. If it is unpopular because members enjoy an unfair share of resources as well as power, how can it continue when the material benefits that attract party members are denied to them?

Indeed, the problems facing the Soviet Communist Party seem to extend to all other key institutions of the Soviet state. With internal dissent growing, the KGB also seems to be being confronted with a need to mount a stronger counter-subversion effort at precisely the same time as it has to move with *glasnost'* and greater demands for the rule of law to replace the interests of the state. The armed forces face declining budgets and redundancy for some officers. With all three pillars of the Soviet state being forced to lose power and resources and to face unpalatable change, Gorbachev's support looks somewhat uncertain. One estimate was that as few as 10 per cent of the population actually supported his reforms. The rest of the population seems divided between bureaucrats anxious to secure their present positions, workers seeking economic betterment but not at the price of uncertainty, unemployment and price rises, party officials trying to retain what they enjoy and those seeking ethnic objectives not necessarily compatible with the survival of the Soviet state in its present form.

CHALLENGES TO GORBACHEV?

All of this poses several questions about the Soviet Union's future and the sort of threat it may pose to Western interests. The first issue is whether current policies, and the personalities associated with them, can continue. Here, at the time of the Conference, there was substantial agreement that Gorbachev, now President Gorbachev, would survive partly because of the inherent nature of the problems facing the Soviet Union. Although there might be a debate about how far and how fast to go, there seemed to be general agreement in the Politburo that something had to be done. The status quo crisis was not an acceptable option. Any course of reform carries risk. It was felt likely that Gorbachev faced by a deteriorating political situation would continue to be able to use this as an argument for reform on the basis that past policies of suppressing or ignoring problems had not worked. If the problem posed a major threat to the state and Party, he had already shown an inclination to side with the Party and use as much force as was needed to restore control. Whilst Gorbachev continued to take the necessary action to ensure just enough party support, no opposition seemed to have a convincing argument for replacing him.

A coup against Gorbachev also looked unlikely, and remains so, on other grounds. Gorbachev had had considerable success in changing the leadership of Party, state and KGB in his own image. As time went on this supporting group from his own generation has become stronger. Public elections had made the case for reform difficult to argue against as well as weakening traditional elements. Most importantly, there did not seem to be any alternative policies or leaders to hand to replace Gorbachev. Given the task in hand, it would be surprising if many people relished the leader's mantle, and the intra-party debate seemed to be between those arguing caution in the face of crisis and those who demanded even faster reform. Anyone seizing Gorbachev's position would also find themselves in a nearly impossible political situation. Replacing a leader because he had failed, they would inherit the same intractable economic and political problems that had caused his fall. Moreover, by removing Gorbachev they would create a preceedent for their own fall when they too 'failed'. People might be driven by emotion or 'duty' to challenge Gorbachev, but prudent politicians were likely to leave well alone. Holding the reins of power, surrounded by his own nominees and steering a middle course in policy Gorbachev should survive. There was, however, some risk that if reform failed and internal dissent rose, Gorbachev would himself be forced by circumstances and colleagues to reassert party control and slow reform. As long as his colleagues felt the situation was under control, his position seemed secure. Whether he would end up in history as the great reformer or the leader who was forced to reimpose control and make do with a stagnating future, remained to be seen.

THE MILITARY

Attention also focused on the role of the military. There was seen to be a major problem here in understanding what the military's attitude to Gorbachev would be in the future. There was a strong logic that the military had come to share the perception of a worsening social, economic and political crisis. It was pointed out that one feature in Gorbachev's calculations may have been the fate of Poland where party collapse and economic crisis had left the military as the only possible alternative power centre. It seems probable that the Soviet military would have been as dismayed by this prospect of Bonapartism as would the Party. On a more pragmatic note, without *perestroika*, the Soviet Union's ability to maintain its position as a military superpower must have seemed threatened by the Soviet economy's inability to keep up with Western technology. An army based on a third-world economy could not be a first-rate army, therefore the economy had to be sorted out today to provide the weapons required tomorrow. In this sense the long-term interests of the Soviet armed forces, as well as the inclinations of those officers who sought a more efficient, more capable, posture today, were entirely congruent with *perestroika*.

Whether this relationship with the military will hold is more difficult to see. Gorbachev's unilateral cuts in 1988 seemed to represent a triumph of his determination to cut, over the military's wish to negotiate bilateral reductions. The history of mutual balanced force reductions (MBFR) negotiations, where discussions continued for fifteen years without agreement, must have seemed a depressing alternative to Soviet political leaders who wanted to make an early start on economic regeneration by cutting defence budgets drastically by 1991. Yet there seems a limit to how many unilateral cuts the military leadership will accept. There also may be some danger that speedy reform which means sacking officers without adequate recompense will create political opposition to the leadership. Managing change will, clearly, be difficult. The problem will grow if the Soviet economy does not produce the growth rates intended in the 1990s. The logic of reduced force levels and reduced procurement today, offset by more advanced technology and defence budgets growing again with a revitalized economy, is under threat. If the Soviet economy does not grow, the reward for today's abstinence will not be forthcoming. Like the Soviet workers, the Soviet military may also conclude that they are facing turmoil today for little or no result tomorrow. In the case of the defence forces, however, economic failure will raise the question of how to defend the Soviet Union from an unimpressive economic base in an even starker form.

DANGERS FOR THE WEST?

Against this background, assessing the future Soviet threat becomes very difficult. Smaller armed forces benefiting from the success of *perestroika* would pose a formidable, if different, threat to the West – or at least there would be the capability within Soviet forces to mount such a threat if Soviet political leaders so desired. At the other extreme, if the more nationalistic tendencies awakened of late should grow to influence Soviet policy, we might find an even more unfriendly and desperate government in power in the Soviet Union than any seen so far. Economic crisis could produce unforeseeable changes in Soviet foreign policy – particularly if the aspiration to superpower status increasingly outstrips economic capacity. Nationalist ferment has obvious dangers – particularly if it should break out in a violent form and spread through from one ethnic powder keg to another. The potential for such disputes to spill over into tension with bordering Muslim states (or even East European neighbours) is slight but conceivable. Then there is the whole question of whether Eastern and Central Europe will be stable when and if Soviet military power declines. A worst case scenario would see increasing internal dissent in the Soviet Union matched by instability in Eastern Europe – with the Soviet Union itself falling into the control of harsher characters determined to use force to restore a crumbling situation. This is still unlikely. However, in a situation where central Politburo control of spade-wielding Georgian militiamen is clearly imperfect, where communism has succumbed to the masses of decidedly unconvinced voters in Eastern Europe, predicting what cannot happen seems dangerous.

A WORSENING CRISIS?

Indeed, events since the Greenwich Conference suggest that Gorbachev's road may be even more fraught than was imagined in February 1989. Events in 1989 suggested that a crisis was developing.[2] Soviet reviews of the Nazi–Soviet Pact of 1939, stressing its unconnectedness with the subsequent annexation of the Baltic States, suggested that political convenience still reigned over *glasnost* – the government still seemed not to trust, or understand, or to earn the trust, of its people. The growth of nationalist sentiments in Latvia, Estonia, Lithuania, Moldavia, Georgia, Azerbaijan, Armenia, and among the Tartars bordered on the uncontrollable and in some places actually fell over into a state of civil war. Nationalist movements in the Baltic States seem determined to push their claims to have their former independence restored. In the south, civil war and fundamentalist Islam have already emerged in ways that threaten the survival of the empire. Andrei Almalrik's predictions of imperial collapse look daily more prescient. The economic crisis has already reached its logical conclusion with the Soviet Union's largest strikes for sixty years and $5.5 billion promised to the Siberian workers in quality of living improvements and purchasable goods. Future success is already mortgaged to pay for present incentives. Also bizarre is the new policy of paying farms that produce more than past norms bonuses in Western currency. Economic policy may not yet have reached the point of panic but it does seem to look increasingly desperate and continuingly unsuccessful.

The Soviet Union also seemed to move quickly to the brink of other precipices. The contrasting needs of the Party and reform became clearer and clearer. Commentators like historian Yuri Afanasyev made the pointed comment that the time was coming when Gorbachev would have to face the choice between being the leader of *perestroika* and remaining the leader of the *nomenklatura*. Others pointed out that this seemed unlikely when even the anti-corruption drive had been halted when it got to near to key party members. The logical contradictions between party and economic interests, between rival nationalisms and between workers, farmers, bureaucrats and Gorbachev's interests became increasingly apparent. Even more importantly, they did so in public – with Soviet voters and opponents in the legislature all too clearly able to see both the problems of Gorbachev's solutions and the lack of their success. As the revolutions in Eastern Europe in 1989 showed, once large numbers of people can see a need for change and believe that they either will not, or cannot, be supressed, challenges can grow rapidly overwhelming.

Indeed, on practically every front, 1989 brought bad news. With a 32 per cent increase in crime in the first six months of the year, strikes, violent internal unrest, counterattacks in the press by the Party, bureaucrats arguing that ill-thought-out reform was worsening the situation, a non-communist government in Poland followed by the collapse of communist rule and authority in the other Warsaw Pact states of Eastern Europe, the repudiation of the 1956 and 1968 invasions and 55 per cent of ethnic Estonians wanting independence from the USSR, Gorbachev's *perestroika* seemed to be, rapidly, redrawing the very same map of Europe whose sustainment had been the major role and achievement of the Communist Party.

Some of these developments looked threatening. As nationalists and Russian minorities come into increasing conflict with each other, the possibility increases that a policy of democratization will succeed in producing demands that cannot be met. Nationalists may demand changes that are inconsistent with the survival of the Soviet Union in its present form whilst sizeable Russian minorities may reject even limited autonomy. Central Committee calls to the Baltic states to 'cleanse' *perestroika* seemed to underestimate dangerously the separatist phenomena. The dangers also seem to be mounting on the economic and political fronts. Saying one will have economic improvements and then failing to meet expectations is notoriously dangerous. Imposing sometimes painful change for no obvious benefit can only heighten resentment. Allowing one group to express its political or economic discontents tends to encourage those with other, perhaps more disruptive and insoluble, ethnic, political or industrial grievances to act. Economic growth is of course more difficult still when the workers have now downed tools to demand the final fruits of that growth. Mass discontent also brings its own dangers. Without clear limits to dissent being established, the possibility that some demonstration will get out of control – either through local reaction or because of its own momentum – cannot be dismissed. Gorbachev's greatest success so far has arguably been to indicate just what a failure his predecessors had made of the Soviet system. With economic failure now matched by industrial unrest, and the national and ethnic disputes of previous decades and centuries resurrected as if new, in New Socialist Soviet Man the Soviet Communist Party seems to have created one of the rarest and most endangered species of the century. This situation may not be sustainable – perhaps even in the medium term. When the people strongly want what the Party cannot give, a political crisis may be inevitable.

Such a crisis, of course, became even more likely as communist authority collapsed in Eastern Europe. Rescinding the Brezhnev doctrine in Europe was always likely to have the dangerous side-effect of making Soviet citizens wonder why they, alongside Albania, are destined to live in a political system that all their East European allies have thrown off. Maintaining a soft image abroad, though, requires soft treatment at home. Successful dissent at home in its turn, however, breeds more strife. This could be the road that leads to the breakup of the USSR or a Soviet Tiananmen Square.

GORBACHEV AS A PROBLEM?

It should probably be seen as a testimonial to Gorbachev's power that he has been able to survive this succession of crises. It did look likely, though, by early 1990 that Gorbachev's own authority would soon come under threat.[3] Mr Ligachev's criticisms seemed to be becoming more heartfelt and more strident. Gorbachev's success in removing conservatives seemed balanced by the fact that he still felt it necessary to remove them. Reports in late 1989 of concerted criticism and calls for caution from regional party bosses, leading Gorbachev to offer his resignation, suggest growing tensions. Subsequent suggestions in the Soviet press in early 1990 that Gorbachev's position was threatened, and Gorbachev's statements to Baltic nationalists that they held his fate in their hands, may have been intended to weaken his opponents, but the fact that the issue had to be raised suggested vulnerability.[4] Questions about Gorbachev's programme were becoming more urgent as the scale of change involved became clearer. Suggestions also began to mount in the West, and from Soviet reformers, that Gorbachev had been overrated and that he does not actually understand enough about economics, his people, or their religious and national aspirations.

These doubts reflected specific issues about Gorbachev's assumptions and goals – neither of which are apparent to friends or foes. Did Gorbachev understand the needs and potential of the Soviet people? Is he ultimately in control of the situation or has he lit a flame that he does not comprehend which threatens to burn the entire house down? At times, it looked as if Gorbachev assumed that citizens will both act in an economically beneficial way and continue to accept party leadership. The question was asked, not least by Soviet critics, whether Gorbachev still, at root, believed in the Party, its role setting macro-political and economic objectives and the willingness of others to accept his dreams. What should have been seen as a blinding light from the East European electorates did not seem to many to have moved the mote from Gorbachev's eyes.

Criticism also mounted in 1989 of Gorbachev's style. The logic of reform and his own goals seemed hidden. While Gorbachev's adherence to five-year plans – even for nuclear arms control – is noteworthy, other analysts began to argue that, by nature, he is not one to establish any detailed plan for getting from A to B. Instead, his forte lies in his willingness to try new solutions and his ability to spring political surprises on his domestic and international opponents. Surprise, of course, is incompatible with a detailed, declared, plan leaving the onlooker to perceive confusion and indecision. Gorbachev's emphasis on the politics of propaganda and exhortation also appeared, at times, to be incompatible with the need to take real, hard, economic decisions.

Gorbachev also appeared open to other challenges as the new decade opened. Politically, the pace of domestic and international change opened up the charge that he had allowed things to get out of control. It looked as if Gorbachev had adopted a series of positions he wished to move to – only to abandon them when events overtook him. Whatever his own, concealed, goals might be, it was questionable if anyone could hope to get there by regularly setting a goal one month that changes four weeks later. Nor, some argued, was it clear how well Gorbachev actually understands economics – in a system where even his most open-minded economic advisers have difficulty understanding just what a market mechanism is and does. Recent Soviet criticism of early decisions to emphasise investment – instead of consumer production – suggests that mistakes have already been made. If anyone sought to apportion blame for the failure of *perestroika*, it looked likely that Gorbachev would have to take his share.[5]

SLOWING DOWN OR SPEEDING UP?

Criticism of Gorbachev also focused on whether he was proceeding fast enough with reform. The Soviet Union by the end of 1989 seemed to have arrived at a crucial point where the case for slowing down was balanced by the need to press ahead with even more vigour. Question marks were raised over how much further Gorbachev could go when key values like the unity of the Soviet Union and control of the Party are already being challenged by their own shallow roots. There were already signs of retrenchment at home – with *glasnost* continuing but real power staying with the Party. Reports that the proposed legislation to allow republics to leave the Soviet Union will require approval from all other republics suggested that little had changed and political reform is still intended to make reform impossible.[6]

Similar problems appeared to be mounting on the economic front. Whilst there is room to debate how serious Gorbachev is about his continuing, changing, programme for political reform, he actually seemed in 1989 to be undermining this by stepping back on economic *perestroika*. Economic reform seems to have been slowed where it has produced adverse, short-term, party and public distaste. Market forces are now to be controlled to stop price rises and the further descent of the Soviet system into the black market. Increased economic caution may seem wise as Soviet leaders reflect on the fact that the current wave of unrest has all happened before the really contentious issues of price and currency reform have even been attempted. The worst in a real sense is yet to come.

THE FEBRUARY REVOLUTION

By the beginning of 1990, then, the storm clouds were looming over Gorbachev's reforms. It looked to some as if Gorbachev had gone far too far – producing a collapse in discipline and unity at home and the loss of all Stalin and Brezhnev's gains abroad. To others it looked as if Gorbachev the reformer had become Gorbachev the defender of the Party and the man who was slowing the pace of his own economic reforms. In many ways, with public opposition rising, nationalist impulses stirring and economic deterioration threatening political consequences, it seemed that the Soviet Union had reached a crucial point of no return.

Gorbachev's answer, the Central Committee meeting of February 1990, was a truly revolutionary response to a situation that seemed to require one.[7] The tone of criticism, with Gorbachev accused of presiding over the 'total democratisation of society without discipline or order' and *perestroika* depicted as producing 'crisis, anarchy and economic decay', clearly showed the scale of resentment in some quarters. Gorbachev's success in winning the day, strengthening his own position whilst weakening that of the conservatives and moving on with the reform of the Soviet Union's political structure, is clearly important. At least it has allowed the case for slowing reform, or even retreating to past forms to be aired and defeated. At best it has ensured the emergence of a new political system that will remove the political constraints the old Party continues to place on social and economic reform.[8]

QUESTIONS AWAITING ANSWERS

Revolutions, though, rarely solve all issues and, although some answers were suggested in February 1990, the vast majority of key questions remained unresolved. If Gorbachev has not thought things through and cannot provide convincing, acceptable answers, he must be at some risk because the questions are, indeed, profound.

Five key sets of questions remain. The first of which concerns the integrity of the Soviet Union. Gorbachev's own drawn features as he confronted the people of the Baltic states on the streets suggests that he has, indeed, been unprepared for the scale of change he has unleashed. Will he allow the Soviet empire to disintegrate leaving a healthier Russia, or is this anathema? One of the more ominous sides of the Central Committee meeting of February was the strong stance taken against allowing the Baltic parties, let alone republics, to break away from the centre. Gorbachev may himself be prepared to allow nationalism to run its course, but it remains to be seen if he can retain enough control over a situation where key party, armed forces and economic interests may become involved. He could produce a situation where maintaining the Soviet Union intact will have a high price in terms of lives, treasure and repression but where the alternative of allowing whole republics to go proves unacceptable. He may find himself squeezed between, on the one hand, the nationalists and the mothers demonstrating that their sons should not die in some far-flung republic, and, on the other, the political pressures and, indeed, the moral arguments, not to allow the borders of the USSR to descend into a series of messy pogroms.

Second, there is the question of how far Gorbachev will let foreign policy change go. It can be convincingly argued that Gorbachev has been flexible enough to accommodate himself to developments in Eastern Europe – even to the extent that a united Germany within NATO is no longer the anathema it was months before. This, however, is another issue where the conservatives have expressed clear reservations and where Gorbachev may be forced to make some moves to reassure critics. It is clear that any alternative Soviet government might not take the same view on issues like German re-unification – although there would be few options open to the USSR to shape change in more acceptable ways. More crucial, though, is the question of whether he intends to allow the Soviet Union to lose its superpower status or is he intent on building it up? The early Gorbachev seemed to believe he was saving a superpower. Has the realization dawned that the future of the Soviet Union may lie as a lesser power, perhaps one geographically confined to the Russian and Far Eastern republics?[9]

Third, there is the question of the role of the Party. Even after the amendment of Article Six and the removal of its constitutional monopoly on power, it remains unclear what Gorbachev expects to emerge. He may have moved, finally, to the position that a democratic system, with himself at the helm in a revived presidency, is optimal. A parliament that was either ineffectual or supportive of his goals could well prove acceptable. On the other hand, the suspicion remains that Gorbachev still thinks that a reformed Communist Party – one in his image, deserted by the conservatives and adopting the positions of the radicals – would actually survive, in power, in a democratized system. Of course, whilst he is moving the Party to reform, Gorbachev is unlikely to reveal his true objectives, but the questions of how far Gorbachev will move on this issue, whether the move will be genuine, whether the moves of 1990 towards weakening the Party's leading role should be seen as a calculated step forward, or as a wave from a drowning man, are, almost certainly, the key issues facing the Soviet Union in the 1990s.

Fourth, there is the question of Gorbachev's support. It looks as if Gorbachev is either an exceptionally clever manipulator of trends in furtherence of a series of goals that he arrived at sometime between 1982 and 1988 or, far more realistically, that he has had the flexibility to ride with forces that he has unleashed. In either case his support looks questionable. Though some analysts like Hough and Gordievsky have stressed that Gorbachev still enjoys the support of the Party and the KGB and may not, in fact, be intent upon challenging their position, his position may not be entirely secure. Though the Party may still see a need for reform and hope for its own survival, support from conservatives like Ligachev, who stay with him whilst criticizing him *en route*, looks conditional. Beyond this circle Gorbachev seems to have to rely on an intelligentsia which is outnumbered by those wanting signs of economic improvement rather than decline, radicals who articulate the demand for more reform and, lastly, a general sense of desperation. The Party has been educated by the need for reform, pressures from the radicals and public opinion and the sheer impossibility of turning back the clock. Gorbachev, or circumstances, have created a series of positions where the only alternative open to the Soviet Communist Party is to move forward in the general direction demanded by the public, intelligentsia and radicals. Comforting assumptions about fall-back positions and limits to change, however, have fallen by the wayside. It now looks as if the next stage may be for Gorbachev to use the prospect of electoral justice to force even further reforms.

What is noteworthy, though, is that there may not actually be much support for Gorbachev's own position. His power lies from position rather than popular enthusiasm and his opponents may be growing in number as success fails to arrive and his promises of moderation are swept aside in the next wave of reform. There may be something to Boris Yeltsin's analysis that Gorbachev is actually becoming more dependent on the conservatives who have chosen to ride with him at the same time as his agenda is increasingly set by East European crowds and Soviet radicals.[10] Indeed, in some ways it looks a very negative form of power. Although there may have been an intention to win support for Gorbachev, it was notable in February 1990 that Gorbachev's Secretary for Ideology, Vadim Medvedev stressed the danger of 'an uncontrolled deluge and fall under the influences of populist demagogues or even fanatical leaders of pogroms'[11] whilst Foreign Minister Shevardnadze commented that 'if we cannot consolidate healthy forces, tomorrow there may emerge chaos and anarchy. It is easy to foresee the entry of dictators with nothing to prevent them turning back the development of our country.'[12] There may be a very real threat that alternative futures for the Soviet Union will come on offer if Gorbachev fails in his dual race to secure economic success and outpace his political opponents.

Finally, there is the issue of just what needs to be changed. Gorbachev seems now to have moved again against the Party – or at least those elements he sees as obstructing his plans. His economic reforms, however, seem to be losing momentum – although a renewed offensive on this front was promised for 1990 and 1991. This raises the question of whether removing the party bureaucracy is anything more than a necessary, rather than a sufficient, condition of economic success. Although Soviet Socialist Man does not behave as he should, one wonders here if the real problem is not party control but the attitude of the people. Support for socialist values like equality and dislike of those who succeed in the market seems a genuine problem, as do ingrained attitudes to authority, initiative and change. Moves to give incentives to workers and to revise the political system to mobilize individual aspirations may not work in a society where different values prevail. Indeed, it may be that by removing the trappings of a communist state, Gorbachev will only unveil the, rather unsuccessful, body of Mother Russia. The revival of Pamyat' and the tendency to blame continuing economic failure on 'the Jews', suggests that, just as nationalism and religion seem to have survived communism, other older values also lie lurking.

Time may, also, still be ticking away here. Although he has not faced the need to succeed in the four or five-year period dictated by Western election cycles, there may be some limit to Gorbachev's ability to promise but not deliver. Gorbachev's success or failure should be apparent by 1993 or 1994 – as time goes on it may be increasingly difficult to avoid some accounting for what, if anything, he has achieved to match the wave of change he has unleashed. Perhaps, by then a. pluralist Soviet parliament will decide to continue down Gorbachev's road or, perhaps, there will be another change at the top if there are no results to match the turmoil created. Any Western defence policy designed now for the mid/late 1990s ought at least to acknowledge the possibility that the more friendly Soviet Union of today may, by then, become a less amiable one – perhaps with a new leadership. Even if Gorbachev remains, current desperation may be as nothing compared to what the Soviet Union may feel forced to try if it still has not achieved economic success by the mid-1990s. If Gorbachev does not succeed sooner or later, the Soviet Union may have to face up to its economic and political crisis again. We could actually see cycles of reform and repression reminiscent of past Russian history. Predicting what, if any, threat the USSR will pose to the West in 1995 or 2005, seems to get more rather than less difficult as President Gorbachev continues to spear some windmills and stir up not a few hornets' nests as he goes on his reforming way.

THE WESTERN RESPONSE

The final question from all of this is what the Western response ought to be. Mr Gorbachev, it was generally agreed in early 1989, was better than any other obtainable Soviet leader for Western interests. It is arguable that the West itself has a keen interest in *perestroika* succeeding because a successful, even a competitive, Soviet Union would be preferable to some of the alternative Soviet Unions that might emerge if the multiple crises of 1985 went on to their natural conclusion. Foreign policy success was one of the few demonstrable pluses that Gorbachev could show his people and opponents – it both demonstrated his ability to secure benefits from the West and provided continuing evidence that the new leadership was effective, respected and, unlike the old gerontocracy, respectable. Gorbachev might well need external successes to tide him over until he could report some domestic achievements. This calculation, plus the need to be seen to match Gorbachev's initiatives with his own, seems to have influenced President Bush's proposals to cut European force levels and, perhaps, even the suggestion of $180 billion defence cuts that came late in 1989. The United States seems to have decided that it can work with Gorbachev, that he does mean real reform and that the alternatives are worse. It may even be that US support for Gorbachev now responds favourably in inverse proportion to the growth of Gorbachev's own problems.

Prospects of benefits accruing from the West were also seen as important to ensure that reform in the Eastern bloc continued. The carrot of favourable economic and political relations with the West helped ensure in 1989, except in Romania where the Soviet writ did not run, that East European dissent did not suffer the same fate as the Peking students and workers. Soviet dissidents – apart from some in Tbilisi and the anarchic southern republics – shelter under the same umbrella. Gorbachev's new image requires a universal application of new principles – a crackdown in one place would destroy credibility elsewhere. Making sure that the carrot was always tempting, whatever the present difficulties, is possibly an important bolster to whatever qualms Gorbachev or his colleagues have about ever resorting to old methods to solve new problems.

There were, some argued, limits to how far the West could go in this. Economic support for the Soviet Union was seen as dangerous – both to the potential borrower and lender. The size of Soviet deficits, trade deficits and inflation argued for caution lest another Mexico should result. There was concern on these grounds about lending to Eastern Europe as well, but subsequent events suggest that there may be a limited role for Western aid here. The long-term integration of Eastern European economies into the Western economic system seemed far more likely at the end of the year than it did at the beginning.

On the defence front, there were dangers. The prospect that NATO would be undermined by Soviet propaganda worried some. Clearly, a certain level of military capability was necessary whilst the Soviet Union remained so powerful – the very size of the Soviet Union suggests that even the most peaceable Soviet government would have to be considered as a potential threat by its neighbours. Worse than this, the scope of Gorbachev's changes undermined most of the old assumptions of threat assessment. Soviet capabilities and intentions are now changing more dramatically than at any period since 1917, as viable routes open up to all possible Soviet futures from economic decline, through nationalist revival, democratization, imperial breakdown, and growing desperation. In the current state of flux in Eastern Europe and the USSR, caution seemed prudent.

Not least worrying, was the likely impact on Western and Eastern Europe if something dramatic occurred to change the comforting picture of a benign USSR. If Western voters pressed for disarmament only to see repression and a military threat return, the result could well be terrified Western publics seeking some security with no reassuring defence against attack available to fall back on. The result of precipitate disarmament could be unsustainable crisis if events ever changed circumstances. Nor did there seem to be any need for the West to weaken its own security to maintain Gorbachev in power. Soviet willingness to negotiate seriously on arms control suggested that reasonable compromises were available – whilst Gorbachev had some scope both in terms of current force levels and political capital to make unilateral cuts. It was important, too, not to overrate the importance of foreign affairs in the Soviet dilemma. It seemed likely that the key issue in Soviet political development would not be foreign policy success but Gorbachev's ability to achieve a revolution in attitudes, working practices, politics and the economy generally. Though the West ought to think more about what it could do to help, there was only a limited amount the West could do here. The future of the Soviet Union, and the future threat it poses to the West, remain in Soviet hands.

NOTES AND REFERENCES

1. See 'Reform spending cuts necessary says Gorbachev adviser', *TASS*, 4 October 89.
2. 'Riding the tiger', *Newsweek*, 4 December 1989, pp. 14–20; R Cornwell, 'The year of revolution – USSR', *The Independent*, 28 December 1989; L. Morrow, 'Man of the decade – Gorbachev the unlikely patron of change', *Time*, 1 January 1990, pp. 14–17; B. W. Nelson, 'The year of the people', ibid., pp. 18–25; M. Kramer, 'The Gorbachev touch', ibid., pp. 26–7; 'The new USSR – special issue' *Time*, 10 April 1989, pp. 14–78.
3. *Newsweek*, 4 December 1989, op. cit.; R. Cornwell, 'How Party rose against Gorbachev', *The Independent*, 14 December 1989; B. Yeltsin, 'Gagged by Gorbachev', *The Sunday Times*, 18 February 1990; R. Clark, 'The world will watch our bleeding land in horror', *The Sunday Correspondent*, 28 January

1990; S. Cranshaw, 'Can Gorbachev bounce back one more time?', *The Independent On Sunday*, 28 January 1990; J. Blitz, 'United it stands . . . divided it falls', *The Sunday Times*, 7 January 1990; J. Blitz, 'Less food under Gorbachev, the shops' grim tale', *The Sunday Times*, 4 February 1990.

4. R. Cornwell, 'Izvestia warns of risk to Gorbachev', *The Independent*, 24 January 1990.

5. *Newsweek*, 4 December 1989, op. cit.; F. Coleman and R. Watson, 'Perestroika isn't working', *Newsweek*, 13 March 1989, pp. 8–11.

6. R. Cornwell, 'Gorbachev's secession offer muddies the constitutional waters', *The Independent*, 13 January 1990.

7. T. Fishlock, 'Gorbachev critics decry his reforms', *Daily Telegraph*, 7 February 1990; M. Dejevsky, 'Gorbachev's revolution', *The Times*, 8 February 1990; R. Cornwell, 'Soviet conservatives in last stand, *The Independent*, 7 February 1990.

8. R. Cornwell, 'End of the communist state', *The Independent*, 8 February 1990; J. Blitz, 'Out of the ice age', *The Sunday Times*, 11 February 1990; J. F. Hough, 'Why Gorby is defying the pundits' predictions', *The New York Times*, 11 February 1990.

9. R. Cornwell, 'What would remain of the Soviet Union', *The Independent*, 13 January 1990.

10. 'Yeltsin – Russians risk a civil war', *The Sunday Times*, 11 February 1990.

11. M. Dejevsky, op. cit.

12. T. Fishlock, 'Kremlin vote gives victory to Gorbachev', *The Daily Telegraph*, 8 February 1990.

4 Soviet military strategy in an age of new thinking on international security*

Phillip A. Petersen

Much in the same way as Ronald Reagan dreamed of a space-based alternative to mutual assured destruction, Mikhail Gorbachev offers an alternative grand vision focused on avoiding the perils of our contemporary international security system. Reflecting their respective cultural environments, Reagan sought technical solutions where Gorbachev looks to the perfectibility of mankind. Their meeting in Reykjavik only confirmed for others their mutual intention to transform fundamentally the strategic environment. Thus, for both East and West, the strategic context of security policy is changing at an accelerating pace. Military planning in both the Warsaw Pact and NATO is being forced to confront 'new realities' in the form of shifts in intra-alliance relationships, intensive re-evaluations of defense spending, and the implications of a quickening scientific-technical revolution in military affairs.

Gorbachev's redefinition of national security in the nuclear age constitutes a direct challenge to the zero-sum assumptions that shaped the traditional Soviet military approach to security. Soviet advocates of the indivisibility of security in the nuclear age are not only heightening the importance of political as distinct from military-technical variables in the security calculus, but place unusual emphasis on threat reduction, unilateral restraint, and collaboration with adversaries. Perhaps again reflecting their respective environments, it is interesting to note that whereas Americans frequently surpass the Soviets in the application of Soviet theoretical literature in scientific-technical fields, the Soviets are now making practical application of the work of American psychologists on the meaning and function of diabolical enemy images.[1] Thus, shortly before the 1988 Gorbachev–Reagan Summit meeting in Moscow, Georgi Arbatov told American reporters that 'we are going to do something terrible to you. We are going to deprive you of an enemy.'[2] Such perceptions about the role of images as defense policy determinants obviously clash with the traditional fixation on 'antagonistic contradictions' in determining military sufficiency. Not since the 'nuclear revolution in military affairs' has there been such an intense debate over the direction Soviet force development should take.

*The author wishes to express his appreciation to Captain Jose Palacios, William Pratt, Charles Pritchard, Joshua B. Spero and Dr Graham Turbiville for their research assistance in preparing this manuscript.

PERESTROIKA AND THE ART OF WAR

Soviet military strategy has, since the mid-1960s, been directed towards attaining victory with conventional arms under nuclear-threatened conditions. So long as an opponent maintained a survivable nuclear retaliatory capability, the Soviets had no intention of initiating nuclear use. In the case of NATO, Soviet strategic planners hoped, instead, to exploit what they perceived as internal contradictions which plague the alliance to undermine its political and military effectiveness.[3] Their concept of operations was focused on obtaining the synergistic effect of destroying much of NATO's nuclear capabilities and quickly taking a conventional offensive beyond the point at which the remaining assets could alter the outcome of the conflict.

The military-strategic objective was to win a quick victory in the main Theater of Strategic Military Action (TSMA),[4] while defending in secondary TSMAs. Operationally, victory was to be obtained by conducting breakthroughs against the weakest ground forces in the main continental TSMA to encircle the strongest of the enemy's forces (see Figure 4:1). Beyond the military implications of operational success, the Soviets hoped to obtain greater political leverage against the smaller states in the NATO coalition. Encirclement and destruction of NATO's forward deployed corps, and a successful effort to coerce Denmark, the Netherlands and Belgium out of the Western coalition was perceived to offer the greatest hope of ending a war before it escalated to nuclear use or became so protracted as to create unmanageable strains on the Warsaw Pact coalition (see Figure 4:2). The forces and means required for such an ambitious concept of operations, however, provoked an 'enemy image' problem for the Soviet Union.

The Western reaction to the Soviet military buildup of the 1970s led to an arms race which the Soviet economy could not sustain and from which Gorbachev wanted to disengage. He rejected security requirements based upon a calculation of the forces necessary to balance any possible coalition of states that might oppose the Soviet Union. In an effort to generate better alternatives, Gorbachev created new security study centers in the international and propaganda departments of the Party Central Committee and in the arms control and policy planning departments of the Foreign Affairs Ministry. The civilian security specialists argued that force requirements should be derived from the calculation of what is necessary to deter war, not win it.

Nearly two years of discussion in the Defense Council preceeded the announcement of a new military doctrine. The new military doctrine unveiled at a Warsaw Pact meeting in May 1987 should, however, be seen as the socio-political expression of military-technical aspects of doctrine in transition. In military terms, the doctrine conforms to a perceived 'transitional stage' in military affairs in the direction of a far-reaching transformation of 'future war' forecast by Soviet military scientists on the basis of technological trends. The new doctrine tasks the Soviet military with war prevention without relieving them of the responsibility of producing victory in the event war does occur. The subsequent and continuing debate

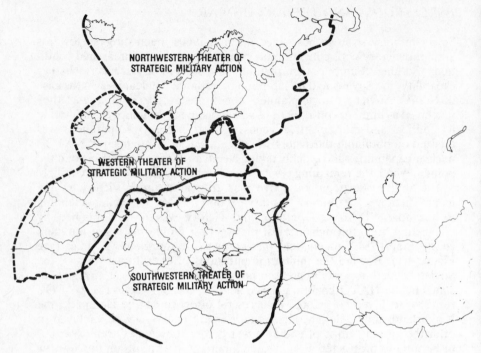

Figure 4:1 European theaters of strategic military action

in the Soviet Union centers on the natural tension between the old mission and the new emphasis on war-prevention.

Although Soviet military scientists recognize that political methods of guaranteeing security (i.e. negotiations, agreements, treaties) can be of great utility, they also warn that 'a mismatch between political and military means and the violation of their harmony, and especially an underestimation of proper military means, can do a great deal of harm to the matter of defending socialist achievements'.[5] For their part, civilian critics of the military point to an excessive tendency in Soviet foreign policy to rely on military force. Aleksandr Bovin, for example, wrote in mid-June 1988 that 'the deployment of SS-20 missiles and the introduction of troops in Afghanistan were . . . typical examples of subjective decisions oriented at the use of military force in foreign policy'. His conclusion was that 'in both cases we clearly overestimated our possibilities and underestimated what could be called the resistance of the environment'.[6]

The tension between deterring war and developing the ability to win the war if it should occur generates conflicting requirements. Defense Minister D. T. Yazov, for example, has emphasized that 'despite the fact that a start has been made on the positive process in the military-political situation, there are no guarantees yet to their irreversibility'.[7] Similarly, Deputy Chief of the General Staff Colonel General M. Gareyev has chosen to stress the 'harsh reality' of the West's military preparations and the undeniable fact

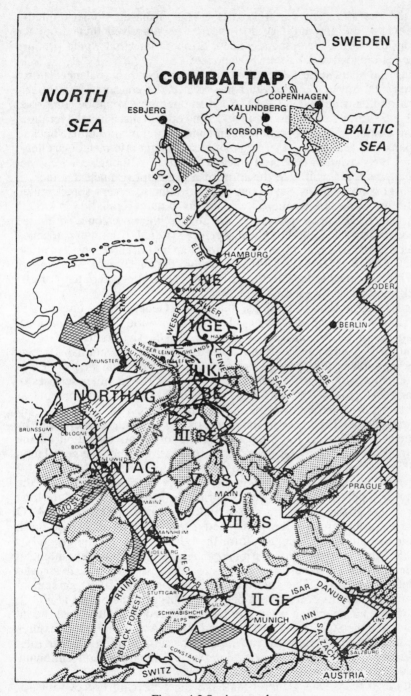

Figure 4:2 Soviet attack axes

that the 'real threat of war still exists'.[8] Thus, from the Soviet military's perspective, the new military doctrine has not absolved them from the responsibility for developing a concept of operations that would produce victory at the lowest risk to the Soviet state.

Over the years since taking the decision to acquire a 'balanced' force posture, the Soviet General Staff has refined the concept of a strategic operation in a continental TSMA. Such an operation would be comprised of air and anti-air operations, *front* and army operations, a naval operation, and an assault landing operation. If an enemy attempted to utilize nuclear weapons, the Warsaw Pact strategic offensive might also include artillery, missile, and aviation-delivered nuclear strikes.[9] Although such Soviet nuclear use could well take the form of a pre-emptive nuclear attack, it is also possible that the Soviets would be willing to accept some limited theater use of nuclear weapons by an enemy without retaliation in kind.[10] If nuclear assets were employed by the Soviets, their use could be limited for both military and political effect. Lecture materials from the Voroshilov General Staff Academy, for example, note that 'political reasons may affect the selection of areas of the TSMA for action, the selection of the countries to be hit by nuclear strikes, or the nations not to be attacked or temporarily attacked by nuclear weapons'.

Under non-nuclear conditions, the Soviet General Staff intended to substitute a modernized version of a Second World War conventional air operation for an initial mass nuclear strike. The contemporary air operation is a non-nuclear, joint operation on the operational-strategic scale, comprising the aggregate combat activities of strategic aviation in coordination with other branches of aviation as well as other services of the armed forces.[11] Assessing that, under both nuclear and non-nuclear conditions, at some point in the mobilization process as much as 50 per cent of NATO's firepower in the Western TSMA could be delivered by aviation,[12] the Soviets focus the main effort of an air operation on the neutralization of enemy air assets so as to decisively shift the correlation of forces and means in the probable main TSMA.

Perhaps the most crucial requirement of the air operation plan is the ability to suppress NATO airfields during the early minutes of the first mass strike. If the Soviet air forces could not catch most of the NATO air forces on the ground, the West's better trained pilots might well finish the air battle quickly enough to turn the tide of battle on the ground as well. Seeking to avoid this possibility, Soviet military planners intended to employ surface-to-surface missiles to suppress time-critical air and air-defense activities. The Intermediate Nuclear Force (INF) agreement turned out, therefore, to have a negative impact on the Soviet ability to execute the air operation when Gorbachev offered to include operational missiles like the SCALEBOARD and the SS-23. As a solution to pressures to reduce the numbers of theater missiles because of their nuclear role, Soviet planners are now showing interest in employing conventionally armed ICBMs against such targets as airfields.[13]

Although the Soviet General Staff has more Ground Forces forward-deployed than is required by their own calculations for the conduct of offensive operations, this situation probably reflects Soviet respect for NATO airpower. According to a study by the USSR Academy of Sciences, 'if 45 years ago 100 aircraft could destroy 1,000 ground combat vehicles, on the average, in 35 days, now a similar mission may be performed in 36 hours.'[14] The perceived impact of NATO airpower on the correlation of forces is so great that in 1988 the then Chief of the Soviet General Staff Marshal of the Soviet Union S. F. Akhromeyev was willing to trade 20–40 tanks per ground attack aircraft.[15] Despite Akhromeyev's strong opposition to a Soviet unilateral force reduction, when the West held firm to its commitment to parity in conventional forces, Gorbachev proceeded with his new thinking on international security. As with the military's policy preferences in Afghanistan, Gorbachev gave them time to work out their own solutions, but when they failed he simply imposed his own.

Essentially, Gorbachev's

new way of thinking in security matters presupposes a revision of the previous requisites and views and a greater conformity between foreign policy and military doctrine, on the one hand, and the development of the art of war and military buildup, on the other.[16]

Yet even Soviet civilian international security specialists appreciate the difficulty of changing military strategy and operational plans, and restructuring the armed forces along defensive principles. Clearly, 'the same elements can perform either offensive of defensive operations' and, no matter how strong the defense may be, 'an aggressor, by concentrating forces in one sector and resorting to a surprise attack and free maneuvering, will in any case have a good chance of breaking through and advancing deep into the territory of the other side'.[17] It is understood even among these civilian theorists, therefore, that 'what is needed to repulse this kind of aggression is a huge counteroffensive potential which, from an operational-tactical point of view, would carry out offensive tasks, and from the strategic point of view, defensive tasks.'[18]

Evaluated in terms of these requirements, the force reductions announced[19] by Gorbachev in December 1988 unquestionably preserve for the Soviets a counteroffensive capability and have worked to reduce, at least in the minds of Western publics, the fear of an unprovoked Soviet attack. Yet it should be understood that 'a huge counteroffensive potential' may be used pre-emptively and, thereby, become an offensive. It should also be understood that lower force levels may, in fact, create less stability rather than greater stability.

The thing is that the advancing side, which has the initiative, usually can use its men and equipment more intensively in the active zones of operations (in the decisive place and at the decisive time) and thus more fully realize its general potential capabilities in comparison with the defending side.[20]

CALCULATING SUFFICIENCY

When calculating sufficiency, it is important to understand that the lower the general density of forces, that is, the lower the overall force to space ratio, the easier it is to obtain a sufficient concentration of forces and means on the main sector. The defending side may need fewer forces than the offensive to succeed at the point of attack, but the attacker selects the main sector of combat and, thereby, may more easily concentrate its forces at the decisive point and time. Thus, when in the course of force reductions the defender is left with even fewer forces to cover the same frontage, it becomes more difficult to defend everywhere in sufficient strength to slow the attack enough to maneuver adequate forces to prevent breakthroughs from occurring.

For the Soviet General Staff, the objective in preparing the plan for an offensive operation is 'to create, at the decisive moment and in the principal region, such a ratio of forces in one's own advantage that the assigned mission can be accomplished with a probability, let us say, of not less than 0.8'.[21] In fact, Soviet military theorists believe that 'victory may be achieved . . . with equal or even inferior general strength of forces and means than the enemy'.[22] This can be accomplished, however, only if local superiority can be obtained in the decisive sector through the creation of strike groups. The success of such strike groups, in turn, would depend upon 'the nature of the terrain, the capacity of the accessible sectors, the conditions for employing weapons and combat equipment, and the possibility for the covert concentrating of troops'.[23]

Skill in creating an overwhelming superiority over the enemy at the decisive place and time requires the massing of forces and means sufficient to conduct a successful offensive without providing 'the enemy the capability, firstly, to conduct a successful offensive with a goal of outflanking the strike group from the flanks and rear area, and secondly, to transfer forces from other sectors to the sector of the main strike'.[24] In terms of this operational requirement, Soviet military scientists have concluded that with a 1–1.5:1 general ratio of forces and means, it is possible to achieve a 3–5:1 forces and means advantage on the main sector (see Figure 4:3). Although the Soviets would seek as much as a 7:1 superiority to reduce casualty rates,[25] once the ratio of forces on a breakthrough sector reaches 5:1 in favor of the attacker within a given division sector the attacking unit will have a 0.9 or greater probability of achieving its objectives.[26] Since the Soviets believe it possible to defend successfully at a 1:2 negative correlation, even with as low as a 1:1 general ratio of forces and means within the 700-km wide Western TSMA, the Soviets could generate 4 army-level breakthrough sectors of approximately 20 km in width.[27]

Four army-level breakthrough sectors are sufficient to launch a general offensive in the Western TSMA directed at the encirclement of the I German Corps in the Northern Army Group (NORTHAG) and the two German and two US Corps in the Central Army Group (NORTHAG). Thus, even with a 1:1 correlation of forces the Soviet General Staff would have sufficient forces and means to execute the strategic offensive plans developed in the 1970s if the air operation was successful in neutralizing NATO's air power. A mutual balanced force reduction (MBFR) agreement in the Western TSMA, therefore, would not necessarily reduce the Soviet capability to accomplish their encirclement plans. In fact, by reducing force to space ratios, a MBFR agreement could facilitate the Soviet ability to execute such a concept of operations.

None of this is to argue that Gorbachev's new thinking on international security is directed at facilitating the execution of Soviet General Staff contingency planning. In fact, if anything, the Soviet General Staff is less confident that it would receive authorization for the conduct of a pre-emptive strategic offensive from the present Defense Council than it was during the Brezhnev years. Soviet military writings clearly betray concern that insufficient attention has been paid to the full range of contingencies and conditions under which a war might break out. Thus, military spokesmen such as General Gareyev have alluded to potential constraints that might hamper effective mobilization and military preparedness in a crisis period.[28] Although better integration of offensive and defensive efforts might provide a hedge against the potentially disastrous consequences of less than full preparedness at the start of conflict, the emerging offense–defense relationship raises additional questions concerning military stability.

PROBLEMS OF MILITARY STABILITY[29]

The introduction of high-accuracy systems, and particularly the depth to which they may be employed, has led Soviet and Warsaw Pact military theoreticians to undertake 'a complete reevaluation of the very essence of the defense on the future battlefield'.[30] According to this analysis, defensive objectives were formerly achieved by actions conducted within the tactical zone designed to 'pulverize' the enemy in a series of defensive battles. The introduction of deep-strike, precision-guided weapons changes this calculation in several ways.

First, the defender's strike will not be limited simply to the tactical zone,

Forces and Means	Last Ops of WWII		Concepts of 1945-1953		With Nuclear Employment		Without Nuclear Employment	
	General	Main Sector	General	Main Sector	General	Main Sector	General	Main Sector
Motorized Rifle Battalions	1.4-5.5	3.0-8.5	1.1-1.5	3.0-4.0	1.0-1.5	2.0-3.0	1.0-1.5	3.0-4.0
Tanks and Self-Propelled Artillery	1.1-6.0	4.5-9.0	1.5-2.0	3.0-4.0	1.0-1.5	2.0-3.0	1.0-1.5	3.0-4.0
Artillery	1.5-6.5	4.2-8.5	1.5-2.0	3.0-4.0	1.0	1.5-2.0	1.0-1.5	3.0-5.0
Aircraft	2.0	3.5	1.5	2.0	1.0	1.0	1.5	2.0

Source: 'Lecture Materials from the Voroshilov General Staff Academy, Army Offensive'

Figure 4:3 Correlation of forces in main attack sectors and secondary (active/passive defense) sectors (indicated as Relative Superiority over Opponent, X:1)

but may be conducted across the depth of the enemy's deployment. This would be part of a progressively increasing scale of operations over the coming decades. By Soviet definition, the scale of military operations is determined not only by depth and breadth, but also by duration.[31] As far as depth is concerned, by every indicator Soviet military planners have concluded that future non-nuclear systems may play an expanded role not only at operational-strategic depths, but even at global strategic depths.

With respect to the geographical breadth of potential conflict, Soviet General Staff planners continue to focus on the five TSMAs contiguous to the Soviet Union, namely on the Eurasian landmass, as the central arena of a future war. Beyond this arena, however, Soviet military theoreticians have for some time been probing the prospect of conventional warfare conducted on a global scale. Indeed, authoritative statements of Soviet military doctrine and military strategy have clearly traced the outlines of a war which, while global in scope and decisive in nature, would not necessarily escalate to the use of nuclear weapons.[32] In a 1984 interview, then Chief of the General Staff Ogarkov predicted that, as a consequence of the increasing range of emerging conventional weapons technologies, the 'zone of potential strategic military actions' would be expanded as many of the new weapons become 'global' in application. Ogarkov's prediction, which has been reiterated by other Soviet sources, seems based on a somewhat different set of planning assumptions than those commonly employed in the West.[33]

With regard to the duration of a potential conflict, for some twenty-five years the Soviets have acknowledged the need to prepare for a war that could last at least one year.[34] Soviet military scientists appear to see no contradiction between the anticipation of an extended conflict on the one hand, and the likelihood, on the other hand, that the new systems would dramatically increase the tempo of conventional operations. They apparently have concluded that the combination of attrition, interdiction of forward-deploying forces, disruption of control, and simply the increased complexity of operations may entail prolonged operations. Consequently, some military theoreticians argue that, regardless of whether the war is fought with nuclear or conventional-only means, 'it is necessary to be prepared for a long, stubborn and bitter armed struggle'.[35] Some Soviet civilian international security specialists note, however, that contemporary local wars suggest that the intensity of modern conflict is such that, 'in the case of the same intensity of combat operations in the European theater (although it would certainly be higher) . . . all NATO and Warsaw Pact Treaty basic combat equipment . . . would be "knocked out" altogether in no more than 30 days'.[36]

A second way in which deep-strike, precision-guided weapons are changing the nature of defense on the future battlefield concerns the relationship between surprise and readiness. The availability of long-range 'defensive' strikes throughout the depth of the enemy's disposition could purchase time for completing the mobilization while substantially improving the conditions for subsequent offensive operations. This is usually put in the context of wrestling the initiative away from the attacking side before it obtains sufficient momentum to sustain its offensive. The actual timing of the combat actions of the defending side, however, raise the issue of crisis stability. Should the defender pre-empt the attacker's preparations, the opportunity would arise for the defender to seize the initiative and launch a counteroffensive under very favorable conditions. Thus, such a capability increasingly blurs the distinction between offensive and defensive operations, since both attacker and defender would attempt to fulfill their mission 'by active offensive methods'.[37]

A third way in which deep-strike, precision-guided weapons are changing the essence of defense on the future battlefield relates to the offense-defense mix in both offensive and defensive operations. The enhanced capabilities of the defense provide greater flexibility in the offense-defense mix to cope with the problem of attrition, particularly with respect to forces operating on critical axes of advance. By improving defensive capabilities, the new technologies allow forces operating on secondary axes to more readily transition to the defense and release forces for redeployment to more critical areas. This enhanced flexibility would appear to apply equally to forces operating on operational or strategic directions and, perhaps, even to entire TSMAs. This latter capability is especially relevant in an era of economic retrenchment and arms control where fewer forces and means may be available.

POLITICS AND MILITARY STRATEGY

As was suggested in the beginning of this chapter, *perestroika* is being advanced in the area of Soviet doctrine, strategy, and military development as it is in all other spheres of Soviet society. Soviet civilian international security specialists have argued that the 'goal is to bring military policy more in line with economic and international political realities'.[38] Urging 'statesmen and politicians as well as military leaders (strategists) to take careful account of economic factors, of the country's industrial and economic resources', and stressing 'the importance of an optimum distribution of the always limited resources among the armed forces', they warn that 'decisions made at the boundary between politics and strategy may have fatal and irreversible consequences'.[39]

Noting that 'the general public, too, should have a knowledge of the main military strategic questions, which means that openness is needed in this particular sphere as well', it is argued that 'this is one of the main conditions for policy to exercise real and not nominal control over military strategy, so that there can be complete correspondence between the political and military technical components of the state's military doctrine'.[40] The discussion itself is centered on

a certain absolutising of the experience of the Great Patriotic War (for all its unquestionable value) to the detriment of full consideration of all the new political, economic, scientific, technological and strategic factors which are now thoroughly changing the entire 'strategic landscape'.[41]

Appreciating that 'the depletion of the economy by the mounting burden of military-political expenditures will increasingly affect the military-technical component of [Soviet] military power as such, particularly if the arms race spills into outer space',[42] the security debate in the Soviet Union is about ensuring security at a lower cost. 'In the context of the reforms under way in the USSR the task is being advanced here of ensuring security chiefly by political rather than military means.'[43] Discussion over how to proceed with this task has been summarized in the following manner:

Individual public figures and scholars in the USSR are advancing at present the idea that security does not require equality of military potentials with the other side. Considering the absurdly high levels of destructive arsenals that have been amassed, and the exhausting and destabilising nature of their further buildup for the sake of maintaining parity, it is proposed to proceed on the principle of reasonable sufficiency and drop out of the West-imposed race for parity, which is understood as equality of military potentials.

On the other hand, in a number of statements and articles by Soviet authors (especially military) the point is made that security today can be ensured solely by approximate military equality or parity, no matter what level it may rise to. Precisely it, these authors contend, is what is used to determine the limit of reasonable sufficiency of the military potential of the USSR and its allies, but on minimal levels, which now depends on the possibility of agreements with the West. Thus, confinement of military potentials to the limits of reasonable sufficiency is being made dependent on the stand of our partners in talks.[44]

This latter line of argument, however, has already been soundly rejected in the documents of the CPSU Central Committee for the 19th All-Union CPSU Conference:

Seeking military-strategic parity, we did not always draw in the past on the possibilities for ensuring national security through political means and as a result allowed ourselves to be drawn into the arms race, which could not but affect the country's socio-economic development and its international position.[45]

In the words of one of the Soviet civilian defence critics, 'the optimal correlation between the economic, international-political and military foundations of security was broken. The latter developed increasingly at the expense of and to the detriment of the first two.'[46] As a result, the security debate in the Soviet Union will increasingly focus on the question of sufficiency for what, for the accomplishment of what strategic and operational tasks?

By late 1988, oblique attacks on the Soviet Navy were being framed over the advisability for the Soviet Union to maintain a large surface fleet which diverts a significant portion of the sums appropriated for defense and may, thereby, deny Soviet ground forces appropriate technical equipment.[47] In fact, according to testimony by the US Director of Naval Intelligence (DNI) before the House Armed Services Committee, the Soviet Navy took more surface ships out of active service in 1988 than in any year in recent history and began selling major combat ships for scrap on the world market.[48] Beyond the recent reductions in the surface fleet, nearly one-half the Soviet submarine fleet has reached the end of its normal lifespan. Professor Jan Breemer of the Naval Postgraduate

School in Monterey has written that the Soviet submarine fleet is faced with 'massive block obsolescence'.[49] Suggesting that many of the older submarines have become more dangerous to their own crews than to their Western opponents, he predicts the strength of the Soviet submarine fleet of the mid-1990s will fall to about 200 non-strategic types that are twenty years old or less.[50]

The DNI, Rear Admiral Thomas A. Brooks, did note in his testimony, however, that the future Soviet Navy is likely to be 'smaller numerically but certainly more capable than today's'.[51] Admiral Brooks also stated that by 1993 the Soviets could have their first two large-deck aircraft carriers operational. In addition, although Soviet submarine production has dropped off sharply, the Soviets continue to add new subs to an inventory that by early 1989 numbered thirty first-line anti-submarine warfare (ASW) platforms.[52] This force development is in consonance with the following three strategic missions:

1. Repulse of an enemy aerospace attack. Primary missions of the navy in support of this mission are:
   Hunting and destroying strategic missile submarines;
   Hunting and destroying surface combatants armed with long-range ship-to-shore missiles;
   Hunting and destroying aircraft carriers.
2. Neutralization of the enemy's military-economic potential. Primary missions of the navy in support of this mission are:
   Strategic strike;
   Sea lines of communication (SLOC) interdiction;
   Disruption of seabed (above all, oil) production.
3. Destruction of groupings of enemy armed forces. Primary missions of the navy in support of this mission are in support of a strategic operation in a continental TSMA and include:
   Destroy enemy personnel and equipment;
   Capture enemy territory, straits zones, and island areas.[53]

Understanding that he will be required to do more with less, the Commander-in-Chief of the Soviet Navy has asserted that countering NATO naval strike forces is a task that only a modern navy is capable of fulfilling. In trying to do more with less, Admiral of the Fleet Chernavin has noted that 'all defense construction must henceforth be oriented principally on qualitative parameters both with respect to equipment and military science and to the composition of the armed forces.'[54] The objective conditions of development require that the Soviets clearly define their economic interests and display more selectivity in identifying goals and commitments abroad. Since 'the depletion of the economy by the mounting burden of military-political expenditures will increasingly affect the military-technical component of [Soviet] power as such', it is being argued that 'it would be expedient to gradually abandon [Soviet] global rivalry with the USA and refrain from the costly support of unpopular regimes, political movements, parties, etc.'[55]

At the political level, the policy flowing from new thinking reflects the thesis that the Soviet Union 'has no valid reason to remain in a state of class confrontation with the USA or any other country, provided certainly that [the Soviets] do not proceed from the absurd theory of permanent revolution'.[56] At the military level, the central question

is how political aims concerning averting war and strengthening strategic stability find their reflection in the military-technical portion of military doctrine, in strategic and operational concepts, in the development of the armed forces and their stationing, in plans for mobilization of industry, etc.[57]

In a June 1988 attempt to contribute to the examination of the 'criteria and conditions of stability of the military-strategic equilibrium', Andrei Kokoshin and Valentin Larionov offered military and civilian specialists the following four hypothetical variants of counterpositioning conventional forces and armaments as 'one of the analytical instruments for an advance in the elaboration of the problem of strengthening strategic stability in Europe':

1. **Strategic-scale offensive posture**: Characterized by high combat readiness, immediate offensive operations in the initial period of war, severe risk of escalation, and war aims defined in terms of capture of the enemy's territory (Historical analogue, '1914').
2. **Strategic-scale counteroffensive posture**: Characterized by high combat readiness, 'premeditated defense' during initial period of war followed by counteroffensive to destroy enemy forces and set stage for successive operations deep into enemy territory, escalatory risk still high and no change in war aims (Historical analogue, Battle of Kursk from July–August, 1943).
3. **Operational-scale counterstrike posture**: Operational-tactical forces kept at high state of readiness, forces configured to defeat aggressor and recapture lost territory, serious problem because most collateral damage inflicted upon attacked country and so pressure exists to carry war across frontier, although *political* factors can act as a restraint (Historical analogues, Khalkhin-Gol in 1939 and Korea from July 1951–June 1953).
4. **Operational/strategic-scale defensive posture**: Characterized a 'strictly defensive posture' in which high combat readiness only among forward forces, but these have been stripped of offensive capabilities (i.e. heavy armor, etc.) and manuever is limited to tactical scale (i.e. units up to and including division in size) *Political* factors condition creation of posture itself, and both sides have sufficient trust to limit capabilities to tactical-scale combat actions (no historical analogues are offered).[58]

The concept of 'victory' in the Kokoshin-Larionov construct varies from strategic in the first and second variant to operational in the third variant and tactical in the fourth. While the first variant may clearly be provocative, and therefore destabilizing, the second, third, and fourth variants are perceived as non-provocative, although only the fourth variant could properly be called 'defensive defense'. Kokoshin and Larionov conclude their article by noting that 'one of the elements of going over to a non-offensive defense can be the transfer of regular formations into the reserves'.[59]

During the course of 1988 and into 1989 a debate occurred over which of the following types of armed forces most reflected new thinking in international security and was best suited to the requirements of *perestroika*: 1. A regular army based on universal service; 2. A regular army based on volunteer service; 3. A territorial-militia; or 4. A mixed system incorporating both regular and militia forces.[60] Returning to their previously concluding notion concerning the non-offensive nature of a non-regular army, Kokoshin and Larionov argued in February 1989 for the adoption of a 'mixed system'. According to their argument, a 'mixed system', combining cadre units with territorial-militia formations was found to be more economic and eventually accepted as the model for military construction of the mid-1920s. This system was said to have permitted qualitative improvements in the armed forces with a minimum of expenditures for their support. At that time the country was laying the foundation for a socialist economy and accordingly, a maximum mobilization of materials and resources was required. For this reason, Kokoshin and Larionov note 'the situation is similar somewhat with the demands of *perestroika* today. A mixed system, relying on a small permanent cadre could successfully prepare reserve contingents, practically without diverting citizens with military obligations from productive labor and their area of residence.'[61]

Quite obviously, the type of armed forces required depends largely upon the skills required of the troops to fulfill the tasks assigned. Although Defence Minister Yazov complains of the 'incompetence' of 'sensation-seeking' proposals based upon 'shallow arguments', he also notes

there are proposals to reduce the duration of active compulsory military service to 1 year, to replace existing formations and units with national formations stationed in the place where the draft contingent is resident, and so on and so forth. These are serious political questions of *vital importance* for the people. They require a responsible approach and comprehensive substantiation.[62]

In assessing these political questions of vital importance, Yazov notes that manning the Army on the basis of voluntary hired recruitment 'is at least several times more expensive for society than an army manned on the basis of universal compulsory military service'.[63] On this particular point, the fact that 'it is calculated that a professional army would be 5–8 times more expensive for [Soviet] society'[64] would suggest that this option was given some degree of serious study. In addition to rejecting a volunteer service regular army, Yazov rejects 'arguments for a transition to a territorial-militia system'. In his opinion,

the most important thing is that a territorial-militia system objectively precludes both the mastery of modern weapons at short-duration periodical camps and, especially, the achievement of the necessary combat harmony . . . that transforms a subunit, unit, or ship into a combat-capable organism.[65]

It is also interesting to note that Yazov argues that 'militia units are stationed not where the situation requires but where they are manned and camps are held, and as a result they cannot gain control of a theater of operations.'[66] In other words, a territorial-militia system would neither be able to take the fighting to the enemy's territory nor recapture its own lost territory. 'The guaranteed fulfilment of these tasks is ensured by the existing system of manning the USSR Armed Forces on the basis of universal military service.'[67] In particular, 'the proposals made by certain members of the national intelligentsia to switch to a military organized on the basis of republican principles', are judged to be a reflection 'of their enchantment with national separatism rather than their concern for preserving national independence and national culture'.[68]

What does not seem to have been rejected is the creation of a mixed regular-militia system so long as it reflects universal service in multinational units and is not a 'unilateral transition to a defense under militia principles'.[69] Since it has been argued that continued development of the current peacetime army is 'too much of a burden on society, because it diverts large masses of people from their productive work for long periods',[70] some mixed system incorporating a reduction of the strength of the army to control spending seems probable.[71] The outline for such a, if not less offensive then certainly less provocative, defense was suggested in an address by Colonel-General M. A. Gareyev in October 1988. According to the Deputy Chief of the General Staff,

such a defence would presumably be of a local nature and would be based on holding major key areas and positions and making widespread use of various obstacles. Possibly on some axes it will be necessary to organise reinforced areas equipped with the latest reconnaissance systems and automatically-guided high-accuracy weapons. The fewer forces there are allocated to defence, the more importance will be attached to the establishment of highly-mobile reserves for rapid maneuvring towards threatened axes. But the specific organisation of the defence in a particular theatre or on a particular axis will depend on which likely adversary one is confronted with, on the features of the terrain and on other conditions.[72]

What Gareyev is describing sounds rather like the 'operational-scale counterstrike posture' in the Kokoshin-Larionov model. Forces restructured to support such a posture in the Group of Soviet Forces in Germany (GSFG) and the Central Group of Forces (CGF) may both create a less provocative image as well as result in greater operational capability. By reducing the number of tanks in tank and motorized rifle divisions, the Soviet General Staff expects to create a better combined arms balance between infantry and armor within maneuver forces. Like the *Bundeswehr*, the Soviet General Staff had concluded that its maneuver forces were 'infantry poor'. On the other hand, restructuring a number of motorized rifle divisions into 'machinegun-artillery divisions' may substantially increase their capability to preform the defensive mission in an offensive or counteroffensive operation.[73] When reinforced by 'an increase in the number of antitank and antiaircraft means, means for creating obstacles and laying minefields, and engineering and position camouflage equipment,'[74] these new machinegun-artillery divisions could, with fewer forces and means, cover Soviet deployment and the mobilization of reserves, as well as facilitate economy of force among the manuever elements.

The contemporary machinegun-artillery division, which would probably be a varient of the organization depicted in Figure 4:4. The division would have something like two machinegun-artillery regiments, a combined tank and self-propelled artillery regiment, an artillery regiment (perhaps self-propelled if the division is not garrisoning a fixed fortification), an air-defense battalion, an engineer battalion, and a signal battalion. Thus, the limited counterstrike capability of the division would be found in the one combined tank and self-propelled artillery regiment with a single battalion of about forty tanks. This structure would be compatable with what Major General G. Batenin told Phillip A. Karber during a February 1989 visit to the Soviet Union:

First, tank divisions, which now have 328 tanks, will be trimmed to 260 tanks, but increase in the number of antitank and air defense means, means for creating obstacles and laying minefields, and engineering and camouflage capacity. Secondly, motorized rifle divisions, which now have 270 tanks, will be trimmed to 160 tanks. Thirdly, some divisions in the border Military Districts will be restructured as machinegun-artillery divisions for the defense of fortified regions.[75]

Although machinegun-artillery units are employed to garrison fortified regions (*ukreplennyy rayon*), such formations were normally elements of combined-arms armies.[76] As noted by Graham Turbiville, 'notable in this regard, was the "combat path" of the 159th Field Fortified Region, which began in the defense of Moscow in 1941, and ended in 1945 in Prague, Czechoslovakia'.[77] Thus, while in the defense permanent fortified regions

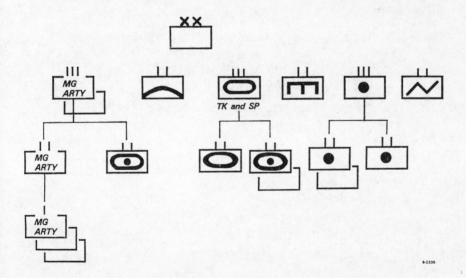

Figure 4:4 1950s machinegun – artillery division

were built on the important operational directions in order to prevent the development of an enemy attack along those paths, in the offense temporary fortified regions were employed to shield the deployment of assault groups reliably and repell any attempt by the enemy to conduct spoiling attacks to break up the deployment.

Examination of the Khalkhin-Gol operation cited by Kokoshin and Larionov provides useful insight into the 'defensive nature' of the new thinking on theater operations. Khalkin-Gol was an army-scale encirclement operation involving the use of machinegun-artillery units to garrison field fortifications built to shield the deployment of assault groups and to misinform the enemy as to the offensive intentions of the Soviet forces.[78] This army offensive operation was called to a halt at the restoration of the border for *political* reasons, and just as easily could have become a general strategic offensive but for the Soviet concern over German military aggression in Europe. If Khalkhin-Gol is the ideal 'type' operation and the 'operational-scale counterstrike posture' is adopted by the Soviet armed forces, Soviet forces will be smaller in manpower and numbers of maneuver units, and have fewer tanks. They will, however, be more balanced in terms of the ability to survive on a multithreat battlefield. Whether in the course of a conflict Soviet operations would remain more limited in scope as against the Japanese at Khalkin-Gol in 1939, or expand to follow the 'strategic-scale counteroffensive' as in Kursk, or even assume the nature of a 'strategic-scale offensive' as in the 1945 Manchurian operation, is a *political* decision to be taken at the time.

Planning parameters for the Soviet General Staff
Christopher Donnelly

Although I work from very different sources, I tend to come up with very similar answers to those of Dr Petersen, so I would just like to develop one or two of his themes a little, and to link these up with the internal dynamics of the Soviet Union discussed in earlier chapters. How can Gorbachev's peaceful declarations be reconciled with the fact that the General Staff is busy working out how to win any war that might start?

Of course that is the essential function of the Soviet General Staff, to which there is no real equivalent in the West. It has complete authority when it comes to talking about war, and there is no real equivalent to the body of journalists, civilian academics and concerned churchman one finds doing the same thing in the West. For seventy years the General Staff have had a monopoly in talking about war. Until Gorbachev, Soviet leaders came from a military background, and although the party has taken great care to ensure that there is no Bonapartism, and that the party holds the gun, the General Staff's impact on directed policy has been enormous. What Gorbachev wants to do is to break that monopoly and to reform rather than destroy the General Staff by creating a kind of loyal opposition, an alternative viewpoint. This is why new think-tanks have been created in the defence field to encourage, over the past year or so, a debate on issues of policy.

There are two elements to the military doctrine, which aims to prepare the Soviet Union for war: the socio-political and the military-technical. The General Staff have concentrated on the latter and have come up with an extremely effective and logical solution to the problem of how to fight a war; and the result is the current force postures and deployments in Eastern Europe. But this deals with the wrong threat, because there is, in Gorbachev's view, no conventional threat to the Soviet Union here, only a nuclear one. The fewer nuclear weapons NATO has got, the fewer conventional weapons the Soviet Union requires. The real threat to the Soviet Union is the increasing gap between Eastern and Western living standards. In preparing for the wrong threat, in other words, the Soviet General Staff have been making the real threat worse.

Hence military doctrine has a real socio-political impact on Soviet society, and, as Gorbachev now admits, gave NATO legitimate cause for concern. Far from instilling respect in the West for the Soviet Union as a military superpower, it spurred NATO to prepare a counter, and in so doing got the Soviet Union into an arms race which it simply could not afford. This was especially true of future weaponry where they are facing, they believe, a revolution in military affairs equivalent to the invention of nuclear weapons. For example, they think the electro-magnetic gun will fundamentally alter the nature of warfare because it will change the number of people needed on the battlefield, and how they are supplied and structured.

The Soviet Union particularly cannot afford the high-tech research and development investment needed for the future. High technology conventional weapons become more important in modern and prolonged war. The Soviet Union can manufacture current platforms, tanks, ships and planes because its industry is geared to it but in future weapons based on new physical principles, it is a decade behind the West, or more. Preventing that mutual modernisation, therefore, must become a key element of future Soviet strategy.

In a longer war, the Soviet possession of a concept of the strategic-operational and operational levels of war, and their ability to fight war on that scale, gives them their current advantage, because NATO does not have that capacity. This is why the Soviet General Staff is confident at least that they have a *system* that could win.

A degree of surprise is still essential for victory, conventionally. Not surprise in the sense of a bolt out of the blue, but something shorter than the twenty to thirty days that it would take NATO to bring over reinforcements and resupplies from the United States. In that period, NATO's only operational capacity is its airpower, which can be switched from one area to another. A longer war also increases the value to NATO, in Soviet eyes, of navies. This is not the same as saying that it has increased the value of the Soviet Navy to the Soviet Union, however.

The General Staff's advice has also been of particular value to Gorbachev in helping him phrase his arms control proposals. The all-important point is that the lower the level of density on the battlefield, the easier it is to maintain that essential element of manoeuvre which the Russians consider so important to victory. The existence of a cadre system which will allow them to maintain forces at 15 per cent and remobilise them rapidly in case of trouble (a system that most NATO countries do not possess) is a tremendous advantage. It is also important to note the importance of their intended reorganisation of armies away from the old system of basing forces on divisions and regiments for nuclear war to a new and more flexible system.

Gorbachev's view is that the Soviet military need to adopt a less provocative posture in Europe. He needs this in order to carry his own people with him, and to influence the Western population so that they do not vote for modernisation. If he can achieve that with the least reduction in Soviet combat capability he will have the best of both worlds. Less provocative does not, however, mean less offensive. The General Staff is determined to keep its military force structured for the offensive, although it will be better balanced for offence *and* defence. Logically, offensive power is necessary actually to win a war. In any case, they have system-designed for the offensive and it will take decades to change that characteristic.

It is not a question of making washing machines instead of tanks but shifting resources from current military expenditure, particularly in high-tech Research and Development, to the development of Soviet science so that the whole nation can be brought up to date. Then, if necessary, in twenty years' time they could make industrial quantities of weapons based on new physical principles. This then is the first real issue.

A second issue is the ability of Soviet forces actually to carry out their doctrine, and there has been a decline in quality of training and leadership over the last seven or eight years which has become critical in the armed forces themselves. They now have to put a lot of effort into training people to use the kit they already have, let alone come to terms with new concepts of operations. The problem is not the quality gap in equipment between East and West, which has always been something of a myth, but the Soviet difficulty in getting the people to make the equipment work. They need to change the structure of society so they can get the people that will make the equipment work.

So everything politically and militarily is pushing in the same direction. The only way to increase quality without increasing cost is to have less. Better is smaller, but in terms of a less dense future European battlefield, smaller is better too.

NOTES AND REFERENCES

1. See letter to the editor by Murray Krim, 'Toning down rhetoric', *New York Times*, 23 December 1988, p. A38.
2. As cited in Philip C. Clarke, 'Why the Soviets left Afghanistan', *American Legion Magazine*, May 1989, p. 18.
3. See John J. Yurechko, *Coalition Warfare: The Soviet approach* (Cologne: Berichte des Bundesinstitut fur ostwessenschaftliche und internationale Studien, 1986).
4. *Teatr voyennykh destviy (TVD)* has also been translated as 'theater of military operations' (TMO) and 'theater of military action' (TMA). See John G. Hines and Phillip A. Petersen, 'Translating a concept', *International Defense Review*, no. 3, 1986. A *TVD* is defined by the Soviets as 'that part of the territory of a continent with the coastal waters of the oceans, internal seas and the air space above them (continental TSMA); or the water areas of an ocean, including its islands, the contiguous coastlines of continents and the air space above them (oceanic TSMA), within the boundaries of which are deployed strategic groupings of the armed forces and within which military operations are conducted.' *Voyennyy entsiklopedicheskiy slovar' (Military Encyclopedic Dictionary)* (Moscow: Voyenizdat, 1983).
5. Lt. Gen. Serebryannikov, 'Sootnoshevniye politicheskykh i voyenny-khsredst v zaschite sotsialima' (The reliable strengths of political and military means in defense of socialism), *Kommunist vorruzhennykh sil (Communist of the Armed Forces)*, no. 18, September 1987.
6. Aleksandr Bovin, 'Perestroyka i vneshnaya politika' (Restructuring and foreign policy), *Izvestiya*, 16 June 1988, p. 4. It should be noted that the General Staff

is said to have been opposed to the military intervention in Afghanistan. See Bill Keller, 'General recalls Soviet rift on war: says military staff opposed 1979 Afghan intervention', *New York Times*, 19 March 1989.

7. D. T. Yazov, 'Increasing the return from military science', *Krasnaya zvezda (Red Star)*, 14 August 1988, p. 2.

8. M. Gareyev, 'The armed forces in the conditions of glasnost', *Argumenty i fakty (Arguments and Facts)*, no. 39, 24–30 September 1988.

9. Marshal of the Soviet Union N. V. Ogarkov, 'Strategiya voyennaya' (Military strategy), *Sovetskaya voyennaya entsiklopedia (Soviet Military Encyclopedia)*, Vol. 7 (Moscow: Voyenizdat, 1978), p. 564.

10. See Notra Trulock III, 'Soviet perspectives on limited nuclear war', in Albert Wohlstetter, Fred Hoffman, and David Yost (eds), *Swords and Shields: offensive and defense* (Lexington: D. C. Heath, 1987).

11. An 'independent' air operation (*samostoyatel'naya vozdushnaya operatsiya*), in contrast, is an operational-tactical scale operation employing only assets of the air forces. As a smaller-scale operation, an 'independent' air operation would probably only occur subsequent to the air operation in the course of a relatively protracted conflict. See Phillip A. Petersen and John R. Clark, 'Soviet air and antiair Operations', *Air University Review*, March–April 1985, pp. 36–54.

12. Col.-Gen. M. Zaytsev, 'Organizatsiya PVO – vazhnaya zadacha obshchevoyskovogo komandira' (Organization of air defense – an important mission of the combined arms commander), *Voyennyy vestnik (Military Herald)*, no. 2 (February), 1979, p. 23.

13. V. Kuznetsov, 'The lead horse and the trace horse', *Krasnaya zvezda (Red Star)*, 31 January 1986, p. 3, as cited in unpublished paper by Lt. Stephen D. Nichols, USN, 'Weapons of enhanced power and the Soviet air operation', Georgetown University, 1987, p. 47.

14. Oleg Amirov, Nikolai Kishilov, Vadim Makarevsky and Yuri Usachev, '"Conventional war": strategic concepts', *Disarmament And Security, 1987 Yearbook* (Moscow: Novosti Press Agency Publishing House, 1988), p. 364.

15. 'CST and CDE: opportunities missed, but not yet lost', Headquarters, USA, Conventional Arms Negotiations Division, 1988, Draft.

16. Alexei Arbatov, 'Military doctrines', *Disarmament and Security, 1987 Yearbook* (Moscow: Novosti Press Agency Publishing House, 1988), p. 212.

17. Ibid, p. 220.

18. Ibid.

19. See, for example, 'Excerpts from Gorbachev's speech', *The Washington Post*, 8 December 1988, p. A32; and 'In Gorbachev's words: "To preserve the vitality of civilization"', *The New York Times*, 8 December 1988, p. A16.

20. Retired Col. A. G. Terekhov, 'A methodology for calculating the correlation of forces in operations', *Voyennaya mysl' (Military Thought*, hereafter cited as *VM)*, no. 9 (September), 1987, p. 56.

21. Rear-Adm. B. A. Kokovikhin, 'Mathematical modeling of military operations', *VM*, no. 12 (December), 1987, p. 42.

22. Maj.-Gen. A. E. Tatarchenko, 'To the question of the creation of strike groups in offensive operations', *VM*, no. 5 (May), 1982, p. 54.

23. Maj.-Gen. P. T. Kunitskiy, 'Massing of forces on the sector of the main thrust', *Voyenno-istoricheskiy zhurnal (Military Historical Journal)*, no. 4 (April), 1987, p. 14.
24. Tatarchenko, p. 54.
25. Maj. H. F. Stoeckli, Swiss Army, 'Soviet operational planning: superiority ratio vs casualty rates', study published by the Soviet Studies Research Centre, Royal Military Academy, Sandhurst, p. 5.
26. Lt-Gen. of Artillery Yu. Kardashevskiy, 'Tvorcheski planirovat' ognevoye porazheniye tseley' (Plan fire destruction of targets creatively), *Voyennyy vestnik (Military Herald)*, no. 7 (July), 1978, pp. 64–7. Although these calculations are for the tactical scale, 'the larger the operation the less the overall superiority of the attacker over the defender is required, since the opportunities for the intensive use of existing men and equipment are greater as the spatial scope increases' (Terekhov, p. 56).
27. Formula from Tatarchenko, p. 55.
28. Col.-Gen. M. A. Gareyev, *M. V. Frunze – Voyennyy teoretik. Vzglyady M. V. Frunze, sovremennaya voyennaya teoriya (M. V. Frunze – Military Theoretician. The Views of M. V. Frunze and Contemporary Military Theory)*, (Moscow: Voyenizdat, 1985), pp. 243 and 437.
29. This section draws heavily from Philip A. Petersen and Notra Trulock III, 'A "New" Soviet military doctrine: origins and implications', *Strategic Review*, Summer 1988, pp. 9–24.
30. Col. Stanislaw Koziej, 'Anticipated directions for change in tactics of ground troops', *Przeglad Wojsk Ladowych (Ground Forces Review)*, September 1986, p. 4.
31. See 'Scale of operations', *Voyennyy entsiklopedicheskiy slovar' (Military Encyclopedic Dictionary)* (Moscow: Voyenizdat, 1986), p. 618.
32. See, for example, Ogarkov, 'Military strategy', p. 564.
33. Western thinking on global warfare has, for the most part, continued to focus on world nuclear war. Notable exceptions include Carl Builder, 'The prospects and implications of non-nuclear means of strategic conflict', Adelphi Paper Number 200 (London: IISS, 1985).
34. See, for example, Marshal V. D. Sokolovskiy (ed.), *Soviet Military Thought*, (New York: Crane, Russak & Co., 1975), p. 28.
35. Gareyev, *M. V. Frunze*, p. 241.
36. Amirov, Kishilov, Makaravsky and Usachev, '"Conventional War"' p. 364.
37. Maj.-Gen. I. Vorob'yev, 'The relationship and reciprocal effects between offense and Defense', *Voyennaya mysl' (Military Thought)*, no. 4 (April), 1980, as it appears in *Tap Chi Quan Doi Nham Dan* (Hanoi), no. 1 (January), 1982, Defense Intelligence Agency Translation LN-873-86, p. 9.
38. Alexei Arbatov, 'Parity and reasonable sufficiency', *International Affairs*, October 1988, p. 86.
39. Andrei Kokoshin, 'Alexander Svechin: on war and politics', *International Affairs*, November 1988, pp. 121 and 123.
40. Ibid., p. 121.
41. Ibid., p. 125.
42. Alexei Izyumov, 'The USSR in the changing world', *International Affairs*, August 1988, p. 54.

43. Arbatov, 'Parity and reasonable sufficiency', p. 76.
44. Ibid.
45. *Pravda*, 27 May 1988.
46. Arbatov, 'Parity and reasonable sufficiency', p. 81.
47. See, for example, Kokoshin, 'Alexander Svechin', p. 123.
48. Molly Moore, 'Soviet naval cutbacks reported: U.S. intelligence official notes Gorbachev's budget reductions', *Washington Post*, 22 February 1989, p. 12.
49. Jan Breemer, *Soviet Submarines: design, development and tactics* (UK: Jane's Information Group, 1989), p. 164.
50. Ibid., pp. 138 and 165. Also see 'Soviet sub fleet called not so super', *Washington Times*, 27 February 1989, p. 2; and 'Soviets allegedly have withdrawn nuclear subs', *Baltimore Sun*, 5 March 1989, p. 2.
51. Moore, 'Soviet naval cutbacks reported', p. 12.
52. 'Second Soviet aircraft carrier launched: . . . possibility of VSTOL-carrying subs cited', *Defense Daily*, 28 February 1989, p. 301.
53. Rear-Adm. N. P. V'yunenko, Cap. B. N. Makeyev and Cap. V. D. Skugarev, *The Navy: its role, prospects for development, and employment* (Moscow: Military Publishing House, 1988).
54. Fleet Adm. V. Chernavin, 'Prepare yourself for modern warfare', *Morskoy Sbornik [Naval Digest]*, January 1989.
55. Alexei Izyumov, 'The USSR in the changing world', *International Affairs*, no. 8 (August), 1988, p. 54.
56. Andrei Kozyriv, 'Confidence and the balance of interests', *International Affairs*, no. 11 (November), 1988, p. 5. Also see Bill Keller, 'New Soviet ideologist rejects idea of world struggle against West', *New York Times*, 6 October 1988, pp. A1 and A11.
57. Andrei Afanas'evich Kokoshin and Gen.-Maj. Valentin Veniaminovich Larionov, 'Counterpositioning conventional forces in the context of ensuring strategic stability', *Mirovaia ekonomika i mezhdunarodnye otnosheniia (World Economics and International Relations)*, June 1988.
58. Ibid.
59. Ibid.
60. See, for example, *Century and Peace*, no. 9, 1988; *Moscow News*, 6 November 1988; *Moscow News*, 22 January 1988; *Sovetskiy Soyuz (Soviet Union)*, February 1989; Army Gen. A. D. Lizichev, *KZ*, February 1989; Gen.-Col. M. A. Moiseyev, *KZ*, 10 February 1989; and Gen.-Lt. of Aviation V. Serebryannikov, *KZ*, 12 February 1989.
61. A. Kokoshin and Gen.-Maj. Larionov, 'The historical development of Soviet military doctrine', *Sovetskiy soyuz (Soviet Union)*, February 1989.
62. Minister of Defence Army Gen. D. Yazov, 'At the cutting edge of restructuring. All-army conference of military press organ leaders', *KZ*, 7 March 1989, p. 2.
63. Ibid.
64. I. M. Panov, editor of *Krasnaya zvezda* as quoted in 'Notes from the auditorium: two *Krasnaya zvezda* soirees in the Moscow variety theatre', *KZ*, 4 March 1989, p. 3.
65. Yazov, 'At the cutting edge of restructuring', p. 2.
66. Ibid.
67. Ibid.

68. Maj.-Gen. I. S. Danilenko, '*Mezhnatsional'nye otnosheniya i armiya*' (International relations and the army), *Voyennaya mysl' (Military Thought)*, no. 12 (December), 1988, p. 68.
69. Serebryannikov, *KZ*.
70. *Moscow News*, 11 November 1988.
71. *Izvestiya*, 6 October 1988.
72. Col.-Gen. M.A. Gareyev, Deputy Chief of the General Staff of the USSR Armed Forces, 'Soviet military doctrine at the present stage of its evolution', an address at the Royal United Services Insitute (London), 19 October 1988.
73. John J. Fialka, 'Soviets outline troop-cut plan in East Germany', *Wall Street Journal*, 14 March 1989, p. 21.
74. Yazov, 'In the interests of universal security and peace', *Izvestiya*, 28 February 1989, p. 3.
75. See Phillip A. Karber, 'Soviet implementation of the Gorbachev unilateral military reductions: implications for conventional arms control in Europe', Testimony Before the House Arms Services Committee, 14 March 1989, pp. 6–7.
76. 'Ukreplennyy rayon' (Fortified region), *Military Encyclopedic Dictionary* (Moscow: Voennoe izdatel'stvo, 1983 and 1986), p. 710.
77. Graham Turbiville, 'Emerging issues of Soviet military strategy in an era of reform: preparing a new military posture for theater war', unpublished manuscript, p. 19.
78. For two somewhat different perspectives on this battle, see G. K. Zhukov, *The Memoirs of Marshal Zhukov* (New York: Delacorte Press, 1971), pp. 147–71; and Petro G. Grigorenko, *Memoirs* (New York: W. W. Norton, 1982), pp. 105–10.

5 The future of Soviet defence policy: further discussion

Discussion of the two presentations on Soviet defence policy focused on three areas – namely how the Soviet military saw the need for reform, what changes were entailed for NATO by such reforms and finally what the position of the Soviet Navy would be in a changing defence policy.

On the first question, the Soviet military seemed to view the changes taking, or about to take, place in military technology as being as revolutionary as the earlier introduction of nuclear weapons. Weapons like the electro-magnetic rail gun which might arise as a by-product of SDI research would change both the structure of armies and the nature of warfare. In the nearer term improved C³I systems like Lacrosse and JSTARS (the Joint Surveillance and Target Acquisition Radar System), combined with new weapons like the ATACMS (Army Tactical Missile System) already threatened to bring the long-heralded and deadly electronic battlefield to the European Central Front. Soviet changes in force structures had to be seen against a background where massed tank forces were, anyway, becoming more vulnerable. *Perestroika* in the armed forces was just as much a response to an inability to continue as before as *perestroika* generally was a response to the inadequacy of the status quo.

This, revolutionary, situation was also seen as explaining the Soviet military's support for change and, if necessary, austerity today to secure the fruits of reform tomorrow. Despite considerable Soviet success in eroding Western technological advantages – with the Su-27, MiG-29, Mi-28 and T-80 as prime examples, the Soviet military still faced an unsustainable future. Present success in acquiring Western technology, by means fair and foul, had itself exposed the inability of Soviet industry to apply their new-found knowledge. The problem of getting technology to front-line units in turn was compounded by the inability of recruits from a non-technological society to use it when it arrived.

All of this meant that societal change was essential for the Soviet military – both to enable Soviet industry to produce what was required and to breed Soviet soldiers capable of operating the electronic battlefield. Any doubts that the Soviets might have about their ability to keep up in an escalating defence technology race was probably also reinforced by their perception of Western success in this field. Traditional Soviet inferiority complexes seemed likely to have been reinforced – by experience in recent Israeli-Syrian clashes, by optimistic US assessments of Western capabilities and by the unveiling of Western equipment like the F-117 stealth fighter, CG-47 cruiser and M1A2 tank and plans for new equipment like the B-2 stealth bomber, DDG-51 destroyer, ATACMS missile system, ATF stealthy air superiority fighter and the A-12 Avenger stealth attack aircraft.

Whilst the Soviet military seemed to accept political leadership on the grand-strategic questions of what Soviet relations with the rest of Europe should be, there did, however, seem to be grounds for dissent between Gorbachev and the military. As the papers pointed out, Gorbachev did seem to be pushing cuts through in ways, and at a pace, that the military had not agreed, and perhaps did not approve. Internal inconsistencies in the figures for cuts in manpower and equipment offered in December 1988, *inter alia*, suggested that those cuts were the result of hasty political decisions. It was noted that Gorbachev in New York had abandoned earlier efforts by the military to trade Soviet tanks for Western strike-attack aircraft. There might well be some limit to how often the military would happily take such unilateral cuts or allow their own influence over defence policy to decline. If Gorbachev was a man making cuts in a hurry, there was clearly some danger that he might outrun his support if he was not careful. The point was reiterated that much would depend upon how cuts were handled. The spectre of Soviet officers retired by Khrushchev and Khrushchev's subsequent oblivion was one that Gorbachev ought firmly to keep in mind.

There was less certainty about what a new Soviet defence policy would look like. The point was made that Finlandization of Europe would in many ways actually be a better solution for the Soviet Union than the status quo. Relations with Finland were in several respects better than with some East European allies and Finland did not pose any threat itself and did not allow its bases to be used by others. If the rest of Eastern, Central and Northern Europe would accept the minimal constraints accepted by the Finns, the Soviet Union would be left to enjoy the benefits of a new political and economic relationship as military tension declined. Such a policy would only require sufficient ground forces to provide a defence of Eastern Europe (at least while existing Pact structures prevailed) together with whatever nuclear forces were required by Soviet nuclear strategy and START and whatever homeland defence forces were felt necessary.

When it came to considering the military implications of such political change and recent arms control initiatives, the situation was far less clear-cut. Dr Petersen caused some rethinking as he pointed out that even reductions to a 1:1 force ratio on the Central Front might actually lead to a less stable Europe. Reduced force levels would reduce force to space ratios and provide both a weaker front line and fewer, more distant, reserves. This could put a premium on massing forces to attack in one sector where the massed attacking forces would both outnumber the first line defenders and encounter no defending reserves available to quickly block their penetration. In a world where both armies could defend at a 1:2 ratio and both could mass enough of their other forces to achieve 5:1 ratios or better at the point of attack, arms reductions could actually produce a far more 'crisis unstable' position than current force levels. The onus in a crisis would be on pre-emptive attack and covert deployments – just the sort of uncertainties that would make crisis management more difficult.

Prospects that the Soviets would deploy unquestionably 'defensive' forces were challenged as it was pointed out that Soviet operational planning now saw the need for defensive elements to act as the anvil for fewer encircling thrusts. Increasing demands for infantry, new missions for helicopters and increasing invulnerability of modern tanks to all but heavy, modern anti-tank weapons, all created a demand to restructure 'offensive' forces in ways that might look 'defensive' but which could, in some circumstances, also provide greater offensive capabilities. Meanwhile, renewed examination of past successful blitzkriegs suggests that it is not numbers of weapons that achieve success – blitzkrieg is essentially about destroying the morale and coordination of the defending commander and his forces. This can be achieved by better tactics or equipment, by conventional manoeuver or by unconventional means like special forces, helicopter-borne *desant* operations or even using light units mounted on motorcycles or light armour. It is a sobering reflection that Hitler's blitzkrieg in 1940 succeeded using one-eighth the tanks that NATO and the Warsaw Pact would each be allowed under the NATO proposed, and Pact accepted, 20,000 ceiling. Also sobering is the fact that those tanks were less heavily armed than much armour now found in infantry units. Where Soviet ground forces are concerned, it is far from clear that changes designed to create a 'defensive' Soviet Army will, on their own, cease to pose a potential threat to the West.

Turning to the position of the Soviet Navy, the mood of the Conference was that the omens were not good. Recent visitors to Moscow reported that there was a major debate underway and that 'the knives were out' for the Soviet Navy. The Soviet Navy could not escape its share of the cuts if its sister services were being reduced to pay for *perestroika*. Traditional Soviet attitudes stressing the primacy of land warfare (if you can't get there by tank, you can't get there) suggested a decreasing priority for the Navy when there was little money even to provide the tank. Similarly, traditional army domination of the General Staff, Defence Ministry and four out of five armed services, suggested that the Navy should if anything suffer disproportionately if resources were scarce. Further evidence of this likely fate was found, by some, in the sacking of Admiral Gorshkov and the timing of this just before the launching of the first of the Soviet Navy's large, new aircraft carriers.

The Soviet Navy was also seen as facing other dangers from the general questioning of Soviet defence policy that seemed to be going on. Soviet Navy arguments for 'maritime reach' seemed out of keeping with a more introspective foreign policy and a more defensive defence policy alike. Arguments for offensive or defensive naval flanking operations in the Baltic and off Norway obviously seem superflous if the Soviet Army is at the same time removing its capability to pose any offensive threat on the Central Front in Germany. Meanwhile, the Soviet Navy may eventually be caught on the logic of its own lack of capability. Whilst the Soviet Navy's case may have been increased by the articulation of a US Maritime Strategy that threatens the Soviet Union itself if the Soviets should start any war, a close look at the Soviet Navy may not support its current building plans at all. It can be argued that if Mr Gorbachev did want a cost-effective defence for the USSR he might well conclude that, as land-based airpower and submarines pose the major threat to US naval forces, building surface ships as desired by the Soviet admirals was rather an inefficient way to proceed.

Many would conclude from all of this that the Soviet Navy faced major cuts. At the conference, some thought that it was unlikely that any more than two carriers would be launched. There were, however, some caveats. One warning was that carrier procurement did have considerable momentum and they did have continuing strategic defensive and offensive missions. Soviet army thinking about a longer conventional war – perhaps lasting a year with the conquest of Europe being a relatively short initial phase – also seemed to create some need for the Soviet Navy to defend initial gains against subsequent US actions. The point was also made that the question was not one of life or death but about the relative rate of modernization. There also seemed to be some capabilities that the Soviet Union would not want to surrender – she clearly would not want to be unable to defeat any offensive naval forces operating in the Norwegian Sea or the Baltic. Soviet aspirations to reduce Western naval power by arms control were themselves a symptom of the Soviet dilemma.

SUBSEQUENT DEVELOPMENTS

Events since the Conference have only served to make the future of Soviet defence policy and the Soviet Navy less clear than they seemed in February 1989. The Soviet Union has produced more figures on its defence budget – but the utility of these is undermined by Soviet admissions that the figures may have to be revised later as they may not reflect true costs.[1] Soviet force levels have been reduced – particularly in the ground forces – but the timing of reductions is tied to the timetable for cutting the military budget. Procurement trends are only slowly becoming clearer as past momentum continues to be seen in present procurement. Like the fruit of his economic reforms, Gorbachev's new defence policy will only be seen in its full form as we move beyond 1991. There also remain doubts over Soviet objectives – with change still falling into place, political uncertainties growing and some propaganda efforts reminiscent of past objectives, defining the Soviet military threat is, if anything, becoming ever more difficult.

If finding the answers is difficult, however, we may now have learnt enough from *glasnost* and *perestroika* to ask the right questions. This is itself a tribute to the changes Gorbachev has wrought. In the past we knew little about Soviet debates, procurement, strategy or personalities – this time we may at least watch the Soviet debate as it happens. As we watch, certain issues ought to attract our attention.

Who makes Soviet defence policy?
The growth of alternative sources of defence policy mentioned by Petersen and Donnelly and the growth of economic imperatives as a determinant of defence budgets, raises interesting questions as to how Soviet defence priorities are being shaped. If there is a spectrum of ideas, which are influential? The emergence of 'independent' Soviet experts at conferences and other gatherings of strategists and foreign policy analysts is a novel and interesting development which should be watched.

How important is defence now as a national priority for the Soviet Union?
In the Brezhnev years Soviet defence policy seemed to reflect a national view that every threat that could be perceived should be met with an overwhelming ability either to defeat the threat or, in the nuclear field, to respond with a superior option. At times, defence policy also seemed designed to support foreign policy goals by posing a threat to influence other states. Though the military obviously did not get a blank cheque (and bureaucratic politics may have played a role in determining the outcome) the Soviet military seemed in the past to be in the unusual position of actually being given the resources to make any potential attacker aware of the certainty of his own defeat. We may now be in a situation where defence policy is becoming increasingly the result of a complex equation where political and economic forces are more important. It may be the case that the Soviets have now adopted a more relaxed, Western attitude to deterrence that contents itself with providing forces that will be adequate to deter most threats without seeking the surer security of being able to defeat all threats, however unlikely. We may be moving into a situation where security appropriations need to be limited by other demands and where realistic threats are met by less expensive means than the massed weight of the Red Army and counterforce nuclear strikes. In the Soviet view, in other words, deterrence may no longer require the perceived capacity to prevail in all circumstances.

What is the nature of the agreement between the Soviet military and Gorbachev on military procurement?
Although there is a clear trade off between today's procurement and tomorrow's research and industrial base, which seems to have been accepted by the military leadership, the practical implications of this are not clear. The Soviet military actually find themselves at a difficult stage in the procurement cycle. New weapons like the Su-27, MiG-29, Mainstay and Blackjack aircraft, submarines like the *Akula* and the future standard tanks for the first time match fielded Western technology. At present, though, they are in the early stages of procurement. It remains to be seen if the Soviet military will gladly accept limitations on the numbers they can buy, when they have, and now seem very proud of, weapons that could match Western capabilities. On the other hand, many Western generals would still envy the Soviet Army its predicament of only building 1,700 rather than 3,500 tanks a year. The US Army going from 840 to zero is possibly an even greater victim of *perestroika*.[2]

Looking to the longer term, the threat of Western technology seems set to return with a vengeance by the mid-1990s, leaving the Soviet Union in the unenviable position of having to match new technology before *perestroika* has produced a suitable economic base. The incompatibility of military needs and economic reconstruction may lessen with economic success, but it looks unlikely that the timetables of the military and the Soviet economy will prove reconcilable.

The biggest question will be the fate of defence budgets post-1991 and 1995. Soviet spokesmen have suggested that the cuts planned for implementation by 1991 will be followed by a further 10 billion rouble cut by 1995 – bringing the overall percentage cut in the defence budget since 1989 to 25 per cent.[3] It is not clear, yet, whether subsequent defence budgets will remain frozen at 1991 or 1995 levels in real terms or will, thereafter, be allowed to grow with the economy – perhaps matching the 5 per cent growth rates hoped for by then. If the latter occurs, defence spending will rise again in real terms, and if defence growth matches economic growth, will eventually reach real 1987 levels again. If defence expenditure is frozen, however, or choice or economic failure only allow low growth rates, the Soviet military will find themselves with obsolete technology and falling numbers. Mathematics dictates falling force levels if budgets fall and unit costs continue to increase. No growth in defence expenditure after the budget falls to its 1995 target, combined with continuing annual increases in weapons costs at recent historic rates, would reduce Soviet forces to around 50–5 per cent of their present size by 2000 – assuming it was not possible to extend the service lives of military equipment still further. At some point between present force levels and this bleak prospect, the Soviet military may insist that they are not being given enough to ensure Soviet security.

What role do nuclear weapons now play in Soviet thinking?
Soviet statements and actions on nuclear weapons seem contradictory. As Petersen points out, the Soviet perception of the undesirability of any nuclear war explains Soviet decisions on START, INF and SRINF. Indeed, it is arguable that the thrust of Soviet policy, since the mid-1970s at least, has been to deter NATO from first use rather than to use such weapons. Beyond this, though, future strategy remains unclear. Gorbachev's statements seem to foreshadow a nuclear free world and by extension reliance on conventional forces. Yet this seems inconsistent with Soviet actions elsewhere. Soviet positions in conventional and strategic arms control talks have preserved both the Soviet medium bomber fleet and the SU-24 force – this leaves an alternative nuclear force intact for deterring theatre threats from Europe or Asia.[4] Even more strangely, Soviet deployment of SLBM and SLCM off Europe since the INF treaty was agreed, seems to display a continuing desire to maintain numbers of weapons on target using whatever means the treaty does not disallow.[5]

A similar paradox presents itself in the START negotiations. Soviet positions seem to allow the full gambit of strategic replacement programmes for SLBM, SLCM, ALCM, Blackjack bombers and SS-24 and SS-25 missiles to proceed. The Soviets look like producing a strategic nuclear force that mirrors US SLBM and mobile ICBM plans whilst retaining heavy fixed ICBM and a modernized bomber force. This force is not the most cost-effective one could design, nor is its procurement likely to produce any defence savings. It is, however, one that maintains current, redundant, deterrent options – even to the extent of keeping 154 heavy ICBM.[6] Indeed, the Soviet military leadership seems insistent not only on maintaining its SS-18-based prompt counter force capability, but in increasing it by moving to deployment of the Mod 5 variant of the SS-18. This does not mean offensive intent, but it does raise legitimate questions about what has changed in Soviet thinking about peacetime deterrence and wartime deterrence and warfighting needs. Moreover, this force structure, when completed at considerable cost, should last for twenty to thirty years. Soviet nuclear force planners seem to be designing forces for a nuclear future extending twenty to twenty-five years beyond Gorbachev's dream of nuclear disarmament. Whilst Soviet statements on nuclear strategy are still obscured by the rhetoric of nuclear disarmament and whilst nuclear capable forces are still available at the theatre and strategic level, determining what the Soviets might do'with those weapons remains a critical exercise for Western analysts.

How important is homeland defence?
Also unclear is the role of homeland defence in the new scheme of defence priorities. In the past, homeland defence has been the clear priority. Khrushchev's earlier attempt to reform Soviet defence policy to promote an economic revolution is noteworthy not only because it previewed Gorbachev's reforms but because wholesale cuts in Soviet ground and naval forces were accompanied both by an oscillating nuclear strategy designed to deter nuclear attacks on the homeland and the continuence of research on ABM to provide a defence against the ultimate attack. Soviet insistence on the merits of defence as opposed to offence before the signing of the ABM treaty – and, indeed, an inability of the political leadership to accept that strategic defence could be bad showed again that defence continued to enjoy a special priority in the Soviet strategic mindset. The continuance of the Moscow ABM system and the continuing modernisation of those ABM and the PVO's air defences even after the 1972 ABM treaty both suggest continuing interest in providing some security. The argument that this can make little difference when ABM can be overwhelmed and PVO bases destroyed by US forces in the first thirty to forty minutes of any nuclear attack does not seem to have won much support, even today, in the USSR. The PVO seems to be continuing to enjoy a high priority with new SAM, the IL-76 AWACS and SU-27 and MiG-29 fighters being deployed. Strategic defence forces seem disproportionately exempt from Gorbachev's arms reductions proposals and in CFE discussion Soviet insistence on excluding defensive interceptor fighters has been noteworthy.[7]

This could change as a more confident Gorbachev moves on to cuts in new areas, but it may be that homeland defence will survive as a core objective. This may be because defence is in a real sense irreducible.

There is no point in guarding one wall of the castle if the others are left undefended. The Soviet Union's vast borders themselves may impose an absolute numerical minimum that may not be far below existing force levels. Similarly, providing a defence against weapon A is of little use if the target is destroyed by weapon B. Unless the Soviet leadership is prepared to go the whole way and draw the logical conclusion that, as weapon C cannot be stopped, there is no case for bothering to stop weapons A and B, Soviet homeland defence forces must continue to thrive. Unless a decision is made to confine defence forces to warning and peacetime border policing, Soviet generals will be able to continue to argue that they are meeting a threat, helping to reduce the impact of an attack or developing the technology that will one day meet the threat.

This is important. It is possible to see some logic in cuts in forces in Afghanistan, Mongolia or even Eastern Europe if one assumes that these are regarded as less important than securing the defence of Soviet territory itself. If the homeland's defence priority remains as strong as ever, though, there are clear limits to how far Soviet cuts will go and what sort of threat a more isolationist Soviet Union will pose. A Soviet Union that sees no conventional threat from Europe or China, but which does continue to see a US naval, bomber and missile threat will still be interested in securing air and sea space around her borders. She will also be very interested in using Western public opinion to remove these remaining threats to her security. She may even continue to develop new 'defensive' weapons that pose new threats to some NATO allies whilst the threat to others declines.

What military threats do the Soviets wish to pose to Western Europe?
The issue here is whether the Soviet Union has renounced any desire to influence or, *in extremis*, attack, Western Europe with military force. Removal of Soviet ballistic missile INF has still left a bomber force and strategic and SLCM assets targeted, or targetable, on Western Europe. The INF treaty at the same time successfully removed all of the GLCM and Pershing II missiles that threatened Soviet territory. US strategic nuclear forces must still feature in Soviet uncertainties, but essentially the Soviet nuclear threat to Europe remains intact.

With conventional forces the case is more complex. As the Conference speakers pointed out, the difference between defence and offence is blurred and even smaller forces with greater helicopter support and better organization may pose an effective threat. Having said this, however, there comes a point at which reductions must reach levels that make a successful attack improbable. Small forces may be able to concentrate to attack and new technology may overcome numbers, but there must be some point at which small forces become vulnerable to domestic insurrection in the Warsaw Pact or NATO airpower. Occupying Europe is no task for fifteen to twenty divisions. Even if a smaller force might retain a theoretical attack potential, it seems politically unlikely that a Soviet leadership would ever find an attack with fifteen divisions attractive when they never found one with forty or ninety desirable.

Indeed, the events of 1989 suggest that a total re-evaluation of the Soviet threat may now be necessary. It seems that we are heading for a transitional phase where Soviet force levels will continue to reduce to less than half their current level. This may be followed by a complete withdrawal. Even in the transitional phase, it looks as if NATO will far outnumber the Soviet Army on the Central Front – at a time when the loyalty of the rapidly decreasing Eastern European forces looks ever more dubious.[8] Arguments that either the residual Soviet forces left in Eastern Europe by CFE 1 and CFE 2, or a smaller Soviet army stationed solely on its own territory will provide a real threat to Western Europe will have to be extremely convincing to succeed in either the Politburo or Western legislatures.

There may be, however, some strands to Soviet thinking that retain an element of threat to the West. It did look at one stage as if the Soviet Union was simply readjusting its timetables for war by placing greater reliance on Category III divisions. War would not only stay conventional and last longer, but it would begin after warning and mobilization. There would both be time to recall and retrain reservists before war started and also an increased need for additional units to sustain the war as it continued. A Soviet attack force could still be assembled, given two to three months, if required. This might be more rational than the situation where thirty divisions were stationed forward in Eastern Europe regardless of the facts that the Soviet leadership did not want to go to war, the threat posed to NATO was producing a proportionate effort from NATO and that starting the war without mobilizing might lead to a situation where NATO might defeat the unreinforced blitzkrieg. If success in peace could come through arms control offers and success in war depended anyway on mobilizing a full-scale attack, cutting front line forces and relying more on reservists who would be ready when, and only when, needed may well have seemed a far more efficient and productive option to the Soviet leadership. NATO, for its part, would face the dilemma of having fewer forces available forward (probably with fewer European forces in total) and being more reliant on sea lines of communication (SLOC) to bring whatever US forces were available back to Europe if the Soviet Army ever started mobilization.

This line of thinking is logical, but it also seems to have been overtaken by other events. An interesting, unremarked, feature of Soviet acceptance of Western proposals on conventional arms control was acceptance of limits on forces in the Western Military Districts. These drastically reduce the potential also for major increases in Soviet forces on the Central Front following mobilization. It may actually be the case that the Soviet Army does now see itself only in a defensive role with a, reducing, role for forward deployed forces controlling change in Eastern Europe. Talk about military disengagement from Eastern Europe by 2000 increasingly looks genuine and the pace of current reform, including moves to a united Germany, suggests that such a result might come about far faster than anyone thought in 1989. It might also be the case that the Soviet experience in Afghanistan has placed a somewhat large question mark over the capability of invading armies to hold ground and obtain favourable political results. An ability to threaten neighbours with bombers or missiles would seem to be enough of a deterrent to ensure that most behave, without going to the additional expense of building land forces to invade them.

In practice, it seems likely that the Soviet leadership have combined several of these ideas and added other themes from recent debates on the implications of new technology, the new foreign policy and the needs of *perestroika*. If the Soviet Union sees no threat from NATO conventional forces – and SACEUR's comments on NATO's capability must be very reassuring – relying on strategic warning may now seem more acceptable. If there are months or years to prepare for circumstances when conventional forces are required, it hardly makes sense to retain such forces in a ready state. New production technology should also make it possible to produce arms quickly using existing production facilities and if necessary converting them back from civilian use. Most importantly, it also follows recent thinking about the military balance which suggests that aggregate numbers of weapons tell us little. What matters in war are the numbers of modern equipments available in the front line for the first, decisive, phase. Old equipment is likely to be impotent against new technology. This is already the trend for both superpowers – US alarm about the inability of most US anti-tank weapons to penetrate Soviet frontal tank armour may be mirrored by Soviet anxiety about the F-117 here. Both superpowers have also already adopted the practice of putting most of their very best, newest, equipment forward and rotating old equipment out of the front line as new is delivered, so as to keep the technological edge in the early stages of any conflict. Soviet planners may have taken this logic to its natural conclusion. If war is thought to be coming, the Soviet Union will use its superior productive capacity to produce modern technology in large numbers in time to start the war. If technology is what matters, the Soviet Union will be able to re-equip rapidly its smaller standing forces with anything necessary, at the same time as it built up its reserve units.

Such thinking would pose new challeges both to NATO and the Soviet military. Matching a capability that could materialize in a year or two would be more difficult for NATO in the absence of a permanent threat. Mobilization would be more important, as would Western naval power. Regular armies might logically become the cadre for mobilization when war seemed likely. Conscription powers might be needed to provide the manpower needed to match a rapidly expanding Soviet Army. Western politicians would face immensely difficult decisions about when to respond to Soviet mobilization when countermobilization would have all too clear escalatory and economic consequences. The history of 1914 would again seem all too relevant. Meanwhile, the Soviet military would have to accept that they would probably be unable to complete modernisation with the current generation of equipment and would not be able to match Western moves into the next generation represented by ATACMS, MLRS/Terminally Guided Weapon, JSTARS, SADARM, Sensor Fused Weapon, AIWS, Long-Range Conventional Cruise Missile, B-2, ATF, A-12 and AMRAAM. Soviet forces may be able to manage with fewer weapons as technology increasingly overcomes numbers – the success of reactive armour/triple reactive armour in making NATO ATGW obsolete must be encouraging here, as must the success of the MiG-29 and Su-27 in matching Western airpower. Yet, the logic of economic reform has already been expressed in cuts in the vital research and development budgets that ought to be keeping the Soviet military up to date with the threat. The Soviet General Staff must be confronting now the reality that cuts in production of today's weapons – of which they are justifiably proud – are unlikely to produce weapons to meet future needs tomorrow. The Soviet military may well now be looking into the abyss where defence budgets continue to fall, technology continues to advance and once declining capability produces a circular argument that, as threats cannot be met, little effort should be made to meet them.

It is not clear if this scenario will prove acceptable to the Soviet military, but is even less clear what they could do to change what looks like the inevitable consequence of relative (and in some senses absolute) economic decline. The Soviet military's support for *perestroika* is born of the realization that an economic revolution is needed to produce the technology for the military revolution needed. One cannot wish revolutions away. New priorities, therefore, do seem unavoidable whether or not the process is slowed by changing leaders, new coalitions and temporary reprieves for military budgets. Ground forces may be reshaped to provide a minimal peacetime deterrent whilst providing some potential for expansion when needed. The promise to the Soviet military that *perestroika* would bring new technology may have to be met by the military themselves shifting money from other accounts to finance R&D and additional resources may have to be found to build a mobilization base capable of producing modern weapons in numbers if needed. There is likely to be an effort to build as many current generation weapons as possible before defence cuts bite even more in 1991 and 1992.

After this period of transition, procurement objectives are likely to be constrained. Nuclear forces may continue to keep a priority as they assume more of the burden of day-to-day deterrence. Homeland defence forces may continue as a guarantor against surprise air attack. The Soviets may even continue strategic missile defence research as the basis of a defence against less predictable missile-armed neighbours. Interestingly, naval forces could continue to be procured to match a naval threat that probably looks more capable to the Soviets than NATO's ground forces. An offensive bomber and Su-24 force, backed by a navy capable of offensive and defensive operations, might assume some of the dissuasive functions performed by the Soviet Army. If the superpowers do settle down to a conventional face-off across their mutual border, the Arctic, and across the Atlantic and Pacific, this will increase the trend to look for security from air and naval forces. Air and naval forces might also benefit from the logic of their own complexity. Whilst a tank division might be produced, manned, and trained in one to two years, it takes five to six years to build a ship and more time to train air and naval forces. It could be that relying on one to two years of strategic warning would actually see a relative shift in Soviet resources from the Army to the Navy. Navies, unfortunately, cannot be turned on in two years. It may be that the Soviet leadership have concluded that an army can be.

Indeed, even hopes for a residual role for the Soviet Army – providing the nucleus of a mobilization capability to meet threats when required – may not have survived the revolutionary changes of 1989. The Soviet Army may now be forced to consider what roles it has in a world where Germany is united and an independent Poland stands between the USSR and the German border. The capability to mobilize a large army might just still be needed in some circumstances, but the collapse of the Warsaw Pact leaves very few convincing scenarios to justify such a capability. The Soviet Army seems doomed to stare out on neutral East European states, hoping that some East Europeans will welcome some Soviet guarantee against Germany. The only sure role, and one that may not be welcomed, is likely to be internal security. Policing the streets of a disintegrating superpower could prove to be the main role in the future for the army that once frightened a whole continent.

Just how far the Gorbachev-inspired military revolution has gone remains to be seen, but it appears to have gone beyond the point at which more cost-effective ways are found to meet old threats. Gorbachev may not have foreseen where his momentum would lead. He may not actually place a very high priority on Soviet external security when his own time is taken up by escalating political and economic crises and when his own past seems more likely to have turned him into a defence cutter rather than a defence enthusiast like Brezhnev. Gorbachev may actually be able to convince himself that he is producing a better security situation – less defence in a real sense is more security. Here, an alternative agenda comes forward. The army that could never be used in Eastern Europe will come home to protect the USSR. The buffer zone in Eastern Europe will remain a buffer zone without the expense of a Soviet garrison. The conventional military threat from Western Europe will be reduced by removing its *raison d'être*. Soviet theatre nuclear bomber forces, backed by strategic and naval weapons as required, will continue to pose a threat to Western Europe. US forces will be reduced by agreement. Germany will be controlled by the carrot of reunification and, perhaps ultimately, will be swung to the left by the weight of socialist-leaning East Germans. At best, change in Eastern Europe would see *de facto* communist control continue over foreign and defence policy – albeit with fresher faces in control. At worst, Eastern Europe will be led by new leaders from new parties who will continue to feel some gratitude to Gorbachev and are unlikely to threaten Soviet security significantly. Gorbachev may believe in nuclear disarmament, but it seems just as likely at present that he will retain current Soviet strategic capabilities whilst milking the rhetoric of disarmament for any one-sided, or cost-cutting, deals he can strike.

This might all prove a very acceptable alternative to present postures. For the West it could mean that the Soviet Union will continue to remove its offensive capability on the Central Front. It will mean, however, that the West will face a more difficult threat. Rather than thousands of tanks in four days the threat will now be thousands of tanks in months, plus a modernizing navy and a vast nuclear force which will rely more heavily on long-range air power and capable strategic forces. This threat will not be visible, it will be less easy to verify, it will require what will look like offensive capabilities to balance the capability of Soviet nuclear forces to limit a nuclear war to Europe by posing a threat to Soviet territory, it may place a premium on European nuclear forces as the credibility and/or the desirability of US nuclear responses declines with US force levels. One likely development is that the Soviet Union is likely to become even more active trying to shape Western defence policies. Another is that, even if Gorbachev thinks he has thought through all of the consequences, the future he has created is one where uncertainties continually arise to confound the best of plans. The Soviet military revolution may still turn out in ways that both we and the Soviet leadership cannot foresee. The military revolution remains the child of the larger revolution Gorbachev (or the collapse of the Soviet system) has unleashed. Trying to steer a military course in a political whirlwind is not the easiest of tasks. Where the ship will end up and whether the military will have overthrown the captain to put the ship back on some course, remains to be seen.

NOTES AND REFERENCES

1. 'Akhromeyev on importance for Soviet military spending figures', *Summary of World Broadcasts*, 10 October 1989.
2. *Defense News*, 12 February 1990, pp.42–7; *Jane's Defence Weekly*, 10 March 1990, p. 427.
3. R.J. Smith and D. Remnick, 'Soviet urges ban on naval cruise missiles: move suggests shift in Kremlin policy', *The Washington Post*, 14 July 1989; 'Soviet defense spending in 1990', *TASS*, 15 December 1989.
4. *Jane's Soviet Intelligence Review*, December 1989, pp. 556–61; ibid., February 1990, p. 56.
5. *Soviet Military Power 1989*, pp. 42–7.
6. D.J. Pay, 'START – some implications', *Defense Analysis*, vol. 5, no. 1, 1989, pp. 55–9.
7. J.W.R. Lepingwell, 'Stealthy pressures on Soviet air defense', *Air Force Magazine*, March 1990, pp. 50–7.
8. R.J. Smith and P.E. Tyler, 'Warsaw Pact losing its edge. Sources say: sweeping changes blunting Eastern alliance', *The Washington Post*, 2 December 1989; T. Shanker, 'What's left of the pact', *Air Force Magazine*, March 1990, pp. 30–5; D. Ignatius, 'Yes its real: how Gorby is cutting the Soviet threat', *The Washington Post*, 5 November 1989.

6 US defense policy: new answers for old questions

Edward A. Kolodziej

INTRODUCTION

'What are the answers?' Gertrude Stein was supposed to have asked as she was about to expire. 'There aren't any answers,' replied Alice B. Toklas, her lifelong friend. 'Then, what are the questions?' retorted Stein.

What is striking about the defense debate today in the United States is that there appear to be more answers than questions. Everyone seems to have his or her favorite remedy to cure defense policy ills even in the absence of a thorough diagnosis of what their sources might be. Some want cuts in the huge US defense budget simply because, like Mt Everest, it is there. More thoughtful observers, disturbed by Paul Kennedy's reckoning of why empires fall, believe that continued high levels of defense spending will choke investment and economic growth, the engines of military power.[1]

Those who view defense exclusively through a security prism see current spending as an impediment to arms control and greater political cooperation with the Soviet Union. Others, more skeptical of Soviet motivation or the long-term prospects of *glasnost* and *perestroika*, foresee the superpowers at global loggerheads for sometime to come. There are also those who prefer to look at defense issues through the myopic end of the telescope. They never see a weapon system they do not like, since threats expand to the weapons available.

So what are the right questions facing American defense policy-makers? The questions that we already know, but tend to neglect or only partially pose, still seem important. First, what are the threats to American interests? Second, how much defense can the nation afford – or, more precisely, is willing to afford? And, third, what strategy and military posture are best suited to match power and purpose? Like the legs of a three-legged stool, no one of these questions is more important than another. Nor can one be answered without necessarily shaping responses to the others.

The discussion will be divided into four principal parts. To set the stage, we will look briefly at the way the first and second Reagan Administrations answered these three questions. Once we have some benchmarks to guide our thinking, we can address in successive sections the three questions of threat, resources and capabilities in a way that provides some new answers to these old questions in the light of prevailing strategic and political constraints and opportunities. In reformulating security questions in ways that they can be better addressed than they are today, some questions need not be posed and others need not be so preoccupying as they are today.

THE REAGAN YEARS

Early Reagan: 1981–5

The Reagan Administration answered the question of threat in classical Cold War terms. Previous administrations, Republican and Democratic, were accused of a 'decade of neglect' in tending to the nation's defenses. Soviet heavy ICBMs, principally SS-18s, were perceived as capable of destroying all US land-based ICBMs and of seriously damaging long-range bomber forces in a first strike. If the 'window of vulnerability' was created because of what administration spokesmen believed were high levels of Soviet defense spending aimed at attaining Soviet nuclear superiority over the West, preceding administrations were also blamed for legitimating these increases in the SALT II treaty.

President Ronald Reagan and his advisors were unmoved by the rejoinder that the Soviet Union, with approximately 75 per cent of its warheads on land-based ICBMs, was more vulnerable to a first-strike attack than the United States. Nor was much weight given to the fact that even after an attack on the United States, most of its sea-based system would survive. Even before the expansion of strategic nuclear forces was undertaken, the nation would still have some 3,000 warheads available to visit intolerable damage on the Soviet Union.[2] The Reagan Administration resisted pressures to ratify the SALT II treaty. The Soviet invasion of Afghanistan prompted President Carter to withold the treaty from the Senate. The Reagan Administration, while informally adhering to SALT II limits, insisted that it would not enter new arms control talks until the 'window of vulnerability' was closed and until US strategic forces were again capable of assuring US and allied security and of restoring what was viewed as the nation's weakened bargaining position, symbolized by the hostage crisis in Iran.

The Soviet and communist threat was perceived to extend well beyond the strategic arms race. Reaganites were determined to match Soviet nuclear and conventional arms modernization in Europe. The 'zero option' was defined in 1981 as the basis for an arms control agreement on INF deployments. The deployments went forward despite a strong Soviet diplomatic offensive and peace marches throughout Western Europe, aimed at blocking them. The Soviet Union was identified as the principal source of global disorder. In March 1983 President Reagan characterized the Soviet Union as an 'evil empire'. Cuban troops in Angola, Vietnamese control over Laos and Cambodia, and the Sandinista takeover in Nicaragua were attributed to Soviet doing.

Budgetary authorizations and outlays matched the projected threat. As Table 6:1 notes, between 1980, the last year of the Carter Administration, and 1985, defense budgetary authority increased by over $100 billion in constant 1989 dollars or about 53 per cent. Outlays went up in excess of inflation from $207 billion to $277 billion or 34 per cent.[3] All four pillars of the US defense posture – readiness, sustainability, force structure and modernization – were reinforced. Priority was assigned to the acquisition of new weapons and modernization. Between Fiscal Year 1980 and FY 1985, expenditures on new weapons and support equipment jumped 114 per cent and spending for research and development increased 96 per cent. Add to this total an increase of 87 per cent in Department of Energy spending to produce the nuclear material and warheads to arm the new weapons entering the nation's strategic arsenal.[4]

As Table 6:2 sketches, between 1980 and 1985, defense outlay rose steadily from 5.3 per cent of GNP to 6.6. The defense share of central governmental expenditures also expanded from 23.1 per cent to 26.5 per cent. Between 1981 and 1985 the Defense Department received over $1.4 trillion dollars in new obligation authority. By FY 1984 it had exceeded the FY 1968 figure at the height of the Vietnam War.

Table 6:3 summarizes the average spending authority for non-war years since 1950 in constant 1989 dollars. From a low of $202.1 billion on the average in 1954–60, defense spending climbed to a plateau of almost $300 billion during the Reagan years. The number of personnel under arms, however, were increased only slightly. In 1980 there were 2.1 million

Table 6:1 Defense Department budget authority and outlays, fiscal years 1980–9 (in billions of 1989 constant dollars)

| Year | Budget authority | | Outlays | |
	Amount	Percentage change	Amount	Per cent growth
1980	213.4		207.1	
1981	241.1	13.0	217.6	5.1
1982	268.9	11.5	232.8	7.0
1983	290.8	8.1	250.5	7.6
1984	303.9	4.5	259.7	3.7
1985	325.5	7.1	277.3	6.8
(1981–85)		(52.5)		(33.9)
1986	312.5	−4.1	294.2	6.1
1987	301.6	−3.4	296.4	0.8
1988	292.8	−2.9	287.2	−3.1
1989	290.8	−0.7	285.5	−0.6
(1986–89)		(−11.9)		(3.0)

Source: William W. Kaufmann, 'A defense agenda for fiscal years 1990–1994' in *Restructuring American Foreign Policy*, ed. John D. Steinbuner (Washington, DC: Brookings Institution, 1988), pp. 49, 57.

Table 6:2   Percentages of US military expenditures relative to GNP and central government expenditures, 1980–5.

Year	GNP	CGE	Armed forces (in millions)
1980	5.3	23.1	2101
1981	5.6	23.6	2168
1982	6.2	25.0	2201
1983	6.4	25.4	2222
1984	6.3	26.4	2244
1985	6.6	26.5	2289

Source: US Arms Control and Disarmament Agency, *World Military Expenditures and Arms Transfers 1987* (Washington, DC: Government Printing Office, 1988), p. 81.

Table 6:3   Historical trends in defense spending: non-war years
(in 1989 constant dollars)

Years	Average
1954–60	202.1
1961–5	224.2
1975–80	206.1
1981–90 (est.)	292.0

Source: Laurence J. Korb and Stephen Daggett, 'The defense budget and strategic planning', *American Defense Annual: 1989–90*, ed. Joseph Kruzel (Lexington: Lexington Books, 1988), p. 44.

personnel in the armed forces; five years later their number rose to 2.3 million.

Spending for readiness and sustainability, while up, grew at a rate one-third as rapid as for weapons modernization. This gap was not noticeable at the start of new spending on weapons, but it has since widened each year as spending on operations and support has not kept pace with the introduction of new and more sophisticated weapons into the nation's armory. To hold spending in check, the Pentagon and the Office of Management and the Budget have preferred to cut out so-called 'fast money' earmarked for pay, spare parts and fuel and to decrease funds for ammunition, training and exercises.

Military capabilities, particularly for strategic nuclear forces, prolifer-ated. The B-1 bomber program was restored after having been cut by President Carter. Funding was also continued for the Stealth bomber program which the Carter Administration had initiated, partly as an alternative to the B-1. Funding for 100 MX ICBMs, each capable of accurately delivering ten warheads on target – an efficient hard-target, first-strike weapon – was proposed although the basing mode was not specifically defined. The Carter Administration's track system, envisioning 200 MXs, was rejected, partly because of domestic opposition from Nevada and Utah where it would have been deployed over large areas. The Trident submarine was accelerated and provision was made to supplant the C-4 with the more accurate D-5 missile. More money was also allocated to protecting and perfecting C^{3}I facilities.

These efforts to bolster the strategic posture of the United States culminated in President Reagan's proposal for a Strategic Defense Initiative in March 1983. Funding rose each year. Despite a storm of Congressional and public criticism at home and abroad, funding authority increased from a little over one billion dollars in FY 1984 to triple that amount in FY 1986.

The Navy was the largest single beneficiary of Reagan largesse. It was to grow from about 480 combat ships to a 600-ship force, including 13 deployed aricraft carriers which were to be increased to 15 by the early 1990s. Army strength was not so much increased as reorganized to expand from 16 to 18 active divisions. Created were 2 light divisions for rapid deployment to trouble spots around the globe. The Air Force was expected to grow from 36 active and reserve tactical air wings to 40 by the middle 1980s.

The defense budget was driven more by the expansion of military capabilities than by a new strategic design. The Reagan Administration was convinced – and the armed services needed little persuasion – that the nation had not received the weapons and support it needed to execute prevailing strategy of flexible response and to respond to what was conceived to be a rising Soviet and communist military threat around the globe. The proponents of more defense spending took little heed of CIA estimates that indicated an actual decrease in the rate of Soviet military spending in the late 1970s.[5] At the start, SDI appeared to be a major departure in strategic thinking, but it has since been disciplined to prevailing nuclear deterrence policy as the vision of a shield to defend cities has been dismissed by most defense analysts as feasible, including some of the most vociferous supporters of SDI. Ironically, more funds for defense actually increased controversy in the American security community as the prospect of more funds whetted service appetites. Wish lists became planning goals. In the case of the Navy a maritime strategy was advanced that fundamentally challenged the priorities and commitments, especially to NATO and Europe, that have been at the core of US defense planning since the Second World War. American defense strategy was threatened with disarray by its very budgetary success.

Later Reagan: 1986–9
The high point of defense authorizations is 1985. Thereafter, defense has been on the defensive. Resistance to further expansion and pressures for cutbacks arose from three principal sources: from those concerned with rising budget deficits which were viewed as much as a symptom

as a cause of the relative decline of United States economic power, a concern fuelled by disclosure of colossal mismanagement and waste and more recently by contract fraud, failings attributable by many to too much money being available to the defense establishment too fast; from fears of an uncontrolled arms race, symbolized by the contentious debate over 'Star Wars' but by no means limited to it; and from positive reactions to Soviet signalling for a relaxation of the arms race and for detente – what might be termed a 'Thermidor in the revolutionary struggle'.[6] The implications of these pressures are addressed in more detail below. What immediately concerns us is how the forces for cutbacks played out in defense spending and the dilemmas that they have created for Reagan and Bush planners, dilemmas faced to date more in the breach than in the observance.

As Table 6:1 reveals, authorizations for the Department of Defense have declined each year since FY 1986, falling from $312.5 billion to $290.8 billion in FY 1989 or 11.0 per cent. Spending has fallen at a slower rate or three per cent because of unobligated authorizations still in the pipeline, estimated at approximately $270 billion at the end of FY 1989.[7] At the same time, the Democratic Congress insisted on progress in superpower arms control talks. Legislative limits on spending were threatened or initiated for strategic nuclear systems like MX, and for SDI. Particular attention was devoted to challenging the administration's broad interpretation of the ABM treaty. If accepted, essentially all restrictions on research, development and testing of SDI systems and components would have been removed by unilateral fiat. Arms control pressures were bolstered further by new assessments of the Soviet military threat and by growing appreciation of the political changes in Soviet domestic society that were generating an imperative for detente with the West. The Scowcroft Committee, composed of bipartisan representatives of leading opinion within the security community, proclaimed in 1983 that the 'window of vulnerability' was closed, ending the debate on the issue if begging the question of whether it were ever open in the first place.

Even as SDI was introduced as a disturbing element in the evolving defense consensus, strategic parity was essentially accepted by an ever-widening number of participants in the security and arms control debate. Neither superpower could disarm the other in a first strike. Stalemate was the real condition under which both superpowers would have to live no matter how much each attempted unilaterally to gain superiority. If arms spending would just produce stalemate at a higher level of cost and risk, why try; hence arms control assumed greater attraction for most hands around except the usual diehards, like Richard Perle, who either left or were edged out of policy circles. The Soviet proclamation of a nuclear-free world in January 1986, the Reykjavik débâcle the following September and the subsequent INF treaty, with the adoption of the 'double zero' option, undermined much of the rationale for the early Reagan buildup, especially with respect to strategic nuclear systems.

What is curious is the failure, by and large, of these messages of limitation to get through to defense budget planners. As late as 1985, the Defense Department was counting on continued annual increases in new obligational authority at the rate established in the early Reagan years. During the period the Congress approved 95 per cent of the requests that were made, pegged at a yearly increase of 8 per cent above inflation.[8] What is clear is that since 1985 the money is just not there. Congress has refused to approve funds at this level and has cut obligational authority each year. The last Reagan budget submitted to Congress in January lowered expectations to real growth in the next five years of 2 per cent above inflation for each year as against the 5 plus per cent real increases enjoyed in the first Reagan period. The revision of the last Reagan defense budget by President George Bush in April 1989 lowered expected growth a notch downward. Defense authorizations were lowered to zero growth for FY 1991, 1 per cent for FY 1999, and returned to 2 per cent after inflation for FY 1992.

The modesty of these budgetary expectations is belied by the priority assigned to new procurement and higher investment in R&D. The DOD budget is not on an even keel. The prow is pushing before it a large wave of future spending on new arms and on developing still newer ones. DOD is requesting more real growth for procurement and R&D than for the total defense budget. These increases are estimated at 3.1 per cent in FY 1990 and 6.6 per cent in FY 1991 in contrast to only 1 per cent and 0.9 per cent for the readiness and sustainability of armed forces in the field. No new major weapons program was cancelled in the final Reagan budget.

Most observers agree that there simply will not be enough money available to meet these procurement and investment goals. One respected analyst estimates that DOD will fall short by almost $1 trillion on its new procurement and investment spending goals if current budgetary trends are maintained through the end of the century, a most optimistic assumption.[9]

Table 6:4, which combines defense authorizations from all sources, comes to a parallel conclusion by contrasting DOD estimates with a budget based only on inflation, and not real growth after inflation, and on no growth at all which would mean a net decrease in real funding as a function of the inflation rate. Between FY 1989 and FY 1994, one can expect a shortfall of $102.9 billion if defense spending keeps pace with inflation and a gap of $236.1 billion if there is no growth at all, real or inflationary. The Bush revision of the FY 1990 budget, which cut $10 billion from the $305.6 billion projected by President Reagan for new defense authorizations, does not bring defense planning into line with resources, but essentially defers hard programmatic choices for a year. President Bush's decision to spend funds both on the MX rail garrison and Midgetman systems, in response to contradictory Congressional signals for more defense spending for some items and for less overall expenditures, actually strains the budgetary process more than relieving it in reducing DOD authorizations for FY 1990. These hard programmatic choices can be better understood once one has a clearer grasp of the forces shaping the availability of resources and of the budgetary priorities as well as fundamental change in the real and perceived character of the Soviet threat.

TABLE 6:4 Potential shortfalls in five-year defense plan: FY 1990–4

	1989	1990	1991	1992	1993	1994	1990 1994
Admin. projections	298.8	315.2	330.8	346.1	361.4	376.6	1,730.1
Growth with inflation	298.8	309.1	318.0	326.1	333.5	340.5	1,627.2
Potential shortfall (in per cent)		6.1 1.9%	12.8 3.9%	20.0 5.8%	27.9 7.7%	36.1 9.6%	102.9 6.0%
Admin. projections	298.8	315.2	330.8	346.1	361.4	376.6	1,730.1
No growth	298.8	298.8	298.8	298.8	298.8	298.8	1,494.0
Potential shortfall		16.4 5.2%	32.0 9.7%	47.3 13.7%	62.6 17.3%	77.8 20.7%	236.1 13.6%

Source: Center on Budget and Policy Priorities, *The FY 1990/1991 Defense Budget Preliminary Analysis,* 12 January 1989. Estimates include authorizations for the Department of Defense and related agencies.

SHIFT FROM A CAPABILITIES TO A RESOURCE-DRIVEN DEFENSE BUDGET

From a logical point of view, strategic analysis should proceed from some assessment of the external threats to a nation's interests to a definition of the military capabilities – readiness, sustainability, force structure and modernization – needed to meet the threat in the near and long term. Estimates of military capabilities, designed to protect the nation's security and to underwrite its foreign commitments and diplomacy, would then be fitted to the resources potentially available to the nation.

As the brief look of the Reagan Administration's policies above suggests, defense decision-making does not always politically present itself in such a logical order. Even when defense issues arise in an expected sequence, there is no assurance that they will be addressed in a logical fashion by decision-makers. Witness the irrepressible optimism shared still by some US defense planners that growth in defense spending approvals will be forthcoming if one assumes so.

Optimism alone does not explain the high priority assigned to procurement and end items. Like the prow of a ship, these expenditures are expected to cut through resistance to increased defense spending and to draw in their wake higher levels of expenditures for readiness and sustainability than might otherwise occur in order for Congress to preserve its initial investment on equipment. That budgetary optimism and political realism are still allied in Pentagon thinking is suggested by the disclosure of the General Accounting Office that the Defense Department continues to maintain two sets of budgetary figures: one for Congressional and public consumption that purports to project lowered defense requests and outlays; the second that operates on the assumption of eventual Congressional approval of increased spending by assuming 'negative funding' that reconciles through accounting legerdemain spending plans with budgetary shortfalls – at least in the expectations of defense planners.[10]

Critics may despair that there is not more order and candor in defense budgeting, but politicians and policy-makers must confront the constraints before them, not those that might arise in the distant future or those that might be relaxed by more fortunate circumstances. What seems clear is that the capabilities-driven budgets of the last several years will have to yield to resource constraints that will compel limits on overall defense spending whatever the merits of the specific claims that might be made on behalf of a particular program by the defense establishment.

First, there is the federal budget deficit. It crowds out defense concerns since it is so volatile a political, and potentially so damaging an economic, problem. While it well may be manageable, as some economists believe, that perception is not universally shared, and perceptions count in Congress and the White House, not to mention with the Federal Reserve which sets US interests rates. Between 1982 and the end of 1989 Reagan budgets will have added approximately a trillion-and-a-half dollars to the federal deficit. This is an astonishing growth, dwarfing the deficits of all previous administrations put together. The deficit stands at over half of the nation's annual GNP. Correspondingly, service on the debt is growing as a proportion of central governmental expenditures. In FY 1970, when the United States was at war in Vietnam, debt service absorbed 7.35 per cent of the federal government's budget. That ratio rose to 8.88 per cent in FY 1980 and is estimated at 14.32 per cent at the close of FY 1989,[11] twice the size of the Vietnam War level.

The real question, of course, is not the deficit *per se*. Despite rising budget deficits (and partly because of them) the American economy has enjoyed the longest peacetime period of sustained economic growth in the post-war period. Employment is at record highs. World stock prices and the value of the dollar have not plummeted. The economy continues to show strength although the current rate of growth is slipping relative to the recent past.[12] In the near term, the problem of the debt is the tax that it makes on domestic and international investment. Interest rates must also be made attractive to maintain the market for government securities. Sale of these securities drain away funds that might have been invested in other more productive areas which would create new jobs and products. Taxes are not a painless solution since they also have the same dampening effect. If market financing and taxes cannot manage or reduce deficits to tolerable levels, then the only and obvious option is to cut governmental spending. The question is no longer whether governmental spending will be cut. The issue is where, how much and at what rate.

President George Bush's campaign pledge not to increase taxes restricts his maneuverability in raising federal revenues through taxation or in taking initiatives, whatever they are called (revenue enhancements, fees, or service charges on federally guaranteed bank accounts), that amount to as much. The cuts introduced by Secretary of Defense Richard Cheney, while modest, indicate that the Defense Department will be expected to contribute to the budget deficit ceilings mandated by Congress. Barring a fundamental reversal of current international trends, pointing towards superpower detente and a relaxation of the superpower arms race, cuts will conceivably fail to accommodate the 2 per cent increase above inflation expectation built into defense planning for FY 1992.

The real question is not the deficit. Nor whether the United States can afford, if it chooses, to spend approximately 6 per cent of GNP for defense or more. It has spent more for defense at other times since the Second World War. The controlling economic question is the long-term competitiveness of the American economy in world markets. It is precisely this question that tends to be lost in the noise of budget cutting and in the harried processes of defense planning as the urgencies of budget deadlines drive decisions.

The defense budget should be viewed not only as a capabilities document but as an economic impact statement. As an impact statement defense spending would be viewed not only as a net consumption item and a tax on national resources, but also as a set of investments, especially in research and development, that could potentially contribute to long-term economic and technological growth and market competitiveness whose significance goes beyond just the sale of advanced weapons and military know-how, such as the F-16 fighter or AWACS. Development of computer and laser technologies, for example, owes much of its initial impetus to defense spending.

It would seem sensible and in the self-interest of defense planners to incorporate these economic and technological impact considerations into their thinking and into their priority setting. A start in that direction is suggested by grouping spending for procurement, research, development, testing and evaluation, and construction under an 'investment' title. The utility of this adjustment remains to be exploited in two fundamental senses. Such an assessment is needed to stabilize defense spending for the long haul and to reach a national consensus on this level of expenditures. Since other pressing needs than defense have to be met and have political clout behind them and since the external threat, to which we will turn in a moment, is receding as a clear and present danger, it follows that the military must develop readiness, sustainability, force structures and modernization strategies that can be economically and politically sustained no matter what partisan winds are blowing in Washington.

Moreover, the military have an obligation to themselves to develop their personnel, procurement, R & D and construction programs by factoring in the contribution that the defense budget can make to economic growth and competitiveness on which the stability of defense spending depends. Such an exercise can easily degenerate into wild claims of added value or in special pleading, but at least these could be examined and measured in some fashion to see if they stand up. That would be better than the current situation in which defense plans proceed with a blind eye towards the question of the viability of the economic and technological base on which a strong defense must rest.

If past is prologue, the question of long-term growth and competitiveness will be ignored or given scant attention as the immediate concerns with budget cutting, on the one hand, and headline-grabbing charges of waste and corruption in the Pentagon, on the other, dominate the public agenda. The latter issues are real enough, as perennial weeds in the garden of defense management. As defense contract-rigging cases reach the courts, they will again emerge as highly visible public issues, whatever one might say about their intrinsic merit on defense or economic grounds. The Senate confirmation hearings on the nomination of Senator John Tower, which led to his rejection as President Bush's first-choice as Secretary of Defense, heightened concerns already abroad in Congress about corruption and influence-peddling in the defense establishment. He was one of the most visible links in the iron triangle of congressional, military and corporate elements that have sustained high defense spending and skewed priorities in favor of big ticket items. The long and tortuous history of the B-1 testifies to the endurance of these special interests.[13]

As pressures to cut defense spending and to control costs mount, one can also expect the issue of 'burden sharing' to again assume greater political force. Until now it has been well managed, both in the recent presidential campaign and in the first public statements of the Bush Administration pledging support for a strong NATO and Western alliance. The appointments of General Brent Scowcroft as National Security Advisor, of Richard R. Burt, currently US Ambassador to West Germany, as the chief American negotiator in the START talks, and of Lawrence Eagleberger to a high post in the State Department, all strong Europeanists and NATO 'firsters', signal a commitment to keep the burden-sharing issue from dividing the alliance. Secretary of State James Baker also has a reputation more as a 'fixer' and problem-solver than as an issue-raiser. His deft diplomacy in lowering the value of the dollar, particularly against the yen, suggest that the Bush Administration would prefer to manage the burden-sharing issue behind the scenes than to pursue it as a lead item, particularly as the West is about to enter prolonged arms control negotiations over conventional and strategic nuclear weapons.

Several otherwise separate and even opposed interests appear to be converging with the effect that the burden-sharing issue may again be a major focus of attention despite efforts to keep it from public view. First, the economic and political forces pushing the burden-sharing issue before them, with a large amount of other baggage, may well prove too powerful to contain. Planners are only partially in control of the forces that are shaping the scope and contours of this issue. Remember the stock market crash of fall, 1987, which appears to have been partly sparked by differences between then Treasury Secretary James Baker and his German counterpart that spilled over into financial circles and helped trigger the selling craze. US economic policy-makers still confront a recalcitrant German economic community. The unexpected increase in domestic interest rates, set by German banks and sanctioned by Bonn in the spring of 1989, evidences continued German independence and single-mindedness in pursuing national interests even at the expense of US and allied economic policies. These transatlantic cross-currents are likely to swell as the European Community approaches its target date of 1992 for the creation of a fully integrated Common Market, raising the spector of increased protectionism and discrimination against American products and investment.

Second, Congressional critics, like Pat Schroeder, are still with us. They are convinced that the Europeans are not pulling their weight. Third, the ghost of Mike Mansfield roams the corridors of the Senate and the House of Representatives. Those of Mansfield's persuasion do not believe that Europeans will spend more for defense unless they are threatened by troop pullouts – and who can fully gainsay them. They are joined, fourth, by those who would prefer to redeploy scarce US military assets from Europe elsewhere – Asia, the Persian Gulf, home bases, or all three – or would prefer to follow an increasingly unilateralist strategy. Grouped under this banner are an odd collection of brand names in the American security community, including Zbigniew Brzezinski, Fred Iklé and Albert Wohlstetter. This viewpoint is given public display in the report of a prominent Congressional commission on long-term defense strategy.[14]

Fifth, the armed services may also be forced to urge greater allied defense spending to compensate for cuts in their own budgets. The Navy would find redeployment and unilateralism consistent with its maritime strategy. The other services, particularly, the Army, need to offset costs for stationing troops in Europe and Asia. Pentagon studies insist that not much would be saved by bringing troops home. Even those who argue this case would like to see a rich Germany and Japan spend more money on US troops, say, for military construction, than on their own forces.[15] Budget constraints may simply force hard choices on the armed services. These cuts may lower NATO priorities. The decision of Secretary of Defense Richard Cheney to cut 8,000 military personnel from the Army reflects these pressures to shift the burden of defense spending onto allied shoulders. The 8,000 figure corresponds to the number of personnel who would have been assigned to US INF and other shorter-range missile units covered by the INF treaty. Even as the Bush Administration argues that NATO must resist Soviet arms control proposals designed to pressure reductions in Western forces, US troop levels will be squeezed to fit a budget strait-jacket.

Finally, there is the question of allied arms production and sales of weapons and military technology. The budgetary and economic constraints confronting the United States are not unique. They impact on all of the Western allies. One way to relax the dilemma between defense preparedness and scarce resources is to re-examine once again the possibilities of Western cooperation in making and marketing arms. It seems pointless and naive to underestimate the powerful state, corporate, and armed service interests at play that sustain autarchic national policies. In the past, they have been formidable obstacles in the path of allied cooperation on weapons development and procurement. There is no reason to believe that under the pressures of cost control and budget cuts these obstacles will be easily overcome.

In three of the eight years between 1978 and 1985, the four major West European states have delivered in value more arms and have signed more contracts for arms than the United States.[16] In 1984, France exported 50 per cent of its arms production; Britain, 42 per cent; West Germany, 20 per cent; and Italy, 70 per cent.[17] Now even smaller European producers

TABLE 6:5 European missile projects

	1946–59	1960–9	1970–9	1980–7
National projects	15	19	18	16
Foreign participation*	6	11	21	31
TOTAL	21	30	39	47

*Major sub-system from a foreign supplier, or formal international program.

Source: Rand Corporation Report, 1988.

are entering global arms markets. Spain delivered arms to thirty-seven developing countries between 1970 and 1986 and the Netherlands filled arms contracts with twenty-two.[18] Meanwhile, the two-way NATO arms market between the United States and Europe has increasingly become a two-way flow. The previous hegemonic position of the United States has eroded from its ten to one advantage of a decade or so ago to only a two to one advantage today.

The likelihood of formalizing agreements between Washington and European capitals on arms is not likely to be great, especially for high prestige arms, like supersonic aircraft. Some of the problem is apparently quietly sorting itself out. As Table 6:5 suggests, the number of exclusively national programs in European missile projects since the Second World War has not appreciably increased in over forty years, hovering between a low of fifteen between 1946–59 and a high of eighteen between 1970–9. Meanwhile, foreign participation in the form of major sub-systems from a foreign supplier or formal international programs, has increased discernibly in each period, rising steadily from six in the first period to thirty-one between 1980–7.

As a recent Rand report observed, 'A government or nation may care deeply about who stamps its name on a missile's rocket case, but appears to care less about who makes the fuse or servo-motor for the guidance and control system.'[19] One of the potentially beneficial implications of this trend towards arms commercialization and interdependence in sub-component supply is a trend towards greater reliance on market over command mechanisms in defense resource allocation. Increased competition may increase efficiencies in allocating scarce Western resources in weapons development and, incidentally, cope more effectively than now with the problems of standardization and interoperability.[20]

REDEFINING THE EXTERNAL THREAT BEFORE IT DEFINES YOU

One of the grimly reassuring aspects of the Cold War struggle was the reliability of the Soviet military threat to the United States and to its allies. The effort of the Soviet Union to gain regional nuclear superiority in Europe, in deploying SS-20 missiles and its heavy-handed diplomatic attempt to split the West by manipulating the peace movements in Western Europe to prevent the counter-deployment of Pershing IIs and Tomahawk cruise missiles, was just one recent example of the Soviet capacity repeatedly to seize defeat from the jaws of diplomatic victory by provocative and counterproductive intimidation of its neighbors and rivals.

Western defense planners will no longer be able automatically to rely on the assumption of an expansionist and aggressive Soviet Union to guide and justify force postures. The Soviet peace campaign, launched almost simultaneously with the arrival to power of Communist Party First Secretary Mikhail Gorbachev, has changed all planning calculations whether planners are willing to admit it or not. It has three integrally related prongs. The first, announced in the call for complete nuclear disarmament in January 1986, puts pressure on the United States for a START accord and on allied independent nuclear powers to reduce and eliminate their nuclear arms. This initiative assumed its most dramatic form at the superpower summit at Reykjavik in 1986. The second thrust was aimed primarily at Western Europe. It took initial form in the Soviet adoption of President Reagan's 'zero option' and the subsequent extension of this principle to include shorter-range missiles in the INF treaty.

The campaign has now widened to include a call for a ban on all short-range nuclear weapons in Central Europe, matched, most recently, by Soviet and East European unilateral initiatives to cut and redeploy both conventional and tactical nuclear arms. Secretary Gorbachev's speech to the United Nations in December 1988 has laid down the gauntlet for the West. Announced are troop reductions of 500,000 men, the withdrawal of six tank divisions from Eastern Europe by 1991 (including their complement of twenty-four nuclear weapons) as well as Soviet armed forces in eastern USSR. 'All told,' promised Secretary Gorbachev, 'in this part of our country and on the territory of our European allies the Soviet Armed Forces will be reduced by 10,000 tanks, 8,500 artillery systems, and 800 airplanes.'[21] These announced cuts were followed by what appeared to be orchestrated announcements from Warsaw Pact capitals of parallel cuts in East European forces.

The third prong of what Secretary Gorbachev has termed 'the demilitarization of international relations'[22] is concentrated on the developing world. Over the past year there has been an astonishing military disengagement of Soviet and client military forces from key trouble spots around the globe – most notably in Afghanistan, Angola and Vietnam. The redeployment of Soviet troops from the Mongolian People's Republic to home bases, also announced in Secretary Gorbachev's UN speech, responds to Chinese conditions for a border settlement with the Soviet Union along with Beijing's demand for military pullouts in Afghanistan and Vietnam.

Not only does the threat of nuclear war or of hostilities in Europe appear less imminent than at any time since the Second World War but Soviet support of insurgent movements or regional strife is waning. US war plans since the 1970s, based on the notion of one and half wars, no longer seem to be justified by what appears to be a declining Soviet nuclear and conventional threat to the United States and to Europe, nor does the prospect of low intensity warfare in the developing world, prompted and supported by the Soviet Union, have as much plausibility as it had just a short time ago.

Two opposing explanations have arisen for the Soviet peace campaign. The first, congenial to most defense planners, attributes the concessions made by the Soviets to Western military strength. The Reagan Administration relied on this line of reasoning to justify ratification of the INF treaty and to meet conservative challenges to the agreement. Partisans of the position opposing major cuts in defense preparedness are cautious and slow in responding to Soviet arms control initiatives and display skepticism about long-term Soviet aims. Why help an adversary now on the ropes to recover his strength, to reform his economy and, in the long run, to pose an even more serious threat to the West than he does now?

Against this view is the school of thought that sees the reform movement in the Soviet Union as driven by fundamentally internal needs for greater socio-economic development. For those who hold this position, the Cold War is over. Efforts to maintain or to increase defense spending risk reversing the progressive forces presumed to be in the ascendancy in the Soviet Union. Unless the West matches Soviet overtures to cut military forces and spending and to signal to reform opponents in the Soviet Union that *glasnost* and *perestroika* can elicit positive strategic, political and economic concessions from the West, there is a danger that Gorbachev will be overturned or compelled to adopt a more stringent foreign posture.

Wherever the truth is – and it very likely lies somewhere between these polar position – the Soviet peace offensive presents both a challenge and an opportunity for defense planners. Neither has been addressed very well to date. On the challenge side, the West must define strategically viable defense postures that can assure long-term Western security and that will enjoy the confidence of stable majorities of the major states of the alliance. That will not be easy. Germany is already out of phase with US and British sentiment over the possibility of negotiating the 'third option' on nuclear weapons in Central Europe. It will also not be easy to maintain the defense budget at its present level even if deficit concerns and welfare considerations were not growing, in the face of what appears to be a declining Soviet and Warsaw Pact threat. If cuts, redeployments and reorganization are now inevitable, what kinds of forces are needed now and in the future? Downsizing and disengagement must be guided by some strategic design and political vision of the future; otherwise, the United States and the West will be at the mercy of Soviet initiatives to define their forces for them. Alternatively, cuts will be made in response to the exigencies of domestic political pressures which may compel reductions where they are most vulnerable to partisan or bureaucratic attack rather than where they are least damaging to Western strategic needs.

The opportunities potentially afforded by the Soviet peace initiative should not be overlooked, either. A persuasive case can be made that the world today is at a watershed as important as the defeat of the Axis powers and Japan in 1945 or as momentous as what proved to be the failed reconstruction of what Hedley Bull would have called the international society of states after the Second World War.[23] The Cold War, understood as the attempt of the Soviet Union to impose its preferences on the world through threat and coercion, is now receding. The Soviet Union is checked by the countervailing military and economic power of the West, by the division within the communist camp, and by the declining relevance of the Soviet model for other states. Nurturing this evolution from a position of strength will not be easy, but some risk would seem worth considering to encourage the prospects of what President Bush might characterize as 'a kinder and gentler' Soviet Union in confronting itself and its Stalinist past and in its dealings with others.

TAILORING MILITARY CAPABILITIES OF FIT RESOURCES AND THREATS

Four questions appear pertinent at this level of analysis. First, what are fundamental American interests and strategic aims? What is the proper weight that the four pillars of defense planning should carry, that is, readiness, sustainability, force structure, and modernization? What balance should be struck between nuclear and conventional forces? And what should be the mix within each category? Answers to these questions are not easy. The discussion below assays some general approaches and principles that might be applied in responding to these questions. In any event, they are the key questions that must be posed if the United States is to live within its means and yet meet its security needs and those of NATO at an acceptable cost.

As for interests and aims, those spelled out by George F. Kennan after the Second World War in his public utterances and writings (except, perversely, in his celebrated Mr 'X' article on the sources of Soviet conduct) still make sense.[24] It is in the interest of the United States to ensure that the human and material resources and creative energies of the West European continent and the Asian periphery, with Japan as its center, remain independent of external control and that the political regimes in control of these areas remain committed to democratic, pluralistic institutions and to open-market economies. These interests, in turn, generate the imperative that needed resources, principally oil, be accessible, particularly from the Persian Gulf, and that the moral and political imperative of Israel's right to exist as an independent state be honored. The United States has other interests than these, but the saliency and significance of these secondary concerns depends on their relation to core interests and aims.

It is misleading to speak of the United States as a global power if one means by that that its interests are of equal value around the globe. Even if one were to accept this assumption, it does not follow that it has the power today (if it ever had) to impose its preferences on the rest of the world. The diversity of the international system of states, with the demise of the Euro-centric system and decolonization, and the emergence of new power centers around the globe, as well as the harsh experience of US efforts since the Second World War to shape the world to its liking, argue against so ambitious an interpretation of American interests and aims. What is also clear is that, however critical military force may be to ensure a security framework for the promotion of these interests, its utility is limited in shaping the world in congenial ways. Vietnam and Afghanistan are useful lessons for both superpowers in this regard. Moreover, just because the United States and the West have enormous military might at their disposal and the potential material capacity to expand it to yet unprecedented levels does not create an interest to pursue such a course. Interest then follows power with no clear limits set to check excessive pursuit.

Strategists and defense planners, perhaps as an inevitable occupational hazard of a profession which dwells on worst case scenarios, have a tendency to reverse the proper order of power and purpose. Former Secretary of Defense Frank C. Carlucci's presentation to Congress in February 1988, illustrates the flaw:

To those who say we should scale back U.S. interests, I would ask: Which mutual defense treaties should we repudiate? . . . . Which American interest should we give up? For these questions, I know of no answers that would enable America to continue along the road that U.S. presidents and Congresses have followed since 1945. Shielding U.S. interests worldwide provides security for our values and future prosperity. A breach or weak spot in that shield could endanger the whole and would call into question America's resolve as leader of the world's democracies.[25]

These claims bear little relation to American strategic behavior since the Second World War and can ill stand the glare of serious examination in light of what has already been said about scarce resources and a declining foreign threat.

If holding the core, as sketched above, should be the focus of defense planning, what should be the priorities assigned to readiness, sustainability, force structure and modernization? We can readily discern that end-item procurement and R&D have been assigned highest priority in the Reagan years. Force structure has not changed much. Readiness and sustainability have been strengthened but they have enjoyed a slower rate of improvement than the purchase of new weapon systems or of investments in developing new ones. This is not to suggest that all of these priorities were wrong when they were made. What is more, the case today is that their single-minded pursuit has introduced distortions in planning and preparedness that need to be corrected.

The two most likely candidates for cuts are new end-item procurement and overinvestment in future weapons development. Cuts in force structure will also have to be accepted in the not too distant future. We will get to the specifics in a moment. Some general principles appear applicable. First, negotiations with the Soviet Union on strategic nuclear weapons within START and on conventional arms reductions and confidence-building measures within the CSCE should proceed with all deliberate speed. The readiness and sustainability of forces should be considered as bargaining leverage in these negotiations, especially with respect to the Central European front.

Cuts of force structure should, ideally, await formal and verifiable arms control accords with the Soviet bloc. That may be a pious hope in the light of seasonally orchestrated Soviet proposals for unilateral arms cuts. The now defunct MBFR negotiations, concluded without positive result after a decade and a half of fitful effort, are not an encouraging precedent – akin in arms talks to 'Waiting for Godot'. The West may not be prepared to wait so long. Unilateral cuts which do least damage to fighting trim – say, reductions in the more than 4,000 tactical nuclear weapons deployments in NATO – would appear easy enough to make without necessarily signalling a weakening either of the US commitment to Europe or of warfighting ability to defend and deter against a Warsaw Pact attack. Previous NATO unilateral cuts furnish a precedent here.

The German proposal, opposed by the United States but supported by most European NATO countries except Great Britain, to open negotiations with the Soviet Union on eliminating all short-range nuclear systems in Central Europe is not necessarily disadvantageous to the West. As Paul Nitze, President Reagan's chief advisor on strategic arms negotiations has observed, the Soviet Union has vastly more European-based nuclear warfighting weapons than NATO. The Warsaw Pact would presumably be obliged to cut more of its nuclear forces than NATO. Moreover, Europe is hardly in immediate danger of de-nuclearization since the British and French strategic nuclear modernization programs remain on track. Even if nuclear weapons were withdrawn from Central Europe, US forces would still have access to nuclear weapons that do not depend on ground-based installations in Germany. Willy-nilly, American soldiers stationed in Europe are nuclearized since the ultimate guarantee of their security is inextricably fused to the US strategic nuclear arsenal that lies outside of NATO.

In the immediate future, conventional force reductions or redeployments should be resisted in Europe to strengthen the West's negotiating position with the Warsaw bloc and to underwrite the US security guarantee in this inevitably fluid and uncertain transitional period. While a controversial point in some security circles, highlighted in the exhausting debate over the INF treaty, the presence of American troops and their dependants on the Central Front, not the deployment of more nuclear firepower, is hostage to the American commitment to defend Europe.[26] The United States should proceed gingerly in paring this military core that, to paraphrase Gertrude Stein, is the core of its core interests until it has reached an acceptable understanding with the East.

Troop reductions which now appear inevitable should be guided by two criteria that must be at the core of any new internal NATO bargain between the United States and its European allies and between the military blocs. First, surprise attack by the Soviet Union or the Warsaw Pact should be ruled out. Substantial progress in defining the military requirements of this criteria have been made under the auspices of the Stockholm Conference on Confidence- and Security-Building Measures and Disarmament in Europe. An accord signed by the thirty-five member Conference on Security and Cooperation in Europe (CSCE) in December 1986 requires a two-year advance notification of military exercises larger than 75,000 and one-year's notice for activities involving more than 40,000 troops. Intrusive and mandatory on-site inspections, under stipulated rules, are also provided for. Any CSCE member state, including the United States, may conduct inspection and furnish its own monitoring equipment; the host state is obliged to provide appropriate transport.[27]

Second, and more importantly, troop and weapon reductions in Europe should preclude quick breakthrough by Eastern bloc forces. While the negotiations now under way in Vienna between the two blocs are encouraging, merely cutting forces on both sides is not enough to ensure against successful attack. Arguably, the West may currently enjoy a relative advantage in defending against a conventional attack which it might forfeit if it does not shape its cuts by a strategic plan aimed at forestalling a surprise attack and rapid breakthrough. The plans presented by both blocs at Vienna risk repeating the errors of MBFR, which approached conventional arms reductions as a bean-counting exercise in which statistical ratios were substituted for military strategy. What is, however, notable about the CSCE talks is that the Soviet Union acknowledges its superiority in most conventional arms, including breakthrough weapons like tanks, artillery and armor. The principle of asymmetrical cuts – greater for the East than for the West – is now accepted by Moscow although with the caveat that NATO air and naval forces, where the West has an advantage, be included in the negotiations.

This brings us now to what should be the balance between strategic nuclear and conventional forces. There seems to be little point in building more nuclear striking power than what already has been produced. Stalemate is the inescapable condition of the current superpower nuclear balance. Preserving that stalemate, principally in the form of verifiable arms control accords with the Soviet Union, is a more attractive strategy than attempts to gain a unilateral advantage through an unregulated arms race, with all the attendant costs, risks and futility of this approach. The counting rules emerging from the START talks, particularly for bombers, are biased in favor of the American posture. The limit on 6,000 warheads, reported in the press, is deceiving. The ceiling would effectively be set higher, perhaps as high as 9,000 warheads.[28]

Under these circumstances, the cuts made in SDI funding by the Bush administration is welcome for sound strategic reasons. Under the most optimistic assumptions SDI adds only marginally to deterrence and cannot provide area defense for cities. From an arms control perspective, spending limits on SDI would help preserve the ABM treaty in some mutually acceptable form that would permit continued research and testing of defensive systems without prompting a full-scale arms race in space.

On the other hand, a research scheme to be funded by the Bush Administration that would ultimately place thousands of small satellites into space, each controlled by a small hand-sized supercomputer, fuels concerns for an expansion of the arms race if such a system is pursued and deployed. The attention devoted to this so-called 'Brilliant Pebbles' solution to the Soviet ICBM threat has also obscured notice of a five-fold proposed increase in space controlled R&D, much of it to be devoted to ASAT. While the SDI authorization was held to $4.9 billion by President Bush's revision of President Regan's scheduled FY 1990 proposal of $5.9 billion (including $400 million for the Department of Energy), funds for space control which includes ASAT research and development jumped to over $300 million. Any restart of fast funding for ASAT, as compensation perhaps for losses in armed service bureaucratic infighting on SDI, should be seriously reconsidered since the United States, more than the Soviet Union, relies on satellites to direct its nuclear and conventional forces. What is the point of creating a new 'window of vulnerability' by stimulating

Soviet progress in this area in the very attempt to decrease vulnerability by developing an ASAT system, especially if an arms control agreement with the Soviet Union can slow the arms race in space on terms advantageous to US strategic forces?[29]

Three other strategic systems might also well be questioned – Midgetman, the MX Rail Garrison Basing program and the Stealth bomber. Midgetman was cancelled in the FY 1989 budget, accounting (in addition to ASAT) for 80 per cent of program terminations and deferrals.[30] Whatever the nuclear stabilization merits of the Midgetman system, present budgetary constraints (not to mention broken bureaucratic bargains on weapons programs that might provoke new interservice discord) cautions against restarting the program as a deployed system.

Before going forward with Midgetman, one should seriously assess what the re-introduction of this program might have on the superpower consensus reached thus far at Geneva. Debate will now be reopened on the Midgetman system for several reasons. President Bush's National Security Advisor, General Brent Scowcroft, has long been on record in favor of the system.[31] Moreover, in early February, a bipartisan group of senior legislators and former Reagan and Carter Administration advisors recommended Midgetman over the MX or its Rail Garrison Basing mode. The implicit alliance between the White House National Security Advisor and important Congressional opinion, particularly Democratic leaders like Armed Services Chairman Senator Sam Nunn and House Armed Services Committee Chairman Representative Les Aspin, will keep the Midgetman program alive. Here the arms controllers appear out of control in pressing a principle of perceived strategic stability over the countervailing principle of political stability and detente between the superpowers.

Similarly, there is no urgent need to deploy the MX Rail Garrison system, pending the outcome of the START talks. The Bush Administration's decision to deploy the fifty MX missiles that have been authorized by Congress on open rail cars and to maintain the Midgetman program would appear to combine the worst of two worlds. The MX is a splendid first-strike weapon system whose sunk costs have been largely covered; the Midgetman, while it may be theoretically more stabilizing as a strategic weapon, carries a much higher price tag, estimated to be about $40–50 billion or approximately three and a half to four times as costly as the MX mobile system.

The justification for a mobile ground system arises primarily from continued US commitment to the notion of a sacred nuclear triad that requires each leg of the US deterrent to survive a Soviet attack and to deliver unacceptable damage on the Soviet Union. Even if the entire US strategic land-based missile system were destroyed by a Soviet first strike – an unlikely event – the United States would still have more than 10,000 warheads on other systems, principally bombers and nuclear submarines, to retaliate against the Soviet Union. What also lies behind the pressures on and within the Bush Administration to work on both systems is the attachment of many in the US security community to a nuclear warfighting stance. The MX is the ideal weapon, given its accuracy, MIRVing, hard-target capability and positive command and control features.

In convincing the Secretary of Defense to assign priority to the mobile MX, the Air Force can also force Congress's hand on Midgetman. In either case, the Air Force will have at least one new mobile strategic missile – conceivably two. Meanwhile, spending on improved cruise missiles and Trident IIs continues with the result that the United States's nuclear arsenal will be expanding at the very time that it will be engaging in negotiations with the Soviet Union on deep cuts in strategic systems. The decision to slow the rate of spending for the Stealth bomber until technical problems in developing a reliable system can be solved is one of the few instances where the Bush Administration did not approve or accelerate work on strategic weapons. At an estimated cost of over a half billion dollars a copy, planners are strongly encouraged to rethink the goal of 132 B-2s as well as their projected mission: to identify and destroy targets deep within the Soviet Union in a post-attack environment.

The savings that can be made in these nuclear strategic categories should not be exaggerated. Only about 17 per cent of the defense budget is attributable to strategic systems. Most cuts will have to be found in conventional forces. The most vulnerable program to budgetary cuts is the 600-ship Navy. An independent maritime strategy no longer appears as politically or economically viable as it did during the tenure of John Lehman as Secretary of the Navy. The resignation of his successor, James Webb, partly over cuts in anticipated funding, is a political straw in the wind which suggests that the Navy will have to absorb its share of reductions in defense spending. Under the best of assumptions, those of the Reagan years, it was problematic whether there would be enough funds available to meet the 600-ship goal.[32] The first major Navy casualties included a reduction in planning from fifteen to fourteen carrier task force groups and cancellation of the Marine Corps program for a new troop transport, estimated to cost in excess of $22 billion. One implication of these cuts, if they are sustained by Congress, would be some retrenchment in the Navy's global maritime strategy, as a consequence of decreased funding and, quite possibly, a refocusing of naval interest in the Western alliance, the Mediterranean, and East Asia, where US interests are primary.

CONCLUSIONS

Like the Cheshire cat in Alice in Wonderland, the Cold War appears to be fading – or at least to be in long recessional. The most persuasive evidence of its slipping grip on our attention is the reform movement now underway in the Soviet Union. The Soviet model is no longer attractive even to the Soviet Union. Certainly a militarily strong West has contributed to the decision by Soviet leaders to launch a fundamental socio-economic reform of the Soviet Union whose repercussions today, not unlike the Soviet Revolution that led to it, can only be dimly perceived today. It would be wrong to conclude, however, that Western military power itself produced this far reaching reform effort. The most that can be said is that it provided a security structure within which the democratic institutions, market economies and concern for individual freedom and welfare of the West could flourish. It furnished an elemental order that fostered the pursuit of equality, not by lowering everyone to a common dry bed, but by elevating as many as possible, much like the tide raises all boats of all sizes and worth.

Recognizing the limits of military power – without, in any way, denigrating its indispensability in a world still at sixes and sevens – suggests some guideline in responding to the signals emanating from Moscow to de-militarize international relations and to promote detente. While Soviet good intentions must be tested and arms control accords must bolster not weaken Western defenses, the West must also learn, as it did in the INF case, to say 'Yes' to 'Yes'. If it is in the interests of the West to cooperate with the Soviet Union to construct a more stable as well as less costly and risky security environment than we have now, then it should have sufficient confidence in its own military and economic strength to accept Soviet concessions if they are consistent with Western security interests.

Cooperation should also not preclude unilateral moves to cut, reorganize, or redeploy military forces if they improve the Western position. As for the United States, defense spending has detracted attention from the long-term problems of global economic competitiveness, growth and public welfare. Military capabilities rather than a balanced strategic design, sensitive to the techno-economic determinants of a viable and enduring defense posture, have tended to drive defense budgets. Within these budgets, strategic nuclear weapons have multiplied with little or no restraint. At a conventional level, investments in new-end items and in developing still newer weapons have distorted defense planning to the disadvantage of readiness and sustainability. We need a strong and staying military force as a guarantee of what we have, but not one so large or uncontrolled that it is an obstacle to what we can yet become.[33]

US defence policy: present and future issues
Phil Williams

The Kolodziej paper is a very useful assessment of past trends and future difficulties, and I intend to go mainly into matters of emphasis and detail rather than the overall structure of the analysis. I thought I would focus mainly on two areas. First of all, the Reagan legacy and then some questions for the future, given the constraints, and problems that US defence policy-makers and planners are now faced with. Kolodziej was rather kinder about the Reagan Administration's defence policy and its legacy than I would have been. That is not to say that Reagan did not make some great contributions. Two were particularly important. In the first place, the Reagan Administration helped to restore American pride, status and self-confidence. However, the Reagan Administration exaggerated the extent of neglect in the previous decade of neglect, and therefore, in some ways, it was fairly easy to exaggerate the extent to which they were putting the problems right. Secondly, and perhaps more positively, its other contribution was to adopt policies which encouraged the Soviet Union to come to the bargaining table and to make significant concessions. This coincided with important developments in the Soviet Union and so there was a real change in the mood of superpower relations.

But against this background, there were a number of problems important enough to warrant more treatment. First, the Reagan Administration had no clear coherence in strategic design. The size of the defence budget, particularly in the early years, was a substitute for strategy. Although, in the earlier years, it did have a broad consensus on defence, its own actions helped to erode and undermine that consensus. The lack of clear management and direction was one factor and disclosures about waste in the defence budget was another. Secondly, in some ways, the Reagan defence policy became a victim of its own success, because it could be argued that the same level of defence was no longer necessary, given the relative decline of Soviet power. It also ran up against problems in Congress, and handled them fairly badly. Weinberger was not particularly good in dealing with Congress, as is evidenced by Kolodziej's Tables. But the big change really came after Fiscal Year 1985. Up to then, Congress had contented itself with something like 5–6 per cent cuts in budget authority from what the Administration had requested, and budget authority still went up every year. From 1985 on, in a more constrained environment, Congress began to cut the defence budget, or the authorizations, by something like 11 per cent. So the Reagan Administration had already lost much of its support.

The Reagan Administration, thirdly, did not solve the vulnerability problem. It came into office, talking about the two great windows, the window of vulnerability and the window of opportunity. It made much play about the vulnerability of land-based missiles but then it had an enormous problem. Reagan cancelled the one system that made sense strategically, even if it did not make sense environmentally, and that was Carter's MPS system. It then went into a basing mode-of-the-month club on MX. The Scowcroft Commission defined away the vulnerability problem partly by stressing the difficulties the Soviet Union would face in coordinating an attack on three legs of the triad and made it less necessary to worry about a first strike. The Commission also suggested that strategic stability could be improved by de-MIRVing and came up with a Midgetman idea which was regarded as stabilizing because it was less of a threat, and presented a less attractive target. I think I do disagree with Professor Kolodziej on the desirability of Midgetman. It seems to me that it is a system of value and it will be interesting to see the extent to which Scowcroft will push it. A Midgetman was actually used to rescue MX, but in a sense they were based on rather different strategic philosophies, with MX based on a countervailing philosophy and Midgetman rather more on a minimal deterrent philosophy. Partly because of this, and partly because of budgetary stringency, they gradually became competitors; the Scowcroft compromise fell apart and the Reagan Administration opted for MX Rail Garrison deployment. It is quite interesting to hear some of the arguments for Midgetman being resuscitated these days; they relate, in part, to the kind of agreement we might get from START. With the kind of START agreement people have talked about, Midgetman begins to look increasingly attractive. But, in a sense, the vulnerability problem, to the extent that it ever was there, is still there.

The fourth problem with the Reagan Administration is that it really left a residue of conceptual confusion. We saw this in SDI and the uncertainty about its ultimate purpose, and its relationship to traditional deterrence. We also saw it in the relationship between force planning and arms control. There was a clear sense of priority on this in the first Administration when the emphasis was on strategic modernization and then negotiation from strength. Yet Reykjavik showed that that sense of priorities could very easily and quickly be skewed.

The fifth problem, I think, is that the Reagan Administration did not fully overcome the Vietnam syndrome. It was able to use force against targets of convenience but found it very difficult to sustain military commitments on situations which were not short, sharp and decisive, and we saw that in Lebanon. And I think that the continuing force of the Vietnam syndrome was evident in the Weinberger doctrine enunciated in November 1984.

The sixth point is that the Reagan Administration was really divided for most of its eight years between the conservative pragmatists and the conservative ideologues, or what Arnold Horlick at Rand Corporation called the dealers and the squeezers. The dealers had increasing successes at the end, but the Reagan years do suggest that fragmentation and lack of coherence in the policy-making system has become a way of life in the US national security policy-making apparatus.

But let us turn now to the Bush Administration and US defence policy in the 1990s. What we might well see is a rather more introspective perspective of the Bush Administration. I think the Administration will be concerned with a lot of domestic problems and will become, in many ways, very inward-looking. This does not mean isolationism but a greater focus on domestic problems. I will try to highlight questions that remain unanswered and that we need to think about. The first question is a very fundamental one, and that is can the United States adapt to a new world in which the limits of its own power are increasingly salient? I prefer this formulation of the limits of American power to rather glib assessments of American decline. It is really about limits. The Reagan Administration came in with the idea that it would transcend these limits; it would ignore them. The limits were attributed initially to the decade of neglect, but the Reagan Administration itself ended up by trying to come to terms with the limits of power. The Bush Administration still has a long way to go in this. There is going to be a very difficult strategic environment in the 1990s and I am not sure it is as benign as we sometimes think. There will still be concerns over the Soviet threat, and part of that threat is technology-driven. We have seen the continued momentum of Soviet strategic problems for example. We have not yet seen the changes in force structure that we would like to see. The traditional threat is not going to go away immediately, although it might be slowly diminishing.

The other point is that there are new sources of turmoil and disorder in the Third World, where the spread of ballistic missile technology is very important. What we currently have is peace by exhaustion in much of the Third World, but as soon as that exhaustion has gone away and we have a degree of recuperation, then we can expect further disorder. So there is a major question for the Bush Administration, namely What kind of defence policy is appropriate for a world which is becoming increasingly multipolar and perhaps increasingly disorderly, and in which the power of the United States and the Soviet Union to intervene very decisively is limited?

But, given the deficits, given the diminished threat, given increased introspectiveness is there a coherent strategy for dealing with resources constraints? What are the most important priorities? Can the United States develop and sustain a coherent posture, given the kind of pressures that stem from the iron triangle of Congress, defence industries and the military as well as interservice rivalries.

What kind of choices will be made in relation to the MX and Midgetman? I differ with Professor Kolodziej on this, because I think, given the START limits, Midgetman makes much more sense than the MX because the United States could have many more of them and the system would be a much less attractive target. Also, what kind of choices will be made in relation to B-1/B-2? What size navy will we have? What would be the implications of a smaller navy? What would that do to the Maritime

Strategy? These are a series of questions which need to be answered. In short, the Bush Administration will have to make the kind of choices that the Reagan Administration succeeded in avoiding.

The third point about the Bush Administration concerns the United States and NATO and the whole question of burden-sharing. We have a new formulation by NATO, and we now talk instead about sharing roles, risks and responsibilities but what does this mean in practice? Can we achieve an orderly devolution of power and responsibility from the United States to Western Europe? Is the United States prepared to yield some of the leadership of the alliance? Is Western Europe willing and able to play a greater role and create a European pillar within the Atlantic framework? The answers to these questions remain uncertain. The process of devolution will be a difficult process precisely because the burden-sharing issue has so much potential to become symbolic and divisive. The controversy will require very careful management indeed. The burden-sharing issue will remain on the agenda for the foreseeable future and I see two distinct strands. First of all there is the Pat Schroeder strand which is really to talk about burden-sharing as burden relief, which I would describe as burden-shedding. Basically, the Europeans should do more so that the United States can do less. The second strand is the Sam Nunn strand. In Nunn's view burden-sharing is a synonym for a continuing strategic debate, but the question is what is the most appropriate NATO for strategy. Nunn wants Europeans to do more, so that NATO will rely less on nuclear weapons. But if that fails, then Nunn could become a much more negative force and go back to the kind of position he adopted briefly in 1984 when he argued that if Europeans did not provide the wherewithal for sustained conventional defence then it would make sense for the United States to go back to a trip-wire.

There are three issues which could actually seriously intensify the burden-sharing controversy. The first is 1992 and the development of a single European market. That has already raised a lot of American concerns about the possibility of protectionism and about Fortress Europe. If those concerns do not abate and if something is not done about reassurance then that kind of argument could feed back into the security debate and the burden-sharing issue. In that case there would be some very damaging linkages between economic issues and security issues. The second issue which could intensify the burden-sharing argument is although Europe and the United States might be redefining the threat downwards, they will do so at different rates. The Europeans will redefine the threat downward rather quicker than the United States. The third is the SNF modernization issue which, again, will become highly symbolic. Will the military benefits of a Lance follow-on actually outweigh the political costs, especially in Germany? Having said that, and if NATO does not go ahead, then that, of course, provokes the Congressional sentiment that we should not keep our boys in Europe without nuclear weapons to protect them.

Finally, the fourth set of issues are to do with deterrence. How stringent will be the requirements of nuclear deterrence in the 1990s? There are basically three different notions of deterrence, and the appropriate posture for it, around in the debate. First, is deterrence through warfighting capabilities, that is like the countervailing strategy for which capabilities such as MX and SDI are required. That was the Carter strategy and in a sense the Reagan strategy too. Secondly, there is what people used to call minimal deterrence, through survival of retaliatory capabilities – capabilities with emphasis on stability – and Midgetman certainly fits in with that second category. The third is existential deterrence. McGeorge Bundy coined the term and his basic argument was that deterrence is a condition, not a policy or strategy, and that nuclear weapons by their very existence make states prudent and therefore deter them from a lot of actions that the other superpower would regard as undesirable. They create prudence, they lead the superpowers to develop certain rules of the game. If you take this view, then precise capabilities, precise strategies do not matter too much, because in this view deterrence is very easy. If threat is declining, then will we see a move away from countervailing deterrence perhaps through minimal deterrence towards existential deterrence? And if we do see that kind of move what would be the implications for Europe?

NOTES AND REFERENCES

1. Paul Kennedy, *The Rise and Fall of the Great Powers* (New York: Random House, 1987).
2. William W. Kaufmann, 'A defense agenda for fiscal years 1990–1994', in *Restructuring American Foreign Policy*, ed. John D. Steinbruner (Washington, DC: Brookings Institution, 1989), p. 57.
3. Ibid.
4. Center on Budget and Policy Priorities, 'The FY 1990/1991 defense budget: preliminary analysis', 12 January 1989.
5. Raymond L. Garthoff, *Détente and Confrontation: american-Soviet relations from Nixon to Reagan* (Washington, DC: Brookings Institution, 1985), pp. 794–6.
6. Edward A. Kolodziej and Roger Kanet (eds), *The Limits of Soviet Power in the Developing World: Thermidor in the revolutionary struggle* (London: Macmillan, 1989).
7. Center on Budget and Policy Priorities, 'The FY 1989 Defense Budget: preliminary analysis', 22 February 1988. Note that figures drawn from Kaufmann, n. 2, and the Center on Budget and Policy Priorities differ for DOD authorizations and outlays, but agree on the general downward trend in over-all defense spending from all sources, including the Department of Defense, the Department of Energy and related agencies.
8. Lawrence J. Korb and Stephen Daggett, 'The defense budget and strategic planning', in *American Defense Annual: 1988–1989* (Lexington: Lexington Books, 1988), pp. 44–6.
9. Kaufmann, p. 83.
10. *U.S. News and World Report*, 1 May 1989, p. 23 and *Washington Post*, 25 April 1989, p. 4.

11. Committee for National Security, *Mission Impossible? An Illustrated Guide to Defense Planning in the 1990s* (Washington, DC: January, 1989), p. 4.
12. See the estimates of slower growth reported by economic analysts associated with the Bush Administration. *New York Times*, 27 January 1989.
13. See Nick Kotz, *Wild Blue Yonder: money, politics and the B-1 bomber* (New York: Pantheon, 1988).
14. Fred C. Iklé et al., *Discriminate Deterrence: report of the commision on integrated long-term strategy* (Washington, DC: Government Printing Office, January, 1988).
15. Kaufmann, pp. 88–9.
16. Richard F. Grimmett, *Trends in Conventional Arms Transfers to the Third World by Major Supplier, 1978–1985* (Washington, DC: Congressional Research Service, 15 May 1986), pp. 1–13.
17. Michael Brzoska and Thomas Ohlson, 'The trade in major conventional weapons ', in *World Armaments and Disarmament: SIPRI Yearbook 1985* (New York: Oxford University Press, 1986), p. 336.
18. Western European Union, *Defence Industry in Spain and Portugal*, 7 November 1988, p. 9. Many of Spain's outlets are in Central and Latin America, traditional areas of US monopoly.
19. Arthur J. Alexander, 'U.S. and European arms collaboration and trade', Rand Corporation, February 1988, pp. 8–9. See also Keith Hartley, *NATO Arms Cooperation* (London: George Allen and Unwin, 1983), for an analysis of free markets in arms production and sales within the Atlantic Community.
20. The literature on RSI (Rationalization, Standardization and Interoperability) is as vast and sprawling as it is inconclusive. For relevant citations, consult n. 40, p. 468 of the author's *Making and Marketing Arms: The French experience and its implications for the international system* (Princeton: Princeton University Press, 1987).
21. *Current Digest of the Soviet Press* XL, no. 49, 4 January 1989, p. 6. See also n. 5.
22. Ibid.
23. Hedley Bull, *The Anarchical Society: a study of order in world politics* (London: Macmillan, 1977).
24. This is not the place to rehearse the long-standing argument of what Kennan meant by containment or to repeat the debate with Walter Lippmann over the Cold War. John Lewis Gaddis sorts out these differences between Kennan and Lippmann and within Kennan himself as well as anyone in his *Strategies of Containment: a critical appraisal of postwar American national security policy* (New York: Oxford University Press, 1982), pp. 25–53 and notes. What is relevant to our purposes here are the interests and strategic aims that should guide US defense policy.
25. Frank C. Carlucci, Secretary of Defense, *Annual Report to the Congress: Fiscal Year 1989* (Washington, DC: Government Printing Office, 1988), p. 67.
26. This point is persuasively made by Jonathan Dean, *Watershed in Europe* (Lexington: Lexington Books, 1987).
27. For a summary of the Stockholm accords, see James E. Doogby, 'The Stockholm Conference: negotiating a cooperative security system for Europe',

in *U.S.-Soviet Security Cooperation*, Alexander George et al., (eds) (New York: Oxford University Press, 1988), pp. 144–72.

28. For a brief outline of these counting rules, consult International Institute for Strategic Studies, *The Military Balance, 1988–1989* (London: IISS, 1988), pp. 233–4.

29. The changes made in President Reagan's last defense budget by President Bush are reviewed in the *New York Times*, 24 April 1989; in the *Washington Post*, 25 April 1989; and *Congressional Quarterly Weekly Report*, 29 April 1989, p. 976. The 'Brilliant Pebbles' program is reviewed in the *New York Times*, 25 April 1989, pp. 19, 23.

30. Korb, p. 58.

31. Brent Scowcroft, et al., 'Come and get us', *The New Republic*, 18 April 1988, pp. 16–18.

32. Two Congressional Budget Office reports reached the conclusion that the Navy would not meet its planning goals. Consult US Congressional Budget Office, *Future Budget Requirements of the 600-Ship Navy* (September 1985) and *Naval Combat Aircraft: Issues and options* (November 1987).

33. I should like to thank the Program in Arms Control, Disarmament and International Security of the University of Illinois and its Director, Dr Jeremiah Sullivan, for assistance in preparing this paper.

7 The future of US defence policy: further discussion

Although the pace has been less dramatic than in the Soviet Union, US foreign and defence policy also faces an era of change. The end of the Reagan era obviously brings with it the potential for a new President to set his own agenda to fit his own priorities. The growth of the US budgetary deficit and the national balance-of-payments deficit both create difficult dilemmas for any new Administration. Relative US economic decline has now been linked in many minds with foreign policy over extension and the argument that the United States must spend less on defence to secure her economic future is firmly on the presidential agenda. This, combined with the need to reduce forces to match Soviet arms control offers and the growing difficulties encountered as the defence budget has declined in real terms every year since 1985, suggests that some sort of defence review may take place over US defence policy in the 1990s.

Such a debate will obviously be important for both the US and allied navies. The experience of the Carter years showed what can happen when a new leader facing changing times seeks a new basis for defence policy.[1] In 1977–8 the Carter Administration decided to concentrate defence resources on the European Central Front whilst it discounted the utility of power-projection forces to assist US foreign policy in other regions. One consequence of this was an attempt to reduce naval forces which was only defeated by mobilized Congressional opposition and the fact that events seemed to call for just the naval capabilities that the Administration was intent on cutting. By way of contrast, the Reagan Administration brought with it a clear desire for maritime supremacy arguing that 'maritime superiority for the United States is a national objective – a security imperative, an essential condition for the success of any national security strategy'.[2] This produced a return to old principles and demonstrated clearly that new Presidents can, and do, bring major changes in defence policy in their wake.

If anything, the situation facing a Bush Administration is probably even more complex than that which faced President Carter. Carter grappled with economic difficulties which were politically more damaging than current problems, but Bush's deficits are far larger, in both absolute and relative terms, than those that shaped defence budgets in the late 1970s. Carter's strategy was logical – if one accepted that missions beyond building the capability to fight for thirty days in Europe could be assigned a low priority. President Carter's policy, however, was eroded by two persistent problems. The first was that the world refused to behave in the benign way his policies anticipated – this fuelled political anxieties in the United States to the point where voters both called for a tougher defence stance and voted for the presidential candidate to provide it in 1980. Carter's second problem, however, has proved even more intractable. This was the question of how much money the United States could spend on defence in an age of escalating social expenditures. The hidden problem of the Carter period was that his defence budgets were too small to match even his limited goals – by FY 1982 the budget would only fund 214 combat planes and 6 warships.

President Reagan essentially solved this problem of inadequate funding by spending more. Reagan, however, avoided the choice between having his defence budgets dictated by the need to control the deficit and actually taxing in order to meet defence needs, by increasing borrowing. He also added missions to President Carter's rather short list of priorities. The Reagan Administration identified a clear strategy for the US Navy, put some flesh on the skeleton of Carter's Rapid Deployment Force, increased air and sealift capability, boosted special forces, raised spares and operations funding to levels that actually allowed the forces to operate at desired levels and added to strategic forces funding by stressing command and control and the B-1. If we add to this the costs of the SDI, the problem of the Reagan Administration's defence policy becomes clear – with so much going on, and the cost of new capable weapons continuing to escalate, even in the best of times the budget was unlikely to continue to meet all of these demands.

Since 1985, with real reductions in defence funding replacing planned rises and procurement funds especially hit, the problem has become more pressing. Planned increases in force levels have been abandoned. By early 1989 it had already been determined that the US Navy would not get 600 ships and the Airforce would reduce to 35, rather than rise to 40 tactical fighter wing equivalents. As pressures on procurement rise, perversely as the fruits of past investments in R&D become available, difficult choices look inevitable.

Discussion at the Greenwich Conference indicated that the strategic debates of the 1970s had still not been resolved on the continental – maritime, nuclear – conventional or the 'to use force – or not to use force' issues.

The role of military power, and the associated question of the role the United States should play in the world, seemed to lie at the heart of the debate. On the one hand, there was a view that Vietnam, Afghanistan, and perhaps Beirut, demonstrated very real, and growing, limits on the capacity of military power – even when wielded by superpowers – to determine events. Some saw indiscriminate global involvement as an unneccessary and ineffective means to secure US interests. There were, it was claimed, entire, large, regions of the world where the United States in fact had no real need to be involved – Africa being particularly unimportant. US interests, in fact, lay in a relatively small number of areas which could actually be summed up as Europe, Oil, Japan and Israel. Where lesser interests were involved, there would be scope for exploiting local discontents to secure US goals – perhaps relying on the divide-and-rule principle. This line of analysis tended to be associated with those who stress the importance of land forces for the Central Front whilst de-emphasizing maritime and intervention forces for other contingencies.

The contrary view was stated with some vigour, with many of the arguments of the Kolodziej Chapter coming under question as the case was made. One of the main problems with efforts to restrict the scope of US interests, it was argued, was the unpredictability of the international political environment. It was just not possible to predict who would challenge US interests – Libya and Iran were both obvious examples of formerly friendly, relatively weak, states that had recently threatened US interests with real effect. There also still seemed to be dangers in defining which areas lay outside the US defensive umbrella: the experience of Korea in 1950 showed that items excluded from the list tended to come back to haunt US Presidents. Equally, some areas excluded from some people's lists, like Central America, looked vitally strategically important to other Americans. It was likely, anyway, that, even if strategic interests were not immediately at stake, few US Presidents would like to be put in a position where they could not intervene when they did feel it necessary because the resources were no longer available. Few Presidents were also likely to relish being placed in a situation where public opinion demanded action and they were unable to respond. The old arguments about credibility, deterrence, real security needs and political pressures still applied.

Even if one accepted that US interests were limited, some felt that there still seemed little scope to reduce commitments and, thereby, deployments. In fact, the United States was not engaged in anything that could be called indiscriminate global involvement. US forces were actually only deployed at present ensuring the security of Europe, Japan, Persian Gulf Oil and Israel, and a few other concerns including US interests in Central America, Korea, the Philippines and Pakistan. The reduced list of interests offered by advocates of 'finite deterrence', unfortunately looked rather like the list of actual US deployments. The reality was that talk of 'indiscriminate' commitments was simplistic nonsense. The commitments were already finite. The problem was that even finite commitments required large forces. What many advocates of finite deterrence had actually done was to assume that core interests from Israel to Japan could actually be protected by smaller forces than history suggested or US military leaders recommended. The issue was not really what interests should be defended but how, and how assuredly, they should be secured.

The notion of an over-extended USA also came under attack. The US defence burden as a percentage of GNP was hardly unsustainable at 5.4 per cent of GNP. In 1955 it stood at 9.1 per cent and began and ended the 1960s at around 8 per cent.[3] The increase in the budgetary deficit since 1981 mirrored not only a return of defence spending to its pre-1973 priority but also continued increases in non-defence items in the federal budget. The real question was not one of economically determined reductions but in political willingness to pay the price of various defence postures. The comparison with the decline of Britain as a world power – implicit from the Kennedy thesis – was rejected both because the United States did not share Britain's economic weakness and because the United States did not have its own America to pass the burden to. If the United States chose not to assume the role of a wide-ranging superpower, no one else was ready to fill the vacuum. The essential issue for the United States was whether she would find it tolerable to live in a world where allies like Saudi Arabia, Kuwait, Honduras, South Korea, Israel, Pakistan and Salvador were threatened, US citizens, in perhaps larger numbers, were abducted by disparate terrorist groups and US economic interests were vulnerable to increasing international conflict. While it is possible to argue that core US interests might survive and that the recovery of the odd US citizen from his fate would not be worth much expenditure of time or money, it is not clear that US Presidents or publics would feel happy in such a world.

There was also strong dissent from Kolodziej's proposals on procurement. Modernization was sometimes necessary, not all new weapons were superfluous – one could not rely on ten, twenty, thirty, forty-year-old weapons to do the job for ever. There was even some scope for new technology to open up new possibilities – allowing conventional forces to do more, more quickly and opening up the gap between US forces and Third World opponents. The real problem was in prioritizing procurement requests and funding the defence budget at a level adequate to meet the minimal demands imposed by the minimal commitments. Here, there seemed to be real room for debate. The US Army still seemed to believe in the centrality of the Central Front whilst the US Navy, suitably supported by the other services, was building a case that stressed its utility in both general war and limited campaigns. A debate seemed to be opening up – if only to the extent that some framework would be needed to decide between current, pressing, procurement priorities.

Given the difficulties facing the United States, it was felt that some changes to existing defence priorities might be necessary, but, again, there was considerable opposition to the Kolodziej proposals. There was consensus that the United States would not regard the numbers of its troops in Europe as sacrosanct and would try to establish some new basis for keeping those that were to remain. The questions of what US forces were stationed forward for, and in what numbers, might be raised. On the naval front, the point was made that the Maritime Strategy did play a role in deterring Soviet attack (and perhaps, therefore, in helping produce recent changes in the USSR) and was part of the national strategy. Rather than being an independent aberration, as portrayed by some critics, it was a strategy that depended upon the other services for its success and was one of the principal deterrent options in the US arsenal.

Which defence priorities would emerge from the current debate was, and is, far from clear. Presidents are limited in their capability to shape the defence budgets they inherited in their first year and, even if new directions were set in 1990, these would take years to implement. Informed US sources believed that these questions still awaited resolution and Europe would have to wait three to four years to see major changes in US defence budgets. There was little support for the idea that the United States was prepared to make dramatic choices over priorities. There was, however, a plurality of US opinion that the arguments for increased reliance on sea and airpower to maintain US interests were at least strong contenders in the policy debate in Washington.

THE DEFENCE DEBATE

Events since February 1989 have seen some movement in US positions but have done little to resolve some key questions. Though there has been some action, the defence policy debate in the United States has been rather constrained. Some contributions have been rather predictable. Anyone who has read any of the proposals of 1974–8 with their arguments for a smaller navy, continuing Central Front commitment and massive cuts in procurement programmes with reliance on older, obsolete weapons, would find very similar arguments being regurgitated in 1989.[4] Calls then for cutting procurement of the B-1, reducing the Navy to eight to twelve carriers and maintaining a short-war Central Front commitment are now echoed by demands to cut the B-2, cut to eight to twelve carriers and concentrate on the Central Front. Again, cheaper weapons are proposed, with calls for lighter, cheaper fighters to replace procurement of more sophisticated types and cheaper frigates for convoy escort to replace expensive Aegis ships. Opponents of such policy options, however, seem to have an easier task refuting them when the Soviet Union itself is buying sophisticated F-15 and F-18 class fighters (the Su-27 and MiG-29) and is, itself, building carriers, large destroyers and sophisticated missile systems. Some of the arguments also seem unusually impracticable this time around – cancelling the US Navy's DDG-51 programme, and replacing it with a replacement FFGX frigate might be an option worth pursuing if it met the needs of a coherent strategy. When there is no design in existence for any FFGX, proposing to stop building everything else in order to build it looks decidedly odd – even if its capabilities were less moot. Also odd, even dangerous, is the suggestion that one aircraft carrier would suffice in the Atlantic, Pacific and Gulf areas to meet any demands – current practice of operating two or three carriers near such foes as North Korea, Libya and Iran seems rather more prudent than sending one with no back up.

The similarity of many recent proposals to the policies of 1977 may be inevitable given the continuity of personalities and organizations. It seems unlikely, however, that this perspective will regain the dominance it had in the 1977–8 period. The policies that were rejected as inadequate by Congress, the US electorate, and even the Administration itself by 1979, are unlikely to prove more appropriate in the 1990s. The reality for the new decade is a political revolution in the Soviet bloc and wide-ranging change elsewhere. In military terms, the debate has now changed in practically all dimensions with an increasing Soviet naval threat, a continuing, and modernizing, strategic nuclear threat and a rapidly diminishing Central Front threat. A US debate centred around whether President Carter's strategic weapons (the MX and B-2) are too costly, looks a strange response to those changes.

Indeed, even when the defence debate outside the Administration has escaped from the bounds of 1977, it often seems not to have progressed far. Old procurement options seem to re-emerge just as often as old strategic priorities. The conventional submarine; the small aircraft carrier; land-based naval airpower; cheaper warships; lightweight fighters; and manoeuvre warfare all seem to be destined to a continous cycle of renewal and re-evaluation as they return as solutions to lack of money, only to be rejected as they prove neither to be truly cost-effective, nor, indeed, adequate to match the threat at all.

Stranger still, US strategic debate seems recently to have been dominated by non-strategic arguments, Vietnam era decision-makers and simple, solutions to single problems that leave other requirements ignored. Burden-sharing or 'the peace dividend', rather than adequate deterrence, are offered as the deciding factors behind troop reductions. Some in the US are proposing 50 per cent cuts at a time when the Soviet Union itself has only initiated 14 per cent cuts by 1991 and talked of a 25 per cent total cut by 1995 – this when much of the US force structure retains missions that are not affected at all by reductions in Soviet forces. Suggestions for reductions mysteriously seize on figures that happen to add up to 50 per cent cuts. Indeed, some contributions to the defence debate do little more than list major procurement programmes and cancel them till the required sum of money has been found.[5]

There have been some positive contributions to this debate – these became more frequent towards the close of 1989 as it became clear that a defence review was occurring and the printing presses finally caught up with change. The US press has given space to some ideas and allowed some argument to proceed. There have been some notable, positive and imaginative, contributions by some Congressmen, Colin Gray, Edward Luttwak and F.E. West. As time has passed, some books have emerged from the publication cycle. The FY 1990 DOD Annual Report contained a useful essay on nuclear strategy and some idea of Administration and service thinking can be learned from the Congressional hearings.[6] We still await, however, a definitive statement of official thinking like PRM-10 or PD-59. Where original ideas have been developed, as with the report of the President's Commission on Integrated Long-Term Strategy, the impact on strategy and priorities has been muted.[7] Even when a strategy has been implemented by the Administration, as in the case of the development of the Stealth bomber to increase US superiority in the air, this seems to have been done in a way that leaves much of the possible consequential strategic change undiscussed. Apart from some reruns of the short-war Central Front argument, the US strategic journals have been rather quiet on future options.

This may be inevitable. Vietnam obviously still shapes perceptions of the utility of force. Political division in the United States is bound to be reflected in prescriptions for its defence policy – although talk of congruence between the Democratic and Republican parties tends to deny real differences. Serious academic debate is inclined to be limited by timelags between the generation of ideas and their publication. Debate has also become more difficult with the increasing complexity of the issues that require it. Defence policy increasingly reflects assessments of military and technological possibilities as well as foreign policy analysis. Intelligent analysis of 'discriminating deterrence', the Maritime Strategy or potentialities for defence in Europe increasingly requires a familiarity with capabilities and concepts that few possess. The result is sometimes arguments based on false assumptions about capabilities, requirements or potentials – a case where ignorance can only produce ignorant solutions.

Even when the effort is made, however, there is a wider problem which goes beyond the sheer difficulty of keeping up with quickening, political, technological and military change. The 1980s have seen something of the growth of a hidden agenda in US defence policy. Nuclear strategy has retired somewhat from public debate and the assumptions of nuclear targeting have lately been little discussed; cooperation between the US services has advanced to the point at which elements of some proposed national strategies are already in place; black programmes provide a concealed range of options. Devising a defence policy for the future is obviously not easy when determining what today's defence policy actually is, is so difficult.[8]

THE POLITICAL PROCESS

The debate has also been affected by wider political trends. The US election campaign of 1989 resolved few specific issues. Its outcome strengthened the trend in US politics to a Republican presidency and a Democratic Congress. As some analysts have suggested, this may itself reflect a subconscious, or even conscious, decision by the US voter as to what he wants. The President is elected to maintain a strong America and defend US interests. Congress is elected to provide local and national economic and social benefits. The results of the 1980–8 elections suggest that a President who is seen to be against strong defences will not be elected – both on the issue itself and because defence has become a litmus test for other issues where strength is desired. The split in the Democratic party between Southern conservatives and Northern liberals may have become less crucial since the early 1980s when Southern Democrats voted with Reagan in Congress, but the presidential votes in 1988 suggest all to clearly that the South does not want a President portrayable as weak on defence. On the other hand, growing House majorities for the Democrats and demands for a gentler, fairer America suggest no decrease in the pressure to spend more on social programmes at the same time as taxes are held and budget deficits are cut. Voters elect a President to ensure a strong America but have little interest in, or knowledge of, what it takes to provide an adequate defence posture. The essential problem of how to fund an adequate defence remains intact.

The capability to reshape US defence budgets is also shaped by increasing Congressional influence. Local priorities seem increasingly influential in deciding authorizations and appropriations – both in the committees and at subsequent floor and conference committee debates. In 1989, efforts to avoid a competition to add favoured programmes to the budget by accepting the Defense Secretary's cuts *in toto* were rejected (albeit on a tied vote on the House Armed Services Committee) with the result that major programmes with substantial support, like the F-14 and V-22 Osprey, were added back into the budget at the expense of other expenditure. Some of the coalitions emerging between defence cutters, proponents of alternative weapons and those seeking better weapons are bizarre. Though in FY 1990 the committees managed to find a series of rational compromises, divisions between House and Senate, and between the House Armed Services Committee (which authorizes programmes) and the House Appropriations Committee (which appropriates money – not necessarily for the same programmes), make the imposition of clearer priorities unlikely. There still appears little hope of Congress agreeing to produce a more rational outcome by combining the authorizing and appropriating functions in one committee instead of two. Money continues to be added for politically high profile items like the National Guard – regardless of any strategic debate as to the utility of reserve forces for likely needs. Nor has there been any move to go beyond an annual budget to an agreed, and honoured, five-, or even two-year plan.

This all looks inevitable given the nature of US politics, the constitutional and economic roots of the political system and the difficulty of agreeing one solution that meets disparate, strategic, economic and local goals. The general trend towards decentralized defence policy-making, in turn, has been exacerbated by other changes. Congressional committees are now less controllable by their leadership. The trend in Congress for single party constituencies to emerge where re-election of the incumbent is the norm has paradoxically produced defence committees where time has removed many of the experienced incumbents who sat through the strategic debates of the 1970s, leaving a situation where leading positions on some sub-committees are now held by younger McGovernite Democrats who have opposed Administration defence programmes under four or five Presidents and hold positions to the left of subsequent, considerably less radical, Carter/Mondale/Dukakis platforms. A system which includes Representatives Schroeder and Dellums as well as Senators Nunn and Warner might even be seen as the natural outcome of a truly pluralist democracy. Compromise around the lowest common denominator may be the price for running such a democracy.

Congress also has its own agenda now. It tends to see security in its wide sense – hence Congressional raids on defence funds to finance aid to Eastern Europe and antidrug efforts; it is inclined to take its role of oversight more seriously following the procurement scandals of the 1980s; nor is it any longer the case that the armed services tend to relay the view of the Defense Department to Congress. The committees now tend to shape a defence budget within the Congressional consensus rather than argue against the rest of Congress. The Armed Services Committees which tested their weight in 1978 and 1979 against President Carter's naval programme, continue to exercise their own judgement on Administration proposals. As Pat Towell has put it: 'The Armed Services Committees . . .

are still prodefense – but they are no longer automatically pro-DOD.[9]

All of this oversight of course adds to the complexity of the process and the outcome, which may not, of itself, be a bad thing. It does all suggest, however, that hopes of matching threats to capabilities are probably too optimistic for the system to deliver. Although Congress provides some of the most informed commentators on US defence policy, and the efforts of Senator Nunn and Representative Aspin, each in his own way, to produce coherency are particularly noteworthy, it still is not clear if Congress can be a net positive force in the development of a coherent defence policy review. Indeed, talk of a 'peace dividend' in 1989 and 1990 suggested a real danger that Congress could become the instigator of full-scale demobilization such as that which occurred from 1945 to 1949, rather than a measured defence review.[10]

Congress in some ways only reflects wider dilemmas. Congressional efforts to sustain local industry may cause budgetary problems but they do reflect a real need to maintain defence contractors in business. It is questionable, for example, that the United States can afford to lose major defence manufacturers like Grumman. To take two other examples: cutting M-1 tank procurement, now that the US Army has reached its original 7,000 objective, would either reduce procurement below minimum economic rates or, if cut entirely, would leave the United States without a working tank plant. Similarly, failure to continue US naval aircraft carrier procurement beyond 1995 might produce a situation where the ability to produce carriers could only be regained at far greater cost later. Congress at least ensures that these issues are debated. Continuing to fund everything at low levels may be preferable to a policy review that produces irremediable change. Options sometimes close options; whilst a change of direction that leads to a cul-de-sac may not be the best route to follow.

THE FIRST YEAR OF THE BUSH ADMINISTRATION

The willingness of the Bush Administration to conduct a radical defence review was also questioned. Although this may change after the decisive use of force in Panama, and the Administration has argued that time was required to devise the appropriate policies for such a rapidly changing world, the US media's initial assessment of his presidency saw President Bush as an incrementalist rather than a visionary. The President is widely seen as 'cautious', 'reactive', a man who 'likes to split the difference' and a man who respects Pentagon advice and is determined not to 'do anything militarily dumb'.[11] The views of the President's advisers remain obscure with only some speculative grounds for thinking that the National Security Adviser Brent Scowcroft continues to support the strategic solutions originally offered by the Scowcroft Commission in 1983 and that the combination of Scowcroft, a former airforce officer, at the NSC and General Powell from the army as the Chairman of the JCS may tilt the balance slightly against any major changes to the detriment of either the army or the airforce.[12]

Throughout its first year in office, it remained unclear if the Administration would chose salami-slicing all-round cuts or whether clear priorities would emerge between missions and services. The initial review of strategy conducted by the Administration on coming to office seems to have had little impact – it appears neither to have been as complete nor as influential as PRM-10 in 1977 – perhaps inevitably, given the perceived success of President Reagan's defence policy and President Bush's promise of continuity. In so far as they indicated preferences, the FY 1990 reductions suggested shared misery – albeit with the Navy bearing the largest percentage of the cuts.

Another chance to indicate direction came with President Bush's arms control proposals for 20 per cent cuts in European forces. This offered some insights but could be read in a variety of ways as a sign of compromise *or* imagination, and as a move away from *or* a reiteration of, the primacy of the Central Front in US defence policy. It was not clear at the time to many observers if the 80 per cent figure was only the result of a compromise between the Administration and Joint Chiefs or whether it really reflected a foreign policy vision. There even seemed some potential that it could have the side-effect of shaping much of any future defence debate by setting certain force levels in concrete. If US forces in Europe continued to equal Soviet forces at 80 per cent of current levels, the scope for reducing the US Army and Airforce in any subsequent review would be limited. Until Soviet force levels in Eastern Europe decline past first the 275,000 and then the 195,000 levels discussed in US–Soviet negotiations – and Gorbachev actually implements his pledge to bring all his troops home – the European commitment in US defence policy will continue to absorb substantial resources. It still has to be decided what US forces would remain in Europe and what guarantees should be provided after any total Soviet withdrawal to the USSR.

It might be wrong, however, to conclude from all this that change was unlikely. The Bush Administration throughout much of 1989 continued to stress the need to think policy through before announcing new directions and to claim that, in a state of revolutionary change, such as that seen in Eastern Europe in 1989, prudence is important. By winter 1989, however, the dust seemed to have settled enough for the Administration to set out in new directions. Secretary Cheney's announcement, in November 1989, that he proposed major defence cuts, and the mention of $180 billion over five years, suggested that the defence review that looked unlikely in summer had become inevitable by winter as the Administration now found itself in a position to take stock of changes. Cheney's announcement was, however, difficult to assess because it left some confusion over how much might be cut, when, at what prices, and from what planned figure or whether the request for cuts up to $180 billion is an objective or a figure designed to produce a range of options. Interestingly, the reaction of unidentified Pentagon sources to the Cheney 'review' was that there were still no priorities and that this was just a financial exercise with the Defense Department attempting to pre-empt pressure from the Office of Management and Budget to cut the defence budget. This, some suggested, indicated that the Administration was more interested in economic success, Gramm-Rudman expenditure targets in FY 1991 and beyond and its 'no more taxes' pledge than having a major review of missions, interests, priorities and procurement.[13]

More evidence that real change was underway came in January 1990 with the submission of the FY 1991 Defense Budget. This clarified a number of issues.[14] The Administration does now intend to reduce US defence budgets in real terms – by two per cent per annum for each of the next five years. It has accepted the need to cut key Army programmes like the AH-64 helicopter and M-1A2 tank and the damage that such cuts will do to the US production base. Other cuts have been made in US Navy procurement, ships have been retired, fleet strength is falling and the Pentagon will try, again, to axe the Osprey and the F-14D. The Airforce faces the end of F-15 procurement, slower production of the B-2 bomber and C-17 transport and the loss of more units.

Some of the major questions, however, remained unanswered. On the one hand, it was notable that the US Army and Airforce took the brunt of manpower cuts whilst the US Navy was lightly cut and the US Marine Corp remained intact. The US Army lost two divisions whilst the US Navy limited its losses to two battleships and a large number of older SSN, cruisers and DDG whilst preserving its fourteen-carrier objective. The carrier force had been specifically excluded from further cuts with indications that decisions here would only be taken in later years. This, and reports of further cuts in the US Army, suggested that there was a definite shift on the way towards maritime, air and lightweight intervention forces.

The question remained unanswered, however, whether this was the result of reshaping priorities between the forces or just the short-term outcome of a policy of shared misery. Suggestions in the *Washington Post* that the services had been asked to provide three options for 'power projection, expeditionary and mobility forces' – one stressing maritime forces, one land and air and the third a compromise position, suggested that a review of roles within an overall strategic plan was being conducted. The scale of the options being considered – with option one seeing one-and-a-half divisions and two tactical fighter wings cut; option two seeing the US Navy cut to eight carrier battle groups (plus a training carrier) and losing all four of its battleships and one-third of the USMC and option three seeing the US Navy reduced to eleven carriers (plus one for training) and only two battleships – suggested fundamental change was possible. The outcome of the subsequent FY 1991 defence budget – with the Army cuts looking like those described under option one and the Navy losing only the two battleships proposed under option three – suggested at least a momentary success for advocates of the, maritime, option one. This seemed to be confirmed by the emergence of the Navy as the biggest spending service, and cancellation of key Army programmes like the M-1 tank.[15]

Other reports, though, suggested that all was not yet decided. The options chosen may, in large measure, just reflect the easiest way to save money. Interestingly, the options outlined in the *Washington Post* demonstrated the difficulty of cutting the Navy to save money – the choice was between reducing the US Army, in terms of major units, by 11 per cent or cutting the US Navy by 42 per cent – hardly an acceptable choice. There are also reports that the equal misery approach is still in favour in the Pentagon. Secretary Cheney is reported to have expressed frustration at the Navy for refusing to give up its carriers. It has also been suggested that each of the services had been asked to make its share of cuts by 1995, that the Navy would have great difficulty finding its share and that DOD planners assume twelve carriers only by 1994.[16] As yet, it seems that the jury must remain out on whether the Bush Administration will set new defence priorities or impose equal cuts. Indeed, it looks possible that what may evolve is a system where the President and the Secretary of Defense continue to make choices as options for cuts are offered. As with President Carter, the final choice on whether the US Navy is cut by 40 per cent, is likely to be made at the highest level and to prove one of the most crucial decisions of the Bush presidency. The extent of any change will only become apparent as the FY 1991 and subsequent budgets are enacted and Congress, of course, has also yet to have its say.

BUDGETARY PRESSURES

Even without Secretary Cheney's cuts, budgetary pressures on US defence forces were certain to become significant. Gramm-Rudman cuts to reduce the Federal deficit loomed whatever Mr Gorbachev chose to do with the threat. Funding shortages were also unavoidable as soon as defence expenditures stopped growing at a rate adequate to cover the real annual increase in procurement, pay and operations costs in the mid-1980s. If equipment costs continue to grow faster than procurement budgets, the quantity of equipment fielded can only fall. Recent experience suggests that, over time, defence expenditures tend to fail to match increasing defence cost inflation and show a very small real percentage of growth. Although increased competition, reforms of procurement procedures, and keeping weapons in service even longer, may lessen the dilemma, smaller fielded forces are inevitable. Choices will have to be made between pay, operations, training and the host of procurement programmes whose costs now exceed any likely procurement budget. If this was not enough, recent reports suggest that the US defence budget has additional problems in the form of underallowance for inflation and unrealistically low costs.[17] Against this background there will be real questions as to what elements of current force structures can be continued. These questions were already certain to demand answers before reductions in the perceived threat put major defence cuts onto the agenda.

The time may also have come when the problems caused by low-rate procurement of many systems have to be faced. Diseconomies of scale are growing as unit production costs rise with decreasing orders. Arbitrary production ceilings imposed by Congressional whim or budgetary pressures have denied the US capabilities that would have come relatively cheaply given initial outlays. A second batch of 100 B-1B bombers, for example, might only have cost $17 billion – a significant reduction on the cost of the first 100.[18] Spending money developing systems only to cancel them before procurement starts or is completed is a waste of resources. Delay to the B-2 programme has already added to overall costs. Early decommissioning of the *Coral Sea* has a hidden cost in terms of stretch on the remaining carrier fleet. The US defence industrial base is shrinking rapidly as companies prefer the certainties and profits of the civil sector to the unpredictabilities of defence. In terms of maintaining the industrial base and controlling falling orders and rising unit costs the United States may already be approaching an unsustainable position.

The current trend to equal misery is also already throwing up decidedly illogical solutions. Increased spending on the National Guard (often as a result of Congressional directions) and continuing procurement of M-1 tanks both increase US capability to fight the third and fourth month of a European conventional war. At the same time, however, US Army ammunition and spares budgets are being cut to levels which finance only the first forty-five to sixty days' requirements. An interesting debate is opening up whether changes in the threat actually puts more or less importance on reserve forces, whilst the whole issue of how much sustainability the US forces should have is also being questioned. Artillery ammunition is being procured at a rate that could see one year's procurement used up in around five hours of real war if each gun matched British consumption rates in the Falklands, or three days if rather lower Second World War rates prevailed.[19]

A similarly confused situation seems to exist with aircraft procurement. Both the START agreement and the INF treaty place greater emphasis on aircraft as part of the remaining nuclear deterrent force. The need for long-ranged fighter/attack aircraft is clearly increasing as bases become fewer, Soviet aircraft become more capable, FOFA requires new capabilities and an increasing nuclear burden falls on aircraft as other INF are withdrawn. The US response, however, has been to terminate procurement of the F-15E whilst a substantial question mark is posed over the B-2. This might make sense if the new strike aircraft, the A-12, can be procured quickly, but that is far from certain. Meanwhile, the future US air superiority fighter – the ATF – is threatened at just the same time as the Soviet Su-27 demonstrates its capabilities compared to current US fighters. The F-117 Stealth fighter, meanwhile, has ceased production with only 59 of the desired 100 ordered. The list of strange, truncated, procurements and lost opportunities is long.

CHANGING GOALS?

Disjointed procurement and failure to maintain key US technological leads are indicative of a case for change but they do not of themselves dictate change. The more crucial debate and even more critical consequences should be about change in the international and threat environment. The United States finds itself in a situation where it ought to at least consider the cases for retaining present deployments or striking out in a new direction.

STAYING STILL?

Several arguments have been run to support the case that priorities should continue to reflect the post-Vietnam solution with priority placed on the conventional defence of Europe:

1. As Kolodziej argues, Europe is still a key economic and political partner to the United States. The opening of the East European market may actually increase its economic importance to the United States.

2. Conventional forces in Europe may be more important as a deterrent symbol of US commitment as implementation of the INF treaty reduces some of the most visible components of extended deterrence. Popular opposition to nuclear weapons in Europe would seem to make continued, let alone greater, reliance on nuclear forces problematic.

3. If Eastern Europe and the USSR are to go through a period of revolutionary change, with communist power dissolving and with nationalist insurrections in the Soviet Union itself a possibility, a continuing US military presence, of some sort, in Europe will remain important to ensure stability. In stark terms, a period of change in the East, with dramatically unforeseeable consequences, could be more dangerous than past decades of Soviet enforced stability. A continuing US presence in Europe would be a positive deterrent against conflict in the East spilling over into NATO Europe and also a necessary reassurance if Soviet reimposition of central control, either in Europe or within its own borders, shattered European perceptions that they were now living in a peaceful, threat-free, continent. A US presence might also serve to reassure Soviet leaders that change in Western and Eastern Europe would not be allowed to take forms that posed a threat to Soviet security.

4. Arguments for reshaping US forces fail to match the reality that existing commitments already reflect clear, and limited, priorities. The current force structure is the optimal one. Pacific commitments are near an irreducible minimum. Unless the minimal navy advocates win the naval debate, and, even less likely, unless US leaders stop using the Navy as all Presidents have since 1945, the naval case is essentially set by continuing peacetime commitments. Nuclear forces have already been shaped to meet the structures dictated by START and future requirements will be set by that treaty and the unavoidable deterioration of current systems. The Persian Gulf still remains unstable and linked to the crucial interest of access to Saudi oil reserves. Israel still remains threatened. Colonel Gadaffi lives.

CAUTION IN THE FACE OF UNCERTAINTY AND CONTRADICTION?

The case for standing still is reinforced by the very unpredictability of the current international situation. Leaping into the dark is also difficult when it is not yet clear how necessary a jump in a new direction has become. There are no clear criteria for indicating when a defence review is vital. Nor, apart from the experience of retention when the services are called on to do too much with too little, is there any clear indication when a force goes below the minimum level of capability it needs to perform its missions. The US may not only face difficult decisions but the even more difficult task of assessing whether it can afford not to take those choices.

It also faces unique circumstances. The Soviet threat has changed in terms of capabilities, intentions, power structures and personalities. The possibilities that it could change again, in any direction, are not negligible. The Western alliance also faces change with contradictory needs to reassure, negotiate, deter and discuss. Any policy other than a return to complete isolation requires support for the US from some allies and secure land-bases to perform many missions. Technology offers tempting new capabilities. Emerging technology seems, finally, to be about to emerge – if it is allowed to – in the 1990s. Such technology may actually make a conventional NATO defence possible, but does anyone in NATO now, post-Gorbachev's cuts on the Central Front, propose to buy such a defence? Modern weapons also pose problems. They cost more and destroy more, more quickly – this clearly affects what is possible and what can be afforded. Strategy and demographics may mean a shift of focus to the flanks of NATO rather than the centre as the cross-Arctic threat to the US grows and Turkey, Italy, France and Spain emerge among the most populous, important and dynamic members of the alliance. Juggling these competing balls will clearly not be easy and the conclusion that prudence requires caution may well prove tempting.

BACK TO THE PAST?

This position would stress that the United States does not have the option of standing still. The reality is that US defence budgets are likely to fall to levels of expenditure last seen between the end of the Vietnam involvement and the beginnings of a defence buildup in the Carter Administration. In terms of procurement this may see budgets that can buy even less than the Carter 1978–82 budgets. In terms of the level of national effort and, perhaps, interest applied to defence this will mean levels of defence expenditure as a percentage of GNP lower than any seen before Korea, the militarization of the Cold War and the implementation of NSC-68 in 1950.

What this would mean in terms of force levels remains unclear. The services responses to Secretary Cheney's request for proposals for a $180 billion cut, however, are interesting. They do not reflect any attempt to prioritize missions but seem to represent the results of apportioning the $180 billion cut in line with service shares of the budget. As such they represent an example of what equal misery could mean. They are also interesting because the resultant figures are very similar to those reached after the Vietnam War. Proposals to reduce the Army by five divisions would return it to the thirteen-division force level of the mid-1970s – a force level that rose to sixteen with increased emphasis on the Army's European mission and to eighteen when the Reagan Administration added additional light divisions for non-European contingencies. The airforce has suggested that it would find savings by cutting five tactical fighter wings and slowing and reducing procurement elsewhere (including the B-2). This would produce a force level of thirty tactical fighter wings – three below the level reached in FY 1975 and eight below the peak level reached in 1989. The Airforce might well find its reductions by failing to replace the five A-10 close support wings – a mission where replacement aircraft are needed and airforce priorities have been questioned. Finally, the US Navy has indicated that it might be forced to cut to twelve/thirteen carrier battlegroups and/or decommission all of its four battleships. A twelve-carrier, no battleship, Navy would actually have fewer carriers than were sustained in the 1970s.[20] The way would also be open, once this post-Vietnam posture was re-established, to move towards the more ambitious 50 per cent cuts proposed by some of the simpler analyses. These might well produce force levels similar to those envisaged by the McGovern campaign in 1972 with, for example, only six carrier groups.

THE CASE FOR REDEFINITION AND RE-EVALUATION

On the other side of the argument there is also a strong case that continuing generalized cuts will increasingly seem out of step with requirement:

1. Whatever Administrations advise, Congress is unlikely to continue to support existing deployments *ad infinitum* as the Soviet threat changes in scope and relative capability and other threats emerge. In 1989 the defence budget debate in Congress was essentially about whether to add or cut 1 per cent of the FY 1990 budget. Congress could continue to accept Administration cuts of this order, but it may seek further reductions, particularly if it becomes convinced that the money is being spent inappropriately. Evidence was growing into 1990 that the US Congress would demand some strategic blueprint from the Administration or, if none was forthcoming, would make its own, major, cuts.[21]

2. Even before the apparent demise of the Warsaw Pact as a military threat, pressures seemed to be growing to rationalize the role of US forces in NATO Europe. There has been some questioning of why US expenditures over the last forty years have produced a situation where SACEUR still declares he can only hold an attack conventionally for seven to fourteen days.[22] Similar questions may be asked again as the Soviet threat reduces as planned and as arms control also reduces NATO's capability to man a continuous forward defence. NATO may have to choose between the alternative postures open to it – from an alliance that exists as a primarily political entity with the alliance nuclear powers providing some residual extended deterrence, through the possibility of building a weak conventional force

in order to gain a short time to negotiate before escalating to the option of building enough conventional capability to stage an effective, protracted, conventional defence. The failure to meet President Carter's limited goal of a one-month conventional defence capability and to maintain the supporting commitment to increase defence spending by 3 per cent a year – let alone the 4 per cent plus required to implement FOFA – suggest that such a major conventional capability is clearly unobtainable. If a lower level of capability is now needed, it may be necessary to both explain and sell any more complex goal, and the levels of forces it requires, in order to continue to secure support.

3. It may also be necessary to rationalize the differences between different services and NATO planning – both to eliminate paradoxes and build fall-back options. US forces, with sixty-day objectives for ammunition stocks recently found themselves committed to fight alongside allies who have not met thirty-day targets. The Secretary of the Airforce in 1987 acknowledged the logic of this, and SACEUR's predictions of NATO's likely endurance, by questioning whether the US Airforce needed to be able to fight beyond fifteen days. If the United States was going to be 'on the channel' by day fifteen and the USAF only planned to fight for fifteen days, it is far from clear why the US Army has continued to try and buy sustainability into months two and three.[23] Conversely, it may be the case that some forces assigned to some missions ought to be able to fight on for longer than at present. What is clear is that Congress is unlikely to continue to fund a situation where some forces can fight on when their partner services can not.

4. US strategy has to be in tune with the desires and efforts of NATO allies. If West European forces reduce and the Soviet threat changes, US force levels in Europe are unlikely to remain static because both the US Congress and European voters will question the mission of those forces in a world where both the external threat and any allied response are lacking.

5. Changes in the Soviet threat themselves seem to call for reciprocal changes. The INF treaty has already brought reductions in US forces. As the House Armed Services Committee has already noted, conventional forces will also have to change. If warning times grow, the role of ready forces may decline and the case for spending more on reserves like the National Guard may grow. It may be less justifiable to continue to keep a ready army to meet a Soviet mobilized threat *and* a mobilizable army to meet the same threat. More spending on reserves and the mobilization base might be necessary if NATO set itself the goal of meeting a Soviet threat with a counter-matching mobilization potential and then sustaining war for as long as the Soviets, but this would prove difficult given the high cost of any long-war capability.

6. Arms control is already reducing US options. The President's proposals of 1989 and 1990 to reduce US force levels in Europe to 275,000, and then 225,000, already make further reductions in the US Army inevitable. The question as to whether European NATO or US forces should be cut seems to be being resolved as part of the CFE process. Congressional hopes of a peace dividend for the United States may preclude any possibility of

bringing units back to the United States rather than disbanding them. US forces could also face particular problems. Although there has been some progress on the issue, prepositioned equipment could be difficult to retain, let alone increase, under any arms control regime that counts each tank. The sum of the cuts may also exceed their total as particular capabilities wither away faster than others because of arms control agreements. Cuts in airpower, for example, seem likely to be made in close-air-support forces rather than long-range strike fighter units. As close-air support needs cooperative training in peacetime, even minor cuts might threaten large capabilities here.

7. Other missions are challengeable. The Rapid Deployment Force has acquired real capability in the 1980s. It remains, though, unclear how the full potential of the force could be used. Deterrence of the USSR may require less capability, whilst warfighting may require more. Against an Iraqi, Iranian or even terrorist threat, the force may be inadequate given the size of these states' armies and the problems encountered in the Lebanon in dealing with an omnipresent fanatical threat. Reports in 1990 of changes in US strategy to a war involving Iran suggest that the Administration itself has re-examined needs in this area.[24] Although Grenada and Panama show a real need for some light intervention forces, US public or Congressional opinion, or even the executive branch itself, may still not be ready for major, bloody, commitments of US ground forces. Divisions that can respond to particular demands (like the 82nd Airborne and at least some of the light divisions) seem to have a secure role, but the role of other units may be questioned. Arguments about the utility of having a RDF as well as a US Marine Corp also seem to be returning to the fore.[25]

8. At present the United States (and with it NATO) have some degree of superiority at sea and in the air which is counterbalanced by Soviet landpower and a *de facto* balance of nuclear forces. Both of these advantages are challenged by new Soviet equipment ranging from quiet attack submarines and nuclear carriers to the SU-27 and MiG-29. Maritime superiority requires a continuing emphasis on ASW, carrier-based air-power, AAW and strike capability. Superiority in the air, against an increasing Soviet fighter, SAM and offensive threat will increasingly rely on 'stealth' (creating a need to defend the B-2, ATF and ATA from cuts), together with increased stand-off strike capability and superior air-to-air missiles and ECM. These cannot be procured if resources for budgets fall much below present levels. There is a real question whether scarce resources are best spent on staying ahead where one is ahead or trying to improve the position where one is weak. The fact that the United States itself provides the most significant elements of NATO's air and sea capability, whilst the US Army is more dependent on allied success (or the lack of it) might argue here that, as shoring up the weak area is impossible, priority ought to go to maintaining superiority where it does exist.

9. Reductions in US Army heavy forces appear logical with arms control reducing the Soviet Central Front threat and the possibility of a reunified

Germany, a disintegrating Warsaw Pact and a withdrawn Soviet Army. Reductions in the US Navy, though, seem illogical when the Soviet Navy is building up its capital ship forces to US numbers and when the Soviet submarine fleet is increasing in capability at the same time as the scrapping of obsolete units reduces overall numbers. With increasing capability in the Soviet Navy matched by improvements in many of the larger regional navies and airforces, cutting the US Navy would seem a strange option. Even more strange if the US Navy were cut to preserve heavy Army units with no home in Europe and no means of getting into combat from the United States, unless the US Navy still existed in roughly its present minimal strength to secure its passage and arrival.

THE SHAPE OF FUTURE INTERESTS?

Any debate about US priorities ought also to be set in the context of some appraisal of changing US interests. Here a number of factors argue against any simple concentration of effort:

1. The growth in importance of the Pacific as a trading and economic partner may call for some shift of US defence resources. Even if Pacific forces are cut by the proposed 10 per cent, they should perhaps be treated relatively well compared to other areas. There may even now be a need to defend certain key suppliers as well as a need to preserve market stability.

2. Calls to remove US forces in Korea seem incompatible with suggestions of a more isolated, and potentially more desperate, North Korean regime falling further and further behind the South. The democratization of South Korea seems to have removed any real objection to the continuing presence, if invited, of US forces at precisely the same time as the possibility of attack is logically stronger and declining Soviet involvement and interest in the Third World may make North Korea less responsive to Moscow. Reductions in US Army forces in South Korea – 5,000 men being announced – may be logical given increases in South Korean Army capabilities[26] but there is a case that total withdrawal could invite a repeat of 1950 or leave US ability to control any crisis or war on the peninsula fatally weakened.

3. US protection for Japan seems likely to continue as a priority as the Soviet Pacific Fleet and Airforce increase their capability. Soviet–Japanese relations may improve, but the Soviet Union may feel that it needs to maintain a military threat against an economic superpower that is nearer to its territory than Germany, important as a possible economic partner to China and a state that has a continuing territorial dispute with the USSR.

4. The growth of Soviet SSN/SLCM and bomber forces, together with US persistence with new manned bombers and interest in under-ice anti-SSBN operations and air defence of the continental US all suggest that greater priority will be given to defences around, and offensive options over the Arctic. This is likely to require considerable US investment. It may also increase the importance of US security relationships with Japan, Korea, Denmark,

Iceland, Norway, the United Kingdom, the Netherlands and Canada.

Other priorities are also likely to continue, and some even grow, in importance the further one looks ahead. As US spokesmen have acknowledged for several years, threats to US interests are more likely to emerge outside the Soviet–US confrontation and outside Europe. Indeed, it is possible, even probable, that many of the large-scale changes likely in the international system over the next ten to thirty years may call for some military response from the United States. Global population increases, resurgent Islam, the growth of nationalist and tribal factions, international crime, terrorism and the growth of regional powers already threaten US trading interests, individuals and access to crucial materials. Local tensions may grow as regional powers vie for position. Energy is likely to grow increasingly scarce – making areas like the Gulf even more important to the United States. Nuclear and conventional weapons proliferation seems to increase the potential threat here. With question marks hanging over the future of states as large as India and China and several regional powers building major naval capabilities, the range of contingencies that might call for US forces to be deployed is clearly growing. It is far from clear that the defence policy of 1958, or 1968, or 1978 will continue to meet the requirements of 1998 or 2028.

A SHIFT TO AIR AND SEA?

If the nature of the threat to US interests has declined, and with it both the case for, and the possibility of, the US providing forces in Europe on their current scale, a case can be made that the time has come to move the United States to a new defence posture that does meet likely threats. Such a policy does seem now to be on offer. In some ways it mirrors the strategy suggested by Walter Lippman in 1950 with his call for the United States to 'recognise the limitations and to exploit the advantages of our island character . . . our superiority in technology . . . the oceans of sea and air around us which offer us the means of flexible defense and a highly mobile defense'.[27] At present, it seems to have some support from airforce and naval quarters. It is also consistent with the ideas of the *Discriminate Deterrence* strategy proposed in 1988 and it is in line with Senator Nunn's suggestions that the United States should emphasize sea and air roles within the alliance and 'Naval, Marine, light Army, [and] Special Forces [for] Third World contingencies, Middle East type contingencies, even contingencies relating to Korea'. Even Representative Aspin, Chairman of the House Appropriations Defense Subcommittee, is reported to have recently suggested that the time may have come to emphasize aircraft carriers as opposed to submarines because the aircraft carrier is the answer to tomorrow's force projection needs, whereas the utility of the submarine lies, almost solely, against the Soviet threat.[28] The US Navy may not accept the logic of this for their submarine force, but it is interesting that Representative Aspin now seems to find some case for maritime forces in a power projection role.

Any such strategy – emphasizing peacetime power projection, flexibility and maritime and air power – would probably require the continuance of existing naval options, possibly some increase in SAC bomber capability and increased efforts to develop stand-off conventional bombs and missiles. This would allow the United States to maintain its present areas of maximum advantage. It would meet the US demand to improve continental air defences. It would allow SAC and the US Navy to pose a number of conventional deterrent threats to the Soviet Union – when, and if, necessary. It would threaten the USSR with a unwinnable, long war if any reshaped Soviet Union threatened aggression. Aircraft could be flown to Europe quickly if needed to back up forward deployed wings. Carrier-based aircraft would become more important as forward bases became fewer in number, and would provide the only means to assist more distant, but increasingly significant, allies like Turkey.

Against Third World threats, the United States could, if necessary, use both the US Navy and whatever overseas bases were available to react. SAC bombers and carrier-based aircraft, supported by forward-deployed Airforce tactical units would be a credible response against most limited threats – with a role, for example, for the B-1, B-2, F-117 and ATA covertly delivering attacks on terrorist bases without the military and political risks seen in the 1986 Libya operation. The US Marine Corps, airborne and special forces could be deployed as needed to deal with those situations requiring ground forces to take territory. At sea, the Maritime Strategy would continue to provide the full range of options from a single-ship presence to multi-carrier group offensive operations. An important argument against cutting the US Navy would be that this is precisely what the US Navy has been doing in peacetime since the Second World War. Present force levels have been proven to be the minimal needed to do this job – indeed in terms of numbers of carriers deployed forward, the peacetime mission may be more of a constraint than the requirement to assemble enough carriers in certain areas for wartime missions against the USSR. Carrier force levels have also been set by requirements other than the need to fight a global war against the Soviet Union – in a very real sense, a decline in the Soviet threat does not logically have much impact on the need for forces that have spent most of their time, and continually demonstrated their utility, dealing with other peacetime threats to US interests. The true flexibility of the carrier battlegroup is that it is a weapon that can be used to look after smaller threats whilst preparing for the ultimate enemy. Unlike the army unit deployed in one place for one mission, its utility does not decline if the ultimate enemy begins to look less likely as a threat.

Such a strategy has both a consistent logic and notable advantages. It uses technology to the maximum – keeping casualties (and hostages) to a minimum by keeping men out of contact with the enemy. It exploits US technological advantages – although reliance on sophisticated, technology will have the side-effect of making much US equipment unexportable on grounds of cost, secrecy and preserving the margin between US forces and potential opponents. It emphasizes mobility, in response to the problem that threats may emerge worldwide. It offers an answer to local resistance to the deployment of some weapons by allowing them to be based always on US territory – either in the United States or at sea. In short, emphasis on air and sea power seems likely to provide a logically coherent defence policy whilst meeting US technological, political and foreign policy imperatives.

This does not mean that any move to such a strategy is inevitable. Talk of a continuing need for maritime supremacy in the FY 1991 *DOD Annual Report* and the balance of cuts suggested it may be being accepted by the Bush Administration, but it remains to be seen if this priority emerges in subsequent budgets. Nor should we, necessarily, expect dramatic change. A maritime–air strategy might not deter some Soviet leaders – nuclear weapons, as now, would still be needed for that mission. Nor should it be seen as a panacea. It might, also, fail to offer any response to some Third World crises – situations like the Lebanon hostage problem would still find no easy solution. No strategy can meet all problems. Indeed, it may be that the strategy will only be acceptable if Congress is convinced that the capability will only be used wisely – the caution of US Presidents post-Vietnam may be an important factor in convincing some Congressmen that such capabilities are needed and will not be used irresponsibly.

Indeed, it seems unlikely that any strategic shift will become definite until the second half of the decade. By then, cuts in European forces may be finalized, decisions will be taken on the next round of carrier procurement and new technology will either have been deployed, will be nearing operational status or will have been cancelled. Other reasoning may preclude any early declaration that policy has changed – not least the fact that this is not a strategy that US leaders could move to overnight without worrying allies. It is also one that will only really become viable if, and when, smart munitions and conventional cruise missiles are deployed in adequate numbers to pose a real threat of effective conventional strategic bombing. If any US President is ever tempted to adopt the logic, change is likely to be slow – unless one capability is removed before another is born to replace it. Perhaps the ultimate hurdle to jump will be that any, even one-third, cuts in US ground forces (which enjoy a rather small procurement budget) may not solve the budgetary crisis – let alone fund any new initiatives. Changes might produce a more useful, sensible, allocation of resources, but it might prove to be the case that what the United States really needs is a review that sets budgets in relation to minimal demands for military forces rather than an arbitary figure derived from last year's funding and current political debate. A system that leaves US forces funded at 1983 levels to meet the unforeseen threats of 1990, 1995 or 2027 is bound, sooner or later, to produce its own unforeseen consequences for US servicemen and future Presidents.

NOTES AND REFERENCES

1. Phil Williams, 'Carter's defense policy', ch. 5 in M. Glenn Abernathy et al. (eds), *The Carter Years – The President and Policy-Making* (London: Frances Pinter, 1984); D. J. Pay, *The Carrier Debate 1976–1980*, PhD Dissertation, University College of Wales, Aberystwyth 1985.
2. *Senate Armed Services Committee Hearings FY 1983*, pt 2, p. 1155.

3. *DoD Annual Report FY 1990* (Washington: USGPO, 1989), p. 221.
4. G. J. Church, 'How much is too much', *Time*, 12 February 1990, pp. 20–5; P. Mann, 'Brookings study suggests halving U.S. defense budget in 10 years', *Aviation Week and Space Technology*, 27 November 1989, pp. 19–20. S. M. Watt, 'The case for finite containment: analysing US grand strategy', *International Security*, summer 1989, pp. 5–49; cf. J. A. Pechman (ed.), *Setting National Priorities: the 1979 budget* (Washington: Brookings, 1978); ibid. 1980, 1979.
5. P. Finnegan, 'CBO report: cancel B 2, C 17, NASP programs', *Defense News*, 26 February 1990, p. 53.
6. E.g. C. S. Grey, *The Geopolitics Of Superpower*, (University of Kentucky Press, 1988); E. N. Luttwak, *Strategy: the logic of war and peace* (Cambridge, Mass.: Belknap, 1987); F. J. West, 'Maritime strategy and NATO deterrence', *Naval War College Review*, September–October 1985; E.K. Hamilton (ed.), *America's Global Interests – A New Agenda*, (New York: WW Norton, 1989); M. Mandelbaum (ed.), *America's Defense* (New York: Holmes and Meier, 1989); E. N. Luttwak, 'Ready or not: cut Pentagon "readiness" spending now', *The Washington Post*, 19 February 1989; J. Lehman, 'Pentagon: cut the fat, build the muscle', *The Washington Post*, 22 January 1989; J. R. Schlesinger, 'Cut US forces in Europe – now', *The Washington Post*, 4 February 1990; *DoD Annual Report FY 1990*, pp. 34–7.
7. *Discriminate Deterrence, Report Of the President's Commission on Integrated Long-Term Strategy* (Washington: USGPO, 1988).
8. P. Finnegan, 'Funding for black programs drops', *Defense News*, 5 February 1990, p. 41.
9. P. Towell, 'The Pentagon vs Congress', *Airforce Magazine*, February 1990, pp. 40–5; C.A. Nash, 'Spending, mending, defending and pretending', ibid., pp. 34–9; C.W. Corddry, 'The chairmen size it up', ibid., pp. 28–33; M. Moore and P.E. Tyler, 'Hill hearings may suggest radically different path on defense', *The Washington Post*, 23 January 1990.
10. T. Kenworthy and M. Moore, 'Democrats gird to lower boom on military budget', *The Washington Post*, 14 January 1990.
11. M. Duffy, 'Mr consensus', *Time*, 21 August 1989, pp. 24–30.
12. J. W. Canan, 'Scowcroft urges caution', *Airforce Magazine*, March 1990, pp. 96–9; 'USMC, army clash on LIC', *Jane's Defence Weekly*, 24 March 1990.
13. J. D. Morrocco, 'Defense dept. grapples with massive spending cuts', *Aviation Week and Space Technology*, 27 November 1989, pp. 16–18.
14. *DoD Annual Report FY 1991* (Washington: USGPO, 1990); R. Lopez, J. Batman, B. Starr, 'Bush – the builddown years', *Jane's Defence Weekly*, 3 February 1990, pp. 18–19; M. E. Morrow and R. R. Ropelewski, 'Peace dividend elusive in FY91 budget', *Armed Forces Journal International*, March 1990, pp. 9–16.
15. M. Moore and P. E. Tyler, 'Services may face major changes in size, mission; Cheney is presented with 3 options for deploying forces In 21st century', *The Washington Post*, 17 December 1989.
16. J. D. Morrocco, 'Pentagon begins drawdown but offers no new strategy', *Aviation Week and Space Technology (AWST)*, 5 February 1990, pp. 26–7;

see also P. Finnegan, 'Specter of new defense cuts is deceptive', *Defense News*, 27 November 1989, pp. 1, 8.

17.   G. C. Wilson and P. E. Tyler, 'Pentagon struggle far from over; services face budget cuts of up to 135 billion dollars, documents show', *The Washington Post*, 26 January 1990.

18.   FY 1989 $, *AWST*, 24 July 1989, p. 25.

19.   *Defense News*, 12 February 1990, pp. 47–55.

20.   *Department of Defense Annual Report FY 1975*, p. 236; ibid., FY 1982, p. A3; ibid., 1990, p. 232.

21.   Towell, 'The Pentagon vs Congress', Nash, 'Spending, mending, defending and pretending'; Corddry, 'The chairmen size it up'.

22.   B. Schemmer, 'Must we go nuke? Let's mop up first', *Armed Forces Journal International*, January 1989, p. 5.

23.   *Senate Armed Services Committee Hearing FY 1989*, pt 1, p. 581.

24.   B. Amouyal, 'Defense plan gives broad latitude', *Defense News*, 12 February 1990, pp. 1, 60; P. Tyler, 'US finds Persian Gulf threat ebbs; a strategic shift over Iran's oil', *The Washington Post*, 7 February 1990.

25.   E. H. Simmons, 'Go marines beat army', *The Washington Post*, 8 October 1989.

26.   *Defense News*, 15 January 1990, p. 22.

27.   Cited H. Brandon, *Special Relationship*, (London: Macmillan, 1988) p. 92.

28.   Corddry, 'The chairmen size it up'; *Defense News*, 22 January 1990, p. 2.

Part II

Maritime Strategy of the Superpowers

8 Developments in Soviet naval strategy

Robert Weinland

This chapter has six topics in all. It will begin with some general observations about the Soviet military press and how we tend to read and misread it in the West. The second topic, included in part to illustrate a main point arising from the first, concerns a mission that the Soviet Navy appears no longer to have. It has, quite simply, disappeared from their discourse. For that reason alone it seems worth drawing attention to it.

The third, fourth and fifth topics are the three missions that appear to have been elevated to form the Soviet Navy's current *raison d'être*. A good deal has changed during the last couple of years – old priorities have fallen by the wayside – new priorities have been substituted in their stead – old myths have been replaced by new myths and possibly some new realities as well. The last topic is either one of those myths or one of those realities – I am not really sure which, but it does seem worthy of attention.

THE SOVIET MILITARY PRESS

Most of what I say is drawn from a single source – a new Soviet book entitled *The Navy: its role, prospects for the development and employment*. This book is authored by a retired Rear Admiral in N. P. V'yunenko, one of Admiral Gorshkov's former ghost writers, by Captain First Rank B. N. Makeyev, a serving officer who writes frequently on naval planning and by a retired Captain First Rank V. D. Skugarev, a noted weaponeer. It is introduced by the former Commander-in-Chief of the Soviet Navy Admiral Gorshkov himself – his contribution being, in all likelihood, one of the last things he wrote before his death in December 1987. The book was sent to press in October 1987, appeared in 1988, and remains the subject of lively discourse both there and here in the West.

In February 1989 the US Naval Institute *Proceedings* contained an interview with the Commander-in-Chief of the Soviet Navy Fleet Admiral Chernavin. One of the questions posed to him there concerned this very book and what it says about new mission priorities. His answer, in essence, was that the book reflects the authors' opinions, but those are the main strategic tasks of tomorrow and are the general principles of the creation and development of simply navies. He could have just made the first of those points, that the book reflected individual opinions – but he did not.

Not surprisingly, some people have questioned the authoritative nature of this book – some always do. That question arose very definitely in the early 1970s when Admiral Gorshkov began a series of articles on 'Navies in war and peace'. The question was asked again in the late 1970s when he published the articles in a revised and expanded form as *The Seapower of the State*, assisted by Rear Admiral V'yunenko. Was he advocating, or announcing, an enhanced role for the Soviet Navy at the time? Analysts of renown, grown men of mature vision came close to fisticuffs over that question. Subsequently, of course, it became clear that what Admiral Gorshkov had said about the Navy's prime task being to pose to its enemies the same threat that they posed to the Soviet Union, and to use the same means of doing so SLBMs deserved their full attention. It took more than five years and the failure of the Soviets to deploy the Delta/SS-N-8 combination, as some of us thought they should, for Admiral Gorshkov's message to receive the attention it deserved, however. I am not sure we can afford to wait that long this time. This time the implications of what is being said are even more urgent.

The point is that the Soviet military press is very significant and we need to be attentive in what we read out of it and regrettably sometimes into it. They are very careful about what they say and how they say it. If we were equally careful about what we read and how, we could understand much of what they intend their words to convey. We will always be at a disadvantage, however, because we are reading after the fact and what we are reading, in the open literature at least, is never the entire story. Frequently, the most important part of whatever argument they are making is the part that is left out. That is hard to remember when you are 150 pages into a 200-page essay still searching for the point on which the whole argument hinges and contemplating going back to page 1 and re-reading it through again more intensively. You may not have missed it, it simply may have never been admitted. Let me illustrate this point.

When Admiral Gorshkov began talking about allocating general purpose forces to the defence of sea-based strategic offensive forces his arguments regarding the advocacy of the use of ASW ships in that role were given less than full credence in the West. Everyone saw the apparent hole in Gorshkov's argument. Soviet ASW ships lacked the sensors required to detect undersea targets and everyone completed Admiral Gorshkov's argument with his/her own conclusions.

Neither then, nor subsequently, did any of the numerous Soviet discussions over the echelon defence in depth of their sea-based offensive forces point out that, thanks to the Walker and Whitworth and Company, their ability to read our operational and message traffic gave them the functional equivalent of a highly effective, broad area, ASW protection system which made that defence a viable proposition. For obvious reasons, this fact was left out of the argument. That they did not talk about such a capability did not make it any less real, however. The issue is raised here because some of the arguments advanced by V'yunenko et al. are also far from complete, but the urge to fill them in from our own understanding of the situation should be resisted.

LOSS OF THE INTERNATIONAL MISSION

Now, having raised the general issue of dogs that don't bark I am going to point directly at one good example.

In *The Navy* the peacetime political mission has disappeared in its entirety from the list of Soviet naval roles. V'yunenko et al. present every detail of the rationale that has been advanced for this role over the last two decades, describing, in excruciating detail, actions of US and other imperialist naval forces intended first to start local conflicts in the Third World and then to intervene in order to determine their course and ensure that their outcomes are unfavourable to newly independent states, national liberation movements and other progressive forces. And they state, as clearly as Admiral Stalbo ever did, that local wars are dangerous to peace since they can escalate into world-wide nuclear conflict. But, at no point in their disquisition on the subject do V'yunenko et al. indicate that the Soviet Navy retains its mission of the defending forces of peace and progress. They used to speak, in very straightforward terms, about actively deterring imperialist interference in progression – meaning by the seen and unseen presence of Soviet naval forces. And at no point in this interview in the USNI Proceedings does Admiral Chernavin correct that omission. Quite to the contrary, he makes it clear that the Third World now has to defend itself, and that the Soviet Navy's responsibility is to the Soviet Union itself.

Some might not find that particular admission significant, but I do. While that mission never provided a rationale for sizing or shaping the Soviet Navy, it unquestionably determined the scope and character of that navy's force deployments and operations from 1964 (when it first came out into the Mediterranean to put a damper on that year's Cyprus crisis) until, who knows when, it ceased to be a motivating factor in their operations. Maybe 1979, maybe 1983, maybe later. Admiral Chernavin talks at length about forward deployments, and like his predecessor keys their location and magnitude directly to the presence in those areas of US and other imperialist naval forces. But, it is clear from what he says that the rationale for maintaining Soviet counter-deployments is now the defence of the Soviet Union itself against the long-range strike capabilities of those Western forces – not protecting local forces of peace and progress. The internationalist mission in the Soviet Navy has disappeared.

Eliminating that mission may well represent an exercise in cost-cutting, and, hence, a bow in the direction of *perestroika*. But if it is such an exercise, the costs they are cutting are political not economic, or at least the economic costs are not significant. One, crucial, element in their attempt to restructure the international security situation is the effort to reduce the level of threat the West perceives them to pose, thereby permitting the West to relax its defensive efforts, and the Soviets, in turn, to relax their defensive efforts, thus, in the end, bringing them equal security at lower cost. Turning down the volume on the internationalist content of their peacetime naval operations, or perhaps even eviscerating it, is a clear cut step in that direction.

WARTIME MISSIONS: SOME NEW EMPHASES

Turning up the volume on the defensive content of their doctrine and strategy is another step in that same direction. That is what is happening in the organization of their wartime mission structure.

Here, however, is where the wolf begins to peek out from underneath the sheep's clothing. That increase in defensive content is not good 'passive' defence but bad 'active' defence – there is nothing benign about active defence and, unlike the elimination of the peacetime political mission which may bring some modest reduction in their cost of doing business at sea, the adoption of active defence at sea, in particular the adoption of active strategic defence at sea, is going to cost them – and us – a pretty penny. If their apparent move in that direction turns out to be real, it involves the acquisition of real capabilities, and effective systems in significant numbers. The essential free ride enjoyed, until now, by Western sea-based strategic offensive forces may be over. The Soviets have spent the last twenty years buying general purpose forces to give their sea-based strategic offensive forces combat stability. We have not thought that necessary. If what they are saying now has substance, we may have to rethink that proposition.

That brings us to the new missions, or more accurately, to the new mission priorities. None of the three is really a brand new task. The three are, in apparent order of priority: repelling an enemy's aero-space attack, suppression of its military economic potential and destruction of groupings of his armed forces. The first of those is more or less what we used to refer to as damage limitation. The second resembles counter-value strike but it includes anti-SLOC action as well. The third is essentially general purpose force action in pursuit of the immediate goals of the war – assistance to ground forces being the defensible part of it. All three are wartime missions, although the first two have important peacetime components.

I said they were not really new, the first in essence being the defence of the homeland which was the Navy's primary responsibility from the end of the Second World War until roughly 1963 when it was displaced by the strategic deterrent task, which, in turn, is now collapsed into the second mission. The anti-SLOC part of the second mission is new, but it is not exclusively a navy mission. The third is what the Marshals have been calling for all along. Each mission will be discussed in turn, but, here, we will give disproportionate attention to the first.

Repelling aero-space attack represents the greatest departure from the recent past, it appears to pose the greatest challenges for the future, and in my view, at least, it is the most enigmatic of the three. For the Soviet Navy to take this on, and be successful, three separate tasks, each of formidable proportions, need to be performed. These are strategic ASW, suppression of submarine and surface cruise missile launch platforms and anti-carrier warfare, and success in the mission calls for them to accomplish all three, as the situation dictates, simultaneously if necessary. That would be a very tall order. Here, as in the other two mission areas, the navy would be operating in concert with other components of the Soviet armed forces, but, at sea, in its traditional area of responsibility it would be playing the leading role.

And, as that statement regarding combined arms action implies, it may be playing the leading role there – even if under central direction.

There is no hint here, as was the case a decade ago, that the Soviet Navy now aspires to an independent existence or to an independent role in combat. Soviet naval writings used to address the requirement for establishing command of the sea, at least in specified areas for specified periods, before actions and pursuit of other more immediate wartime objectives could be undertaken. It was often depicted as a critical point of success in those other areas. They, V'yunenko et al. included, still talk about establishing and maintaining command of the sea, but, now, it is obtainable at any time, including during the course of the conflict. It facilitates a success in the immediate task but is not a precursor or a prerequisite, and it is discussed in conjunction with the mission of supporting the ground forces. Not only has the Navy's role changed, the Navy has been put in its place. Unfortunately for us, that place may prove more important than the one it o ccupied before.

V'yunenko et al. clearly recognized that the combat actions they were discussing could well be initiated in a conventional context, or one in which nuclear weapons have seen only very limited use, and they suggest that some of those actions would retain their currency in such environments. But, the primary focus in *The Navy* on the world-wide nuclear scenario, something which they on several occasions note, constitutes a combat situation with no precedent for which no potential participant can turn for guidance.

Let us sketch out the first, and what is clearly the most important, of those new mission priorities involved in repelling an enemy aero-space attack. The scenario is surprise attack involving the enemy's entire nuclear arsenal, the primary means involved being SLBMs and ICBMs, and possibly IRBMs. The objective of the repelling operation is to disrupt or weaken as far as possible the strength of the enemy's attack by its combined arms operation. The naval component takes the form of large-scale actions, carried out in all spheres of naval warfare: sub-surface, surface, air and against the enemy's territory. The targets of those actions would be nuclear submarines with SLBMs and long-range cruise missiles (described as the primary enemy target) and surface combatants with nuclear capable aircraft and cruise missiles.

In the context of those actions is peacetime surveillance, localization and tracking by deployed countering forces in preparation for pre-emptive attack at the first available opportunity. Nothing could be more straight-forward, as they describe it, and nothing at this juncture is harder to swallow. It is hard to believe that they believe they have the wherewithal even to attempt, let alone accomplish, this task. They talk at length about the problems that must be overcome in the process; detecting and classifying nuclear powered missile armed submarines, especially given their diminishing signatures and expanding operational areas; the problem with establishing and maintaining trail on them by prosecution forces; handing-off trail from one prosecution unit to another; surging additional prosecution forces as conflict becomes imminent; and achieving a *coordinated* pre-emptive attack on those submarines at the appropriate moment. Each of those problems receives its dues as a problem and the argument marches on. At no point, however, is the overall level of difficulty declared too tough, and at no point in there is a mission killer identified.

We should resist the temptation to supply our own mission killer to fill the void with our own conclusions. This has proved a poor approach to understanding what they are saying in the past, and would not probably be any better now. They have some reason for advancing this argument, and some basis for believing it to be as credible as the remainder of their discussion. It just is not clear at this point what those reasons and bases are. Maybe, as indicated earlier, the passage of time, and a closer look at how they end up using whatever forces turn out to be associated with the adoption of this new task, will clarify those enigmas.

Let us turn to the second of the new missions, namely suppressing the enemy military economic potential. This is the Navy's part of a larger national level combined arms task and has three components. The first is maintaining in place, throughout peacetime and up to the appropriate point of wartime the capability to strike industrial, energy and administrative targets, political centres, naval bases and ports, command, control communications and intelligence installations and other important strategic installations. These strikes would be nuclear, delivered by ballistic and cruise missiles and launched, primarily, from nuclear powered submarines. This was the principal mission of Admiral Gorshkov's navy and everything necessary, including the general purpose forces required to guarantee favourable conditions for its execution, was allocated to him. Those general purpose force allocations continued to be mentioned by V'yunenko et al. but no quantifiers were attached, perhaps because some of the same general purpose forces now had an important role to play in the second component of this task, which is anti-SLOC operations.

The anti-SLOC task has two parts, one is the disruption of the flow of resources to military industrial complexes, the second is the disruption to the flow of resources from those complexes to forces in the field. Which part receives attention, and when, in the conflict would depend on the situation. V'yunenko et al. point out that the success of military action in land TVDs, even to the extent of the ability of states to keep fighting at all, can depend on the outcome of the SLOC battle, especially in prolonged conventional war. Submarines, aviation (including but not necessarily limited to naval aviation) and missile troops will all play a role – as will mines and as can nuclear weapons – the use, or threatened use, of which will disrupt convoy operations significantly, thereby increasing SLOC vulnerability to other, primarily conventional, forces and means.

The third component, the military economic suppression mission, involves interdiction of seabed oil and other mineral extraction operations and is not, in itself, exceptional.

The third complex of naval missions is, in essence, that traditional Soviet Navy mission of rendering assistance to ground forces. It involves combining ground, air and naval forces in continental oceans and sea theatres with the objective of destroying personnel and military equipment and capturing enemy territory, straits, zones and island areas. The primary focus is merely placed on supporting existing ground forces in coastal sectors but that can require operations over vast spacial areas and operations of a high command intensity, especially when it involves forcing enemy carriers out of strike range, and those operations can require large numbers of varied types of naval forces and means.

There are three principle tasks that are identified under this mission – one is covering ground forces and, in essence, protecting them against strikes from the sea and preventing seaborne assaults of the flanks and rear. The second is combat support of ground forces. In essence, this involves strikes against enemy ground and support forces, landing one's own assault forces, blockading enemy groupings and forces from the sea and disrupting enemy tactical sea lines of communication in the immediate combat area. The third portion of that task is combat service support, in effect providing the logistic support and movement services to friendly forces. V'yunenko et al. noted that aircraft are the most effective forces for accomplishing the second of those tasks concerned with providing combat support, but they do not press the issue.

The issues they do press, on the other hand, are the requirement for a large number of service combatants to perform those three functions. The utility of exploiting the potential of naval forces to help ground force advance speedily, particularly in crossing large water areas, and the navy's other more traditional anti-enemy navy actions can make a fundamental contribution to the fulfilment of this particular mission.

This brings me to my last point. At the beginning of this chapter I admitted I did not know whether this topic dealt with myth or reality and this is exactly true. V'yunenko et al. discuss strategic ASW and its importance and they make the following point. Anti-submarine warfare was waged in past world wars, but, under contemporary conditions, it includes a wider range of problems, going far beyond the bounds of traditional anti-submarine defensive combatants, auxiliaries and naval bases. The fulsome manner in which the book addresses the prospects of this mission indicate the possibility of a substantial growth in its importance. In the immediately foreseeable future the mission of combating submarines may be elevated to the level of a national mission and then one will be able to speak of national anti-submarine defence – 'PLO Strany' – just as today we speak of national air defence, PVO Strany. They do not say it is in place now, but they do imply that it is on its way. That shows a seriousness of purpose, and a level of commitment to the enterprise, that can only be characterized as disturbing. This is all they say directly about a 'PLO Strany' but, indirectly, the passages that follow provide some of the rationale for its establishment. First, the complexity of the detection problem and consequent necessity for deploying complex, costly and, therefore, national level surveillance systems, mostly located in overhead platforms. Second, the large number of prosecution forces that will be required, the vast scope of their areas of operation and the consequent difficulty of coordinating their actions. And third, the hostile character of the environment in which those prosecution forces will be operating, which will require actions by other forces to give the prosecutors combat stability. None of these, of course, are unrealistic concerns. Whether a 'PLO Strany' is the appropriate vehicle for meeting them is a separate issue, but for them to decide, not us.

Prospects for Soviet naval strategy in the Gorbachev era

Bryan Ranft

Nowhere have there been more significant changes in the last four years than in the Soviet Union. The advent to power of Mikhail Gorbachev has been followed by a re-examination and the beginning of a restructuring of every element of Soviet policy, internal and external. Declarations on defence policy have been frequent and radical in tone, emphasizing two main objectives; the reduction of the burden imposed by military expenditure on economic, industrial and technological resources, and a replacement of confrontation between the socialist and capitalist world by negotiation, leading to cooperation on global problems. In this context Soviet defence policy will be entirely defensive in character and the size and shape of the armed forces will be based on sufficiency, with no aspirations towards superiority. It is against this background that the future nature of Soviet naval strategy and forces must be considered.

There are further general questions about Gorbachev's policies to be taken into consideration; not the inane one, 'is he sincere?' but the more practical ones on what are his ultimate aims and his chances of achieving them and within what timescale. The answer to the first is clear. He wishes to achieve an economically successful and politically more cohesive Russia, secure in its frontiers and able to play the part in world affairs which its superpower status merits. The likelihood of success and the time needed to achieve it can only be expressed in terms of probability and generality. His skills in operating the Soviet political machine have already established his personal authority and seriously weakened the power of the Party conservatives to obstruct his internal reforms. But as yet there has been no visible improvement in ordinary living standards and the degree of internal unrest arising from political dissent and even more from militant nationalism is producing strains which could well result in doubts, even in his own mind, about the pace and extent of possible reform.[1]

Internationally, the withdrawal from Afghanistan and Gorbachev's frequent declarations on arms reductions and the need to cooperate on environmental global problems, have met with strongly favourable responses in Western public opinion, while the personnel changes he has made in the Soviet defences establishment suggest that a newer generation of senior officers are willing to accept his military reforms. On the other hand, increasing prospects of instability in Eastern Europe, and consequent security implications, the certainty of continuing conflict in the Middle East and the eternal ambiguities of the international behaviour of China and Japan, make up a world scene in which no Russian leader, including Gorbachev would wish to leave his country militarily weak.

In such a time of change and uncertainty an attempt to identify likely future developments in Soviet maritime (a more useful term than naval) strategy can best begin by looking at underlying general factors rather than detailed analysis of public utterances by naval leaders, specialized publications, perceived changes in emphasis in staff college teaching, the *raison d'être* and authority of all of which it is impossible to establish. Substantial changes in construction programmes would be a different matter, but none are publically apparent at the time of writing. Reconsideration of blinding glimpses of the obvious can sometimes be better guides to the future than sophisticated analysis, however logical and well informed.

Major decisions on maritime affairs will continue to be made by the political leadership, certainly not by naval staff. If they follow the doctrine of sufficiency political leaders will look for the minimum level of power needed to defend the state's maritime interests in the light of their perception of the developing international situation and of Russia's industrial and economic well being. Such decisions on maritime matters will only be a part of their overall conclusions on the whole level of national defence and will be made after consideration, though not necessarily acceptance, of the advice of the General Staff, and perhaps, in a new development, that of independent civilian experts. For the outcome to be favourable to the Soviet Navy, its leaders will need to be able to convince the predominantly land-oriented General Staff, and through them the politicians, that their Service can make an essential contribution to the country's declared defensive strategy, which in terms of efficiency and cost effectiveness cannot be provided in any other way. In other words, can the admirals, during a period of financial and resource restraints on defence, consolidate Gorbachev's achievement of a navy second only to that of the United States in capabilities and reach? If they are to succeed they will have to dissociate themselves from what could be interpreted as their old leader's unacceptable claims to independent naval doctrine and operations and his now unfashionable stress on the unique potential of naval forces for furtherance of Soviet prestige and interests abroad.

In pursuing such advocacy the Soviet Navy has some forceful arguments to deploy. If the keywords in overall strategy and forces structures are to be defensiveness and sufficiency it could claim that these are what it has always aimed at in its aspirations to be able to defend the homeland and its maritime frontiers from the wide range of threat offered by the maritime predominance of the United States and its allies. With the recent increases in the US Navy's strength under President Reagan the threat from sea-based nuclear missiles, nuclear capable maritime aircraft and the alarming new capabilities of sea-based cruise missiles has grown in significance. The United States' possession of unequalled amphibious forces and strategic mobility is a conventional threat which cannot be ignored in any defensive strategy. By the proclamation of its Maritime Strategy the United States has made clear the offensive doctrine which governs the design and proposed employment of all its maritime forces, and its technological and industrial superiority guarantees its ability to remain in the forefront of all elements of ship and weapon design. Is this a threat to national security that even the most pacific and economy-minded Soviet administration can afford to neglect, and are not appropriately shaped maritime forces the only effective method of response?

Whatever reductions in strategic missile systems the Soviet Union is prepared to advocate and accept, there is no doubt that it will maintain a SLBM component and will expect its potential adversaries to do the same. In the light of the certain failure to secure mutual agreement to establish inviolable SSBN sanctuaries, Soviet naval advocates should have little difficulty in establishing the necessity of possessing heterogeneous maritime forces to protect the deployment of their own submarines. Similarly, they have an equally strong case, within a totally defensive strategy, for the necessity of having a capability to harrass, and if possible prevent, all forms of nuclear attack on the homeland from the sea. To go beyond this and convince a sceptical General Staff and an economy-minded government that what is really needed is a navy strong enough to contest the command of the sea with the United States would be an argument naval advocates would do well to avoid and to make a more indirect approach.

Well before Gorbachev's accession to power in 1985 there were strong indications that Soviet general strategic thinking was moving away from dependence on nuclear weapons of any kind, even in a European war with NATO.[2] Success in such a conflict would be critically affected by early disruption of NATO's transatlantic supply lines. Maintenance, and better still strengthening, of the navy's general purpose forces to accomplish this, could be presented to the General Staff as a strategically significant form of the Navy's traditional role of support for the Army. Similarly, in the Baltic, Northern Europe and on NATO's Southern Front the navy could point out how rapid success on land could be hastened by offensive and defensive maritime operations. In all these arguments stress should be placed not on what the Navy can do by itself but, on what it alone can do to contribute to the success of an integrated land, air and sea strategy.

In this context Rear-Admiral V'yunenko's book can be seen as an important example of advocacy. In the main it is a clear exposition of the traditional naval case but it puts particular emphasis on 'repelling an enemy aero-space attack' and 'suppressing the military-economic potential of the enemy', the latter including the importance of the capability to interdict maritime lines of communication in long wars. The navy's role is support of land forces, and in operations figures largely and throughout the book the essentiality of tri-service integration at all levels is given primary importance. All of this lays a reasonable foundation of the naval case, although the fierce ideological flavour of part of Admiral Gorshkov's Foreword is completely out of tune with the political leadership's current approach to Soviet-American relationships.[3]

The best advice which can be offered to Soviet, or indeed any advocates of strong maritime forces would be: never to use the term 'naval strategy', to treat 'maritime strategy' as a synonym for the principles of sea operations and to base all their arguments on the undoubted truth that power to use the sea in peace and war is an essential component of national security.

NOTES AND REFERENCES

1.   Archie Brown, 'A giant step for Reform' presents an optimistic view of the permanence of Gorbachev's internal reforms. *The Times*, 27 April 1989.
2.   Bryan Ranft and Geoffrey Till, *The Sea in Soviet Strategy* (London: Macmillan, 2nd ed, 1989) chapter 8, contains an extended analysis of the foregoing.
3.   See Ibid., pp. 1–5 particularly.

9 The Soviet Navy 1990–2010: problems and prospects
A.D. Baker, III

That this paper[1] should follow discussions of Soviet naval strategy, Soviet military strategy, US defense policy, and arms control is entirely appropriate, for the material strength, composition, and platform characteristics of the ships and aircraft of the Soviet Navy are distinctly subordinate to – and governed by – the former subjects. To project authoritatively the future size and force composition of the Soviet Navy, one would need not only a thorough grasp of the above topics but also of the economic developments, resource constraints, and overall historical and sociological trends within the Soviet Union – a tall order indeed.

The roles and missions of the Soviet Navy, which govern the design of its hardware, are enmeshed in a very different political and economic context than those of the US Navy, NATO, and the other major world naval powers. Even the categorization of the Soviet Navy's ships is radically different, being a two-dimensional matrix of four 'rates', or levels of capability, plus a set of type designations that are very different from those employed by other fleets. When predicting the future composition of the Soviet Navy, for example, one should not work in terms of carriers, cruisers, destroyers and frigates, but rather in 'anti-submarine cruisers', 'missile cruisers', 'large anti-submarine ships', 'destroyers' and 'guard ships' – the latter category (*Storozhevoy Korabl'*) being a quite distinct type from the Western frigate.

Added to the different roles, missions and force structure are a set of missions not shared by most other navies, notably responsibility for such 'coast guard' functions as aids-to-navigation maintenance (the *raison d'être* for many of the '700' or so Soviet naval auxiliaries), search-and-rescue and salvage. The police patrol functions normally assigned to coast guards elsewhere are carried out by the separately subordinated KGB Border Guard fleet, whose several hundred ships and craft range from what we would call a frigate, to armed ice-breakers, to an impressively large if not particularly capable force of inshore, anti-submarine-capable, patrol boats. Lumping the KGB Border Guard fleet in with the Soviet Navy (despite the fact that it draws non-rated ship and craft complements from the same pool of basic training inductees as does the navy) is a mistake made all too often by writers comparing fleet strengths in those inevitable tables that appear in press and official publications in the West. On the Western side of the balance sheet, those same simplistic 'us versus them' tables usually neglect to incorporate the forces of such sizeable and combat-worthy paranaval fleets as that of the US Coast Guard.

Our understanding of Soviet naval mission, role and doctrinal changes is time-late – and, I believe, getting more so. In retrospect, for one important example, it now appears that a major check was put on the expansion of the Soviet Navy as far back as 1977, when Ustinov came to power as Defense Minister. Only about 1984 was it recognized that the Soviet Navy was no longer growing steadily in all of its many categories, as it had seemed to be doing during the decades of the 1960s and 1970s. Since 1984, of course, we have also seen so marked a diminution of the Soviet Navy's 'out of area' activities that no less a figure than former US Secretary of the Navy John Lehman, never one to denigrate Soviet capabilities or to downplay their possible intentions, felt compelled to note Soviet naval retrenchment in his final posture statement to the US Congress in 1987.

Many obstacles, of course, face scholars and the general public in attempting to assess Soviet military and naval capabilities. Because of Soviet secretiveness, we are dependent on official information furnished by our own governments, whose understanding is not only imperfect but must also be tempered by caution so as to err on the high side. When, in October 1988, Soviet Deputy Foreign Minister Vladimir Petrovskiy told the United Nations Conference on Disarmament that the Soviet Navy possessed 1,380 warships, including 4 'carriers', 376 submarines and 97 ships in the cruiser, destroyer, and frigate categories, and that it had 1,142 aircraft and 12,000 'marines', his figures could not be reconciled with those published either in official Western documents like the US Department of Defense's *Soviet Military Power* or in such standard privately published references as the Institute for Strategic Studies' *The Military Balance*, the US Naval Institute's *Combat Fleets*, or *Jane's Fighting Ships*. Conceding that Petrovskiy probably did not falsify his numbers, then their context still must be defined.

Most probably, Petrovskiy's 1,380 ships and craft included only those units actually operational. This brings up yet another problem for Western 'bean counters', for Soviet concepts of what constitutes reserve equipment are very different from our own. Suffice to say, in all probability – and particularly in the small combatant, mine countermeasures and amphibious warfare categories – far more Soviet Navy ships, craft and aircraft are reckoned by their owners to be out of service in reserve than are realized – or acknowledged – in the West. Where this becomes important, of course, is in those already cited 'us versus them' tables, where, for example, the latest in nuclear-powered cruisers is equated exactly to a worn out *Skoryy* class destroyer in the 'major surface combatants' category, or a three-decade old *November* is counted as equal to an *Akula* in the 'attack submarine' total.

Added to the difficulty of realistically 'counting the beans' is the propensity for the Soviet Union to retain obsolete ships and other equipment far longer than would be the case in the West. Most of these items are little better than candidates for the apparently inefficient Soviet scrap industry, yet they remain afloat (or, at least, awash) and tend to be counted against the Soviet totals.

In October 1988 two *Kanin* class guided missile destroyers ('large anti-submarine ships', of the third rate, in Soviet parlance) left the Northern Fleet under tow for scrapping in Spain (one was run aground *en route*). Despite these vessels having originally been completed as recently as 1960 and 1961, and despite they and their sisters having completed major modernization reconfigurations between 1968 and 1974, both the *Kanins* had obviously been out of service for many years. This gives one license to speculate as to how many of the even older Soviet naval ships of such formerly familiar submarine classes as the *Foxtrot*, *Whiskey*, *November* and *Romeo* and surface combatants like the various versions of the *Kotlin*, *Skoryy*, *Riga* and *Petya* classes are actually operational or are even considered by the Soviet Navy to be reactivatable assets.

Even without accepting Petrovskiy's unverifiable and largely undefined figures, the size of the Soviet fleet – both in numbers and in total tonnage – has been acknowledged as shrinking. In the most recent edition of *Soviet Military Power*, the point where expansion became reduction is placed at 1984 in two of its most revealing and useful graphs.

That Soviet fleet totals are coming down should be of no particular surprise, for the ships and craft built over the last decade or so have obviously been of far greater size and complexity within their Soviet type categories than the earlier generation units they have been replacing. Greater complexity in the face of greater threat begets greater size and a greater drain on Soviet resources – a trend wholly familiar to Western naval planners. Thus, the 220-ton *Osa Raketnyy Kater* of 1958 is being supplanted by far smaller numbers of 540-ton *Tarantuls*, whose virtually identical principal payload – 4 anti-ship missiles – must now be defended by a far more complex and expensive array of weapons and sensors in order to achieve an acceptable chance of mission success. Similarly, but on a far vaster scale, the 10,000-ton *Akula* was a necessary follow-on to the 6,000-ton *Victor* III made in order to keep with – or, perhaps, in hopes of outpacing – the steady improvements made to the US and British submarine forces.

In the mid-1970s it was possible to determine that the output of steel from the Soviet Union's warship building yards was actually pretty steady over time, being, as I recall, about 100,000 tons per year, a little over half of which went to the submarine force. The figure does not include the significant tonnage in amphibious warfare ships and auxiliaries built for the Soviet Navy abroad, and with the current extensive investment in titanium for submarine construction the proportion of steel devoted to submarine construction may no longer be the same. Assuming the annual tonnage to have remained fairly constant over the years, however, and acknowledging that, with the period of major shipyard expansion now over and no new yards having been introduced (Soviet naval shipbuilding capacity has not notably expanded its capacity in recent years), the 100,000-ton figure may still have relevance.

Thus we are now seeing the completion of far fewer but much larger and more complex ships in virtually every Soviet naval combatant category. In 1987, production for the Soviet Navy (as outlined by Rear-Admiral

William O. Studeman, USN, the then Director of Naval Intelligence, in his 1 March 1988 public testimony before the Seapower and Strategic and Critical Materials Subcommittee of the House Armed Services Committee on Intelligence Issues) included the launch of only five submarines, three of which were nuclear-powered and one of which was an experimental, non-combatant diesel boat. Major surface ship deliveries during 1987 included only two of what we would call destroyers, while one 'frigate' was completed for the KGB. In 1988, of course, not only was the fourth and last of the 43,000-ton *Kiev* class 'anti-submarine cruisers' delivered but so were the third 28,000-ton *Kirov* 'missile cruiser' and the usual two destroyers and a frigate. In other categories, however, such as small combatants, the numbers are down, while there have been no deliveries of seagoing mine countermeasures ships for at least six years and no significant new replenishment vessel has been completed for a decade.

Part of the reason for fewer deliveries to the Soviet Navy has been the upswing in the construction of major warships, submarines, small combatants and mine countermeasures units for foreign customers, in particular India, whose priorities seem almost to take precedence over those of the Soviet Navy. A building position tied up for three or more years in constructing a *Kashin* for India is unavailable to build something better for the USSR. The need for hard currency foreign exchange, and the need to extend foreign dependence on the Soviet military logistics infrastructure, may outweigh the need to rejuvenate the ageing Soviet Navy.

At the same time that we are watching the inexorable decline in the Soviet Navy's numbers, there is no doubt whatever that there is also a corresponding increase in individual ship, submarine, and aircraft capabilities and, perhaps even more important, in the surveillance, command, control and communications network that would be used to manipulate the Soviet Union's naval assets in wartime. The trick for the Soviet Union has been, and will continue to be, to ensure that their side of the 'correlation of forces' equation results in at least a retention – within their current and planned operational context – of equality or superiority to the fleets of their perceived enemies. That will be no small feat to accomplish, especially during a period of apparent overall Soviet military retrenchment, increasing resource and manpower constraints, growing demands for force modernization from other more senior branches of the Soviet armed forces in the face of Western developments, and the geometrical progression in the complexity – and cost (by any definition) – of modern naval weapon systems.

Because we have seen – or have been shown – so many seemingly spectacular examples of Soviet naval technology in recent years, there has been a tendency to assume not only that it all works but that all aspects of Soviet development may be as seemingly advanced. Thus great hullabaloo continues to be raised about the impressive maximum speed and depth achieved by the handful of *Alfa* class submarines, to the extent that major naval weapons have been delayed interminably in order to counter a capability that is found in only a tiny percentage of the Soviet submarine force, and that is, in any case, not the major tactical factor in modern submarine warfare. Since irresponsible speculation always sells better than reasonable analysis or established facts (especially when the facts must remain classified in order to protect the means of obtaining them), we must also continue to endure the fantasists who attempt to portray, say, the towed array pods on some modern Soviet submarine classes as actually being magnetohydrodynamic propulsors à la *The Hunt for Red October*.

In point of fact, the Soviet Union is very good at some aspects of naval technology and not so good at others. There are excellent surface-to-air missiles and superb naval guns coupled to fairly primitive acquisition and guidance systems. Hydrodynamics, a speciality in a nation that is reported annually to graduate literally thousands of naval architects, has resulted not only in the speed-optimized hull forms for submarines like *Alfa* and *Akula*, but also in innovative forms for conventional surface ship hulls, and a willingness to experiment with advanced concepts like the *Ekranoplan*, or WIG. There are also innovative propulsion systems that are driving ships like the *Kirov* that, however, had it been built in the West, could have achieved as much capability on perhaps half the displacement.

The Soviet Union as a whole is, by its own admission, woefully deficient in computer technology, and that crucial deficiency simply must have a deleterious effect on the design and operation of their navy. Obvious to anyone who has ever examined Soviet equipment up close, they have a continuing inability to make things *small*; simplicity and durability take precedence over performance.

No doubt ships like the *Kirov* are impressive to the eye, but it is still the case that there is not yet a single ship in the Soviet Navy with the surveillance and control capabilities of an Aegis cruiser or anything approaching the massed firepower of a US Navy aircraft carrier. In fact, if it is accepted that the *Kiev* class are 'aircraft carriers' (and I agree with the Soviets that they are best described as 'anti-submarine cruisers' or by their more recent appellation, 'aircraft-carrying ships'), the combined fixed-wing aircraft complements of all four ships do not add up to that of a single CVN – and, of course, the, unimaginatively employed, Yak-38 *Forger* is hardly a match for a *Sea Harrier*, let alone an F-14 or an F/A-18.

The above too brief discussion of technology, however, perpetuates another problem in comparing Soviet naval power with that of the West: the tendency to discuss relative fleet strengths as if each fleet had the same set of missions. That is, however, not the case, and the Soviet Navy can be considered a 'balanced fleet' for the purposes of the Kremlin where, particularly to US eyes, it might appear deficient in afloat support resources and to have far too many coastal combatants. The US Navy must operate far from home waters, and, indeed is not at all well-equipped to act as a coast defense fleet; the Soviet Navy, in time of war, is really intended to be a seaward extension of the Soviet land defenses, and for that role it is more than adequately equipped.

Because the assigned title for this chapter points towards a projection for the years 1990 and 2010, the author really ought to make the attempt. The following 'single-point' projection, however, must be defined as one in which the Soviet Navy continues to receive about the same absolute and relative allocation of resources as is now the case; if Gorbachev and his program survive, things may be more than a bit leaner for the Soviet Navy in the short term, but two decades from now, assuming he succeeds in reviving the Soviet economy, the Navy's programs should be nearly back on the track projected here. If Gorbachev fails and is replaced by conservative hardliners, then the complete economic collapse of the USSR is a good possibility, and before that occurred, we would have a lot more to worry about than the Soviet Navy.

In an era of billion-dollar *Seawolf* class submarines, the effort to keep up between the Joneses and the Ivanovs will be enormously expensive for both sides. It will, however, be utterly necessary for the maintenance of seapower, for the submarine is the one naval platform with a reasonably assured chance of survival in the three-dimensional, undersea/surface/air-space warfare environment of the twenty-first century.

The strategic ballistic missile submarine force will number about sixty-two units in 1990 and will consist of not more than six operational, SS-N-20-equipped *Typhoons* (with another one or two under construction), eight *Delta* IV with SS-N-23 missiles, the present complement (barring accident) of thirty-six earlier *Delta* variants with SS-N-8 or SS-N-18 missiles or, just possibly, some backfitted with SS-N-23; at most a dozen *Yankees* will still be in SSBN configuration and assigned to the theater attack role being vacated by the *Golfs*.

By 2010, the eight *Typhoons* and perhaps eight to ten *Delta* IVs will have been joined by sufficient numbers of a new class introduced in the early 1990s to ensure the continuity of the SLBM deterrent. Any surviving earlier *Deltas* will have been relegated to subsidiary duties. At the same time, the build up in facilities, command systems and ASW capabilities will have made the force relatively far more secure than it is today.

Barring a verifiable sea-launched strategic cruise missile limitation treaty, the Soviets will probably further develop the capability inherent in the SS-NX-24 long-range weapon, whose long-expected production launch platform submarine has yet to appear. The SS-N-21, although roughly analogous to Tomahawk in size, has been publicly adjudged to be a theater attack weapon by US intelligence, and, over the near term, it is likely that we shall see additional *Yankees* converted to the 'Yankee Notch' configuration revealed in 1987. SS-N-21, like Tomahawk, in US Navy submarines that lack dedicated vertical launch tubes, displaces other torpedo tube-launched weapons, and, because the Soviet submarine force has so many other different types of weapons to carry at once, devoting significant capacity to the theater-attack cruise missile is really not an attractive option for the *current* SSN force. For the future, however, an increase in the number of launch tubes, installation of external vertical launch tubes, or provision of an enlarged reload capacity in new classes is a strong possibility.

The dedicated short-range anti-ship missile launching submarines of the *Charlie* series were a dead-end line of development that will be unlikely to necessitate functional replacements; the Soviet submarine has yet to receive a torpedo tube-launched weapon like Sub-Harpoon, but, with its long-range, large-diameter, wake-homing torpedoes, it may not consider such a weapon necessary or desirable. The submarine cruisers of the *Oscar* class, with their large, 250-mile plus ranged 'strategic' (meaning, in Soviet terms, that they are intended for use against strategically significant targets like carrier battle groups) SS-N-19 missiles are a viable weapon system in the Soviet context. *Oscar* has a very differerent role in the Soviet Navy than the *Charlies*, and it isn't the fault of the Soviet Navy that we have chosen to type both classes as 'SSGNs'.

Perhaps the real successor to the *Echo* II/*Oscar* series will be the above-mentioned SS-NX-24 submarine, with the weapon usable against land or sea targets. Because of the large number of bulky missiles that it must carry to perform its 'strategic defense' role, the production rate for the *Oscar* series has been slow, only about one submarine every year and a half. A faster production rate for an *Oscar* successor class is unlikely. Such submarines, however, will be able to take far better advantage than the *Oscar* of the space surveillance resources of the future for targeting their weapons, and, if their weapons are reduced in size or employ 'stealth' concepts, the *Oscar*/*Oscar*-successor force will be a formidable threat.

The force of what we choose to call 'SSGNs', however, will inevitably shrink to a small number of ships, perhaps two dozen at the most by 2010, with the demise of the *Charlies*, the already obsolescent *Echo IIs*, and their contemporary diesel-powered cousins, the *Julietts*, occurring by the middle to the end of the 1990s.

The modern Soviet nuclear-powered attack submarine force is already well outnumbered by NATO SSNs, and new units are joining at the rate of only two to three (at best) a year – in a still bewildering variety of classes. By 1990 the *Novembers* and *Echos* will have had near or over thirty years' service and can virtually be disregarded as a significant threat. That will leave the *Victor* I and later classes, totaling fewer than sixty units, with one or more of the undoubtedly noisy *Yankee* SSN conversions doing little to swell the threat. By 2010, and assuming such submarines are retired after roughly thirty year careers, the twenty newest *Victor* IIIs will be the oldest boats, with *Akula, Sierra* and their successor design(s) bringing the total SSN force to between sixty-five and eighty units. Thus, the first-line quiet and deep-diving attack submarine force could not only be significantly more numerous than at present (while NATO's totals are likely to decline), it will also be significantly quieter and more combat-worthy.

The Soviet diesel submarine order of battle is rapidly declining and is being renewed at only a token rate. By next year there should be only about seventy such vessels left in operation; by 2010, even with the probable introduction of new classes, a force of a dozen such ships in each fleet is likely to suffice.

Unannounced and undetected submarines are worthless for projecting naval presence, as Great Britain should have realized from its unheralded late 1970s dispatch of two SSNs to the South Atlantic, in response to an Argentine pressure over the Falklands. The diminishing survivability of surface warfare units, however, in the face of the almost certain development of near-constant space surveillance of the oceans, while it may not be a reality by 2010, will be a trend that must be dealt with and that will cost dearly to counter.

In the Soviet Navy the surface forces have as their primary responsibilities the defense of the homeland and the protection of the ballistic missile submarine component of the strategic deterrent. The present hardware and operational trends all indicate a realization that accomplishing those missions requires a massive investment in equipment and the development of the means for close cooperation between land and sea-based aviation, the surface forces, and the submarine fleet (and, in the future, space-based forces as well). In the coming years, we are told in the recent and greatly overrated Soviet book, *The Navy, Its Role, Prospects for Development, and Employment* (*Voyenno-morskoy Flot: Rol', Perpektivy Razvitiya, Ispol' zovaniye*), introduced and allegedly edited by the late Fleet Admiral of the Soviet Union Gorshkov, the Soviet Navy will also have to take on the mission of countering strategic cruise missiles – again, an expensive and complex undertaking. While the mission will be aided by high-performance aircraft, airborne early warning aircraft, space-based detection systems, and new weapons that will probably include, by 2010, an operational directed energy or laser weapon system, it will have to be accomplished with fewer individual platform resources than are now available.

Sea-based aviation, developing with painful slowness in the Soviet Navy after overcoming doctrinal resistance in the 1970s, will in 1990 receive its first true aircraft carrier. Although without catapults the *Tbilisi* will be sorely handicapped in the operation of high-performance fixed-wing aircraft. Later carriers – and at least one more is definitely in the offing – should join the fleet at roughly three-year intervals and, with the announcement last year that a navalised Su-27 Flanker B variant is being readied, will probably have the long-delayed catapults.

Equipped with the Su-27 (or, at least, capable of servicing and relaunching land-based squadrons), the new Yak-41 Forger successor and a sizeable helicopter complement, the Soviet carriers will have as their wartime role not the projection of power in the US maritime strategy context but, instead, the seaward extension of Soviet air defenses and the protection of the strategic submarine fleet, a point made very well in a US Naval Institute *Proceedings* article by Floyd D. Kennedy of the US Center for Naval Analyses, 'The reorganization of Soviet military aviation and its impact on the new Soviet aircraft carrier'. By 2010 the carrier force, still including the by then aged *Kiev* and her later three sisters, might number ten to twelve ships – five or six each in the Northern and Pacific Ocean Fleets.

The massive investment in these enormous ships will have its effect on the size of the rest of the surface fleet. To protect the carriers (which themselves will probably have far more in the way of defensive systems than do US carriers, even at the expense of aircraft capacity), the Soviet Navy will almost inevitably evolve a 'carrier battle group' structure in which the smaller ships escort the larger ones. That is already possible now to a limited degree with the introduction of the SA-N-6 missile, but, even today, most Soviet surface ships are intended to defend themselves against air attack independently rather than in cooperation. The need to build ever more sophisticated escorts will drive their sizes upward and the numbers that can be acquired downward.

To return again to Petrovskiy's figures, his ninety-seven 'cruisers, destroyers and frigates' appears to include everything from the two *Moskva* class ASW cruisers, the surviving handful of operational *Sverdlov* class conventional gun cruisers, the 'missile cruisers' (*raketnyy kreyser*) of the *Kirov, Slava, Kresta* I and *Kynda* classes (thirteen ships to date, with two *Slavas* and a *Kirov* coming); the forty-six or so 'large anti-submarine ships (*bol' shoy protivolodochnyy korabl'*) of the *Kara, Kresta* II, *Udaloy* (nine completed, at least three more coming) *Kashin* series and *Kanin* classes; perhaps two of the only 'large missile ship' class, the Modified *Kildins*; the twenty-seven destroyers (*eskhadrennyy minonosets*, literally 'squadron minelayers') of the *Sovremennyy* (nine completed, at least nine coming) *Kotlin* series and, just possibly, *Skoryy* classes; and, presumably, the thirty-two large *storozhevoy korabl'* ('guard ship')-designated ships of the *Krivak* I and II classes.

The problem is that the total of the above is on the order of 115 ships, while eliminating the *Krivaks* results in too few; the Deputy Foreign Minister may not have been counting ships in long-term refit – or there may be far fewer of the older ships of the older classes through the *Kanins* than we think. In support of the latter conclusion, deleting all of the *Kotlins* and *Skoryys* would just about result in Petrovskiy's number. Time will shortly tell, for there are at least ten more Soviet Navy ships, including submarines, scheduled to be scrapped in the West, and it is reported that upwards of 50,000 deadweight tons of discarded Soviet warships are for sale on the scrap market.

Since 1980, the Soviet Navy has received, in our terminology, an average of one 'cruiser' every other year and two 'destroyers' a year. 'Frigate' deliveries stopped with the last *Krivak* II in 1982 (subsequent *Krivak* IIIs, for the KGB Border Guard, have been delivered at the rate of one per year). During that same period, by way of comparison, the US Navy alone commissioned four battleships, eleven cruisers, ten destroyers, and forty-eight frigates.

For the immediate future, there does not seem to be much prospect for an increase in the production rate of Soviet Navy major surface combatants, although the US Director of Naval Intelligence stated in his public testimony a year ago that the prototype for a new frigate class was then under construction and was expected to begin trials during 1989. Of the current construction designs, the *Kirovs* appear capable of performing an escort role for carriers, although that was probably not the original intent for the design, while the *Slava*, a 12,000-ton general purpose ship with the SA-N-6 system, is none the less handicapped by being equipped primarily with weapons and sensor systems first introduced in the mid-1970s. *Udaloy* is primarily an anti-submarine vessel, while the *Sovremennyy*, a true general-purpose destroyer, has only a limited, essentially self-defense, ASW capability and, since its design is based on that of the *Kresta* series, represents basic platform and propulsion technologies introduced over a quarter century ago.

Thus the stage really is set for a new series of major surface combatants if the Soviets intend, as it appears that they do, to be able to maintain against the contemporary threat an ability to continue to operate at will in the contiguous waters they consider vital to their national defense. Because of size, cost and shipyard capacity constraints (including a continuing export program), however, it does not seem likely that with the likely exception of the new 'frigate' program production rates will rise.

This means that by the year 2010 the major surface forces will have shrunk in total number, however greatly they may improve in quality. If these forces are increasingly tied to the protection of carrier battle groups, then the Soviet Navy will probably need about two-thirds to three-quarters as many major surface combatants as it currently keeps operational.

The development of the Soviet carrier battle group, although its mission will be very different from that of its American counterpart, will inevitably transform the Soviets' surface fleet force composition into one more closely analogous to that of the US Navy. What we have not seen for over a decade, however, is any program for new ships that would provide underway support for extended out-of-area wartime operations for such a fleet. That glaring lack (from our perspective) adds support for the growing consensus that the Soviet surface fleet (and, to a lesser extent, the submarine fleet with which it is intended closely to operate) will not venture any great distance from the homeland in time of war. I would even go so far as to conclude that the Soviet fleets will not venture far beyond the limits of land-based aviation support, although, of course, those limits are being expanded beyond their current limits through the introduction of longer-ranged, more capable interceptors, new and more capacious aerial refuellers and AWACs-type aircraft – all operating under the control of a greatly enhanced C^3I network.

The 'other' Soviet surface fleet is being catered to at about the same level of effort that has prevailed for the last three decades, and it is likely that short-seas patrol and ASW types like the *Grisha* (now in production for well over twenty years and probably due for a production successor in the near future), coastal patrol types like *Pauk* and the whole family of seagoing coast defense anti-ship missile craft like *Tarantul* will continue to be built for operations in Northern Fleet home waters, the Baltic, the Black Sea, the Sea of Japan and elsewhere. There is a definite, long-term Soviet Navy layered coastal defense mindset, and there is no reason for such forces to disappear, at least not by 2010. Indeed, current R&D programs, like the SS-N-22-toting *Utka ekranoplan*, are an indication that coast defense will continue to be a major – and resource-consuming – Soviet Navy mission.

Although the Soviet Navy is perhaps the most mine warfare-conscious of any of the major fleets, there have been few recent platform or capability developments that could be said to match Western European technology. Although it is possible that, based on the lack of progress in the development and production of new mines within NATO, the Soviets have reallocated resources elsewhere, it is far more likely that the 1990s will bring a new generation of mine countermeasures platforms, including a truly capable aerial mine countermeasures helicopter, to maintain or exceed their current capability.

Although Petrovskiy and the US Department of Defense disagree by a third on the size of the Soviet naval infantry (he said 12,000; DOD says 18,000), it cannot be disputed that the Soviet amphibious warfare capability has been greatly enhanced in recent years and looks to continuing to improve in the years ahead. Although the Soviet naval infantry will still have a wartime role in support of the massive Red Army forces, the introduction of sizeable numbers of large air cushion vehicles and *ekranoplans* for the delivery of shock troops and their light vehicles will enhance the already formidable ability of the USSR to mount an amphibious assault within relatively short distances of the homeland. The growth in size and versatility of the Soviet merchant marine's strategic sealift capabilities will certainly facilitate the amphibious deployment not only of the naval infantry but also of large numbers of Red Army troops, if required. There does not, however, seem to be any doctrinal or hardware trend to indicate that the Soviet Navy is in any way headed towards an ability to project power ashore during a general global war beyond the limits of the defensive perimeter established by the sea/land/air-space shield around the nation.

As to the trends in the auxiliary forces, it can merely be said in summary that the Soviet Navy has continued to renew these over the years and that, because of the greater number of roles and missions assigned to such organizations as the Naval Salvage and Rescue Service, the Hydrographic Service and the Naval Auxiliary Service than are generally assigned to Western 'navies', there will continue to be built what appear to us to be large numbers of ships in large numbers of diverse classes.

To repeat the caution that began this paper, those who hope to analyse and project the current and future capabilities and intentions of the Soviet Navy must do so from within as complete and thorough as possible a Soviet historical, cultural, social and economic framework. Our official (and unofficial) efforts to understand Soviet military power should be couched within an overall understanding of the Soviet Union's past and likely future and not tied to narrow 'bean-counting' exercises or to mirror-imaged technological feasibilities.

Finally, it must always be remembered that a military force with a strong doctrinal foundation and a clear view of its mission has distinct advantages over an opposing force that has concentrated on technology for technology's sake or on acquisition over strategy. Whatever the Soviet Navy may lack in platform sophistication, now and in the future, it may make up for in operational organization and planning.

The Soviet navy 1990–2010: a commentary
John Jordan

It is difficult either to take issue with Baker's analysis of the current status of the Soviet Navy, or significantly to dissent from anything he has said about its current missions, and the achievements and limitations of Soviet military technology. However, the task of projecting construction programmes into the future on the basis of current trends is even more difficult than he has suggested, given the radical nature of the political changes in the Soviet hierarchy over the past few years. I would, therefore, like to broaden the angle a little and look at some of the fundamental issues which cannot fail to have an impact on the Soviet Navy over the next two decades.

We are faced with the most radical Soviet leadership since the Revolution of 1917. The only parallels which can be established are with the accession to power of Khrushchev following the death of Stalin. Khrushchev, like Gorbachev, believed that it would be necessary to reduce expenditure on the military in order to raise the standard of living of the average Soviet citizen. For Khrushchev the advent of nuclear warheads, delivered by long-range missiles, presented the opportunity to reduce the size and capabilities of conventional forces. However, Gorbachev is in a very different situation, because relatively 'cheap' nuclear weapons no longer offer a solution to the problem. The current Soviet leadership appears to have come to the conclusion that the *use* of nuclear weapons is no longer practical as a method of waging war, and that nuclear weapons, therefore, cannot provide a substitute for more expensive conventional forces.

The Gorbachev solution to the reduction of military expenditure lies therefore in *political* initiatives aimed at undermining Western perceptions of a Soviet 'threat'. In the view of the current leadership, mutual arms reductions will provide the same level of security as obtains at present because the military balance – and our perception of the military balance – will be unchanged.

Another factor which we must take into account is that *glasnost'* and *perestroika* have created within the Soviet Union a destabilization of the entrenched industrial, bureaucratic and military establishments. In future the Soviet armed forces cannot assume that programmes will be funded simply because they constitute a logical development of those currently running. New systems will have to be justified in terms of their place in the overall political and military strategy.

In this respect the concept of 'reasonable sufficiency' espoused by Mikhail Gorbachev may have far-reaching effects on the Soviet Navy. Naval force structures will be tailored closely to the perceived threat offered by the US Navy in particular, and by the navies of its allies. If that 'threat' can be reduced, whether by mutually agreed arms reductions, by international agreements to limit naval deployments in sea areas close to the Soviet Union, or by undermining the aggressive stance of the US Navy as embodied in the Maritime Strategy, then the Soviet naval construction programme can be reduced accordingly.

What are the perceived threats from the US Navy which the Soviet Navy will have to deal with over the next two decades? I would suggest that they are the following:

1. The threat of strategic anti-submarine warfare directed against the Soviet ballistic missile submarine fleet.
2. The threat to Soviet territory and military installations posed by the US Navy's carrier battle groups.
3. The threat to Soviet territory and military installations posed by surface and submarine-launched Tomahawk missiles.

How will these threats be countered? The threat of incursions by Western submarines armed with cruise missiles and/or antisubmarine torpedoes will be countered within the framework of the bastion concept, with the perimeters of Soviet sea space being guarded by a combination of high-performance surface ships, submarines and aircraft. Soviet coastal waters will continue to be guarded by large numbers of relatively cheap, small vessels with relatively basic equipment.

The threat posed by the carrier battle groups will be countered by the traditional combination of platforms equipped with stand-off missiles – 'rocket cruisers', large SSGNs such as the 'Oscar', and especially maritime bombers.

GORSHKOV VS CHERNAVIN

The current Soviet naval construction programme has been inherited from Admiral Gorshkov. It remains to be seen how far this programme will be carried through under his successor, Admiral Chernavin.

Gorshkov from the early 1970s openly championed the view that naval warfare constitutes an independent branch of military science with its own disciplines, and its own special problems susceptible to its own particular solutions. This view may be considered perfectly legitimate in the West, but in the Soviet Union it has been attacked as heresy. And during the struggle for influence which preceded Gorshkov's demise, Admiral Chernavin was one of its foremost critics.

The current Soviet construction programme emphasizes *self-sufficiency* and *endurance*. Its centre-piece is the new through-deck carrier programme, intended to provide protection to Soviet surface forces operating outside the land-based air umbrella. The *Kirovs* – the world's largest cruisers – are equipped with a formidable array of air defence systems to enable them to operate independently. The large destroyers of the *Udaloy* and *Sovremenny* classes are similar in size to the US Navy's *Spruance*, and twice the size of the latest NATO frigates and destroyers.

The appointment of Chernavin to succeed Gorshkov represents a return to the traditional Soviet school of naval strategy. Chernavin has reaffirmed the combined arms approach to naval operations. He has 'reigned in' the large-scale ocean exercises favoured by Gorshkov. These have been replaced by small-scale combined arms exercises taking place within the Soviet fleet areas, practising the interception of hostile carrier battle groups. There has been a renewed emphasis on the value of training and coordination of forces.

This fundamental change in operating policy inevitably puts a question mark against some of Gorshkov's more ambitious projects. Clearly the new through-deck carrier will be completed, as will the sister ship already under construction. However, there may be a slowing down of the programme, and the programme may not run its intended course – which I would estimate at four ships.

It would appear that there has already been an important modification to the original proposal to provide these ships with their own squadrons of navalized fixed-wing CTOL aircraft. Latest reports suggest that the new carriers will be closely integrated with an increasingly elaborate maritime theatre air defence system, and that land-based SU-27 variants may use their flight decks as 'staging posts' in order to extend their effective operating radius and time on station. The ships' own air complements may be limited to a more traditional mix of Ka-27 *Helix* anti-submarine helicopters and the new Yak-41 VTOL *Forger* successor. Certainly the return to operations aimed primarily at defending Soviet sea space reduces the requirement for fixed-wing carrier aviation.

Other possible long-term changes affecting the surface fleet include a reassessment of the balance between blue-water ships and smaller, less capable vessels for the defence of Soviet sea space. It is reported that a replacement for the SKRs ('guard ship') of the *Krivak* class is now in hand, and this may signal a tailing-off of the large destroyer programme exemplified by the *Udaloy* and *Sovremenny* classes. Construction of the large 'rocket cruisers' of the *Slava* class at Nikolayev on the Black Sea has already all but ground to a halt, in part because of the demands for skilled labour made by the carrier programme, but also because of the dramatic growth in Soviet naval exports to friendly countries over the past few years.

In the near term, the only opportunities for cuts in the Soviet blue-water surface fleet appear to be the retirement of a number of elderly classes of dubious military value such as the *Kotlins*, the *Kildins*, the *Kanins* and the *Kashins*. It is in any case unclear how many units of the former classes remain in service, as many are thought to be either in reserve or in a disarmed condition, awaiting disposal.

The new SSN designs are clearly very important to the Soviet Navy, as under the new operational policy attack submarines will be virtually the only Soviet weapons platforms capable of an offensive outside the bastions.

The emphasis on quietness in the latest types is evidence that they will also be increasingly important to the defence of the bastions themselves.

However, it is of interest to note that Admiral Chernavin, in his recent interview with USNI *Proceedings*,[3] stressed the value of diesel-electric submarines for defensive operations, especially in the shallow waters surrounding the Soviet Union. It is therefore unlikely that the Soviet Navy will move towards an all-nuclear submarine force. Diesel boats are cheap, make fewer demands on specialist manpower, and if employed in the right environment have a number of advantages over nuclear-powered submarines.

NOTES AND REFERENCES

1. The opinions and the projections made in this paper are entirely those of the author and do not in any way pretend to represent the views of the US Navy or Department of Defense. The information employed in the analysis was derived entirely from open-source official and unofficial publications.
2. Floyd D Kennedy, 'The reorganization of Soviet military aviation and its impact on the new Soviet aircraft carrier', USNI *Proceedings*, March 1989.
3. Interview with Admiral V.N. Chernavin, USNI *Proceedings*, February 1989.

10 The future of the Soviet Navy: further discussion

As is often the case when any number of experts on the Soviet Navy come together, discussion at the Greenwich Conference revolved around three closely interlinked issues. First, there was and continues to be, a debate about the quality and nature of the evidence upon which Western assessments are based. Secondly, there is the issue of the Soviet Navy's mission structure, that is, what its essential tasks are and are likely to be. Thirdly, there is the problem of the Soviet Navy's future prospects – now quite definitely an issue with a maritime arms control dimension – and how the West should prepare to respond.

THE DEBATE ON EVIDENCE

The debate about evidence has been dominated by the appearance of the book *The Navy* by V'yunenko et al.[1] This is a difficult work, with some fairly bizarre passages, which appeared in Moscow in 1988, with a Foreword by Admiral Gorshkov. Work on it probably began about 1984; it was apparently sent for typesetting in June 1987 and cleared for printing in October of that year.[2] It seems to have had a substantial print run and is widely available.

The missions outlined in *The Navy* appeared to demonstrate a return to a combined arms philosophy – in contrast to the independent roles that Gorshkov seemed to have sought. Command of the sea was not seen as an end in itself but was set in, and justified by, a specific context. The primary focus was on how the navy would operate in a protracted nuclear or conventional conflict. There was no sign of former interest in the use of navies to secure foreign policy goals. Instead, the Soviet Navy was now moving to emphasize defence of the homeland from aero-space attack, the offensive strike mission, attack on Western Sea Lines Of Communication and assistance to Soviet ground forces. The first of these missions, homeland defence, was given a higher emphasis – with forces explicitly needed for strategic ASW, anti-SLCM missions and traditional anticarrier operations. *The Navy* even envisaged a role for the Soviet Navy in any future strategic defence of the homeland against ballistic missile attack. Attacks on Western SSBN, early in the conventional phase of any global war so as to remove Western SSBN before nuclear escalation occurred, were also given a high priority. From this perspective, *The Navy* was an important signposting of the way ahead for the Soviet Navy – one that clearly indicated new priorities and new challenges for the West.

Among those who think the book *is* significant can be detected at least two schools – and probably more! These two schools are those who think *The Navy* is saying something interestingly new, and those who think, on the contrary that it is saying something interestingly old.

To take the last school first, *The Navy* can be seen as a confident reassertion of what might be regarded in Western terms as 'the naval case', of course with some differences in emphasis. In a recent article, for example, MccGwire has argued that the Soviet Navy ran into trouble in the late 1970s and that, paradoxically thanks to the new maritime thrust of American policy, it then launched an at least partially succesful claw back campaign. One step of the campaign was the much remarked upon debate about the nature of military doctrine and the Navy's place in it, '*The Navy* . . . can be seen as a further step in the process of reasserting the navy's contribution to the assessment of military requirements. Developments in the US maritime policy would have highlighted this process.'[3] An essential part of the campaign was to emphasize that the naval dimension was an important, indeed an indispensable part of military doctrine as a whole.

The Soviet Navy's discussion of this issue has certainly been widely misinterpreted in the West in the past. The notion that in Gorshkov's last years in office he was publicly criticized by his then subordinate, and eventual successor, Admiral Chernavin for arguing too strongly for the Navy to have 'independent missions' is inherently implausible. Certainly, Admiral Chernavin has written of the need to integrate naval thinking within 'the framework of a unified military science', but there is little in this that could be seen as substantive criticism of Admiral Gorshkov's views. In the second, 1979, version of Gorshkov's book, references to the existence of a separate 'naval science' had, in fact, already disappeared. Instead, the emphasis throughout was even more strongly than in the first edition on the Navy being an indispensable constituent of a unified military establishment. This was, indeed, the burden of the new section in the book, entitled 'The strategic employment of a navy'. Finally, the whole *Morskoi sbornik* series on the nature of naval theory was rounded off in due course by an article by Admiral Gorshkov himself.[4]

Scepticism about the view that this rather esoteric debate at the time signalled a dramatic decline for the Soviet Navy is reinforced by the fact that it is by no means clear why the new emphasis on the combined arms approach should be regarded as necessarily against the Navy's institutional interests. Indeed it is possible to argue the precise reverse (which may help explain why so many Soviet admirals seem to have supported the line). If the services were to disintegrate, the weight of tradition and manifest strategic legitimacy of the Army and the sheer power of the Strategic Rocket Force would still lead to their overshadowing the Navy. Being semi-detached might simply lead to the Navy's being ignored. In short, being integrated does not necessarily mean less resources for the Navy, and being independent would not necessarily lead to more. The debate about military theory and the reorganization of the Soviet Union's command structure therefore does not in itself yet lead to clear-cut conclusions about the future of the Soviet Navy.

On the other hand, there is the view of another group of experts who would argue that *The Navy* is important, but not for its readiness to restate traditional naval verities. Instead, it can be seen as a significant text outlining, or advocating, a new slant to some old missions and some new missions altogether. Weinland approaches *The Navy* in this sense and so does James McConnell, both of whom attach a great deal of importance to the discussion that V'yunenko provides of the Soviet Navy's task in repelling aero-space attack. We will look at these discussions in rather more detail later.

Interestingly, support for the notion that *The Navy* is a significant book, though for rather different reasons, comes also from James Kipp. In a recent article he argues that the book concentrates on identifying the basic requirements of naval modernization in the light of a huge range of technical possibilities, of likely constraints in Soviet defence expenditure and the new strategic thinking. The increasing dangers and difficulties in making technological choices for the future explain the stress in *The Navy* on forecasting, a subject all too often dismissed as arcane by Western observers who do not understand the serious professional approach the Soviets have to the analysis of military problems.

V'yunenko's et al.'s work can also be seen as an attempt to identify those characteristics of the US Navy that the Soviets would most like to dispose of through maritime arms control, especially those which cannot be realistically countered by military-technical responses. Perhaps the book, then, is an attempt by the Navy to set the agenda in a difficult future on how to manage a 'rapidly changing naval threat to the Soviet Union by military-technical, tactical and political means'.[5]

So, for a variety of reasons, a substantial body of expert opinion has concluded that the appearance of *The Navy* is intrinsically significant, and worth paying the kind of attention that it received, particularly in the United States.[6]

At the opposite end of the range of analysis were, and are, those who argued that the book should be effectively dismissed. At the conference and subsequently, the detailed technical contents of the book provoked a good deal of scepticism from those who thought *The Navy* was essentially written like a book intended for the credulous teeny-bopper market. In places there were surprising technical errors which sometimes reflected poorly on the quality of Soviet information about Western navies. Some of the technical solutions suggested such as 300-knot torpedoes or 100-knot submarines looked both technically impossible in principle and impossibly expensive in practice. Lapses in present fact and unconvincing prognostications about the technical future undermined the general credibility of *The Navy*, especially where it discussed fanciful missions such as the Soviet Navy having an anti-SSBN capability or a substantial role to play in a Soviet strategic defence system against missile attack.

To the scepticism of Western technical experts about the real significance of *The Navy* might well be added the publicly expressed opposition and

even ridicule it generates among some Soviet observers. Western analysts
in contact with their opposite numbers in or around the Soviet Navy have
certainly encountered the view that the book should simply be dismissed as
outdated 'Gorshkovshina', the last echo of a vanishing era of naval growth.[7]

Nor is it difficult to find Soviet analysts willing publicly to attack the
traditional naval arguments and values to be found at the heart of works
like *The Navy*. Alexei Arbatov, for example, has made his opposition to
the continuation of certain past naval policies, and the naval contruction
programmes associated with them, perfectly clear:

Special mention should be made of naval forces in view of the high cost and
complexity of modern surface ships and submarines and of the time it takes
to build them. Logically, defence sufficiency in the case of these forces implies
restricting their combat tasks to defending the Soviet coast against stikes from
the sea by carrier task force forces and amphibious landings of the West as well
as defending strategic submarines with long-range missiles in coastal seas against
antisubmarine enemy forces.

Such functions as interdicting Atlantic and Pacific communications are hardly
consonant with a defensive strategy, especially where ground troops and air forces
dependably ensure defence in the main continental theatres.[8]

To people of this persuasion, the Soviet Navy as part of the general
military establishment in the Soviet Union is engaged in a process of
wholesale change in consequence of the new military thinking, and almost
by definition, *The Navy* represents outmoded thinking, is substantially so
regarded by the Russians, and, therefore, ought to be treated with disdain
by the West.

It is difficult to know what conclusion we should come to about this
issue. In some ways, Western analysts are confronting a new situation in
the Soviet Union since *glasnost'* might well be encouraging the growth of
a kind of pluralism in military thinking. There has in fact always been
more variety of military thought in the Soviet Union than some Western
analysts have given their Soviet opposite numbers credit for, but now we
have a much increased problem in distinguishing pieces of advocacy from
pieces of announcement, and of determining private thought from official
conclusion. In effect, was *The Navy* a naval view, or *the* naval view?

On the whole, it seems wisest, for the time being at any rate, to take *The
Navy* seriously but not as gospel. In particular, simply ignoring it, or even
rejecting it altogether seems unwise. It is worth remembering that Western
analysts went through this very same process when Gorshkov's works first
appeared. Similarly, the detection of earlier shifts in Soviet thinking has
previously been rejected by some on grounds of inherent unlikelihood
or insufficent evidence. But as Robert Weinland pointed out, later new
evidence, say in the shape of the then unknown benefits we now know the
Soviets must have had in consequence of the Walker spy ring, often seems
to show that when Soviet naval leaders say they can do something, then that
is actually true, whatever we in the West may think at the time. At the very
least, then, *The Navy* looks like the expression of view of at least a segment
of naval thinkers in the Soviet Union, and is intended plainly to influence
an unfolding debate by an explanation of the Navy's missions and the

contribution their successful accomplishment could make to Soviet security. On the success of this campaign might depend the Soviet Navy's ability to get what it needs to carry out the tasks its leaders think important.

THE DEBATE ON OTHER TYPES OF EVIDENCE

Another, much analysed, type of evidence of course are Soviet exercise and deployment patterns. It is often pointed out that in striking contrast to its exercise assertiveness in 1983–5 there have been no major oceanic exercises since then and a dramatic fall in such measures of the level of Soviet naval activity as 'ship-days out of area'. The Northern Fleet continues to be the most important of the Soviet Fleets but, even here, there has been a sharp drop in the exercise rate. In 1985 the Fleet achieved 456 ship-days in the Norwegian Sea, in 1986 207 and in 1987 a mere 114.[9]

In early 1989, the new US Navy Director of Naval Intelligence, Admiral Brooks told Congress,

OPTEMPO is the number of days that an operational Soviet ship is at sea, either in local training or operations, involved in an exercise or deployed out of area. . . Overall Soviet Navy OPTEMPO remained at reduced levels last year, continuing the trend begun in 1986. In 1988 Soviet naval units spent more time in port and at anchor and less time at sea than in previous years; they also reduced the extent of distant deployments and exercise activity, especially out-of-area exercises. OPTEMPO for Soviet general purpose forces since 1986 has been lower than in previous years. Additionally, although overall SNA (Soviet Naval Aviation) strength continues to grow, SNA sortie rates have declined since 1986. Such reduced OPTEMPO has an immediate impact on reducing costs for major consumables such as fuel, and may also reduce the burden on shipyards since required repairs can be scheduled at longer intervals.[10]

But what should be made of all this? Admiral Brooks himself went on to argue that reduced OPTEMPO did not necessarily mean a less capable navy. Holding a higher percentage of exercises close to home meant there were more forces in home waters ready to meet an enemy attack and, therefore, able to offer effective resistance to forward maritime operations by Western powers. The fact that the Soviet Navy seemed now to be operating less as a blue-water global navy, might actually make it more capable in some aspects of its work. In the past, active naval diplomacy and operational effectiveness have sometimes seemed to be inversely related, and they may well be so again. Ship-days out of area in themselves were not a good indicator of naval performance. They may be thought to indicate the reduced importance perhaps attached to Soviet naval diplomacy or even something as prosaic, but eminently believable, as a reduction in fuel allowances for the Soviet Navy. They do not need to imply that the Navy is regarded as less important or that it is less effective across the board.

Nor in fact, should the extent of the Soviet Navy's retreat from the open oceans be exaggerated. As Admiral Chernavin himself remarked in February 1989,

In 1988 our ships paid 7 official visits and 438 routine port calls and around 40,000 servicemen went ashore. In other words, Soviet ships were in a foreign state virtually every day of the year. In 1989 we are due to pay at least 17 visits.[11]

Training levels which may, or may not be related to OPTEMPO, were perhaps a much better indicator of efficiency. In this connection, it is interesting to see the extent to which Admiral Chernavin of late has been emphasizing the need for more effective training and use of manpower. He appears to believe *glasnost* will help this, but the nationalities problem inside the Navy is an increasing problem militating against efficiency. As he recently remarked:

the armed forces have now begun to receive people who found themselves caught up in a wave of problems between nationalities. Some have diminished international feelings which pander to national egoism between nationalities . . . [Th]is having an effect . . . [which is] . . . difficult to deal with because of . . . young officers' lack of practical experience in regulating relations between nationalities.[12]

The last source of evidence about the Soviet Navy is of course the Soviet Union's naval construction programme. Here there is little doubt that reductions in overall totals are in prospect for the Soviet Navy in many classes of combatant. But assessing the threat posed by such a reduced navy is a difficult task. On their own, numbers are a poor guide to naval capability. Recent Soviet ship and submarine designs were noticeably larger as well as more capable than their predecessors. With new submarines like the *Akula* consuming 40 per cent more resources than the previous *Victor* III class, and similar examples from the surface fleet, reductions in numbers look inevitable. Reductions in numbers, however, do not equate to reductions in overall relative capability when each new unit has far more capability than those it replaces.

Other caveats also had to be entered into when dealing with the Soviet Navy. Many of the units being scrapped were older corvettes and frigates with little capability against a modern threat and no deep water capability. Unclassified Western estimates of Soviet capability notoriously failed to distinguish operational from non-operational ships. Ships partially manned, ships in reserve, ships awaiting scrapping, obviously did not all have the same capability as units in full commission. As a more general problem, there was also too little information available on Soviet capabilities – just how effective were Soviet equipment, tactics and training? This was the key, and most expensive, problem facing Western intelligence services. What mattered was what worked, how reliably, how well, in Soviet Navy hands – this was far more difficult to assess than just counting units or weighing their capability by their cost.

Information on Soviet capabilities was seen to be important, both in an arms control context and for a realistic naval, as well as public, appreciation of the threat. Although the Soviet Navy did offer a potent threat, and an increasingly capable one, there was a need to keep a sense of perspective about Soviet achievements. Some would argue, for example, that even some of the most powerful new Soviet ships were still in cases only marginal advances on what had gone before – the *Sovremmeny* and

Udaloy classes had much design commonality with the *Kresta* 1 class of the 1960s. Soviet design practices and procurement difficulties also sent warships to sea without their designed weapons systems being fitted even more often than the less successful Western navies did. Even more telling, was a comparison between the US *Ticonderoga* class Aegis cruisers and the Soviet *Kirov* class battlecruisers. In terms of air and strike warfare capability, the US ship offered more capability on a ship of only half the tonnage. Western advantages should not be underrated. At the same time, real increases in Soviet capability deserved more highlighting than they now received.

One interesting final issue in the matter of evidence on the Soviet Navy, and in particular its construction programmes, is that, with *glasnost* and *perestroika*, a good deal more information about Soviet building plans should shortly begin to appear. Soviet commentators frequently maintain that the new parliamentary aspects of the Soviet system will make a good deal more information available than has traditionally been available to Soviet citizens, and others. Indeed, this has already begun to take place; media analyses of the military have far more substance to them now than was the case even quite recently. While, no doubt, there is still a huge information gap between the Soviet and American navies, the gap is narrowing. In the future, this could be a significant factor in assessing the balance between them or in improving the maritime relations of East and West.

THE DEBATE OVER THE SOVIET NAVY'S MISSIONS

Much of the evidence suggests that this debate over what the Soviet Navy's mission structure is, and should be, is taking place in the Soviet Union as well as in the West. In the Soviet Union it is clearly part and parcel of the general issue of adapting the military establishment to the new strategic thinking apparently sweeping the country. There are plenty of signs that naval leaders have acknowledged that they cannot expect, nor would wish, to remain immune from these developments. According to the Chief of its main political administration, Admiral Valil Panin, the Navy is in the throes of 'fundamental changes . . . [which] concern all aspects of its development, from military-technical programmes all the way to planning potential'.[13]

Especially in an era of defensive sufficiency, *air defence* was clearly a growing priority and this would have important implications for the future of the Soviet carrier fleet. The Soviets, apparently, seem to be interested in an enhanced, layered, air defence network with space-based sensors, AEW aircraft and over-the-horizon radars. With detections far enough from the Soviet border, an air defence grid system would attempt to intercept US B-52s, B-1Bs, B-2s, ALCM and ACM. To get fighters forward into the far zones of the grid the carrier would play a key role. It would carry fighters further out than any available land bases and could also act as a forward airfield for land-based interceptors to stage through. Geography, and the need to intercept US bombers before they reached cruise missile release areas, meant that the alternative to carrier-based interceptors would be even larger fighter resources to maintain an adequate number of fighters on combat air patrol stations far enough north. If carriers are, indeed, more cost effective than land-based fighters in this, crucial, mission, the case for building enough of them to meet the air defence demands of homeland defence would grow accordingly.

As far as the wider aspect of 'repelling aero-space attack' is concerned, there is considerable debate about the role that the Soviet Navy might actually play in the defence of the Soviet Union against ballistic missile attack in the age of SDI and START. Some argue that the required technologies are simply not available – especially to the Soviets – and that the apparent stress given the matter in *The Navy* is simply science fantasy. Others are not so sure. Some, admittedly ambiguous, indicators imply that Soviet naval leaders may really believe they have something to offer here. Thus Admiral Chernavin: 'American plans to translate the arms race into space, if they materialize, will also change the nature of the activities of the Soviet Navy.'[14] Might there be, for example, a naval role in launching quick-reaction space-based SDI type sensors over the oceans?

Connected with this, of course, is the Soviet *anti-SSBN* mission, a role also given some prominence in *The Navy*. Thus V'yunenko et al. 'Under modern conditions the possibility of destroying missile-carrying submarines at the outset of war is of special significance.' For some years now, at least according to some leading Western analysts, there has been the view that the Soviets believe themselves to be on the verge of a technological break through that would make this kind of strategic defence feasible.[15]

Despite this, though, the majority Western view is that Soviet technology is not up to the task. Soviet computer technology is a restraint on Soviet ASW processing capability and restricts Soviet ability to match Western strategic and tactical towed array systems at the same time as technological inferiority and the disadvantages of geography conspire to stop the Soviets developing a system equivalent to SOSUS. Unless some means of detection from space proved possible – and there was, as yet, little evidence of this – an oceanic ASW area-detection capability was impossible and with it any real capability to destroy Western SSBNs by triggering Soviet SSNs.

The reverse of this is the so-called *pro-SSBN* mission, namely where the Soviet Navy seeks to defend its ballistic missile-firing submarines from Western attack. Clearly, the Soviet SSBNs in question will have to be provided with sufficient 'combat stability' to allow them to operate effectively in the face of a Western ASW threat which Soviet writers seem to take very seriously:

The fact is that the US is not only putting counterforce-type submarines into service but is also simultaneously creating a system of anti-submarine forces and means capable of destroying an opponent's submarine missile carriers on combat alert duty.[16]

These anxieties were partly based on the Soviet Union's experience in the 1960s and 1970s and have, doubtless, been increased by the declaratory intention to change the nuclear correlation of forces that is so pubic a part of the US Navy's current concept of the 'Maritime Strategy'

As far as operational responses to this putative threat are concerned, the Soviet Navy appears to have concentrated its resources on the procurement of SLBMs with a range sufficient to be fired from submarines operating in home waters. This means they can be deployed into defended bastions where they can look for protection to the rest of the Soviet Navy and the geographic advantages of proximity. It is worth remembering that Alexei Arbatov specifically included this as an important and legitimate task for a future and possibly reduced Soviet Navy.[17]

It should, however, also be noted that the idea that the Soviet Navy *does* deploy its SSBNs into defended bastions is by no means universally accepted. There have been signs that the Soviet Navy is also interested in other deployment options (such as under the Artic ice-cap) which would release a proportion of their other naval assets for other tasks.[18]

Some Western analysts have expressed their alarm about possible Soviet responses to any such Western anti-SSBN campaign since these might well include further escalation and the possibility of a pre-emptive nuclear strike. This view was firmly rejected by the assembled experts on Soviet strategy at the Conference however, and for a great number of reasons. The 'lose them or use them' argument is not one that was likely to appeal to the Soviet General Staff because suicide in response to a reduction in one's assets is not a rational policy. The Soviet Navy itself laid considerable emphasis on trying to sink Western SSBN, and would hardly be surprised if the West responded in kind. The Soviet Union also seemed to be placing less emphasis on SSBN – with Soviet proposals in the START negotiations demonstrating a willingness to see the proportion of nuclear warheads on the SSBN force decline from its 1989 level of 30 per cent of the total, back to 1980 levels of around 20 per cent.[19] Moreover, new mobile ICBMs could now carry some of the burden of providing an enduring nuclear force in any protracted exchange. Soviet thinking on nuclear strategy had also changed to the extent that any use of nuclear weapons – let alone in response to an attack on a submarine – was now much less unlikely. Soviet military thinkers were unlikely to be surprised by the likely loss of SSBNs in any protracted conventional war (where even a limited Western anti-SSBN capability could prove successful as time went on). There was evidence, indeed, that the Soviet Union itself had thought through the conduct of a long conventional war to the extent of considering long-range, protracted, conventional ballistic missile exchanges. The real challenge to the anti-SSBN mission outlined in the Maritime Strategy was not the danger of uncontrolled escalation but that it could not provide the leverage its proponents assumed. There was even a logic that SSBNs would become less important as START reduced their numbers and other systems provided more cost-effective alternatives. The rundown of the SSBN force, in turn, would either create less demands on, and justification for, the rest of the Navy or alternatively it would free more of the fleet for other missions.

Among these was the *anti-SLOC mission*. Many felt that this was unlikely to be a major Soviet priority. The Soviets might make some effort to interdict NATO's supply lines, but only as part of a concerted combined arms effort to target lines of communication from US depots and factories, through US ports, across the Atlantic and between disembarcation points and the front line. Soviet efforts at sea would fit into the General Staff's appraisal of what needed to be destroyed at sea and what could be destroyed by other means. The Soviet Union would not try to cut the hosepipe linking the USA to Europe if it could put a foot on the hose just behind the outlet. Even if the Soviets did put a major effort into the attack on shipping, it seemed that an offensive Maritime Strategy was the only way of dealing with it. The point was made that, in the Second World War, the allies had needed 1,000 escorts to keep the sea-lanes open but there were now less than 300 available against a larger, and more capable, Soviet submarine fleet. The weakness was compounded by the inability of escorts to detect submarines if the escort had to move at modern convoy speeds, the inability of most cheaper escorts to meet the current air threat and the difference in kind between the attacking U-boat of 1945 and the faster SSN, with unlimited endurance, of the modern day.

None the less, V'yunenko et al. *had* devoted attention to this mission, specifically remarking that the ability of states to carry on fighting will depend on sea communications and this dependence in turn 'will be especially strong in the course of a long war conducted with the employment of conventional means of destruction or with partial employment of tactical nuclear weapons'. But there is another possible motive for such an attack. An assault on Western shipping in the Atlantic might turn out to be the best way of defending the Soviet Navy's defended SSBN bastions. However an anti-shipping campaign fitted into the overall picture though, it could hardly fail to work to the strategic advantage of the Soviet Navy if it meant the West devoted more resources to the defence of maritime communications than the Soviet Union committed to their attack.

In view of the developing idea in the West that CFE would make transatlantic reinforcement more important and would, therefore, increase the strategic profile of both the Soviet anti-SLOC and the Western pro-SLOC missions, it was interesting to note the view expressed by some Soviet commentators that they did not regard this as a justification for the maintenance of maritime supremacy by the West. The argument is built, they claim, on a number of false premises. In fact, the Soviets would not be able to reinforce Central Europe either, because the required military equipment would probably not exist since CFE would require its destruction. Moreover, Soviet forces outside the CFE area were already constrained by unilateral cuts and would be needed to meet other commitments like keeping China quiet (or maintaining internal order) and, in any case, their movement by rail would be easily interdicted by the West. The Soviets were not, therefore, likely to be very sympathetic to any special pleading by the West on this point.

There was at the Conference, and generally remains, a high level of consensus that the *homeland defence* mission of the Soviet Navy has always been important and that given the stress on defensive sufficiency this was if anything likely to increase. The only problem is that, given the increasingly long range of Western sea-based attack systems, this might require Soviet forces to move further and further forward. Moreover, it is clear that the Soviets do not interpret this defensive role necessarily in a passive sense. Thus Admiral Chernavin recently:

What is meant by defensive? Some people understand this in a simplified and primitive way. They consider that once we have adopted such a doctrine, we must be only the passive side, defend ourselves, and in the event of conflict retreat into the depths of our territory. But modern warfare, whether on land, sea or in the air is first and foremost manoeuvre warfare. How can a warship fight today as if sitting in a trench? A submarine must find the enemy and sink him. The aim of the surface ship is when necessary to conduct missile attacks on the enemy without waiting for him to enter our territorial waters.[20]

In other fora, it became clear that the Soviets have informal lines which when crossed by significant naval forces – especially those armed with SLCMs – cause concern in Moscow. These lines have been described as 1,000 km off the Kuriles; 1,000 km off the Norwegian coast south to Trondheim; north of the Muscat–Karachi line and east of a line a little west of Crete. Beyond that, Soviet reconnaissance forces would monitor Western naval activity without, in normal times, being that alarmed about it.[21] The importance the Soviets attach to preventing Western naval buildups in contiguous sea areas by political means in peacetime and by close marking and early attack in wartime has been reinforced recently. The justification often used by the Soviets is of the danger of surprise attack (such as the German attack on Russia in June 1941 or the Japanese attack on Pearl Harbor in December 1941) with destructive modern weapons.

Seen from Western perspectives, however, and especially those of people living behind these Soviet defensive perimeters, wherever they were, Soviet naval activity might not look so defensive. What was at issue in effect was the question of perception. There was, and is, some apprehension in the West that the Soviet ability to portray their force levels as inferior and their deployments as defensive could be politically significant when it came to persuade Western electorates of a continued need for naval expediture, or to frame sensible responses in the field of maritime arms control.

This may be connected with the final 'disappeared' mission of *naval diplomacy*. This mission, in the past a focus of considerable interest and concern among analysts both inside and outside the Soviet Union, was, in fact, little discussed at the Conference directly. Nevertheless, it soon became clear that the Soviet Union was engaged in a related and major effort to extract political advantage from the forces it deployed at sea, namely in the area of maritime arms control to be discussed later. The ability to make cuts at sea, and press for parallel concessions from the West, was, in its way, an important mission for the Soviet Navy.

To conclude, there are good reasons for continued agnosticism about the Soviet mission structure. Categorizing the Soviet fleet as a defensive navy is, moreover, inadequate when some of its defensive objectives call for domination of Norway and Japan. Saying that the anti-SSBN mission is now in favour tended to obscure the fact that some Soviet assets are probably always assigned to it – however impossible a full counterforce strike on all Western SSBNs might be. Today's shipbuilding might well represent the plans and aspirations of ten to fifteen years before and tomorrow's ship would reflect the momentum of past plans rather than this year's decisions. None of this allowed neat and easy conclusions.

THE SOVIET NAVY: FUTURE PROSPECTS

For some time there has been a widely held view in the West that, in Moscow, the knives were out for the Soviet Navy. Certainly it is not difficult to find Soviet naval leaders ready to make at least oblique, and sometimes quite direct, criticism of the earlier efforts of Admiral Gorshkov. According to such critics Gorshkov, and the political leadership of the time, built the kind of ships and prepared for the kind of missions most likely to cause alarm in the West and, so, were partially responsible for the renaissance of US naval power which has, in turn, put added pressure on the Soviet Union.[22] In other words, the rise of the Soviet Navy could be portrayed by its critics as essentially counterproductive. However hard the Soviet Navy has tried, it has not improved the country's overall strategic position to an extent that would justify the resources devoted to it. The Navy's case will not have been helped either by its political failures in the Third World or by the more recent series of embarrassing accidents at home and abroad.

Bhrezhnev and Gorshkov are said by their internal critics to have built big ships simply as status symbols. The whole stress on the Soviet Navy becoming a global and blue-water fleet now seemed to be anachronistic in an age of defensive self-sufficiency to a political leadership more interested in maritime arms control. There were two angles to this debate, and indeed to the Western debate about it and the Soviet Navy's future structure. The first was the question of hardware and the Soviet naval construction programme and the second aspect is the matter of speculating about what the Soviet Navy's future missions might be, but these two issues are of course very closely interrelated.

Turning to the question of future building, there seemed little doubt that the Navy was vulnerable here anyway because it already faces something of a block obsolescence problem in the 1990s as it seeks to address the problem of replacing the large number of ships and submarines that, by then, will be approaching the end of their first-line operational lives. This problem of block obsolescence, paradoxically, is a consequence of the rapid increase of the Soviet fleet in the 1960s. Ship and submarine classes largely completed in the 1960s would in the normal course of events need to be replaced or at least substantially refitted in the 1990s. A large tonnage falls into this category, including 10 *Kresta* Is, *Kynda* and *MOD-Sverdlov* cruisers (and, by the end of the decade, a further 10 *Kresta* IIs would be getting rather elderly), 13 *Kashin* destroyers, 38 *Kanin, Kildin* and *Kotlin* destroyers and at least 20 *Krivak* frigates would be well past their best. The submarine situation is still worse, and would include 29 *Yankee* Is, 8

Hotel IIs, 20 *Golfs*, 17 *Charlies*, 34 *Echos*, 16 *Juliet*, 13 *November* and any of the, very large, number of *Whiskeys* and *Foxtrots* that survive that long. The replacement process should of course be well under way by now.

The problem for the Soviet Navy is exacerbated by the fact that the relentless march of naval technology, has made ships and submarines much larger, much more capable, and, therefore, much more expensive than their predecessors. A size comparison of fairly comparable warships of the 1960s and 1980s makes the point quite well:

Heavy Cruisers	*Sverdlov*	17,000	tons (full load)
	Kirov	27,000	"
Cruisers	*Kresta* I	7,500	"
	Slava	12,500	"
Destroyers	*Kashin*	4,750	"
	Udaloy	8,000	"
Frigates	*Riga*	1,320	"
	Krivak	3,800	"

The most likely consequence of all this is likely to be a further reduction in fleet size. All the indications are that the Soviet Navy is indeed engaged in a major exercise in reduction of its fleet units. More units were decommissioned in 1988 than for any other year in recent history. In May 1989, the process of scrapping ships and submarines reached new heights when the Pepsi-Cola Company took a cruiser, a destroyer, a frigate and seventeen submarines as scrap in part-exchange for its products sold in the Soviet Union. There are estimates that in the course of 1990 the Soviet Navy will dispose of at least thirty-five diesel submarines and seventy ships, with many more to follow later on. However, it has to be said that the military value of these units is negligible, and the Soviet Navy is probably better off without them. Fleet Admiral Kapitanets, First Deputy Commander-in-Chief of the Soviet Navy recently confirmed the limited military effect of the cuts so far like this,

Certain warship formations, naval air regiments, coastal artillery and naval infantry units will be affected by cuts, but this will not result in any structural changes in the four Fleets, nor in the supporting arms of the Soviet Navy. In the first instance, it will be obsolescent ships, aircraft and equipment which will be disposed of.[23]

The real indicator of a substantially reduced future role for the Soviet Navy would be a drastic trimming of current and future building activity. While this activity has obviously not expanded to compensate for the increased level of disposal, there is as yet little sign of any significant cut-backs either. So far, then, the hardware evidence about the present and future prospects of the Soviet Navy remains ambiguous. The absence of more substantial indications is usually put down to the long lead-times of naval progammes, but at some stage soon there should be much clearer evidence of a reduction in naval production if such is in prospect.

The shape of the Soviet Navy that emerges from all of this is difficult to see but its outline is becoming clearer. Ambiguity extends, moreover, far beyond the carrier programme. Reports of follow-on cruiser classes being built in the Baltic suggest that the carriers will not be the only large ships in the Navy. Existing building programmes will see 4 *Kirov* class battlecruisers, 4 *Slava* class cruisers, around 30 *Sovremenny* and *Udaloy* class destroyers added to quite large numbers of still viable cruisers, *Kiev* class ASW carriers and *Krivak* class frigates. The addition of *Akula* class submarines to the Northern Fleet for the first time is another unwelcome increase in Soviet naval capability for Western navies. Current annual procurement figures show roughly the following ships being produced per annum for the Soviet Navy (excluding the considerable numbers going for export) (see Table 10:1).[24]
With thirty-year lives for most ships probable, and many not extendable beyond this time, this will inevitably produce a smaller Soviet fleet which seems destined to have around 8 carriers, 20 battlecruisers and cruisers, perhaps 120 destroyers and large frigates (allowing for some trade-off between destroyers and a future frigate class) and around 120 SSN. Such a technically advanced force would still pose formidable problems for NATO, but, split between four fleets, they may not be insoluble. Indeed, looking at the future size of the Soviet Navy with, perhaps, only 4 carriers, 6–8 cruisers, 20 destroyers and 60–70 SSN and SSGN in the Northern Fleet, the Soviet Navy may well be able to argue that they have already been reduced to the level of prudence. Once past numbers are offered up to the inevitable scrapyard, with a suitable arms control fanfare, the Soviet Navy will also actually begin to look like the streamlined, effective, and not unduly large, fleet that a Soviet leadership who want a homeland defence would build.

Viewed from a Western perspective, however, this declining fleet will look less benign. The problem for the West will be that this smaller navy's ships will be individually far more capable than those that have gone before. Many will be more capable than their West European counterparts. The Soviet fleet that emerges will pose new threats that far exceed old capabilities. The supreme irony of the navy Gorbachev is continuing to

Table 10:1   Annual Soviet construction

Aircraft carriers	1/4	
Battlecruisers	1/3	
Cruisers	1/3	
Destroyers	3	
	SSN/SSGN	4
SSK	1	

Source: IISS, *Military Balance*, US Defense Depart. The Soviet Military Threat etc.

finance is that, in terms of the number of capital ships it has (battlecruisers and carriers), Gobachev's homeland defence navy will look very much like the blue-water, foreign policy-supporting, navy Admiral Gorshkov is thought to have dreamed of. Moreover, it will have, for the first time, a similar number of capital ships to the US Navy as Soviet carrier procurement offsets declining US carrier and battleship numbers. The US Navy will still be more powerful, but one does wonder if even Mr Gorbachev, with his ideas of efficiency and reasonable sufficiency, finds himself attracted by the status symbol of the big ship. As his other military status symbols wither away, his navy may soon appear as a highly visible sign of success against a sea of decline. Even if no such thoughts ever enter Soviet leaders' heads, the momentum it has built up in the 1980s will ensure that it poses major problems for European navies. The Soviet Navy will be smaller in terms of numbers but it will be more flexible, less predictable, and for those unfortunate enough to find themselves behind the Soviet defensive frontier more frightening. It will still be a navy that gets itself noticed, and certainly whenever its new carriers go for a cruise.

This brings us to the carrier question – surely the crucial indicator of the Soviet Navy's future. In early 1989 there were two distinct positions on this question. One suggested that the carriers were the most controversy prone ships in the Soviet naval programme and like their Western equivalents, the most likely to come under attack. The two carriers then known to be building ought probably to be seen as the fifth and sixth of the *Kiev* class rather than as a completely new programme. The Navy might well find itself in competition with the Airforce – just as Western navies had been in the past – and such interservice rivalry might become more prominent as former, less restrictive, goals like matching all threats were no longer accepted. Overall, it looked from this viewpoint, very unlikely that more than two carriers would ever see the light of day.

The alternative view at the time was more optimistic on the fate of the carriers. This put more stress on momentum and missions. The Soviet Navy had spent fifteen to twenty years working out its plans for the ASW and air defence of the homeland. The system was now geared to produce carriers and the political and economic inertia of the Soviet military-industrial complex might well carry it forward regardless. The carrier plan might be delayed from full fruition by six to eight years as problems with catapults had to be overcome, but it might still proceed. If its mission was to protect the Soviet homeland from the US Navy and Strategic Air Command, the carrier still had a crucial role as a forward offensive and defensive platform and the programme might well continue.

Subsequent events seemed, in the main, to support the second of these two views rather than the first. The evidence from the *Tbilisi*'s trials suggests that this 'heavy aircraft-carrying cruiser' will eventually deploy a variant of the formidable Su-27 *Flanker* fighter, perhaps backed up with MiG-29 *Fulcrum* and Su-25 aircraft. Earlier Western scepticism about the *Tbilisi*'s capacity to operate effective conventional aircraft was plainly misplaced.[25] Taken with the ship's SAM and SSM batteries, the developing

Soviet carrier air wing will present a significant threat to Western navies, airforces and shore installations.

It was, moreover, interesting to see that far from keeping quiet about the carrier programme Soviet *glasnost* on the progress of the *Tbilisi* amounted virtually to publicity. Of course one could perhaps expect Western journals to be full of dramatic pictures of the new ship launching and recovering its aircraft on the open sea. But what was perhaps more surprising was extensive coverage in the Soviet press of the *Tbilisi*'s sea trials and references to the ship being 'the flagship of the Soviet Navy'. On 22 October 1989 *Pravda* even went so far as to call the ship an aircraft carrier, though it tendered an apology and correction the following day.

Moreover, it became known, in 1989 that a third carrier had been laid down, according to some sources, in November 1988.[26] Soviet sources suggest that this carrier, *Ul'yanovsk* is actually likely to be bigger than the first two, being 75,000 tons rather than 65,000 and the first to be nuclear-powered. All this was in strong contrast to the widespread view in the West in 1988 and early 1989 that a cancellation of the carrier programme was imminent. Furthermore, the carrier programme continues to have its critics in the Soviet Union. Some argue that they simply cost too much and the money would be better spent 'solving the social problems of the Soviet military'. Others claim that since they are not 'real' aircraft carriers, they would prove too vulnerable to the US Navy to have a role that would justify their expense.[27]

None the less, for the time being, the programme seems to be going ahead. Is this because it simply managed to slip through before the major manpower and budgetary cuts announced by President Gorbachev in December 1988? To compound the mystery, Admiral Chernavin has defined the ship's mission in terms of defending the fleet instead of what might seem the more vital all-arms mission of defending the homeland.[28] But this may be an unreal distinction if the task of the fleet itself is to defend the homeland.

To return to the wider issue, the Soviet Navy seems, so far, to have escaped the scythe of *perestroika*. There are three possible reasons for this. The first is the familiar one of production momentum; programmes are inherently hard to stop. In the Navy's case, moreover, it is possible that the advantages of converting production facilities to civilian purposes are not so apparent as they may seem to be for tank factories and the like.

More interestingly, though, it is possible to argue that the way the doctrinal debate is going is also working to the eventual benefit of the Navy. As we have seen, academic defence critics like Alexei Arbatov have claimed to see the need for a navy to defend the Soviet Union from air and amphibious attacks from the sea, to support the Army and to protect Soviet ballistic missile submarines from attack in 'coastal' waters but no more. Such critiques tend to place their emphasis on land-based air and missile power. Interdiction of SLOCs tends to be rejected as 'offensive' whilst attack on Western ballistic missile submarines is regarded as impossible, or out of keeping with Gorbachev's offers of ASW-free havens. There has been considerable questioning of past tendencies to copy Western thinking, which has been specifically linked to attacks on the carrier programme.

Against this, the Soviet military seem to have highlighted the threat posed by Western naval power and recently the defensive potential of the new Soviet carriers. Admiral Chernavin has argued vigorously that the Navy cannot be cut responsibly, unless the threat is reduced and the publicity given to the carrier as it nears the point of emerging from the Black Sea has had the effect of very firmly nailing the Navy's colours to the carrier's mast.

Perhaps this is why the Navy, so far anyway, continues to enjoy relative success. Perhaps the stress on homeland defence found in *The Navy* has actually provided the Soviet Navy with both a methodology so that its case could be rationalized in the cost-effectiveness terms required by *perestroika* and missions that are difficult to challenge. An interesting reading of Arbatov's work suggests that, by conceding the need to defend the homeland, critics of the Soviet Navy have actually given anyone intent upon naval cuts the difficult problem of having to disagree with the professional military assessment of what is needed to defend the homeland. There is a difference between a political decision that an offensive capability in East Germany is not necessary and a decision that carriers or cruisers are not necessary for effective homeland defence.

In this case, we might even be coming round to the conclusion that the survival of the Soviet Navy may depend, in some measure, on the continuation of what Soviet leaders believe to be an assertive maritime policy by the United States. In this situation, 'defensive sufficency' is a positive factor in military procurement and not the negative one it is usually thought to be. Interestingly, Admiral Chernavin has made his position on the matter quite clear. Describing cuts in naval power as in keeping with the 'reasonable defence sufficiency' principle, he said,

This sensible initiative cause me, as Soviet naval commander-in-chief, much concern, since dialogue with the other side just doesn't come off.

Both NATO and the United States preach the 'forward sea basing' doctrine as before. They are unrelentingly building up their naval forces and do not agree talks on their reduction.

Their advantage over Warsaw Treaty countries, in the meantime, is palpable: 3 to 1 in surface ships, 2.5 to 1 in marine aviation and 2 to 1 the overall deadweight (tonnage) of warships, not to mention their overwhelming superiority in aircraft carriers and amphibious ships.

In this situation, should we scrap naval vessels? I trust that every patriot, every Soviet person will give this unequivocal answer: if we don't want to become hostages in the hands of aggressive forces, we should not.[29]

Finally, it may be that other considerations such as specific political and economic pressures in particular areas are also supporting the Navy. It might even be that even Mr Gorbachev sees some role for powerful naval units to convey the image of Soviet power that is denied him by the need to cut elsewhere and the general decline of the Soviet economy. Although it is more likely that large ships will appear an inefficient adjunct to the new foreign policy, it is just possible that such ships could look like a relatively cheap status symbol. Whether Mr Gorbachev, consciously or subconsciously, thinks like Mr Brezhnev, or whether he still expects the status of a superpower are two unanswered questions which continuing production of large surface combatants may cast light upon. While the Soviet military stick to, or are allowed to maintain, the priorities they have settled on – including a commitment to homeland defence – the Soviet Navy may continue to enjoy its relative success so far.

NOTES AND REFERENCES

1. Rear-Adm. N.P. V'yunenko, Capt. Ist Class B. N. Makeyev and Capt. Ist Class V.D. Skugarev (eds), Foreword by Fleet Admiral of the Soviet Union S.G. Gorshkov, *The Navy: its role, prospects for development and employment* (Moscow: Military Publishing House, 1988).
2. M.MccGwire, 'Gorshkov's Navy, Part 1 and II, *Proceedings* of the USNI August and Sept 1989.
3. Ibid.
4. Admiral Chernavin, *Morskoi Sbornik*, no. 11, 1982. For discussion on these points see R. C. Suggs, 'The Soviet Navy: the changing of the guard' in *Proceedings* of the USNI, April 1983 and I. Paparella, 'La theorie de la flotte', *Defense Nationale*, August 1984.
5. J.W. Kipp, *From Another Perspective: the overlooked message in The Navy. . . .* Unpublished Paper from Soviet Army Studies Office, Fort Leavenworth, 1988.
6. For example, see the 'Naval review' of 1989 by *Proceedings* of the USNI.
7. These were the views of Admiral N.N. Amelko and some of his colleagues at a symposium organized at a Foundation for International Security symposium at Adderbury in July 1988, Moscow February 1989 and Adderbury November 1989. See Eric Grove, *Maritime Strategy and European Security* (Adderbury, Oxfordshire: FIS, 1989).
8. Alexei Arbatov, 'How much defence is sufficient?', *International Affairs* (Moscow) April 1989, p.41.
9. Tonne Huitfeldt, 'Major drop in Soviet Norwegian Sea exercises', *Jane's Defence Weekly (JDW)*, 6 March 1988.
10. Statement by Rear-Adm. Thomas A Brooks, US Navy, Director of Naval Intelligence, before the Seapower Subcommittee of the HASC, 23 February 1989, pp. 13–14.
11. Adm. Chernavin, interview *Izvestiya* 23 February 1989.
12. Ibid. See also his articles in *Morskoi Sbornik* 1984, vol. 1 and 1986, vol. 1.
13. 'Soviet Navy set for fundamental change' *JDW*, 11 November 1989.
14. Adm. Chernavin, 'The Navy' *Morskoi Sbornik*, no. 1, 1986.
15. These views are especially associated with James McConnell of the Center for Naval Analyses, Washington.
16. G.M. Sturua of the Soviet Institute for the United States quoted in J.M. McConnell, *A Possible Change in Soviet Views on the Prospects for Anti-Submarine Warfare* (CNA: Alexandria, 1985).
17. Arbatov, op. cit.
18. See note 15. McConnell is currently working on a paper on the implications of SDI for the Soviet Navy.

19. These proportions are extrapolated from *The Military Balance* 1980/1 and 1989/90. (London: IISS, 1980, 1989).
20. Adm. Chernavin, 'A higher level of vigilance and readiness is the order of the day', *Morskoi sbornik*, February 1988.
21. The views of Vice-Adm. N. Markov at the last FIS seminar listed in note 7.
22. Ibid.
23. Fleet Adm. I. Kapitanets, 'How is the Navy developing?', *Krasnaya Zvezda*, 15 August 1989. See also reports in *JDW*, 17 February 1990, *The Wall Street Journal*, 21 July 1989 and Michael L.Ross, 'Disarmament at sea', *Foreign Policy*, Fall, 1989.
24. Extrapolated from *The Military Balance* 1975/6 and 1989/90 (London: IISS, 1975, 1989).
25. See reports on the *Tbilisi*, *JDW*, 11 November 1989, 9 December 1989 and 16 December 1989. In contrast, see 'Soviets may cancel carrier programme', *JDW*, 4 March 1989.
26. S. Elliott, 'Soviet sea power', *Flight International*, 13 February 1990.
27. Georgi Sturua, 'Does the Soviet Union need aircraft carriers?', *Moscow News*, 28 January 1990.
28. Adm. Chernavin, quoted in *Tass*, 19 October 1989.
29. Adm. Chernavin, Interview, *Tass* 28 July 1989.

11 The US Maritime Strategy in transition

Joseph Metcalf

Over the years our maritime strategy has been very much like the British Constitution–unwritten but thoroughly understood by those who must practice it.

Admiral Carlisle A.H. Trost, USN

Like many basic tenets of the US Navy the Maritime Strategy began with John Paul Jones. He was also the first executor. How else can one describe his forays in *Ranger* about the British Isles?

With these observations we dismiss those who continue to portray the Maritime Strategy as something new, a radical strategy invention on the part of the Navy, or a creation of the Reagan Administration as a rationale for a 600-ship Navy.[1] The Maritime Strategy is a warfighting concept. As such it is a resource allocation guide, a guide for planning naval operations and a policy statement to the Soviets and US allies. To remain viable the strategy must evolve with changes in the warfighting environment.

A strategic planning process is a dynamic one. Fundamental theories of a strategy may not change, but plans for implementation are continually altered and updated as circumstances dictate. Unchanging is the mission of the US Navy which is to 'conduct prompt and sustained operations at sea in support of national objectives.'[2] Mao Tse-Tung said that political power comes from the barrel of a gun.[3] For the past fifty years the US Navy's Maritime Strategy was founded on the principle that the 'gun' flew from the deck of an aircraft carrier. Technology may mean that in the next century the Maritime Strategy may be based on the missile, and in particular, the cruise missile. This alone means that the Maritime Strategy of the US Navy will be in constant transition. At the same time that the Navy is evolving to a different warfighting environment the nation and the alliances which it supports are changing. Mr Gorbachev's *glasnost*, the realities of the Third World and fiscal priorities are forcing changes in political and military thinking both in the United States and in NATO Europe. Within the United States political and military leadership will be responding to demographic and fiscal challenges and, most significantly for the maritime leg of the National Strategy, technology.

There is one constant in all of this, the perspective of military and political leadership in the United States, thus the US National Military Strategy and commitment to NATO, will remain undiminished. This means the basic concepts of the US Navy's Maritime Strategy will remain, but the execution of the strategy in war and thus its translation into war plans and weapons procurement will most certainly change. Change will come in the way that wars are fought on and from the sea.

What is the Maritime Strategy of the United States? Although it is not the purpose of this paper to either lay out or argue strategy, a review of the precepts of the three phases of the strategy is in order (see Figure 11:1).[4]

- Phase I: Deterrence/Transition
              Objective: Escalation Control

    _____   If Deterrence Fails   _____

- Phase II: Seize the Initiative
              Objective: Establish Maritime Superiority

- Phase III: Carry the fight to the Enemy
              Objective: Favorable War Termination[5]

Figure 11:1 The Maritime Strategy

The Maritime Strategy of the US Navy is not a scheme for going to war but one that positions the United States, in concert with allies, to win if efforts to avoid conflict fail. Although the Maritime Strategy deals primarily with the Soviet Union, the concepts are just as easily applied to Mr Khadafy and Libya. The strategy speaks to those who would promote instability and trouble in the world. The tactical warfighting fist of it is in the details of deployment, employment, tactics and weapons.

Forward deployment of forces is the fundamental warfighting principle of the Maritime Strategy. It is a tactical as well as a strategic principle. The US Navy will take the fight to an adversary rather than wait for the war to come to the Navy. In the world today most of the forces for change reinforce this traditional strategy of the US Navy. The popular idiom for warfare and conflict may have changed over the years to 'small wars', 'police actions', 'single unit actions', and the latest, 'low intensity conflict'. However, the US Navy expects to fight the same way it always has, with a forward strategy.

If the Maritime Strategy is not new there certainly has been in recent years a renaissance in naval strategic thinking. In the two decades that followed the Second World War there was an apparent erosion of the Navy's strategic concept. The US Navy was a victim of its own success. Potential adversaries had been removed from the seas. At the same time the Navy failed to enunciate publicly a clearly stated, offensive, strategic concept for applying power against a non-naval, non-maritime state. The Navy did not effectively articulate its basic mission of supporting national objectives at sea.

Where did the modern concept or interpretation of a strategy for the US Navy originate? The force behind the revival of a clear US Navy strategy is a matter of debate. At least one Secretary of the Navy and two Chiefs of Naval Operations can lay claim to the honor. Secretary John Lehman in his memoir writes 'I began hammering away on strategy from the very first day.'[6] He also says that after repeated requests for a briefing 'on the overall naval strategy . . . it was never put on my schedule: it did not exist!'. The Maritime Strategy as it is articulated today clearly has the imprimatur of Admiral James Watkins, who as the Chief of Naval Operations in 1984 approved the Maritime Strategy. In 1986 a special supplement to the January *US Naval Institute Proceedings* outlined the unclassified elements of the strategy.

The early tactical force behind today's Maritime Strategy should be attributed to Admiral Thomas B. Hayward. As Commander-in-Chief, US Pacific Fleet (CINCPACFLT) he and his staff developed a contingency carrier task force strike plan against the Soviet Far Eastern bases. It was an imaginative plan embodying many of the forward deployment concepts of the Maritime Strategy. When he became the Chief of Naval Operations in 1982 he began publicly to articulate the idea that the US Navy would have to carry 'the war to the enemy's naval forces with the objective of achieving the earliest possible destruction of his capability to interfere with our use of the sea areas essential for support of our own forces and allies'.[7] Hayward called for the integration of the American naval effort with that of the other services and the nation's allies. He argued that a Navy as small as the US Navy stands a good chance of completing its wartime tasks only if it adopts a forward, offensively oriented strategy. He was repeating a theme of a former CNO, Admiral Elmo Zumwalt, that the US Navy's 'current narrow margin' of advantage left no alternative. This 'forward strategy' is the bedrock of the US Navy's Maritime Strategy.

A forward naval strategy was only part of what Admiral Hayward had in mind. His goal was the revitalization of the Navy. As CNO midway in the Carter Administration he was under no illusion that he could call for a larger Navy. (600 ships and 15 carrier battle groups as a force objective came with Secretary Lehman.[8]) The post-Vietnam Navy was in a period of physical and psychological decline. It was faced with increasing global demands and an expanding Soviet Navy. Lacking 'quantity', the Navy would need 'quality': good leaders, sailors, material and a coherent strategic concept.[9] Hayward stressed the importance of skillful operational performance by commanders, who in executing naval strategy would have to be bound by the reality of a strategy based on calculated risk. This philosophy has continued under Admiral Trost as Chief of Naval Operations. In particular he has written, 'the Maritime Strategy was not – and is not – a force builder, and it was certainly not the origin of the 600-ship Navy'.[10]

How does the leadership of the US Navy view the Maritime Strategy as we enter the 1990s? There is no doubt that those responsible for preparing the US Navy for war consider the concepts of the Maritime Strategy as the intellectual *raison d'être* for the Navy. They certainly do not view it as John Lehman's strategy. (To Robert W. Komer and the coalition or continental defense point of view, it is probably still a John Lehman run on the Treasury at the expense of the US Army.[11]) On the other hand, to many there is reason to question the Navy's consistency of purpose. Recent articulation of the strategy by senior naval officers and civilians in the public forum has not been as vigorous as in the past. (Failure of senior navy leadership to answer the article in *The Atlantic* magazine of May 1987,

'In harm's way' is a case in point.) This is not a new phenomena: Secretary Lehman was critical of senior uniformed leadership when he observed that 85 per cent of the CNO's staff is involved in the grimy task of programing and budgeting and not strategic thinking.[12] However, strategy is neither a numbers game nor public relations exercise. The facts are that as long as deterrence, forward posture and coalition defense are key elements, the US security strategy the Navy will live by will be the Maritime Strategy. It will dictate the allocation of resources, from forces to procurement. It will be part of the war-gaming syllabus at the Naval War College. For the Fleet Commanders it will form the strategic foundation of their war planning. The failure of the Navy continually to spell out the elements of the strategy to the public may leave the field to its critics but it will not alter the strategy.

As stated above, strategy, maritime and otherwise, is constantly changing as circumstances and the world political and economic environment changes. Underway in the world today is a diffusion in the balance of economic power. Asian economic growth rates continue to outpace the United States, Western Europe and the Soviet Union. Between NATO and the Warsaw Pact there is essentially nuclear parity with a concomitant decrease in the credibility of nuclear weapons. In Central Europe reductions in nuclear weapons are being made with unknown consequences to the balance of deterrent force. Secretary General Gorbachev has declared a policy of *glasnost*. In the West there is a widespread public sense that the Soviet threat is diminishing. Related to the perception of a decreasing threat from the Soviet Union there is growing support for all manner of arms control. The pundits of the world press cannot figure out whether we are living in the best or worst of times, but for the man in the street, his politicians and military planners, one aspect of life is understood, these are times of uncertainty.

Uncertainty breeds change, but what will these changes be? Under ordinary circumstances change is difficult to predict. In the United States there is unusual ambiguity with the confluence of a new Administration and the well-publicized budget deficit. In Europe many of the same factors are present. Add to this the uncertainties of arms control and you have the peacetime equivalent of the Fog of War.

While governments and politicians talk of schemes to reduce the threat of nuclear war, military leaders in NATO, as well as the Soviet Union, must accommodate to a revolution in the means of putting ordnance on target. In fact about the only thing that has not changed in warfare since Caesar landed in Dover is that a man with a weapon is still required to occupy territory. Satellites, stealthy missiles and aircraft, cruise missiles, small ballistic missiles, lasers and zap guns, are flowing from the laboratories of the West, the East and smaller nations in between. Inexpensive missiles that can be easily launched from a variety of platforms proliferate. State-supported terrorists and old fashioned anarchists armed with powerful weapons that make every man a rocket launcher will test the metal of nations and navies with civilized rules of engagement. In the 'large' weapon category the long-range, non-nuclear cruise missile has arrived with accuracy to rival the precision of the best air delivered weapons. This weapon more than any other factor, political, economic or fiscal will change warfare at sea and thus the Maritime Strategy.

Arms control, the cruise missile and the Maritime Strategy are closely linked. The statesmen and politicians of the Western world may not be able to see through the mist to know what the next decade will bring, but to the US Navy it is clear what changes the Soviets would like in NATO's maritime power. To the leadership of the US Navy the Soviet arms control strategy seeks to 'capture the Navy' by limiting its capabilities and mobility. In the words of Vice-Admiral Henry C Mustin, Deputy Chief of Naval Operations for Plans and Policy: 'they want to capture at Geneva what they can't defeat at sea'.[13] For example, General Secretary Gorbachev has publicly suggested initiatives such as those listed here:

- Zones of peace
- Nuclear-free zones
- ASW-free zones
- Safe SSBN havens
- Elimination of SLCM
- Numerical limits

The Soviets have put forth these ideas in terms that are achieving some receptivity. The problem is that every one of them goes after maritime strength, an area in which the Free World has the edge on the Soviet Union. The Soviets say, 'If you won't come up and conduct antisubmarine operations in our home waters, then we won't conduct operations in your home waters. We do not want to see the US Navy in the Norwegian and North Sea.' They have tried to make the Tomahawk missile a START (Strategic Arms Reduction Talks) treaty buster.

The Soviet Union recognizes that while they are a great landpower, NATO is a great seapower. They do not see any way that they can solve NATO superiority at sea without spending a lot more money on naval forces. They are comfortable with the land balance but are uncomfortable with the balance at sea, 'they are trying to solve that maritime problem through a massive, sophisticated campaign of disinformation and diplomatic assault.'[14] They would like to secure their flanks without firing a shot. They would like to disarm the cruise missile.

The Soviets may understand better than the US Navy that the long-range ordnance delivery equation based almost totally on the aircraft carrier will eventually be rewritten. When the Tomahawk went to sea in the early 1980s in a submarine and in the battleship *New Jersey* a *modus operandi* that has sustained the US Navy since the Second World War died. At this moment the warfighting posture of the Navy changed and implicitly so did the Maritime Strategy. The cruise missile became part of a 'revolution at sea'[15] in the US Navy. The Navy went from fifteen power projection platforms to a force capable of putting ordnance on target from on and beneath the seas and from hundreds of launch points. This distributed offensive capability means that the map on the wall in the Kremlin that tracks US Navy ships capable of striking the Soviet Union went from a few pins to a forest.

The impact of this on Soviet strategy must be significant. In fact the Soviet Union has been much more attuned to the potential of the cruise missile at sea than the West, and particularly the United States. Lacking aircraft carriers the Soviet Navy installed cruise missiles in their ships and aircraft long before the US Navy. It was clear during SALT I that the Soviets understood the potential of the sea-launched cruise missile fired at land targets. At that time, even though the US Navy was ten years away from introducing an effective, long-range, cruise missile, the Soviets wanted them banned. The reason is obvious. Maritime forces from waters controlled by NATO firing cruise missiles 2,000, or even 1,500 miles can reach Eastern Europe and the Soviet Union. The same situation exists in the Far East and from waters close to the Soviet Union where in wartime submarines can operate. The Soviet strategist sees that cruise missiles can potentially rise from the sea from almost anywhere around the periphery of the Soviet Union. This represents an enormous defensive challenge.

That challenge, which during SALT I was only one of undemonstrated potential, is at sea today.[16] Recent developments in the accuracy of guidance systems means that cruise missiles will rival the precision of the best air-delivered weapons. Concentrated in great numbers they can be as destructive as small nuclear weapons. Their strategic value, thus their deterrent value, will be in direct proportion to their numbers available and inversely proportional to their accuracy.[17]

How will the non-nuclear cruise missile affect warfare and power projection from the sea and the Maritime Strategy? It will affect them in at least two important ways: the missile makes militarily plausible the execution of the first two phases of the Maritime Strategy and it will alter the tactics of forward strategy.

In conflict with the Soviet Union, deterrence, seizure of the initiative and avoidance of escalation to the use of nuclear weapons are strategic objectives. To be successful in both their deterrent and warfighting roles, maritime forces must be credible. They must be able to deliver ordnance with high confidence. Adversaries must believe in and fear potential weapon effectiveness. The accurate, non-nuclear cruise missile will deliver ordnance that does not have to be nuclear to be effective.

The Soviets are also aware that the world-wide development and proliferation of effective air defenses has put the US Navy on the horns of a dilemma. Since 7 December 1941 the US Navy's best means of projecting power has been from an airplane launched from an aircraft carrier. Now the twin issues of mission accomplishment and aircraft attrition are being debated. Manned aircraft versus Soviet anti-air warfare defenses is the main issue but is not the only threat. Modern air defenses are not just the province of the Soviet Union. Any nation can procure highly effective, inexpensive, portable, easily employed weapons in the world market. Manned aircraft are at risk in almost any combat situation.

To counter sophisticated air defense systems, expensive defense sup-pression weapons have been developed. These systems are effective but they have become a tactical and cost 'overhead' of aircraft strikes. Aircraft that carry suppression weapons are not carrying ordnance to strike targets. Stealthy aircraft are also on the drawing boards to counter modern defenses, but will they be silver bullets? Are they to be affordable in numbers? 'Stand off' weapons allow aircraft to launch their ordnance from outside defense zones. Does this not make the airplane an expensive missile booster? The combat utility of the airplane is its unrivaled ability to mass and put a lot of ordnance on target in a short period of time. Defensive technology directed at the manned aircraft is cutting into that capability.

Perhaps even more critical than aircraft attrition, particularly in peace-time, are the consequences of hostages and casualties. It is a political, not military decision to use force in the Third World against a terrorist target or to get the attention of a malevolent state. A conventionally armed cruise missile leaves no prisoners. If it is also surgically accurate or, in numbers, devastatingly effective will it replace the airplane as a weapon of choice in peacetime?

Finally, the non-nuclear cruise missile brings new dimensions to the meaning of 'forward' in a forward strategy. In the NATO context ordnance from warships can now be delivered to the flanks and to the Central Front from such dispersed places as fifty miles off Cape Fear, the Bay of Biscay and the Gulf of Genoa. This means that the Navy can support forces defending northern Norway without first defeating the submarine threat in the Norwegian Sea. NATO land forces in the central region could receive deep interdiction support from ships in the Mediterranean. Targets in highly defended areas where manned aircraft attrition would be unacceptably high are now vulnerable to attack by cruise missiles.

In summary, the Maritime Strategy is changing as the world changes. The single most important change has been the introduction of a long-range, accurate, non-nuclear cruise missile. The HMS *Dreadnought* at the dawn of the twentieth century revolutionized naval warfare by extending the battle space of warships from yards to miles; the cruise missile will extend the firepower of maritime forces from miles to hundreds of miles. The challenge is that the land and the naval strategists must come to grips with the cruise missile. It is the engine of transition in the Maritime Strategy. Whatever the outcome of the debate, the genie is out of the bottle. . . .

The Maritime Strategy – an historical comment
Ian McGeoch

The Maritime Strategy is, in Admiral Metcalfe's words, 'a warfighting concept', and as such 'it is a resource allocation guide, a guide for planning naval operations and a policy statement to the Soviets and US allies.' But, 'to remain viable the Strategy must evolve with changes in the warfighting environment'. Quite so. Remembering the immortal words of J. P. Jones himself: 'Without a Respectable Navy . . . alas America!', the question which Admiral Metcalfe has posed, therefore, is: 'Given all the changes now taking place – in the warfighting environment, in the perception of the threat, in "the realities of the Third World and fiscal priorities" – what should a respectable [US] Navy look like?' For what is under discussion is not 'maritime strategy', or even 'a maritime strategy', but 'The Maritime Strategy of the United States'. As Britain's Admiral Fisher put it before the First World War, 'strategy governs ships – weapons govern tactics'. The shape and size of a 'respectable' American Navy is governed, therefore, by 'The Maritime Strategy'. Hence it is critically important to know that: 'Although the Maritime Strategy deals primarily with the Soviet Union, the concepts are just as easily applied to Mr Gadaffi and Libya' and that 'to those who would promote instability and trouble in the world' the warfighting fist of the strategy is 'in the details of deployment, employment, tactics and weapons'.

According to Admiral Metcalf, these concepts (as listed in Figure 11:1) constitute 'The Maritime Component of the US National Military Strategy' (unclassified version, 1989), 'Forward deployment of forces is the fundamental warfighting principle of the Maritime Strategy. The United States Navy will take the fight to an adversary rather than wait for the war to come to the Navy.'

This is the offensive spirit made flesh. Winston Churchill, in his capacity as First Lord of the Admiralty, would have approved – but would he have been wise to do so, unconditionally? What about the Dardanelles disaster? What about the failure to introduce convoy? And in the Second World War, what about sending fleet aircraft carriers to hunt U-boats, with the immediate loss of HMS *Courageous* and the near miss on HMS *Ark Royal*? What about the priority given to bombing Germany over the provision of long-range aircraft to close the convoy escort gap in the Battle of the Atlantic, which was thereby almost lost? What about the futile sacrifice of the *Prince of Wales* and *Repulse*, sent into action without an aircraft carrier in support or adequate shore-based air cover? What, for that matter, about the long-planned Japanese pre-emptive strike on Pearl Harbor, which not only failed to sink a single aircraft carrier, whereby the Imperial Japanese Navy signed its own death warrant, but brought into being the coalition which ensured the total defeat of Japan and her Axis allies.

So let us take for granted the determination of the American Navy, however constituted, to get to grips with the enemy, and leave aside the offensive rhetoric. In classic terms, the situation of the United States *vis à vis* the rest of the world corresponds to that of Britain *vis à vis* the rest of Europe, as outlined by Sir Eyre Crowe in his famous Foreign Office Memorandum of 1 January 1907:

The general character of [Britain's] foreign policy is determined by the immutable conditions of her geographical situation . . . as an island state . . . whose existence and survival as an independent community are inseparably bound up with the possession of preponderant sea power . . . Sea power is more potent than land power . . . its formidable character makes itself felt the more directly in that a maritime State is, in the literal sense of the word, the neighbour of every country accessible by sea.

He went on to argue, from this, that the 'national policy of the insular and naval State' should be so directed 'as to harmonize with the general desires and ideals common to all mankind', and that [it] has a direct and positive interest in the maintenance of the independence of nations, and therefore must be the natural enemy of any country threatening the independence of others and the natural protector of the weaker communities'.

Sir Eyre Crowe did not leave it there. He recognized that for Britain's security, predominance at sea was not enough. It was an abiding imperative of British policy that the Low Countries, with their ports, should not fall under the control of a potential and powerful enemy of Britain. Hence the long-established commitment to preserve the balance of power in Western Europe. The analogy today is with American naval predominance in the world, coupled with regional pacts designed to deny to 'a potential and powerful enemy' the ports, hinterland and industrial base of Western Europe, as the primary theatre, but also in the Pacific and elsewhere.

It is thus reasonable to take the view that 'The Maritime Strategy' is no more, and no less, than a phrase descriptive of American foreign policy. Since the end of the Second World War disentanglement from the power struggles of the rest of the world has no longer been a valid option for the United States. Both the geographical extent and the military power of an expansionist Soviet Union have seen to that. The advent of nuclear-armed ballistic missiles of intercontinental range confirmed the imperative. The prediction made by Alexis de Tocqueville, long before Karl Marx wrote *Das Kapital*, has come to pass:

The Anglo-American relies upon personal interest to accomplish his ends, and gives free scope to the unguided exertions and common sense of the citizens; the Russian centres all the authority of society in a single arm; the principal instrument of the former is freedom; of the latter servitude. Their starting point is different, and their courses are not the same; yet each of them seems to be marked out by the will of Heaven to sway the destinies of half the globe.

In this context, what the United States is called upon by the will of Heaven to do, is to maintain:

A credible deterrent to the initiation of nuclear warfare by any power or group of powers hostile to the United States or her allies and friends.

Non-nuclear armed forces, sea, land, amphibious and air, of sufficient strength to be a credible deterrent, in conjunction with those of allies and friends, to the use, or threat of use, of armed force by any power or group of powers in pursuit of any political aim hostile to the United States, her allies and friends.

The shape and size of the naval and associated air forces of the United States and her allies are therefore to be determined by their perception of the forces which they may be called upon to counter, in defence of specific strategic objectives the loss of which would be decisive. What are these objectives? Here, we have a paradox. The political purpose of collective defence is to preserve the independence of the countries that subscribe to it but, from the point of view of military effectiveness, the more nearly the allied forces can be organized as a single entity the better. In order to resolve this tension in a positive sense, so that military unity may be achieved through consensus, strategy should be founded upon recognition of the following first order strategic objectives as common to all members of the alliance, although not necessarily in the priority accorded as follows.

Defence against bombardment by:
  ballistic missiles, land-launched, nuclear-armed or non-nuclear;
  ballistic missiles, submarine launched, nuclear-armed or non-nuclear;
  cruise missiles, land-, air-, surface ship- or submarine-launched, nuclear-armed or non nuclear;
  bombing from aircraft, nuclear-armed or non-nuclear.

Defence against invasion by land forces, amphibious forces, airborne forces.

Maintenance of uninterrupted use of the sea for whatever purposes are indispensable to national survival and the successful prosecution of war, and in general to provide 'security to such as pass on the seas upon their lawful occasions'.

The assurance of continued access, on politically and economically acceptable terms, to indispensable supplies of food, fuel and raw materials.

The preservation of public order and the maintenance of internal security.

It will be noted that these first-order strategic objectives are defensive, relating to the national security policies of governments which have themselves repudiated the use of armed force except in defence. But, once attacked, the right of self-defence, and alliance undertakings, bring into being an additional first-order strategic objective to which the exercise of military strategy must accord primacy if the remainder are to be achieved, namely, the destruction or neutralization of the hostile armed forces and hence the capacity of the aggressor to continue the war.

The strength of an alliance is proportional to the enhancement of the security which it confers upon its members; that is to say the extent to which, by combining resources, the first-order strategic objectives of each ally can be made more secure, or maintained with greater economy of force. It follows that alliance planning, as for example in NATO, should seek to bring superior forces to bear on those of the enemy which most immediately threaten first-order strategic objectives. It is axiomatic that no plan is valid, the aim of which cannot be expected to be achieved with the forces allocated, in the circumstances prevailing. What constitutes 'superior forces' in any given situation is the most difficult question to answer; rigorous planning should assume that, unit for comparable unit, the fighting power of the enemy is equivalent to one's own. Surprise may be exploited, in space and time, and technological surprise in countermeasures, or counter countermeasures. Above all, planning should involve the combination of all arms to the best possible effect.

As Admiral Metcalfe pointed out, 'about the only thing that has not changed in warfare since Caesar landed in Dover is that man with a weapon is still required to occupy territory'. And, apart from bombardment by one means or another, invasion is the threat feared most by sovereign states. Hence the primacy accorded, in NATO strategy, to the deployment of land forces on the Central Front where they can engage invading forces at once. Hence, also, the primacy which should be accorded, in NATO strategy, to the maintenance of uninterrupted use of the sea for reinforcing and resupplying from North America and elsewhere the alliance land forces, and for the transportation of essential foodstuffs, goods, materials and oil.

Since the advent of the nuclear-powered submarine, capable of remaining fully submerged and almost undetectable for weeks on end, and the long-range aircraft which from remote bases can strike shipping in mid-ocean, the protection of shipping has seemed to present an almost insoluble problem. The US Navy's preferred solution, namely 'forward deployment of forces', seeks to bottle up the enemy's submarines, by mining and anti-submarine submarine patrols; and to reduce the air threat to manageable proportions by bombarding the hostile airfields and installations.

But it is inconceivable that a force of submarines, capable of running as silently as one's own, could be bottled up by anti-submarines, since the outcome of every encounter between one of one's own and a hostile submarine might go either way – the odds being even.

On the other hand, it cannot be too strongly emphasized that fully submerged submarines cannot operate as a concentrated force, tactically, owing to the constraint of the relatively slow speed of sound in water, which precludes the reliable exchange of position and other data between submarines rapidly enough for cohesive manoeuvre. In consequence, the saturation of convoy escorts by U-boat 'wolf-packs', operating on the surface, which proved so effective in the Second World War Battle of the Atlantic, could hardly recur. Furthermore, the nuclear-powered submarine, being capable of sustained high speed, could itself form part of the escort of a convoy today, using its sonar in the active mode, with a high probability of detecting enemy submarines approaching the convoy. For these reasons, it would be in order to regard the deployment of submarine, surface and air escort and support forces with convoys as carrying the war to the enemy's naval forces 'with the objective of achieving the earliest possible destruction of his capability to interfere with our use of the sea areas essential for support of our own forces and allies'.

It must be emphasized, however, that the sea areas themselves are of no intrinsic military worth, and cannot be attacked or defended. What matters is the shipping which uses the sea, and it is the shipping which must itself be defended against attack, by the destruction of the attacker. In the case of the submarine, which counts on achieving surprise, the likeliest place to locate him is in the vicinity of his target, the movement of which places constraint upon his own. The case of aircraft attack is different: first, because their movements can rarely be concealed for long; secondly, because their radius of action constrains their operations – and thirdly because concentrated air attack is feasible, and might be timed to coincide with submarine attack. Nevertheless, as with attacking submarines, the likeliest place to be sure of engaging hostile aircraft is in the vicinity of their target, with the advantage in both cases thereby facilitating the concentration of force needed to meet the enemy.

'I consider the protection of trade the most essential service that can be performed', wrote Nelson, and no doubt the leaders of the US Navy would agree. The difference of opinion, if any, would be in the method of achieving such protection. It is worth while recalling, when considering this, the experience of early 1942 when a dozen German U-boats, at the most, destroyed in the month of March alone twenty-eight ships of 159,340 tons off the eastern seaboard of the United States, and fifteen more of 92,321 tons in the Gulf and Caribbean commands.[18] No U-boats were sunk in those areas during this period because the shipping was sailing independently. Where is the evidence that, for example, Soviet submarines deployed forward at the outbreak of hostilities would not wreak havoc similarly on independently sailed shipping, and without themselves being brought to action?

It sounds fine to say 'the US Navy will take the fight to an adversary rather than wait for the war to come to the Navy', but macho sentiments are no substitute for sound strategy. Nevertheless, the mighty power of the US carrier battle groups which form the backbone of the NATO Striking Fleet Atlantic demonstrated recently in Exercise 'Teamwork 88' the effectiveness of forward deployment in providing cover for the transit and landing of an amphibious force 15,000 strong in northern Norway. And in so doing the NATO fleet would undoubtedly have drawn into battle a large proportion of the enemy's forces which might otherwise have been deployed against shipping in the Atlantic. But, as we have seen, quite a small anti-shipping force can bring about critical losses if directly protective measures are non-existent. 'Forward deployment' should most emphatically not, therefore, preclude adequate protection of shipping. And because the United States and its NATO allies between them now possess barely enough ocean-going shipping of the required types to meet the minimum strategic needs, failure to organize and protect shipping worldwide would risk the interruption of sea use with consequent defeat of the alliance.

Of the many factors which are currently changing the 'warfighting environment' Admiral Metcalf states with conviction that:

the long-range, non-nuclear cruise missile has arrived with accuracy to rival the precision of the best air-delivered weapons. This weapon more than any other factor, political, economic or fiscal will change warfare at sea and thus the Maritime Strategy . . . The cruise missile became part of a 'revolution at sea' in the United States Navy. The Navy went from 15 power projection platforms to a force capable of putting ordnance on target from on and beneath the seas and from hundreds of launch points.

Unfortunately, there is no prospect, as yet, of the cruise missile putting ordnance on submarine targets. What it can do, in the NATO context, is to enable warships to deliver ordnance 'to the flanks and to the Central Front from such dispersed places as fifty miles off Cape Fear, the Bay of Biscay and the Gulf of Genoa'. This certainly 'brings new dimensions to the meaning of "forward" in forward strategy'. At last the surface warship can have an offensive role comparable in importance with those of the aircraft carrier and the submarine. But can the cruise missile not be shot down even more easily than manned aircraft? Until we know more about the capacity and cost of countermeasures to cruise missiles it is too soon to go all the way with Admiral Metcalfe.

NOTES AND REFERENCES

1. The term 600-ship Navy was an invention of Vice-Adm. Stasser Holcomb who at times was Director, Systems Analysis Division, OP–96 to Adm. Thomas B. Hayward. He was responding to a particularly inane Office of the Secretary of Defence question: 'how big should the Navy be?'. The response was '600 ships'. The number has stood the test of time and constant analysis, so it must be considered 'about right'.
2. *NWP – 1* (*U.S. Navy Warfare Publication Number One*).
3. Mao Tse-Tung, *On Guerilla Warfare* (Peking: 1937).
4. For an excellent, but brief, overview of the pros and cons see Capt. Peter M. Swartz, 'The Maritime Strategy in review', *USNI Proceedings*, February 1987.
5. 'The maritime component of the U.S. national military strategy', 1989, unclassified version, Office of the Chief of Naval Operations, The Pentagon, Washington DC, slide 15.
6. John E. Lehman, Jr, *Command Of The Seas* (New York: Scribner, 1988), p. 128.
7. House Committee on Armed Services, *Hearing on Military Posture and H.R. 1872 (H.R. 40401, 429), Departmental Defense Supplemental Authorization for Appropriations for Fiscal Year 1979 before the Sea Power and Strategic and Critical Materials Subcommittee, Pt 4, 96/1, 1979, pp. 37–71.*
8. The introduction of the concept of the Maritime Strategy into the lexicon of navy programing came in 1981 when the author, as OP-90, requested that OP-06 prepare a Maritime Strategy input to the Program Objectives Memorandum (POM), which is a basic Department of Defense resource allocation document.

9. Thomas B. Hayward, 'The Future of U.S. Sea Power', USNI *Proceedings*, May 1979.
10. Carlisle A. H. Trost, 'Looking beyond the Maritime Strategy', USNI *Proceedings*, January 1987.
11. Robert W. Komer, *Foreign Affairs*, vol. 60 no.5, Summer 1982.
12. John F. Lehman, Jr, *Command Of The Seas*, p. 128.
13. Vice-Adm. Henry C. Mustin, 'An infinite number of hypotheses – and a finite fleet', *Sea Power*, June 1988, p.20.
14. Ibid.
15. Vice-Adm. J. Metcalf, III, 'Revolution at sea', USNI *Proceedings*, January 1988, p.36.
16. A 1500 to 2,000 mile cruise missile does not exist today in the US Navy, but the technology to build one is known.
17. Rear-Adm. W. A. Owens and Cdr J. A. Moseman, 'The Maritime Strategy: looking ahead', USNI *Proceedings*, March 1989.
18. S. W. Roskill, *The War at Sea*, vol. II, p.96 (London: HMSO, 1956).

12 The US Navy 1990–2010: problems and prospects

Norman Friedman[1]

INTRODUCTION

This is probably a watershed year for the US Navy. Under the Reagan Administration many of the gaps left by the post-Vietnam rundown were finally filled, in the overall context of a foreign policy which had been very nearly stable since about 1947. It seems likely that future historians will see the current changes in the Soviet Union as at least partly a demonstration of the success of that policy.

What of the future? Some likely lines of world development are already somewhat clear, in the changes in the Soviet Union, in the growing independence of Third World powers, in the rise of regional powers, probably also in the solidification of a European economic and defense community. The other extremely important factor seems to be that both superpowers apparently now accept that nuclear weapons are very nearly unusable in war, with the vital exception that they can be used to counter the use of other nuclear weapons.[2]

This last seems to mean that war, if it should come, would be protracted, more like the First World War than the nuclear blitzkrieg which many commentators have imagined.[3] The evolving political situation suggests that within a decade it may become much more difficult for war to break out with the sort of stunning suddenness now commonly imagined. Many have suggested that the underlying East–West tensions will go the same way, but that seems most unlikely, on historical and geopolitical grounds. It seems more likely that the world will return to something like its pre-1939 state, in which war was by no means inconceivable, but a considerable period of war warning could be expected. That would have important implications for the character of defense forces, and particularly for the character of ground forces.

For navies, reversion to an earlier protracted war stance would have profound effects. Since about 1955 the Western navies have operated on the basis that the only units which could be expected to fight were those already in commission, or at the least in partial commission manned by reservists. Ships laid up in reserve were discarded on the ground that they could not be ready to fight in less than six months or a year, by which time the war would already have ended. Similarly, measures intended for survivability were largely discarded on the ground that a ship put out of action was as good as sunk, because it could not be repaired to re-enter service in less than six or eight months. Mobilization of warship construction, on a Second World War scale, was unthinkable, because new ships would not appear until after the war had ended. These points were not always made explicit in the policy papers of the time, but they are very clear in retrospect. Fortunately, because they were not made so clear, they were not always wholeheartedly adopted. USS *Stark* is still in service because her design retained survivability features which a thoroughgoing review might well have eliminated as uneconomical.

It takes many years for policy decisions to wash through a large military establishment, particularly since those decisions are so often implicit rather than explicit. However, it seems reasonable to imagine that long-war thinking is coming back. Such thinking makes survivability extremely important, because a ship which can be repaired in a year may well still be needed. Mobilization is essential, because no democratic country can buy in advance the massive numbers needed in wartime. Nor is any democratic country likely to maintain the sort of warm mobilization base wartime conditions really require. The solution adopted in the past has been to plan the conversion of the massive *non-military* industrial base.

There is room for considerable optimism here. Military electronic systems are not too different in nature from the commercial systems which are manufactured in very large numbers. They are better, and they are designed to work in harsher conditions, but in an emergency commercial equipment might well be adaptable. Ships themselves can be built in modular fashion, and it seems reasonable to imagine that in wartime commercial metal fabricators can be ordered to produce the requisite modules. If that is practicable, then a small number of yards can assemble substantial numbers of ships from modules.[4]

What sort of policy should the United States adopt? What sort of fleet will evolve to execute that policy?

THE BACKGROUND FOR US NAVAL PLANNING: THE MARITIME STRATEGY

The fleet of the next two decades will reflect current political-economic and technological trends. By and large the former will determine its size and probably its operating level; the latter will determine its character. However, there is an important meeting point between the two. A fleet designed primarily to face the Soviet Union in a global war may be quite different from a fleet designed primarily to deal with Third World contingencies. The US Maritime Strategy of the 1980s calls for a fleet designed to do both, but the design of other navies, for example in Europe, shows that this need not be the case.

The basis of the Maritime Strategy as it is now understood is that power projection and sea control need not be alternatives but that they are, instead, two aspects of the same strategy. In a war against the Soviet Union, the United States and her maritime allies would threaten to project power around the periphery of the Soviet Union so as to draw out Soviet naval forces, particularly naval air forces, into decisive engagements. The threat of power projection would also limit Soviet flexibility in naval and ground force deployments, and above all would keep the Soviets from threatening Western control of the world oceans. In this context power projection includes forward submarine operations against Soviet strategic submarine in bastion areas, the object being to force the Soviets to meet an immediate threat instead of deploying at will into the world oceans.

Although it has attracted considerable criticism over the past few years, the Maritime Strategy is actually a recapitulation of classic naval thinking. For example, it mirrors quite closely British and US naval war plans of the late 1940s. It can be argued that, given the parallel rise of technologies both offensive and defensive, is not an unreasonable thing.

ECONOMICS

Most importantly, the Maritime Strategy, particularly as it applies to ASW, is a reflection of the hard facts of economics. Given the sheer number of merchant ships required to maintain connections between North America, the Far East, and Europe in a protracted war, it is virtually impossible to imagine producing a sufficient number of sufficiently effective escorts to maintain convoys on a Second World War scale. Yet the experience of the Japanese in the Pacific strongly suggests that convoy, which is the strategy generally opposed to the Maritime Strategy by its critics, fails horribly when the escorts are insufficient.[5]

On a physical basis, the Maritime Strategy emphasizes power projection forces: the carrier battle groups, the attack submarines, the Marine amphibious ships and their consorts. The battle groups are backed by underway replenishment forces, which themselves require escorts. In addition, as currently constituted, the US Navy includes sufficient general-purpose escorts (frigates) to provide some convoy support, in the context of an overall NATO strategy which includes convoys.

There seems to be very little question but that the US defense budget as a whole will come under heavy attack over the next few years. To the extent that the Soviets, under Mr Gorbachev, reduce their own defense spending, the threat which has been used to justify the US budget will shrink. At present the defense budget is the largest single item of discretionary spending in the federal budget, and the pressure of fears of the deficit is very strong. The question is just how this cut will be accomplished.

The problem is exacerbated by the growth of 'black' development programs during the Reagan Administration, particularly in the US Air force. These programs were never subject to the standard Defense Department reviews, and their production costs were not, apparently, ever included in long-term projections. Thus it is an unpleasant surprise to discover that a single B-2 bomber will cost almost $600 million, particularly when the need for this particular weapon has not really been examined in great detail. As programs have emerged from blackness into production, the overall defense budget has not grown to accommodate them. It seems unlikely that a major review, with heavy bloodletting, can be avoided on this score.

The other major potential source of short-term defense savings is manpower, particularly in forces stationed abroad (and therefore contributing to the ongoing deficit in balance of payments). In Europe in particular, large US forces reflect the fundamental strategic decision made in 1949–52 that the loss of Western Europe to the Soviets would be unacceptable. That decision was made when Europe was virtually prostrate, only beginning its recovery. Now Western Europe is quite prosperous, to the point that US troops stationed there cannot afford many local products. The basic strategy, and its implementation, have not really been examined for nearly four decades.

THE SOVIET INFLUENCE ON US MARITIME THINKING

The apparent changes in the Soviet Union may well occasion a re-examination. There are, broadly, two interpretations of the Soviet situation. One is that Mr Gorbachev badly wants to back away from confrontation for the next decade or so, in the hope that he can rebuild his country's economy. Once it is rebuilt, the Soviet Union may well return to its old threatening character. The other interpretation is that failure in the Cold War has convinced Mr Gorbachev that the entire program of ultimate world power is unrealistic, and that it should be discarded. Pessimists and cynics will adopt the first view, optimists the second.

A pessimist would suggest that Mr Gorbachev will forego the next generation of systems in hopes that he can have the generation after, or the one after that. If that is a realistic appraisal, then it can be argued that the West would be extremely foolish not to do likewise, i.e. not to cut current forces and current production in favor of research and development.[6]

It seems very unlikely that any form of *glasnost/perestroika* will eliminate the underlying hostility between the superpowers. As it currently exists, the Soviet system justifies itself too much on the basis of its supposed historical mission to support and protect the spread of communism throughout the world (i.e. our defeat by the forces of history). For the Soviets actually to abandon the idea of struggle against capitalism would have shattering, possibly fatal, effects on their own political system. Such problems might well push Mr Gorbachev from office. It is also possible that underlying geopolitical considerations mandate the basic hostility between the Soviets and ourselves.

One interesting effect of relaxation of tensions between the superpowers is likely to be the creation of a market in surplus advanced weapons, as the Soviets draw down their forces and also as they try to satisfy their need for capital to rebuild their economy. Given a less ideological approach to their own foreign policy, the Soviets may well see the disposal of weapons (such as anti-aircraft systems) as a very useful way of earning hard currency, and they may not really care very much about the ideology of the customers. There are some modest indications of such a trend in reports of the Soviet advertising of a new fighter as an alternative to the US-supplied F–16; the publicity accorded the MiG-29 may also be an indicator. One effect of such sales would be to increase economic pressure on the United States, since they would increase the sophistication of the Third World states in which US forces might have to fight.

There is an important caveat to projections of Soviet intent beyond the current period of relaxation. As China modernizes, the Soviets may find her a greater threat than the United States. Although the Soviet government is now trying to reduce tensions in the Far East, it seems unlikely that any Soviet government can give in sufficiently to fundamental Chinese demands that past injustices be acknowledged and (to some extent) rectified. Matters will be even more complex if the Chinese and Japanese somehow combine forces, since then again the Soviets are faced with territorial demands. Any Soviet government will probably find it extremely difficult to accede to such demands.

One other point is well worth making in this context. Ships and aircraft may well last twenty to forty years. It would be foolish to imagine that the Soviet Union will be the sole superpower three decades from now, or even that it will be the sole major enemy of the United States at that time. For example, it is conceivable that by the second decade of the next century the brittle Soviet system will have cracked in such a way as to change the balance of power abroad. Perhaps then the United States would find Japan her greatest rival. Probably not; but it seems wise, in a world growing less bipolar, to seek weapon systems which can be used anywhere, not merely in areas significant for their connection to a war against the Soviets. That has implications for the flexibility and character of future US naval forces.

THE THIRD WORLD

It seems very likely that the Third World will continue to be extremely unstable, and that the United States will continue to depend on Third World countries for vital materials. Therefore the United States will continue to intervene in the Third World for the foreseeable future.

There can be little doubt that the Navy will continue to be the primary military instrument of US foreign policy, at least in peacetime. The Navy is the only means by which US power can be projected abroad on a sustained basis, without the acquiescence of the country into which it is being projected. Land-based aircraft and missiles can, it is true, drop weapons far overseas, but they can do so only on a spasmodic basis. Troops can exert pressures, but they can do so only from bases provided by friendly and acquiescing hosts. Since US territory abuts few of the possible areas in which a future US government may wish to enforce its writ, it seems unlikely that the naval role will diminish over the next two or three decades.

Although since 1945 the Navy has very often been used in the Third World, it has almost invariably been justified publicly in terms of the underlying conflict between the United States and the Soviet Union. Mr Gorbachev has convinced many in the West that this conflict is abating, and that it is likely to abate further in the next few years. In that case, the major public justification for maintaining an expensive US Navy will dwindle, but there is no reason to imagine that the need (in the Third World) will follow suit. If anything, detente between the United States and the Soviet Union will probably provide the leaders of a turbulent Third World with more room for maneuver. They may also have more reason to maneuver, since they may no longer able to play off the two superpowers to obtain economic and military support.

Another important future factor will be the rise of major powers in the Third World (e.g. Brazil, China, India, South Korea). Several of these countries apparently see the development and export of weapons as a means of propelling themselves into the modern world. At present their products are still quite primitive, but one might imagine considerable advances during the next few decades. As a consequence, US forces operating in the Third World may, in future, face more advanced weapon systems, quite aside from any Soviet assistance they may receive.

STRATEGIC CONSIDERATIONS

If in fact the Soviet Union is more or less permanently hostile, then it may be argued that the only appropriate US response to short-term Soviet cuts (designed to cure the Soviet economy) is a combination of US cuts in standing forces (and existing systems) combined with substantial investment in new R&D. Thus the Soviet action might be a valuable window of opportunity for us. If the United States makes deep cuts in standing forces *without* corresponding investment in R&D, it will presumably be caught badly when the Soviets reinvest in standing forces after they have made the requisite economic improvements. There is, of course, a political problem: the Soviets are selling disarmament, not a temporary retreat. It will be up to proponents of continued US preparedness to explain, both to Congress and to the wider public, that Gorbachev's rise does not presage the millennium.

To the extent that naval forces are insurance against surprises, it might seem logical that the United States should cut standing ground forces while maintaining current or even expanded naval forces. One way to do so would be to emphasize the insurance, or stabilizing, role of US naval forces, which allows us to justify cuts on the ground. The Army will of course reject such a policy, preferring to trade Soviet tanks for US ships; one of the major issues will be whether the Navy can properly make the case that without continuing maritime supremacy the Army will soon be defeated on the ground in Europe.

In any case, deep cuts in the US defense budget will occasion severe interservice warfare in the United States. Alternatively, this warfare might be seen as indicating a need for (or perhaps an opportunity for) a new national strategy. To some extent this need has already been stated, but only obliquely. The high ground in such interservice warfare might well be a clearer strategic or long-range view.

Another important political development is the increasing indication of a desire on the part of the Western Europeans to unite politically, and to take control of their own defense (as indicated by the Gulf operations carried out under the aegis of the Western European Union). At present the Europeans are unwilling to increase their own military investment to match that of the United States in Europe. However, should the Soviets be willing to make cuts of their own, then the price might fall to a point at which the Europeans were willing to pay. The European problem is compounded by the possible effects of protectionism, particularly after internal tariff barriers largely fall in 1992. The Europeans may then no longer be willing to cooperate with the United States in buying and developing weapon systems. As a consequence the costs of US systems may well rise. This consideration should limit US interest in developing systems specifically for their export potential.

Neither of the present superpowers is likely to accept the risks of a major war because each has a great deal to lose, and because the political systems of both superpowers do not encourage gambling on that scale. That need not be the case over the long run. For example, some observers of the Japanese system of government suggest that Japan may yet flip back into the habits of thought of the 1930s. It is also possible that the Soviet Union can find a dictator in power who is so secure that he really can afford to gamble. Mr Gorbachev does not yet fit that description, but his attempt to restructure the Soviet government does represent a great concentration of power. Finally, it is possible that a politically united Western Europe might turn against both superpowers, particularly if there came a time when both were perceived as economically weak and as incapable of maintaining their military edge.

For the present, the great obstacle to any such radical development is the general perception that nuclear weapons can so easily eliminate a modern power. However, perhaps the most important message of the Strategic Defense Initiative is that evolving defensive weapons are likely to render nuclear offensive forces (at least ballistic missiles) much less effective. It is not clear that this is as yet practical (probably it is not), but it seems clear that such a development is likely, at an affordable price, within the next three or four decades. That would not altogether eliminate nuclear weapons from the international equation, since they could still be delivered by air, but it would greatly increase the maneuvering space available to the superpowers and to their rivals.

All of these features are likely to remain valid over the next thirty years, with the important likely additions of a more or less united Western Europe and a rearmed Japan as regional or global superpowers. It also seems likely that the fraction of world economic power held by the United States will continue to decline, so that over time it will be more apparent that the United States cannot maintain large garrisons abroad (unless they are paid for almost entirely by those being defended). Ultimately nationalism may well prevent the United States from maintaining bases in countries such as the Philippines. It is by no means certain that the Soviets will be able to operate their own bases freely in the Third World (e.g. Vietnam).

This logic suggests that the United States will find it most expedient to concentrate its national power in some mobile form, e.g. in carriers and their consorts, and that it will be forced to abandon all or most of its forward bases. In the absence of forward bases, naval forces may well have to operate for extended periods without very much underway replenishment. That should mean radical changes in operating practices. For example, carriers will have to operate in a way which conserves their flying time (in terms of spares and fuel). This projection would also seem to emphasize the value of nuclear power, both for the carriers and ultimately for their consorts.

This is not the only possible outcome. For example, the United States may be able to maintain a network of defensive alliances with advanced like-minded states, such as Australia. However, experience since the 1960s shows that such countries tend to withdraw access to their bases when that access is used for limited operations in the Third World outside the terms of the basing or defensive agreement. If the most likely use of US forces is in the Third World, then the question is whether the United States can ever really depend upon bases abroad.

Certainly the US Navy has come to rely heavily on forward facilities. Indeed, the current Navy probably does not appreciate the extent to which the US Navy of the pre-Second World War era, which was designed specifically to carry its facilities with it, has lost that ability. The Navy now resembles much more closely the Royal Navy of the pre-1945 era, which was so dependent upon fixed facilities around the world, and which was so badly upset when those facilities were seized by the Japanese.

The fundamental problem is really that the West's economic strength is best adapted to mobilization (which may be conducted over years rather than weeks). If we could see that war would almost certainly break out in, say, 1993, then we could begin a massive build-up which would swamp the Soviets. In fact, however, we cannot really expect war in 1993, or in 1995, or at any other particular time. War is quite unlikely, but the threat of war is continuous, due to the basic hostility of the Soviet Union. Thus the West must maintain steady-state forces, to the extent it can without excessive damage to its underlying economic strength. Incidentally, the impressive efforts of the first post-war decade, particularly 1949–55, did represent a mobilization to head off what was perceived as a very real threat of war in 1954–7 (as indicated both by the Soviet development of the atomic bomb and by the outbreak of war in Korea); they represent a level of effort which probably cannot be sustained.

COMPETITIVE STRATEGIES

'Competitive strategy' is one way out. If any sort of superpower war is very unlikely on a day-to-day basis (due to nuclear deterrence), then what counts is long-term rivalry. The West plays to strengths which are expensive for the Soviets to match. In a very crude form, that might mean that we are good at ASW, and the Soviets are not, so we should emphasize ASW. That crude form fails because there is no simple Olympics of warfare, in which our ASW is matched against theirs.

At a more sophisticated level, competitive strategy might mean a greater emphasis on maritime warfare because (a) it guarantees that we can buy enough time to use our inherent mobilization base, *which they cannot easily match* and (b) any attempt on their part to deny us the broad seas will (if we are clever) impose disproportionate costs on them, since high technology costs them much more than it costs us.

Here (a) is attractive because mobilization base costs less than mobilized forces, and because building up the mobilization base means building up US industry. It is, moreover, probably impossible for the United States to match Soviet conventional ground forces *unless* it mobilizes. Post-1945 history shows that the only other way is through nuclear weapons, but once the Soviets have such weapons our own lose much of their value. We cannot abandon nuclear weapons (in that case the Soviet weapons overwhelm us), but we also probably cannot really rely on them for solutions through escalation. In that case the only Western escalation solution is superior production: mobilization. This carries unfortunate implications in the event that Mr Gorbachev can cure Soviet economic ills.

There is also another approach. It may be that the Soviets can be forced into technological competition with us, and that they can be forced to build equivalents of systems which, although we find them expensive, they will find horribly expensive. On a primitive level, that might justify Stealth bombers (they will have to build a new form of national air defense, one might hope). On a more sophisticated level, it might justify SDI, on the basis that they will of course have to match it, but that production will be so expensive that they will have to make deep cuts elsewhere.

A skeptic would argue that the Soviets need not commit technological suicide. One advantage of their closed society is that they can *claim* they are matching us even when that claim is false; we cannot be so sure of our intelligence (or so willing to reveal it) that we can easily demonstrate the falsity of such a claim. Khrushchev's missile antics (including Cuba) are a case in point.

The economic problems facing a Bush Administration make some shift in national strategy almost inevitable. One might also note that it was Mr Bush who, during the campaign, mentioned competitive strategy (an idea under development for some years) as a way out of the current problem.

THE US NAVY OF THE FUTURE: INFLUENCES AND CONSTRAINTS

On the physical side, the US Navy of, say, 2010 cannot be very different from that of 1990, if only because so many of its ships already exist. There will still be large-deck carriers, and their escorts probably will be Aegis-armed cruisers and destroyers, not too different from those currently at sea or under construction. Submarines of the *Seawolf* class will probably still be in production, perhaps with a follow-on in advanced design. The other two major fleet components, the amphibious force and the underway replenishment force, probably will also continue much as at present. In none of these areas is there much room for radical change, if only because ships are expected to serve for three to four decades. The main potential for change would have to come from some major addition to the naval arsenal, comparable to the advent of the aircraft carrier before the Second World War, or to the advent of the modern amphibious force during the Second World War.

The main engines for change are likely to be demographics, stealth and improved electronics. For the US Navy, and indeed for the United States as a whole, demographics means a declining pool of military-age individuals. That makes manpower-intensive ships, particularly carriers, more and more difficult to man. The likely responses are either to move some carrier functions to surface ships which require many fewer men, or to reduce carrier manning by cutting maintenance and servicing requirements.

It is also possible to imagine a realignment of the US services, in which the Navy would be provided with a greater percentage of the overall personnel pool. That was entirely impossible a few years ago, since the United States had to (and still does) maintain large ground forces, including forward-deployed forces within NATO and in the Far East. However, should the United States be able to reduce those forces significantly, pressure on the overall pool might ease. That would be the case if standing forces could be converted into reserve or cadre forces based in the United States. Such a conversion might be practical in the context of a general relaxation of military tension in Europe.

Another possible means of relieving pressure on personnel would be to extend the use of women in the armed forces. Several NATO countries, such as Denmark, already employ female sailors aboard combat ships and craft. The Canadians have stated that they plan to enlarge the second series of their 'City' class patrol frigates specifically to accommodate female personnel. Without commenting on the merits of such practices, it would be unwise to look forward two decades without taking them into account. The effect of any relaxation of demographic pressure would be to reduce pressure for reduction in manning, and thus to reduce pressure for radical change within the Navy.

More generally, one might comment that reductions in the personnel pool make it more difficult to maintain forces afield, since most potential servicemen would like to be near their families. Thus it is much easier to man the army in Germany (which keeps its dependents with it) than to man the fleet in the Persian Gulf. One problem of recent operations has been that, with a relatively small fleet, ships must remain forward-deployed for very long periods. As a consequence, sailors are reluctant to re-enlist, and that in turn places a greater burden on the naval training establishment. It also, of course, reduces operational effectiveness, since experience is always very important. All of this suggests that the United States must either reduce its overseas naval commitments (which is most unlikely) or strive to maintain the largest possible number of combatant ships (to reduce the burden on a ship-by-ship basis). If the overall size of the fleet cannot grow, one might suspect that the appropriate trend would be to trade off non-combatants (such as underway replenishment ships) for combatants which can and will be forward-deployed. This particular trade-off probably has not yet been thought through. It would seem to make larger surface combatants, which need less support, more attractive than smaller ones.

Whatever its details, it seems unlikely that the United States will enjoy anything like a monopoly on Stealth aircraft technology into the next two decades. The US Fleet of the future will have to be able to detect and kill future stealthy missiles and aircraft. That in turn may dicate major changes in its composition.

The most likely change will be in greater reliance on cooperation between platforms, and between platforms and offboard systems. For example, no one looking at the B-2 bomber could fail to observe that it is quite large when viewed from above or below. That suggests that, however stealthy it may appear to a radar looking approximately edge-on, the B-2 (and its brethren) can be observed fairly easily by a radar looking directly up or directly down. A single radar of this type would gain only a fleeting detection, since the bomber would soon pass to a less favorable aspect for detection. However, a series of such radars, well separated and linked to a central data base, might well be able to detect and track the bomber. The same might be true of satellite radar.[7]

Cooperative engagement is already an important theme, because it permits a fleet commander to make much better use of his limited assets.

Another aspect of stealth, submarine silencing, is already quite familiar. The likely technological counters are already fairly well known: better signal processing of lower and lower-frequency sound; and the use of low-frequency active sonars (with large passive arrays functioning as receivers). On a strategic plane, the forward submarine operations envisaged by the Maritime Strategy may be the most promising countermeasure. It is possible that the most interesting feature of the likely technological counters is that they can best be exercised by off-board platforms, such as fast helicopters or VTOLs planting and retrieving large passive arrays relatively far from the self-noise of a group of ships.

Finally, there is micro-electronics. The most striking feature of recent development is an enormous improvement in reliability. There is now very little question but that, when a modern radar like SPY-1 is turned on, it works. That may seem odd (when the same applies to commercial electronic devices like personal computers), but it is really quite a recent advance. It means that as ships with unreliable (earlier-generation) electronic systems are retired, their successors will require many fewer highly-skilled technicians. Their electronic systems may also require much less in the way of maintenance workshops and spare parts. Both factors should combine to reduce running costs, and this likely reduction probably has not yet been factored into the cost of buying and operating ships.[8]

The effect of the new electronics can be revolutionary, a call taken up by Admiral Metcalf in his 'Revolution at sea'. Because it requires many fewer technicians per radar or per weapon, ships can dispense with the very substantial accommodations now required. Greater reliability can also mean fewer separate electronic systems. The electronic systems themselves can be much more compact. At the same time, the adoption of command mid-course guidance, as in the Aegis system, makes it possible for the ship designer to break with the classic arrangement of weapons launchers and directors down the centerline of his ship.[9] All of this means that in future warships weapons themselves, rather than electronics or accommodations, can dominate. Because they are volume, rather than weight, critical, modern warships often seem m˙ch boxier than their gun-era predecessors; they often seem to underemphasize their real mission, which is combat. The effect of change is to make it possible to devote a larger proportion of the available volume to weapons. Actually doing that requires some major changes in design and operating practice; hence the need to call for revolution, rather than simple evolution of existing ships.[10]

Modern electronics has another profound implication. Modification to existing hardware is often unnecessary. Instead, much modification is done by changing software. That reduces the requirement to modernize many ship systems. Instead, improved weapons can be accepted into standardized launchers (such as the new vertical launchers) while the associated fire controls are updated through software changes. This method will be familiar to almost any owner of a personal computer, who finds himself buying more new software than hardware.[11]

If indeed this implication is taken correctly, then the Navy of the future will be able drastically to reduce the frequency and cost of major modernization of its ships. Major upkeep will still of course be necessary, but the basic shape of ships will not change greatly over their operating lifetimes. In fact, it may be argued that ship designs will tend to last much longer.

That should mean that ship lifetimes can be stretched without paying a high price in operational value. That is not the case at present. The United States may well have to retire all of the *C.F. Adams* class before new *Arleigh Burke* class destroyers replace them. In numerical terms that will mean a drastic cut in fleet size. In capability terms, however, the *Adams* class cannot be modernized economically, and the ships are obsolete.[12] Even if the *Adams* class could be retained in service, they would not remain useful militarily (at least for their primary AAW mission). By way of contrast, an Aegis cruiser can much more easily be updated with improved software and new missiles, and she will probably remain viable even three decades from now.

Given world-wide commitments, the United States requires a substantial fleet. The unit cost of warships is rising, although with the new electronics that trend may reverse. In any case, the number of new ships to be expected each year cannot be very great. The steady-state size of the fleet is the product of new construction *and ship lifetime*, and the only way to maintain a large fleet is to increase lifetime. That now seems a reasonable goal. It implies that individual ships should probably be made larger, since a larger hull is not strained as badly as a smaller one, and also since a larger hull may make access easier (e.g. for maintenance at sea and for repair).[13] Larger unit size need not mean much larger crews, particularly if robotics can be enlisted for some maintenance.[14]

The other obvious future application of micro-electronics is a new generation of much smarter missiles. Current advertising suggests the emergence of a class of very precise (effectively zero-CEP) long-range conventional cruise missiles.

The great danger of reliance on very small CEP weapons is the supposition, on the part of their proponents, that they are somehow a usable equivalent of nuclear weapons. They are not, partly because they are likely to be very expensive on a unit basis (nuclear weapons are very inexpensive) and partly because it is unlikely that intelligence can be sufficient to support them. Their political attraction may be that a small or stealthy airplane can probably carry very few such weapons. Therefore, if each is the equivalent of a nuclear bomb, stealth pays. If a few pounds of HE in the right place cannot reliably kill the important targets, however . . .

An important issue here is warhead size and weight. Current carrier ordnance is limited in weight and dimensions by considerations such as minimum safe deck clearance. More sophisticated guidance and stand-off propulsion and control all subtract from the available weight. It is by no means certain that very small warheads, no matter how cleverly delivered, can always destroy the important targets, both at sea and ashore. For example, there is probably no way to place 300 pounds of explosives so that it will sink a 23,000-ton nuclear cruiser.

On the other hand, clearly something is gained by the more intelligent use of small warheads. In many cases, commanders will want something approaching concrete evidence that these warheads have actually killed their targets. For example, in war games commanders reportedly refuse to stop ordering strikes on ships until the ships are clearly sunk, even though the existing munitions are unlikely actually to sink their targets (they will more likely disable them completely). This problem is not limited to naval targets. It would seem, then, that there will be a much greater future requirement for what would amount to bomb damage assessment, both at sea and ashore. One possibility would be to provide more reconnaissance aircraft; another would be to sacrifice some ordnance for strike assessment devices aboard each attack airplane.

The political dimension of this argument is that *if* small zero-CEP cruise missiles are like atomic bombs, then a few surface ships or submarines can do the same job, in the Third World or the First, as is currently done by expensive carrier battle groups. For that matter, if the missiles can fly thousands of miles, why have the ships at all?

I have left out directed-energy weapons, because I suspect that, if they enter service, it will be as replacements for current point or close-in defenses. In that case they will not have the sort of fundamental effect which can be expected of the three major drivers listed here.

The Navy, and the entire US military establishment, will have to make do with less. The question is how the inevitable cuts will be distributed, and with what underlying political and strategic rationale. In the past, money has been distributed with very little thought of basic strategy, because the basic strategy was fairly rigid and was well understood. That was containment for basic security, containment achieved by deterring the

Soviets from challenging it militarily. The deterrent had to function most actively in Europe, because that was where Soviet breakout forces (the Soviet Army) were most effectively concentrated. Actual warfighting was a fallback position, and over the 1960s and 1970s the United States gradually and unsteadily adopted a position of being able to fight for a limited time in the event that deterrence failed. However, it relied on escalation to terminate any major war relatively quickly.

These positions were also adopted by the US allies.

Alongside this strategy, the United States also adopted a position of being able to fight a protracted war in the Third World, because it was obvious that pressure on the Soviets could not terminate many Third World conflicts.

Given these positions, first priority went to nuclear deterrence, in the form of SAC and the SSBNs. Second priority went to the ground forces, since they provided the bulwark against easy Soviet breakout (in the event the Soviets decided that the nuclear deterrent was self-deterring, as it has turned out to be). The Navy came into third place, because (aside from its nuclear role) it was associated with the least-desired outcome, a protracted war in which it would be essential to support forward-deployed ground forces.

The Reagan Administration began a tacit re-evaluation of these ideas. Building on ideas first generated under the Carter Administration, it decided that war would almost inevitably be protracted, and therefore that modernized naval forces were essential. However, it never discarded the tacit assumption that any future war would have to be fought by standing forces. As a consequence, very large funds went to standing ground and tactical air forces.

Because the change in US strategy was implicit, there was never any real national debate or national stock-taking. As a consequence, now that money is much less available, it is not so easy to decide on just how cuts should be applied. To the author of this paper, it seems obvious that the cuts should be in ground and tactical air forces, but that is not so obvious in political terms in Washington. In particular, the need to place sufficient men on the ground in Germany is very easy to understand, whereas the influence of two carriers 1,000 miles away is much less obvious. The real determinant of US naval strength will of course be the Bush Administration's review of basic national strategy.

The US Navy: problems and prospects
E. J. Grove

There seems little doubt that the two main premises of Norman Friedman's paper are sound, first that the East–West confrontation is going to diminish in relative importance over the next twenty years and, second, that the uncertainty of a threatened long conventional war is going to increase in importance compared to the uncertainty of possible nuclear use in the deterrent strategies of the great powers. On the whole I take a more optimistic view of the current changes in the Soviet Union than Norman Friedman. The millennium has not yet arrived but the Soviet Union has made some fundamental changes in its approach to competition with the West and the desirability of long term co-existence with it. It is even thinking of cooperative approaches to dealing with some of the problems of Third-World instability that are likely to loom larger as the stabilizing framework of East–West confrontation is removed. The world is indeed going to be filled with 'small violent countries' for some time to come. This means that US and perhaps Soviet naval forces are going to have a great deal of traditional peace-keeping to do: it would be good for the world's two largest naval powers to be beginning to think about how they might help each other if common interest dictates, as well it might.

As for the increased importance of what I have called elsewhere[15] 'long war uncertainty' there is little doubt that shutting off the nuclear escape route will mean that some old dilemmas will have to be confronted once again. Investment will have to be balanced between mobilization infrastructure, not least merchant shipping, and the armed forces themselves. As for the latter, the balance between active and reserve forces will need careful consideration. In terms of maritime strategy, however, the key choice will be, as always, between battlefleet forces and those forces designed to exercise command of the sea. There is absolutely nothing new in this choice and the clear articulation of the American 'Maritime Strategy' has just re-emphasized its existence. I must admit to be getting a little tired of the rather sterile debate of forward strategy versus convoy. *Both* are vital to the successful prosecution of a future campaign in the Atlantic for the foreseeable future

In the Second World War the allies did not follow a strategy of convoy protection alone. There was always a Home Fleet forward deployed from its base at Scapa Flow ready to pounce on any enemy heavy surface units that might sortie to overwhelm the light forces that comprised the convoy escorts. Both *Bismarck* and *Scharnhorst* were thus destroyed and

– excepting the tragic exception of PQ17 when the air threat prevented the Anglo-American battlefleet deploying sufficiently far forward – the *Tirpitz* was more or less effectively neutralized. Without the heavy cover of a main fleet the convoys could not have run. Equally, as Norman Friedman emphasized in his remarks, we need to get our history absolutely clear on how convoy actually worked. But here I must differ somewhat from his presentation. Convoy does not 'fail horribly when escorts are insufficient'. The Japanese never had anything other than the most rudimentary convoy system belatedly introduced and even this had some effect in mitigating losses as D.W. Waters' post-war research proved.[16] As for 1942 in the Atlantic, allied merchant ship losses did not 'mount steadily' that year. According to the British Naval Staff History[17] the story was as Table 12:1 as far as losses to U-boats were concerned.

The true lessons of 1942 and of the Pacific War are that independent ships are always at terrible risk even from the most limited scale of submarine attack. In the first half of 1942 thanks to the American heresy that badly defended convoys are worse than none the Germans were able to concentrate on undefended shipping in the western Atlantic and have a second 'Happy Time'. Once the convoy system had spread it was able to hold the situation against an increased U-boat threat and the convoy loss rate was always substantially below that for independents, even when absence of special intelligence made avoidance of U-boats much less certain. In 1943 the Battle of the Atlantic reached its peak and the U-boats smashed themselves to pieces against the convoy escorts. As U-boats were now too numerous to be avoided the combination of convoy and special intelligence allowed a limited number of escorts to be used with maximum and decisive effect. I agree with Norman Friedman that 1942 and the

Table 12:1   Merchant ship losses 1942

Month	Independently	Ships lost In Convoy	Stragglers	Total
Jan	48	3	9	22
Feb	67	9	2	82
March	88	0	5	94
April	69	4	1	75
May	111	13	1	125
June	121	20	3	144
July	70	24	2	96
Aug	51	50	7	108
Sept	58	29	7	98
Oct	54	29	10	93
Nov	70	39	6	117
Dec	33	19	7	61

slaughter of the Japanese mercantile marine are terrible lessons that must be learned but we must be clear about what lessons we are learning.

This is not to say that one should abandon the forward strategy and just build escorts, only that a balanced policy is required as we need *both* battle forces suitable for forward deployment *and* convoy escort groups that can cope with a threat reduced in scale by the activities of those battle forces. There are no easy ways out of this problem and we kid ourselves if we think there are, fully accepting that budgetary pressures will force reductions in force levels. Given peacetime tasks that are essentially concerned with power projection we should not be surprised to see the US Navy increasingly concentrate on its carrier battle groups and amphibious forces in its active inventory, and making its 'sea control' frigates the primary focus of cuts. There is little alternative to this and if the maximum number of frigates are maintained in reserve harm will be minimized. Indeed, perhaps a more wholehearted reserve policy might allow more frigates to be retained than otherwise. Certainly the emphasis on maximizing the number of active carriers will make it imperative to obtain the maximum possible warfighting potential from them by deploying them forward and early in crisis and war. In this sense far from undermining the forward maritime strategy, budgetary restraint will increase the emphasis upon it.

As Norman Friedman says, a power projection navy is going to be a crucial asset to allow the United States to face the uncertainties of the next few decades. Given the international situation described so well in the paper I agree that such a fleet might indeed be an even more vital asset in the next twenty years than it has been in the last. This will cost money and other resources. The spread of sophisticated weapons will mean that the US Navy will still have to make substantial investment in maintaining its technological edge. With individual platforms becoming more expensive the synergy between them allowed by modern communications becomes ever more important. Investment in secure C^3I may therefore be a most cost-effective option despite its relatively unspectacular nature. Technology may also allow better use to be made of limited numbers of personnel, a word used advisedly. Traditional views on the role of women in warships are luxuries that all navies are going to have to reconsider, not least the American, although it is far from being the most backward in this regard.[18]

I agree with Norman Friedman that the revolution in stealth is going to have fundamental effects on naval operations, although my perspective differs somewhat from his. I do not think that quieter submarines are going to enhance the importance of forward submarine operations, indeed I think one can more strongly argue the opposite. Instead I must agree with the remarks of ACDS (Concepts) at RUSI in 1988[19] when, in a most stimulating presentation, he said he thought the inexorable trend of the stealth revolution was to place defensive assets close around the things one was actually trying to defend. In this sense Admiral Metcalfe's 'Revolution at sea', based as it is on ever wider and more certain sensor performance and accurate three-dimensional picture compilation may well be undermined and we will find ourselves pushed back to what Corbett called the historical 'normal'.

I also agree very much with Norman Friedman when he points to Western Europe playing a relatively much greater role in its own defence. No European misconception is more dangerous than the idea that greater European defence effort and cooperation is somehow corrosive of the Atlantic relationship. In fact the Americans are going to make a greater European contribution a condition for the continued American commitment to Europe's defence. Europe's navies already make an enormous contribution to the joint allied maritime effort. The Anti-Submarine Striking Force, without which the NATO Striking Fleet cannot move, is a European command and multinational in composition. European officers command the eastern Atlantic and Channel battles on, over and under the sea. European forces are able to provide the lion's share of the close escort of NATO carrier battle groups in Norwegian waters as demonstrated on the recent 'Teamwork' exercise. Mine countermeasures is, of course a heavily European activity, given the sad neglect of this role by the Americans themselves. Underfunding here could have some serious effects on the forward strategy as it might literally undermine the fiord option recently developed in NATO exercises.

In such ways the burden can be genuinely shared to mutual benefit, and some of the pressure taken off our American allies. European influence in alliance maritime strategy and operations can also be exerted. The misconception that somehow the Atlantic can be left to the Americans is a most dangerous one and must be strongly opposed. Equally, joint European action 'out of area' is gratefully received by our American allies as supportive even when a relatively loose European framework such as that offered by the WEU allows subtle diplomatic nuances to be made between European policy and that of their American allies – not to mention between the policies of the individual European states themselves.

Norman Friedman offers 'Competitive Strategy' as one solution to the long-term American problem of maintaining US strength in the long term. There is much in the concept of investing in one's own strengths and in those areas designed to exploit opponents' weaknesses. The danger is that the competition might get out of control and help precipitate increased tension. To maintain stability therefore the armed competition that will inevitably remain between the great powers in the future must be mediated by some system of cooperative security. In circumstances where, as Norman Friedman correctly points out, all the pressures on fleet size are downward the US Navy has nothing to fear and much to gain from changing its currently negative approach to maritime confidence-building and dialogue with the East. If Soviet politicians and arms controllers want argument to reduce the size of the Soviet Fleet – and its archaic reliance on nuclear weapons – they should be given every encouragement. The spectre of exchanging tanks for ships as mentioned in this chapter is not one that is very real. The Soviets accept that maritime matters are best discussed separately. But, they insist, they must be discussed somewhere if the Soviet threat on land is to be entirely dismantled. I find it hard to imagine that by

2010 the American fleet, still the world's most powerful, will not be directly affected in some way by the process of East–West dialogue. It might well have proved by far the best way of maintaining that maritime superiority upon which Western security will still depend.

NOTES AND REFERENCES

1. The opinions expressed in this paper are the author's own; they do not necessarily correspond to any position adopted by the US Navy or by any other official sponsor.
2. This begs the very important question of nuclear or chemical weapons in the hands of Third World countries. For many years it has seemed unlikely that proliferation of nuclear weapons could be avoided, although in fact that has very nearly been the case (India is the major exception). Widespread availability of nuclear weapons would radically alter the world situation. For example, naval operations near countries possessing such weapons might be much more difficult than they are at present, assuming that Third World states would not be nearly so inhibited about using them as are the major powers.
3. The analogy to the First World War is taken because, in the presence of nuclear weapons, neither side will be overly anxious to force a decision which the other might take to require the use of its own nuclear weapons. For example, it might be very difficult for NATO to contemplate any invasion (or at least any deep invasion) of Soviet territory. The Soviets do contemplate a blitzkrieg, but their plans tend to require a degree of tactical success which seems unrealistic. The result might not be unlike Brigadier Hackett's stalemated *Third World War*, the ending of which proclaims the difficulty of achieving any decision in such circumstances.
4. Some recent developments make these ideas more practicable. The widespread use of data-busing should greatly reduce outfitting time and expense, since it should simplify wiring. The projected shift to electric drive would make it possible to place propulsion machinery in modules before assembly, since it would no longer be necessary to align long propeller shafts. It may also be that such power plants, which could be modular, would be easier to repair in the event of battle damage. Given multipurpose vertical launchers, ships currently considered in separate categories (such as AAW and ASW escorts) could use common hulls and power plants, and thus could benefit from mass production ideas. In the event that towed arrays remain the principal ASW sensors, sensor installation would be relatively simple.
5. This was true even in the Atlantic. It appears that much of the success of convoy in 1940–2 was due to evasion of U-boats, convoy providing an important degree of shipping control. Once enough U-boats were at sea – in 1942 – convoys could not hope to evade them, and losses mounted steadily. That is why the winter of 1942–3 was the crisis of the Battle of the Atlantic; there were always too few escorts, but now virtually every convoy had to fight its way through. The situation rapidly reversed in 1943, when sufficient escorts and aircraft became available, due to the maturation of building programs set in motion in 1940–1. I suspect that the 1942 situation

was fundamentally different from that of the past, in that the U-boats could cover a much larger ocean area than in, say, the First World War, and so could overcome the effect of convoy in emptying much of the ocean area of shipping. In a future war submarines would probably benefit from space reconnaissance, and in addition they might be faster than their average targets. It might well be 1942 all over again.

6. That would not be a new idea. About 1947 the British government adopted exactly this approach to the new jet and missile technology then coming into existence, scrapping a number of near-term programs in favor of those expected to reach maturity in 1956–7. The latter date was chosen on the basis of estimates of the time it would take Stalin to rebuild his badly damaged industrial base. These calculations were thrown into disarray by the outbreak of war in Korea. It may be that, given the extensive penetration of the British government by Stalin's agents, Stalin could be sure that the allies would not escalate the Korean War to a point dangerous to him. For accounts of British naval rearmament after the Second World War, and the effect of the 1947–57 plan, see my *Postwar Naval Revolution* (Conway Maritime Press/US Naval Institute, 1987) and *British Carrier Aviation* (Conway Maritime Press/US Naval Institute, 1988).

7. The present author would emphasize that these are speculations *not* based on any official data.

8. In the US Navy, this electronic revolution really dates from the Aegis cruisers, and thus it is not really reflected in current frigates, particularly the ASW ships dating from the 1960s. The new electronics also probably cost much less on a unit basis because more of the cost is in software, which is extremely inexpensive to reproduce (not, by any means, to write).

9. The directors need not be positioned to provide illumination from the moment of launch, as in current semi-active systems.

10. In effect, the revolution meant that all aspects of warship design should be rethought in terms of combat capability. That may not seem terribly original; however, in peacetime operations, a navy accumulates many design requirements derived from peacetime circumstances, and it is difficult always to review them in terms of intense combat. The idea is not new: in about 1907 a number of young US Navy officers, led by then Captain W.S. Sims, called for radical changes to the US Fleet to eliminate the peacetime features which they considered inimical to wartime efficiency. The result was the series of extremely austere (i.e. adapted primarily to battle) US dreadnoughts built from about 1910 on. From an organizational point of view, what the reformers accomplished was to shift responsibility for warship design characteristics from the materiel Bureaus to a group of senior line officers constituted as the General Board. It might be argued that the line officers were much more aware of possible wartime requirements than were the materiel men. For the officers' revolt, see my *U.S. Battleships: an illustrated design history* (US Naval Institute, 1985). Sims' biography, by E.E. Morrison, gives details of his fight for a battle-ready, rather than a peacetime, fleet. The experience of the 1907–8 world cruise probably supplied Sims with valuable ammunition.

11. Even when some new hardware is required, it can often be installed in an existing system at relatively low cost, adapted to the system by applying

new software. The key technology here is the data bus, into which new hardware can easily be plugged. Data buses (also known as data highways or data pathways) were the keys to the successful 'open architectures' of the IBM Personal Computer and the Apple II; on a very much larger scale they are also the key to future easily modified warships. In theory the shift to data-busing and the parallel shift to standardized software-controlled consoles and computers ought greatly to simplify both damage control (making ships fail more gracefully) and post-damage repair.

12. The ships are too tightly designed for major modernization, since their technology modernization entails replacement of major equipment, such as computers and radars. Too much of their capability resides in specially designed (and now obsolete) hardware. That is entirely beside the issue of their tightly packaged steam plants, which may be difficult to maintain. Ironically, equivalent modern electronic systems would fit into a fraction of the space taken up by their current computers and associated equipment, but merely to remove the existing equipment would be difficult. An additional expensive factor is wiring. As long as each electronic item must be separately wired, installation and replacement will be very costly and relatively slow. The modern alternative is to plug each item into a common data bus; in effect the ship is wired once at completion time and never needs rewiring. Even if the data bus must be replaced by a higher-capacity bus, that is much simpler than rewiring each major electronic item. The outstanding example of the effect of data-busing on modernization is the Danish Standard Flex 300, whose armament/sensor suit can be replaced in less than twenty-four hours. The key technology is a combination of data-busing and flexible consoles whose operation can be modified by the substitution of alternative software.

13. This assumes that the strains of operation at sea are the effective limit on hull life. It seems noteworthy that the US Navy assumes that current ships will last about thirty years, whereas the Royal Navy takes about twenty as the limit. Reports of structural failures in some older British frigates suggest that the British figure is not far off the mark. The difference may be in frequency of operation in rough northern waters. Given the emphasis placed by the Maritime Strategy on the north, it seems likely that the US Navy will find itself operating under worse sea conditions on a more frequent basis.

14. It may also be possible to reduce the load on the crew by emphasizing durability in internal construction, and relying on shore facilities more than at present. That was the justification for reduced manning in the US *Perry* class. For the United States, the main drawback is that the fleet may well have to operate far from any base, as in the Persian Gulf. In the past, base-like facilities could be extemporized in the form of the Fleet Train, but that seems less likely in the context of the coming demographic and fiscal squeezes. In 1987 a British firm, CAP Scientific, proposed a highly automated frigate with a complement of only fifty. The Soviets may already have gone in this direction in their *Alfa* class submarines, which are reportedly manned only by officers (and which are presumably maintained only at base); the problems of these craft may be a pointer to the practicality or otherwise of future low-manning warships.

15. See, for example, the author's *The Merchant Fleet and Deterrence: a study of the availability of shipping for NATO and national defence purposes*, paper

prepared for the British Maritime Charitable Foundation, London, 1988, p.2.

16. Interviews with D.W. Waters; he claims the graph of sinkings was clearly affected by the graph of number of ships convoyed; the more Japanese ships convoyed, the fewer sunk. Sadly, these graphs have never been published.

17. Naval Staff History, Second World War, *The Defeat of the Enemy Attack on Shipping 1939–45: a study of policy and operations*, BR 1736(51), 2 vols. The figures are from Table 13 in volume 2.

18. In 1990 the Royal Navy placed itself ahead of the US Navy with its welcome decision to allow women to serve at sea in combatant roles.

19. Commodore R.F. Cobbold, 'Future maritime needs and means' lecture presented 16 November 1988 and published in *RUSI Journal*, Autumn 1989, see pp.22–3 for section quoted.

13 The future of the US Navy: further discussion

Discussion at the Conference focused on two main issues. There was a debate about the alleged dangers of the Maritime Strategy which was followed by a discussion about the importance, or lack of importance, of forward operations against other naval missions.

The Maritime Strategy stirred some criticism from various non-naval quarters. The strategy was seen by opponents as being provocative, out of tune with the current state of East–West relations and dangerous because it would provoke the Soviet Union to escalation. In short, the Maritime Strategy seemed incompatible with the ideas on non-provocative, non-offensive defence being promoted by some for NATO's ground and air forces. The fact that this argument could be raised three years after the public announcement of the strategy itself suggested that the case still needs continual explanation. Although there are some who will not listen – there are, it seems, many who simply have still not heard the message.

Those seeking to explain the strategy made a number of points. First, that going forward was the only option open to NATO when NATO had so few maritime assets. Penning enemy forces in, and forcing them to draw back to protect their homeland and SSBNs from attack, was the only strategic option open when NATO had neither the resources to obtain sea control over and under the whole Atlantic or the capability to put a leak-proof blockade line across the Greenland–Iceland–UK gap. Second, the point was made strongly that NATO could not abandon any of its members. Norway could not be left behind the Soviet defensive perimeter. Third, the strategy had to be seen in the context in which it would be enacted – the United States would not move naval forces forward unless NATO was attacked and options for bringing pressure to bear at sea had to be considered against the reality of what would be happening in the land campaign at the time.

Opponents of the Maritime Strategy seemed to have ignored this question of context completely and seemed, to some, to be solely interested in removing any and all potential threats to Soviet security. Why the Soviet Union should be immune from conventional aircraft attack in circumstances when its forces would be invading Norway and, presumably, devastating most of Europe, was not clear. How Norway could be protected without going forward was an unanswered question. Why the West should not hunt Soviet SSBNs when Soviet naval analysts were stressing the importance of hunting Western SSBNs seemed paradoxical. Even stranger was the failure to put the Maritime Strategy in the context of a Central Front war.

The last of these problems was particularly striking. There are only a limited number of things that could happen in a war on the Central Front. NATO could be lucky and find itself facing a relatively minor attack – in which case the war might last long enough to make reinforcement and resupply by sea possible. Alternatively the war could go as SACEUR predicts – with rapid defeat for NATO conventional ground forces and nuclear escalation after ten to fourteen days. Even if SACEUR is slightly pessimistic, escalation would have to come sooner or later as NATO's ammunition ran out. If NATO needs to fight for a long time, removing the Soviet naval threat will be crucial to that fight. If, on the other hand, nuclear escalation is imminent on the Central Front, talk about the dangers of posing a conventional threat at sea in the same time-frame is plainly ridiculous. The Maritime Strategy ought instead to be applauded – precisely because it offers an alternative conventional option to nuclear escalation. The prospects of defeat for the Soviet Navy, conventional attacks on the Soviet homeland, possible escalation and a US capability to fight a protracted conventional war, even after Europe has fallen, all add to the risks inherent in any Soviet calculation to go to war. They also offer NATO options short of prompt nuclear escalation if NATO is attacked. Concentration on the dangers of the Maritime Strategy when, in fact, the strategy adds to deterrence and lessens the likelihood of nuclear escalation on land, is logically bizarre. It seems only to reflect a strange inability to comprehend deterrence and the real risks to security. In short, what appears dangerous in peacetime may appear less so when nuclear escalation on land is already under review.

The second, and clear, divide came between those who saw the roles of navies in terms of protecting merchant ships and those who saw the role of navies in wider power projection and deterrent terms. The problem here was that some still seemed to think in terms of Second World War analogies with a mobilized US industrial base providing ammunition, weapons and men to sustain a long war and massive quantities of shipping required to transport this over the Atlantic. The reality of 1989, however, was somewhat different with the United States itself only having sixty-day munitions stocks, sixteen to eighteen months required to bring US military production up to significant levels and six months required to produce the first 100,000 conscripts out of the training system.[1] With no equipment, or ammunition, to bridge the gap between the point when war reserves ran out and the time when new production became available, and with much of the, limited, war reserve stocks already deployed forward in theatre, talk of vital sea lines of communication to sustain a conventional war was unrealistic.

This was not to say that resupply and reinforcement by sea was not important. War might erupt in circumstances where the Soviet Union could only spare, or would choose only to spare, a limited number of divisions for offensive operations on the Central Front. War by accident, rather than design, looked more probable as existing Soviet hegemony over Eastern Europe broke down. Reinforcement would be important even in a short war and would become more vital as warning time grew longer. Certain equipment would have to come over early, by sea, to support early deploying units. The inadequacy of prepositioned POMCUS stocks and airlift meant that even with short warning, everything would have to be done to get some units over the Atlantic by sea, as fast as possible. If NATO was ever able to fight on past week two of any war, and if money was put into war stocks, resupply would become crucial. The real question about cross-Atlantic resupply was not about imaginative scenarios replaying the Second World War but about what had to be sent across the Atlantic in a relatively short NATO war and how it could be defended. The last mission was felt to be easier said than done given the number of Soviet units that could come out, if not otherwise preoccupied, and the difficulty of escorting 20–30-knot cargo ships when escorts were ineffective at such speeds. There was considerable support for an interim position that stressed the importance of the Maritime Strategy whilst accepting that some provision ought to be made to escort certain ships.

SUBSEQUENT DEVELOPMENTS

The Maritime Strategy is expected to be reissued in a public form in 1990. As might be expected from the revolutionary changes of 1989, some toning down of the overtly anti-Soviet and apparently offensive aspects of the strategy is likely. Although the strategy always stressed the role of the US Navy in non-Soviet contingencies, these are likely to be given even more prominence now. It is also probable that there will be some re-evaluation of the merits of anti-SSBN operations and the nuclear potential of US naval forces. This would seem to meet many of the criticisms of the strategy and should make it appear more in line with the public perception of a changing Soviet threat.

Meanwhile, the US Navy has continued to address the criticism that navies are unable to project power against a land power – particularly one the size of the USSR. The recurrent argument that aircraft carriers carry too few aircraft to cause significant or sustained damage is likely to be countered by increasing reliance on 'brilliant' weapons and new, sophisticated, aircraft whose capabilities belie their limited numbers. The new A-12 (the ATA – Advanced Technology Aircraft) attack aircraft is now reported to be large and long ranged. Admiral Metcalf's chosen option of the conventional land-attack cruise missile also continues towards fruition. Orders for the current Tomahawk are nearing the acquisition objectives set. A follow-on conventional cruise missile is projected for turn of the century service – although its future is not certain yet. Suggestions of orders for 10,000 plus cruise missiles suggest that these would have a reasonable impact on any power they were used on.[2] Similar 'brilliant' technology – offering very high accuracy – is being applied to shorter range stand-off land-attack weapons like the SLAM variant of the Harpoon missile and the AIWS 'brilliant', stand-off bomb. With US naval orders for Rainbow anti-radar drones again possible in numbers over 10,000, current development programmes seem to offer all the capabilities required to conduct, with the US Air Force, a protracted conventional campaign against any state that threatens US interests – including even the Soviet homeland if Soviet actions ever required such a response. Numbers of weapons planned seem adequate for likely target requirements.[3]

On the defensive side of the equation, planned improvements to SOSUS, the *Seawolf* class SSN and the new P-7 Maritime Patrol Aircraft, together with improvements in sonar and processing capabilities, continue to be used to justify the proposition that US ASW superiority can be maintained.[4] Though some systems may be delayed, the components of an improved defence against air attack, including Over-the-Horizon relocatable radars, F-14 updates, the ATF, AMRAAM and the AAAM seem likely to be procured (although perhaps not in the time-scales or numbers now planned) whilst longer-range SAM and other improvements may also see service.[5] This and gradual standardization of the battle fleet on Aegis-equipped ships should dramatically boost defensive capabilities.

Questions, however, remain about the size of the fleet that can be procured, the impact of arms control and the effect of further budget cuts.

The shape of the future US Navy depends, of course, on many factors, but current plans allow some interesting comparisons to be made between requirements and procurement. The US Navy, at the beginning of 1989, had the objective of providing the following forces requiring the stated numbers of battlegroup-capable and frigate type combatants:[6]

	Battleforce combatants	Frigates
15 carrier battlegroups	90	–
4 battleship surface action groups	16	–
Amphibious forces	14	8
Convoy escort groups	–	56
Underway replenishment groups	–	40

The surface combatant force Requirement Study envisaged meeting future requirements by procuring only one class of surface warship (the *Burke* and its variants) and using older ships for less demanding duties. The result would be, eventually, that older Aegis units would move to replace current frigates.[7]

This plan has had some problems from its inception. The most important being that, as planning only assumes five *Burke* class ships will be procured a year, even retaining the ships for thirty to forty years will only produce a force of 150–200 surface combatants. Of these 50–100 might be considered battlegroup-capable – depending on how effective they could remain with what degree of refitting. This force level will inevitably have to deploy less capable escort units in some battlegroups if the required nineteen carrier and battleship groups were to be fielded. The shortage of battle group combatants is, of course, not a new problem. As of mid-1989 there were only 109 cruisers and destroyers in the USN to escort 14 carriers, amphibious shipping and 4 battleships instead of the 114 required.[8] Thirty plus of these were of limited capability and, even by mid 1989, only fourteen out of the required seventy-six Aegis escorts were, as yet, available.[9] The future US Navy, like its present day counterpart, therefore seems likely to be limited in the number of battlegroups it can actually deploy in a high-risk environment

A happier situation can be found with submarines. If procurement of SSNs can be sustained at three per annum it should be possible to sustain the pre-Reagan objective of ninety SSNs and the current objective of one hundred should remain within reach until block obsolescence hits the *Los Angeles* class. The problem with submarines may be the cost of the *Seawolf* class with one SSN costing a projected $1.5 billion. This would mean that three SSNs per annum could cost $4.5 billion from a budget for ship construction that might not reasonably exceed the $11 billion averaged from 1987 to 1991. Completion of the *Ohio* class SSBN programme might release resources, but cost remains a problem here.[10]

The situation with aircraft carriers is more complex. Plans to order one carrier every three years from 1996 to replace the eight, conventionally powered, units of the *Forrestal* and *Kittyhawk* classes were intended to maintain the fifteen operational carrier battlegroup level when the older carriers had to be retired at the age of 45. Early retirement of the *Midway* and *Coral Sea* will reduced planned force levels into the 1990s. Thereafter, whether carrier force levels will drop below the level of fourteen deployable carriers set by President Bush will depend on how many of the conventionally powered carriers are maintained and how many are given a service life extension, and when. Interestingly, the age of the carrier fleet and the sequence of SLEPs so far, suggest that it will be necessary, still, to build new carriers from 1996 onwards. Flexibility in force levels in the medium term will come from decisions whether or not to get full use from existing carriers by extending their lives. Unless the carrier force level is to be reduced below President Carter's figure of twelve in the first decade of the next century, it will still be essential to continue buying new carriers from 1996. A further reason for continuing procurement could be the likely effect of stopping construction in terms of both the increase in costs and loss of capability that would ensue when procurement was eventually resumed. Procurement of more carriers can only be avoided by dramatic reductions in force levels (below ten) or by running some carriers on to the age of 60, if that proves safe.[11]

Just what can be procured, and some of the choices involved, can be seen from looking at the cost of current naval units compared with likely budgets. If we make a few assumptions, it is possible to illustrate some possible consequences.

Assumption 1

US naval ship procurement budgets continue at around the $11 billion level requested in FY 1988 and FY 1991 and funded in FY 1989 and FY 1990. Ship procurement reflects current objectives of five DDG, three SSN, one-third of a CVN a year, with amphibious and support forces procurement continuing in line with recent experience.[12] It is assumed that US SSBN procurement ceases after the twentieth *Ohio* boat and does not resume until the 2002–3 period – this eases the problem considerably, but will pose a dilemma next century if SSBN production costs have to be found again from the SCN budget.

Ships FY 1991–2000	Cost FY 1991 $billion
2 CVN	7.5?
3 CV/CVN SLEP	2.1?
50 DDG 51	36.0?
30 SSN 21	45.0?
Amphibious warfare ships	12.0?
Mine countermeasures ships	3.0?
Support ships/prior year programme costs	17.0?
Total Cost Over 10 years	120.6?
Total available	$110 Billion

This level of funding, over time, might sustain force levels roughly 90 per cent of those envisaged at previously planned building rates and provide 60–80 per cent of existing force levels depending on whether it should prove feasible to retain surface combatants in service beyond the age of 30.

Assumption 2

US defence budgets fall in real terms by 2 per cent a year until FY 2000. Budget cuts are shared between services with no priorities allocated according to utility. Ship construction remains at a level of 12.5 per cent of the total naval budget. The level of SCN (Ship Construction Naval) falls to $9.9 billion by 1995 and 9 billion by 2000. The total funding for ship construction for FY 1991 to 2000 falls to $100.6 billion. This is around 83 per cent of the sum required to meet current building plans and 91 per cent of the funding in Assumption 1. Over time, without even allowing for increasing weapons costs in real terms, this funding shortage would become even more acute. If the funding levels of the FY 2000 SCN budget were maintained for the next twenty years, and allowance made for the need to recommence SSBN construction in this time-scale, the total of SCN funding available over the thirty-year period might only equal around 70 per cent of that required to maintain a five DDG/three SSN/one-third CVN building rate. The decline in numbers of units could also be drastic with perhaps only 60 per cent of the present numbers of combatants available by 2020. Even this might prove an optimistic figure – if it proved impossible to sustain surface warships in service beyond the age of 30 (instead of the forty-year life assumed above) the number of combatants might well fall to nearer 50 per cent of present numbers.[13]

Both of these scenarios pose difficult problems. The second, where the Navy bears a proportion of overall reductions in the defence budget, leads to reducing force levels simply because it is too low to finance a five DDG/three SSN building rate. It will also become more difficult to maintain force levels as money has to be found for SLEPs for the *Nimitz* class and replacements have to be built for some of the remaining CV as they near the end of their extended lives. Under Assumption 1, with ship construction budgets kept at around the $11 billion level, problems remain but are correspondingly less damaging.

Whilst these crucial financial questions remain unanswered, some other questions about the size and nature of the US Fleet seem to have become clearer. The size of the carrier fleet that can be maintained, is, in fact, already shaped by the logic of carrier construction and refit dates and assumed lives. Maintaining fourteen deployable carriers throughout the 1990s would be possible if the *Midway* was retained beyond 1992 and the, originally planned, SLEP of the *Ranger* proceeded. Beyond this, carrier force levels will be determined by three other considerations. The first is the crucial difference between the number of carriers deployable and the total number in service. This gap will grow in the 1990s if the need to refuel CVN coincides with the need to continue SLEPs for conventionally powered carriers. If both of these programmes continue as planned, a twelve-deployable carrier fleet (President Carter's minimum) will actually need fourteen carriers throughout the 1990s. The second factor is the pace of new carrier construction. Because older carriers will begin to reach the end of the fifteen-year life extension gained from a SLEP after 1998, it will almost certainly be necessary to resume new carrier construction as planned in 1996, because, without new construction, carrier force levels will fall to ten by 2011 even if all current carriers are extended to forty-five years. The third key variable will be the number of CV which are given SLEPs. Early retirement for the *Ranger* will reduce the deployable force below fourteen for much of the period from 1992–7 – assuming other CV SLEPs continue and the *Ranger* is retired. Cancellation of the 1993–9 SLEPs for the *America* and *John F. Kennedy*, might look an easy way to reduce the deployable carrier force level to twelve from whenever the carriers were cut. There would, however, be longer term repercussions as these carriers would, then, no longer be available to sustain numbers until 2014. This would place an even greater premium on uninterrupted carrier production after 1996 and, even then, there would probably be a fall in carrier numbers below twelve in the 2005–10 period.

There are many permutations possible here not least of which, on one side of the equation, is the possibility that it may be possible to expand carrier lives further (or at least retain carriers in service beyond the date when they are currently planned to have SLEPs) whilst, on the opposite side, there is the possibility that unforeseen problems and individual ship condition may produce problems. Extrapolating from carrier life histories and standard assumptions of thirty-year lives and fifteen years extra from a SLEP, may, however, identify some of the consequences of various decisions. With all the caveats noted above, it looks as if the retention of a twelve-deployable carrier fleet into the next century could only require the planned refuelling of the *Nimitz* class (plus the, already authorized, CVN 65 refit) and the continuance of plans to build new carriers every three years from 1996. Twelve deployable carriers might be sustainable until 2000 even if SLEPs for the *America* and *John F. Kennedy* were abandoned, but it would probably not be possible to meet that minimum force level in many years and deployable force levels would rapidly fall below ten ships beyond 2005 if new carriers had not been procured. Modernizing the *John F. Kennedy* and the *America* would not stop numbers of deployable carriers sinking to twelve after 1992 but it could allow a return to thirteen deployable ships from around 1996 and a return to the current force level from 1996 to 2005. The difference between deployable force levels of fourteen and twelve in 2000 or thirteen and eleven in 2006 looks like being the cost of two SLEP refits – around $1.5 billion. A 14–17% increase in the carrier force level seems to equate to the cost of one SSN.

This may be an overly optimistic view. It seems likely that correspondingly reduced budgets for aircraft, missile and weapons purchases and for operations and maintenance will prompt further cuts in both carrier and other combatant force levels – the problem may not be in ship construction budgets but in manpower, operations and aircraft budgets. Indeed, it is notable that suggestions that the Pentagon faced a choice between cutting one-and-a-half army divisions or five carriers seemed to have been calculated, not on combat capability or strategic grounds but in terms of how to save outlays for manpower costs quickly.[14]

The situation for surface combatant and SSN force levels is, of course, less satisfactory. Numbers of surface combatants would fall – but it is already envisaged that this will happen and it is assumed that the battlefleet will be large enough to cater for most threats. Logically, battlegroup combatant availability would become the key determinant of the need for sequential operations in any future US – Soviet war instead of carrier force levels – but again this is inherent in the current situation where availability of CG-47 class cruisers must already dictate options.

Submarine force levels may be more problematic, given the high cost of the new *Seawolf* class. In this respect, it is notable that the FY 1991 budget requests only two *Seawolf* SSN and that proposals have been made to augment numbers with a cheaper SSN class. It might be the case that only two SSNs a year will be procured – with perhaps some increase as SSBN funding becomes available or a cheaper SSN design becomes available. It could even be that two other arguments will take off: submarines may be considered a lower priority as attention shifts to power projection roles and situations that do not involve the Soviets. It might even be that having argued that the *Seawolf* will enjoy a 6:1 kill ratio over opposing submarines, the US submarine force will find itself being challenged on the need to field 90–100 SSNs to defeat a Soviet SSN/SSGN force that by then might number only 120 units. Talk of reductions to a SSN force level of eighty by the turn of the century may be realistic.[15]

Some other pieces of the picture of the US Navy's future also seem to be taking shape. First, the scope for naval arms control involving ship numbers appears to have vanished as a result of the unilateral cuts accepted by the US Navy in its force levels. Removal of sixteen *Brooke/Garcia* class frigates in 1988–9 and the thirty-three DDG of the *Coontz/Adams* class from 1989–93 leaves the US Navy with no old warships to surrender and a growing shortage of battlegroup combatants. This trend spread to the SSN force in 1990 with the announcement that eight older SSN would be retired – well before they reached the 'normal' retirement age of 30 in some cases.[16] The scope for SSN reductions also now seems to be closing as reductions already threaten established force objectives. It is inconceivable that the United States would wish to increase these shortages further, just as it is improbable that brand new ships would be offered up for destruction when they too were still to come into service in adequate numbers.

Second, US naval choices when faced with cuts continue to reflect the primacy of the carrier battlegroup. Cuts in MPA force levels, reduced frigate numbers, retirement of older destroyers and cruisers and older SSNS, movement of frigate forces into the naval reserve, withdrawal from the NFR 90 project and proposals to eliminate half, and possibly then all, of the battleship force to save costs and manpower, all reflect a continuing emphasis on high-technology warships capable of battlegroup operations. This reflects both an assessment of the utility of these forces and a continuing assessment that smaller ships cannot meet the demands of likely threat environments.

Third, Admiral Metcalf's Navy may be emerging. Some of the carriers' mission may be being fielded by the cruiser/destroyer force and more may be as larger numbers of conventional land-attack cruise missiles enter the arsenal. The magazine capacity and flexibility of the DD-963/CG-47 and DDG-51 may mean that, where the requirement to put tonnages on target is measured in tens of tons rather than hundreds, and where the attack has not got to be sustained, surface combatants could, indeed, perform some of the carriers' missions. The carrier may find its missions becoming even more specialized: with surface combatants armed with long-range missiles emerging as capital ships in their own right. It is also notable that there have been proposals to build *Ohio* class submarines as carriers for hundreds of SLCM once production of *Ohio* SSBN finishes – the Metcalf tanker or the semi-submerged cruiser of other plans, could emerge as a submarine.[17]

Fourth, reductions in carrier force levels and retirement of older carriers into reserve will have one interesting side effect. At some stage in the 1990s, the US Navy could reach the total of twenty-two carriers designated as the prudent force level for a global war.[18] Though many carriers would be mothballed and might take one to two years to bring back into service, for the first time since the 1950s there would actually be the resources available to fight the protracted three-year war called for in some contingency planning. Another deterrent option looks likely to become available.

All of this leaves the US Navy at a difficult, and exciting, crossroads. Along one road lies decline: with the prospect that a smaller navy would be stretched to perform missions that now take up all the time of a larger fleet. Along another lies the unlikely prospect that the United States will contract its world role to suit the cloth of a reduced navy – history suggests that it is easier to cut forces than it is to cut peacetime missions. Down the final road lies a future where the US Navy could maintain its fourteen carrier force level for the cost of extending the lives of the *America* and *John F. Kennedy* and could increase its capability even more by fielding additional cruise missiles and some of the next generation of aircraft. The logic of the US Navy assuming a greater share of the defence burden as the Soviet ground-force threat declines, appears undeniable. The dilemma facing anyone wanting to cut the US Navy's carrier force is also noteworthy. This could be done by a combination of stopping procurement of the two CVN authorized for FY 1989 and retiring other carriers without extending their lives. Cancelling the procurement of the *United States* or the SLEP for the *America* might, however, prove too symbolic – without allowing for the furore caused the last time a carrier called *United States* was cancelled. Cancelling the *John Stennis* might perturb any president who recalled Senator Stennis's victories over President Carter's previous attempts to reduce the carrier fleet. Scrapping the *John F. Kennedy* early might be even more symbolic – to many it might well suggest that a decision to cut the US Navy was in practice a decision to abandon the United States' position in the world. The choice is there – it remains to be seen which road the Bush and subsequent presidencies will take.

NOTES AND REFERENCES

1. *House Appropriations Committee Hearing 1988*, pt 5, p.218; *Senate Appropriations Committee Hearings 1985*, pt 2, pp.639–41.
2. J. D. Morocco, 'Cheney orders reassessment of major aircraft programs', *Aviation Week and Space Technology* (*AWST*), 8 January 1990, pp.18–19; B Sweetman, 'USN to spend $10b on A-12', *Jane's Defence Weekly*, 20 January 1990, p.92; *Defense News*, 18 September 1989, p.3; *House Armed Services Committee Hearing* (*HASC*) *FY 1989, Title II*, pp.534–45, 581–3; *Jane's Defence Weekly*, 30 September 1989, p.636; ibid., 26 August 1989, p.332.
3. *AWST*, 11 September 1989, p.34; *Airforce Magazine*, April 1989, p.56.
4. *HASC FY 1989, Title II*, pp.493–6, 564–92, 969–1000.
5. E. J. Walsh, 'Carrier battle group AAW: navy upgrades layered defense', *Armed Forces Journal International*, November 1989, pp.77–85. *Senate Appropriations Committee Hearings FY 1989*, pt 1, pp.309–10.

6. *DoD Annual Report FY 1990*, p.144.
7. E. J. Walsh, op. cit.; S.C. Truver, 'Whither the revolution at sea', *US Naval Institute Proceedings*, December 1988, pp.68–74; *House Appropriations Committee Hearings 1989*, pt 6, pp.253, 297–302; E.J. Walsh, 'US surface navy plans ahead to 2020', *Armed Forces Journal International*, July 1989, pp.64–9.
8. *Military Balance 1989/90* (IISS, 1989), pp.18–19.
9. Ibid.
10. *Defense News*, 12 February 1990, p.52.
11. Figures for carrier lives and refit schedules taken from *Jane's Fighting Ships 1989/90* (Janes, 1989), pp.706–12.
12. *Defense News*, 12 February 1990, p.52.
13. Own calculations. See also *House Appropriations Committee Hearings 1989*, pt 6, pp.281–4.
14. M. Moore and P.E. Tyler, 'Services may face major changes . . .', *The Washington Post*, 17 December 1989.
15. B. Starr, 'Goodbye to 600-ship fleet', *Jane's Defence Weekly*, 3 February 1990, p.178; *HASC FY 1989, Title II*, p.1000; R. Holzer, 'Navy's 100-sub fleet unrealistic, Admiral says', *Defense News*, 12 March 1990, pp.1, 44.
16. R. Holzer, op.cit.
17. S.C. Truver, 'Whither the revolution at sea', *US Naval Institute Proceedings*, December 1988, pp.68–74.
18. Richard Halloran, 'Pentagon draws up first strategy for fighting a long nuclear war, *New York Times*, 30 May 1982; George C. Wilson, 'U.S. defense paper cites gap between rhetoric, intentions', *Washington Post*, 27 May 1982.

14 Arms control at Sea
Lawrence Freedman

Maritime arms control has rarely attracted the attention, resources and diplomacy accorded arms control on land. It has always appeared as the 'poor relation' of arms control, too difficult and not quite important enough to warrant the effort. Within NATO, which has a more benign view of sea power, the fact that the majority of actual proposals in this area seem to come from the Soviet Union seals its fate.

Richard Hill, in his excellent survey *Arms Control at Sea*[1] so diligently and patiently explains the impracticality of most measures of naval arms control that I intend in this chapter to pick on only two areas – both nuclear – that might merit consideration. To help both introduce these issues and explain the irrelevance of much arms control theory to sea power it might be useful to explore the tension between the values of arms control – cooperation, predictability, parity and stability – and those of sea power.

COOPERATION

The idea that antagonists can still cooperate is in many ways the basis of arms control. This cooperation might be tacit or informal; it certainly need not involve formal negotiation. It can be understood as setting rules within which conflict can continue to be conducted. In this sense there is no contradiction between arms control and sea power, in that there is a long tradition of maritime law which has had a similar objective, and can be reflected in measures to avoid incidents at sea. Where the arms control perspective is always useful is in encouraging attention to the implications of particular measures (such as, for example, the Maritime Strategy) on the perceptions and concerns of the other side.

PREDICTABILITY

Predictability means that known forces will be at known places at known times. This is the essence of the approach based on confidence-building measures which encourages such a familiarity with the routines, capabilities and procedures of a potential adversary, that anything out of the ordinary will immediately be noticed, and serve as a form of strategic warning. Sea power does not lend itself to the necessary constraints, with its stress on mobility, flexibility and the ability to pop up in unexpected places. It is about movement which cannot be readily bounded, through large open spaces over which no nation has jurisdiction.

PARITY

The idea of parity involves reducing the pressures for competitive military procurement by allowing both sides to claim that they are 'second to none'. It is a contrived symmetry. Agreement on parity has been easiest to negotiate when it already broadly exists, waiting to be confirmed through negotiation, and even then it is not *that* easy.

Naval parity does not exist at the moment. The forces of NATO and the Warsaw Pact have developed in quite different ways for quite different purposes and from quite different starting points in terms of tradition and geography. They may both have developed 'balanced fleets' but the balance varies considerably in each case. Within the total force mix the two sides see naval forces differently. Britain and the United States remain at heart maritime powers just as the Soviet Union is a classical continental power, more at home with land power and aware that its task on land would be easier if seaborne reinforcements could not be introduced by NATO.

A quick glance at the *Military Balance* indicates that any agreement that attempted to limit numbers or tonnage of warships, with sub-limits for different types, would be impossible to negotiate.

An agreement on numbers was reached in the 1920s at the Washington Naval Conference, but that was to use ratios of capital ships as a means of regulating the hierarchy among the maritime powers who were, at least for the time being, also the world's major powers. The normal condition is a competition for status between maritime and continental powers which cannot be regulated through a measure appropriate to only one type. The modern equivalents of the 1925 naval treaty are the strategic arms agreements which can use the modern equivalent of capital ships – nuclear delivery systems – to make the same sort of political point.

STABILITY

At the heart of arms control theory is the idea that it is possible to discriminate intelligently and usefully between different types of weapons. To those campaigning for disarmament all weapons are bad and all should be reduced to promote the cause of peace. Arms controllers, by contrast, argue that certain sorts of military balances are less likely to encourage war in a crisis than others, and so the task is to promote those balances that seemed the most stabilizing and oppose those with the opposite effect. It does not require that antagonists end their antagonism; only that they recognize a shared interest in avoiding a war brought about by military factors being allowed to force the pace of a crisis.

A variety of features in a military relationship might lead to a crisis getting out of hand before the possibilities of peaceful settlement have been exhausted. As often as not, faulty intelligence is as important as anything else. None the less arms control theorists have put particular stress on there being a clear premium attached to getting in the first blow. This creates incentives to pre-empt.

The size of the premium is relevant to the degree of instability around. The incentives are going to be greatest when the initial blow might be decisive. Much of the theory has been developed with nuclear weapons in mind, and in particular the sort of first strike which leaves the enemy disarmed and unable to retaliate. With land war it might be the sort of blitzkrieg which allows for defending armies to be caught off balance and quick penetration to the centres of the enemy's political and economic power. In neither instance can miscalculation be precluded: all that can be done is to remove the grounds for anything other than the most chronic miscalculation.

Discussion of this sort requires that we consider total capabilities and not just types of weapons. Attempts to distinguish between 'offensive' and 'defensive' weapons are even more hopeless at sea than on land. Defensiveness on land is often taken to be synonymous with a static entrenched defence, with the offensive defined through mobility. Warships are by definition mobile and can often perform a variety of missions. Thus the attempts to label submarines 'offensive' during the inter-war years by those who feared their role as commerce raiders was countered by those who saw them as providing an ideal system for coastal defences. Perhaps the aircraft carrier is the closest to an offensive system, in that it provides a means to project air power far from home while land-based maritime aircraft can provide more local cover. Yet if sea lines are to be protected far from home, beyond the reach of land-based air then the carrier may have a critical defensive role.

One way of considering defensiveness is as the concession of the initiative. Although pre-emption can be justified as 'anticipatory self-defence', and undertaken for essentially defensive reasons, the capacity to launch a surprise attack is generally considered to be the most significant source of crisis instability.

Naval power has been used for surprise attacks, which are, after all, often described by reference to Pearl Harbor. More recently naval power has been used to deliver surprise offensives against islands in the case of Turkey and Cyprus, and Argentina and the Falklands. However, these cases indicate that the risk of surprise attack at sea or from the sea is greatest in very special circumstances. These are as follows:

1. When political and economic centres on land are in range of sea-based systems.
2. When land defences are unable to cope with an amphibious assault.
3. When national survival is dependent upon sea control and this might be lost by the enemy seizing the initiative.

By and large the East has been most concerned about the first circumstance and to some extent the second, and has criticized the Maritime Strategy for accentuating both possibilities, while the West has been most concerned with the third. If we move through them in turn we find that in current circumstances none offer the possibility of gaining a decisive strategic advantage.

It is not my argument that capabilities to do any of these things are irrelevant: only that they cannot be decisive. The United States can attack critical Soviet targets from carriers or submarines, but if it lacked both carriers and submarines it could still attack these targets, and attacking them from sea or land could still not prevent Soviet retaliation in kind. Western amphibious capabilities could complicate a number of Soviet strategic moves, most notably on the Northern Flank, but these moves would not by themselves be decisive in a European war. If a future European war was protracted then the outcome of the next battle of the Atlantic might be crucial, but few expect war of this sort to be truly protracted. By the time the Atlantic battle was won the land war would be lost.

SLBMs

This issue can be explored further by taking the naval system that features most often in arms control, the ballistic missile-carrying submarine (SSBN). Given the underlying theme of this chapter it is noteworthy that SSBNs have largely been protected rather than controlled through strategic arms control. This is because of the well-established view – at least in the United States – that of all strategic offensive forces, submarine-launched ballistic missiles (SLBMs) are the most stabilizing. Since the early 1970s it has been a feature of American proposals that both superpowers should therefore be encouraged to 'go to sea' to reduce both the temptation and the fear of a first strike.

Despite – or because of – the fact that they are designed to deliver a highly destructive blow against the opponent's political and economic centres from a mobile and relatively invulnerable base, SLBMs appeared as the answer to the arms controller's prayers. On the one hand they were invulnerable to surprise attack; on the other hand, their relative inaccuracy meant that they could not threaten the strategic forces of the other side with a counterforce first strike. By contrast ICBMs could threaten each other.

Hence the bias in US arms control proposals, looking kindly on SLBMs while penalizing dependence on land-based missiles. In the 1972 SALT I Interim Agreement on Offensive Arms, for example, the Soviet Union was allowed to increase its SLBM force so long as it reduced its ICBM numbers. In the SALT II treaty, signed by Carter and Brezhnev in 1979 but never ratified, there were sub-ceilings on ICBMs with multiple independently targetable warheads (MIRVs) and on bombers carrying cruise missiles, but not on SLBMs. In the proposals put forward by the Reagan Administration in the more recent Strategic Arms Reduction Talks

(START), the main focus has still been on cutting down the number of Soviet ICBMs.

An important reason for this is not only the destabilizing properties of large ICBMs but the fact that the Soviet strategic force structure is dominated by ICBMs, to the extent that they provide some 70 per cent of its total nuclear warheads. As this is seen in Washington to constitute the major area of Soviet advantage it is not surprising that the Americans seek substantial cuts in this area. For the same reason the Soviet Union has been less than sure about the idea of moving its forces out to sea. Although it actually has more SLBMs than the United States (942 as against 640), it is far less confident at sea, reflecting its continental bias. This is indicated by the much more limited time spent by Soviet as compared to American submarines on patrol or on transit to patrol.

More seriously, while the Americans are confident that their submarines could survive a coordinated attack, the Russians cannot be so sure. Western anti-submarine warfare (ASW) techniques are believed to be superior to those of the Soviet Union. This may make the Kremlin nervous lest the relatively small proportion of its submarines on patrol are tracked and caught in a surprise attack. In response to this concern improved submarines have been developed as well as missiles of a longer range. This allows a much greater sea area in which to patrol, including hiding under the Arctic ice-pack which has attractions as a relatively secure sanctuary.

On a number of occasions in the past Soviet leaders have given some indication that they would like to address the problem of anti-submarine warfare as a destabilizing activity. One idea they have proposed is that of an 'ASW sanctuary', an area off bounds except for SSBNs. Defining such areas and ensuring that the sanctuary status is observed present formidable problems. As serious is the fact that while ASW may be destabilizing at the strategic level it is considered absolutely vital by the West at every other level (Britain, for example, is spending twice as much on ASW over the last two decades of this century than on its own strategic nuclear forces, including Trident). The reason has nothing to do with preparations for a first strike, but with the desire to protect vital sea lines of communication. Even if controls on ASW were feasible, they would not be deemed desirable.

The other main feature of SLBMs that once commended them to arms controllers is certainly passing. The first and second generation American SLBMs – Polaris and Poseidon – were inaccurate. This is not true of the new generation. The Trident C-4 missile, now in service, has been reported to be achieving accuracies comparable to those of the Minuteman III ICBM of around 750-foot circular error probable (CEP). CEP is the radius of a circle around a target within which a weapon aimed at the target has a 50 per cent probability of falling. The Trident D-5, soon due to enter service, carries some nine warheads each of 475-kiloton yield, with an accuracy of some 300–400-foot CEP. As it is planned to deploy more than four times as many accurate warheads on the D-5 during the 1990s as is currently planned for the controversial new ICBM-MX, it is surprising that it has not attracted much more publicity. This is largely because unlike the MX there are no problems with basing. However, criticism is growing that this sea-based ability to attack hardened targets from the sea constitutes a dangerous new development. From the Soviet point of view, an alarming picture could be built up of uncertainty over the reliability and survivability of its own SLBM force, with a continuing dependence on a large ICBM force that is itself becoming increasingly vulnerable to attack from the sea.

Nevertheless a substantial lobby has yet to develop against the Trident D-5. The controversial areas in the US strategic posture are the B-1 and B-2 bombers, and the MX Midgetman mobile missiles – not Trident. (One American colleague commented to me that the only thing that will stop Trident 2 is Trident 3.) It is difficult to oppose *every* new Pentagon project in this area, and the survivability point still counts for a great deal. Moreover, it is now hard to imagine a new missile being constructed that is less accurate than its predecessors, just as it is very difficult to imagine a deliberate decision to construct noisier submarines.

That does not mean, however, that Trident will escape controversy lightly. Only part of the strategic arms control process concerns the question of just what is and is not stabilizing. As we noted earlier, much strategic arms control has been concerned with consolidating 'parity' between the superpowers. A key question has been what is the best measure; launchers, warhead, throw-weight.

The very factors that encourage a concentration on SLBMs when the concern is with stability create problems when the concern is with numbers. An effort to keep the numbers down will be felt most keenly in those areas where the natural tendency is to push them up. A START agreement will include a ceiling of 6,000 warheads and 1,600 launchers. The Americans have sought a sub-limit on ICBMs at around 3,300 but may not push this, especially if the Soviet Union insists that this sub-limit also applies to SLBMs. The bulk of American warheads are carried on its submarine-based forces while with the Soviet Union the position is reversed.

In an arms control regime which penalizes MIRVing, the Poseidon missiles which carry up to fourteen warheads and Trident C-4 (up to eight) will become something of a liability. In a regime which penalizes launchers, then large SSBNs become a liability as is now becoming apparent with the *Ohio* class, which carry twenty-four missiles apiece instead of the sixteen carried by their predecessors. Current plans envisage reductions in the number of US SSBNs from the forty-one that were once maintained. The number of boats has already gone down to thirty-six. It may go down without START to as few as twenty SSBNs, and with START to fifteen, which, given the problems of patrol, will make any Soviet breakthrough in ASW problem even more acute. The same reasoning also applies to the Russians – the new Typhoon class carries twenty missiles. As it might be expected that the Soviet Union will find it unpalatable to make over-drastic reductions in its ICBM force it too could find itself more dependent on a few boats in such a regime.

All this suggests that in the future submarine-based forces might not do as well out of arms control as they have done in the past. The very factors that have served to encourage all nuclear powers to emphasize their sea-based deterrents mean that these forces will be at the centre of any attempts to achieve substantial reductions, especially given the disposition to maintain to some degree what was the triad and is now the quadrad of ICBMs, SLBMs, bombers and cruise missiles.

Looking further ahead it is being questioned whether SLBMs actually serve the cause of strategic stability quite as much as had originally been supposed. There has been a growing interest in the sort of instabilities that could result from problems with command and control or the strains that might develop if it were felt that there would be minimal warning of a nuclear attack. On these matters of SLBMs often do not score well.

BRITISH AND FRENCH FORCES

It should be noted that there is no demand at the moment to include British and French SSBNs in START. When the 1972 SALT I agreement was signed the Soviet delegation issued a unilateral statement to the effect that the Soviet Union would consider itself entitled to increase the number of its SSBNs if Britain and France between them should construct more than nine SSBNs. The American delegation did not accept this, and indeed the Soviet Union made no further mention of the matter when the French moved on to their sixth boat (bringing the combined total to ten). However, the 1972 statement indicated the presumption of a credit for the British and the French in the SALT I ceilings.

The propriety of including allied forces has never been accepted by the United States. During the INF talks the Soviets made various proposals linking their intermediate range missiles – especially the SS-20 – with the British and French forces, but this was generally viewed as being a tactical device designed to make a case for expelling all American nuclear forces that could hit Soviet territory from Europe. If we move into START II it may be difficult for the West to argue that while Soviet and American numbers are being severely constrained no constraints at all should apply to those of Britain and France, especially when these countries are modernizing their forces and multiplying the number of their warheads: the new French M-4 SLBM has six warheads, while Britain has ordered the Trident D-5 from the United States.

Britain's position is somewhat more delicate than that of France as it does assign its strategic nuclear force to NATO and uses American systems. Although it is inconceivable that the Conservative government would allow the number of its SSBNs to be reduced for the sake of arms control, as that would make it very difficult to keep one boat on patrol at all times, it might eventually be prepared to contemplate a ceiling on the number of warheads.

CRUISE MISSILES

An interesting test of the proposition that strategic arms control is generally permissive when it comes to sea-based systems has arisen with sea-launched cruise missiles (SLCMs). The Soviet Union has operated SLCMs since the early 1960s, and for a while they constituted an important component of the Soviet strategic forces. However, they were very clumsy to operate and not very reliable, and after a while US intelligence presumed that they were most likely to be used as anti-ship weapons. American negotiators did raise the question of their inclusion during the first strategic arms talks in the early 1970s – only for the very idea that they should be taken seriously to be mocked by the leader of the Soviet delegation who described SLCMs as being akin to 'prehistoric monsters of the triassic period'.

The exclusion of SLCMs from the 1972 SALT I Interim Agreement was viewed by some in the Pentagon as a loophole – which they then sought to exploit. The United States is now producing, or has produced 758 nuclear cruise missiles for deployment on 46 submarines and 25 surface combatants. However, far larger numbers of conventional cruise missiles are being produced for similar deployments but for anti-ship rather than land-attack missions. The Soviet Union is proposing a limit of 400 nuclear SLCMs plus 600 SLCMs, although separate from the global limit on strategic nuclear delivery vehicles. The United States has not opposed limitation in principle but demands adequate verification, a problem that is in fact greater for the Soviet Union than for the United States (at the moment) and is made almost impossible by an American refusal to tolerate its ships being inspected. This is in honour of the 'neither confirm nor deny principle'. If the Danes are not allowed to know then neither can be the Russians!

There is one school of thought which argues that it might be in the American interest to scrap its SLCMs, as the Soviet Union is now in the process of modernizing its SLCM force with the SS-N-21. With an open eastern seaboard undefended by any air defences, the United States is much more vulnerable to these missiles than is the Soviet Union.

TACTICAL NUCLEAR WEAPONS AT SEA

One area highlighted by Richard Hill for possible action is that of tactical nuclear weapons at sea. There has been increasing concern over the numbers of nuclear weapons to be found at sea and speculation that there might be greater temptations to use them at sea than on land – given the lower levels of collateral damage. Hill, on the basis of his analysis of this problem concludes:

First, there will be extreme reluctance on the part of commanders at sea, even in wartime, to recommend to their higher commands the first use of nuclear weapons. They will be unsure of their tactics, of the effectiveness of the weapons themselves, and most of all of the consequences of an escalated conflict. Secondly, there is almost certainly – simply because of the lack of precision in the tactical situations and scenarios – gross over-provision of tactical nuclear weapons at sea.[2]

He notes concerns about the higher risk of unauthorized or accidental use at sea without putting great weight upon them. I would add the inevitable scare that is raised when a nuclear navy is playing a major role in a crisis, as with the Falklands, that somehow nuclear weapons are going to get involved. Hill is reluctant to see all the weapons scrapped but makes a case for 50 per cent reductions. He then finds it difficult to come up with a workable verification regime.

This confirms the extent to which arms control generally, and at sea in particular, often appears to be about a very large verification tail wagging a small dog. It raises the question as to whether reductions might not be achieved by other means. If these weapons are superfluous to requirements we only need a formal, negotiated scheme before we can get rid of the excess. Why not reduce because the numbers do not reflect our own priorities and explore alternatives, such as conventional instead of nuclear depth charges. One of the most insidious consequences of arms control is the presumption that every reduction must be mutual, so that even the unilateralists make the case because of the exemplary effect on the opponent.

If we are moving into a period of budgetary stringency then there will be reductions, and it is best that these are organized according to our own sense of priorities and timed to fit in with our own plans rather than those of the negotiators. Arms control criteria can give us some sort of guidance during this process without everything being handed over to the diplomats.

CONCLUSION

It might be argued that these arguments fail to recognize the powerful political momentum building up behind arms control which, it is claimed, must soon embrace all aspects of military power, nuclear and conventional, land and sea. My own view is that the momentum is building up behind improved East–West relations, and that this can be reflected in a range of political and economic contacts that are, in themselves, generally more productive than arms control. Arms control is often an artificial enterprise that has the unintended consequences of giving trivial military capabilities and outlandish strategic hypotheses far more importance and credibility than they deserve. It has a point when there is an arms race visibly under way or tension is high and crisis stability has become a pertinent question. But neither side is racing very hard at the moment.

There is a case for attending to crisis stability well away from an actual crisis, but in the nuclear area this has been done. There are no serious incentives to pre-empt with strategic arms. START has yet to run its course and the conventional stability talks are only just about to begin, so there is plenty to keep the arms controllers occupied for the moment. It will be surprising if either area appears quite so promising in five years time, with a first START treaty still being digested and conventional armaments and stability talk bogged down in familiar detail. In these circumstances naval arms control will remain a not-very-good idea whose time has not yet come.

Prospects of maritime arms control
Richard Hill

In this section I am simply going to supplement one or two things discussed in the chapter by Professor Freedman.

Freedman talked about submarine-launched ballistic missiles and suggested that the idea of the Trident D-5 being used as a first-strike system was very largely a chimera. I would agree very strongly with that. The great point about the D-5 is that it is carried in a submarine which makes it essentially a weapon of last resort; and that is how I am quite sure it should remain and will remain. Any idea of using it as a first-strike pre-emptive weapon seems to me to be quite out of court, and should not form the basis of negotiation at all.

That then brings me on to the British system, which is also, of course, the D-5. I think it has been admitted by Her Majesty's Government that the theoretical number of warheads carried by a single D-5-fitted British submarine would probably be more than is necessary to fulfil the criterion of unacceptable damage which is the basis of the British seaborne deterrent. The only difficulty in fitting the right number of 'wooden' warheads and the right number of live ones lies in verification, and it does not seem impossible that this difficulty could be overcome if Britain were drawn into a START agreement, maybe START II. My only hesitation here is that things being what they are, Britain in my view would not start such a negotiation without France being part of it, and this does not seem very likely.

In this chapter Freedman does not mention the one type of operational arms control that does, or could, affect the strategic scene – and that is ASW sanctuaries. The notion of the ASW sanctuary should perhaps be very briefly addressed. Although the idea that there should be sanctuaries where SSBNs can lurk unmolested may appear attractive to some, it is in fact a very difficult proposal to carry through; moreover it is probably not inherently stabilizing.

First, let us consider practical difficulties. If you pick an area that is too large it is extremely difficult to police it; if you pick one that is too small it is open to pre-emptive strike. Second, what ASW systems are you going to exclude? Clearly this would be any such systems with a specific ASW mission, but where does that stop? The logic goes to the exclusion of anything that may have a surveillance or intelligence-gathering role and that might lead to the exclusion of all foreign forces. And that in turn leads on to a third question – what is the status of those areas in international law? The effect on rights of user even by neutrals is clearly very severe.

The problems do not stop there either, because, however restrictive the sanctuary regime, the owner state will want to monitor compliance. The mechanics of monitoring present great practical difficulties, not least because all the more effective looking methods depend on the degree of cooperation between the signatory states, between the sanctuary owner and the opposition, a degree of cooperation that would make sanctuaries quite unnecessary anyway. If you do not have that cooperation then you are thrown back on your own surveillance and, as is well known, underwater surveillance and warning is a business with many uncertainties and false alarms. A suspected violation would be extremely sensitive politically, especially if multiplied by the number of false alarms that you are likely to get. For this reason alone SSBN sanctuaries are hardly likely to improve mutual security.

Finally, of course there is the question of negotiability, given the asymmetry of the operating patterns of the two SSBN forces: the Americans far-flung, the Soviets in bastions (as it is said, and still generally agreed, though there are differences of opinion). The sanctuary regime would to a degree legitimize and secure the Soviet system while it would give no benefit to the United States at all. Even if the US Navy were not committed to the maritime forward strategy, it would be very hard to negotiate such a measure. For all those reasons SSBN sanctuaries do not seem to be a workable proposal for maritime arms control.

Leaving strategic systems, let us now turn to the grey area system, the submarine-launched cruise missile (SLCM). This is being addressed in the START talks. Whereas the Americans used to argue that Backfire was a strategic weapon, now the Russians say the same about SLCM: it makes agreement much more difficult to reach. The SLCM issue will probably prove intractable in those talks, intractable in exactly the same way as the Backfire bomber threatened to be in SALT II. One solution, though it is not a very easy one to work, might be that they ought to come back into the maritime fold, to be treated as maritime weapons. Therefore it might be necessary to limit their range quite severely, to make them clearly maritime weapons aimed at targets that were primarily maritime in nature, for example naval bases and, of course, naval airfields, particularly those that threaten the US Fleet. On such a basis it might be possible to include SLCMs in the category of tactical nuclear weapons generally.

And so to move on to tactical nuclear weapons: in my book I argue that there is gross over-provision of these weapons in the maritime field. I have done a few back-of-the-envelope figures and come up with total holdings for the United States of something between 6,000 as a high figure and 3,500 as a low figure,[3] and for the Soviet Union of 4,500 as a high figure and 3,000 low. I have no means of knowing how accurate those totals are but I would be a bit surprised if they fall outside that bracket.

It is not at all clear that the rationale for all those weapons has been carefully thought out; and it does seem that the more you have, the more the possibility of inadvertent use by people mistakenly thinking they could use them simply as war-fighting weapons. In my view financial stringency, rethinking, general cutting back will not necessarily lead to a logical set of reductions on either side. And therefore it does seem to me that this is a possible area for negotiation.

The basis on which such a negotiation might be conducted is that the criterion for holdings of such weapons should be that they are weapons of last resort, for use only when the side holding them is threatened with catastrophic defeat. I call it the desperation criterion. Trying to work out what the holdings would be, given that desperation criterion, is an exceedingly difficult calculation. There seem to be only two possible approaches. One is to say what targets you are going to hit if you are desperate; and the other is what your present holdings are and how much you can reduce them. The second is subjective; the first, which is objective, is far more sensible, and if you look at it from the point of view of maritime targets only (to include, of course, maritime bases ashore) the calculation suggests that a 50 per cent reduction on either side, even allowing for post-launch and pre-launch attrition, would still be possible. Clearly you would have to have sub-ceilings, possibly on above-water systems and under-water systems with a certain amount of freedom to mix, given the complete disparity of the two superpowers' holdings of these weapons. It would be an interesting calculation and it points up the need to arrive at an agreed database.

It is quite likely, however, that if a negotiation was entered into the first year or two would be taken up in working out what the true data were. With the horrid example of MBFR before us perhaps one should go no further than that. About the only concrete result of thirteen years of MBFR negotiations is the tie that the author of this paper is entitled to wear. Nevertheless, it does seem to me that if you are talking about these things you are at least bringing them out into the open. By discussing them in a rational way, you are to that extent alone reducing the possibility of tensions arising.

Finally I would like to go on to confidence-building measures. Lawrence Freedman has said in some of his books that verification itself is a confidence-building measure; and some people have argued that verification is an absolute block to reductions of tactical nuclear weapons for use at sea. Verification is certainly an extremely difficult problem. It does appear, however, that INF verification also looked an insuperable problem for a very long time. None the less, by a layered verification system including the factory gate, including stores, including verification of destruction, the negotiators did arrive at a workable, though extremely complex and heavily policed system. It does not seem to me to be out of the question that tactical nuclear weapons for use at sea could be subjected to the same sort of layered regime: that is to say at the factory gate, in stores and possibly at the point of embarkation. Observers in ships afloat would not seem to be necessary. There are various means of electronic tagging now available – for example, in the United Kingdom there is an organization called Vertic which is working on this very issue – and no doubt there are others in other countries. I have suggested somewhere in my book that if 1 per cent of the resources at present being deployed on R&D for SDI was employed on verification of nuclear weapons, then we might get quite a long way.

With regard to go on to confidence-building measures themselves, the question of CBMs on the Stockholm model of exercise declaration, applied to forces at sea, is an interesting one. The Stockholm figure is 13,000 troops for a notifiable exercise. Actually that is quite large and well above a carrier battlegroup complement, plus an underway replenishment group and a few supplementary ships. And if you get round to two carrier battlegroups operating together, then it is just possible that that is the sort of exercise that ought to be notified anyway.

Submarines are a very great difficulty here. Submarines are a very great difficulty in any sort of confidence-building measure anyway[4] for many obvious and not so obvious reasons.

Again, many people have said that the observation of exercises at sea is an absolute bar to any sort of confidence-building measure, but is that actually so? For a start, many people in the West would be very happy to be able to observe a Soviet naval exercise on the same basis as they were allowed to observe ours. On that basis, I think I know which side might get more out of it provided the arrangements were exactly the same for both sides. I would also say that we did turn over to the press at least (who are, after all a sort of intelligence organization) a large part of one Royal Naval Fleet Auxiliary in our last major seagoing exercise. And I would add that the Stockholm accords make it quite clear that the purpose of having observers is not to gather intelligence for their own side but to confirm that the exercise in question is non-threatening in character; and that is the basis on which they ought to be admitted to such an exercise.

Moreover, of course, there are the incidents-at-sea agreements between the United States and the USSR and now between the United Kingdom and the USSR; I believe a French one is about to be concluded. Those, again, for surface ships and aircraft are very satisfactory and working well, and could well be extended in their scope; but the submarine continues to be a rather difficult vehicle for inclusion in the agreements.

I should also mention question of linkage between conventional land forces and conventional sea forces as a form of arms control. Given geography, and given the asymmetries of the forces of the two superpowers and their allies, such a connection and cross linkage would be a very artificial and an extremely difficult procedure to work. It would probably run into exactly the same sort of problems as MBFR did, would sink slowly into a detritus of paper and is not therefore really worth pursuing. The Russians will wish us to pursue it, but even so in my view it ought not to be entered into.

As a closing question, how should we guard against the dire possibilities of either a catastrophic and dangerous decline in the Soviet empire or the departure of Gorbachev in some way, and perhaps the re-establishment of dominance by the military or KGB, or someone even worse? In the field of arms control at sea, the answer must be considerable caution in making absolutely sure that no negotiations are to our disadvantage. It is quite possible here not to have zero-sum games but to have agreements that are advantageous to both sides. That is the only way in which we can proceed. In short: limited agreements in this field are not at all impossible and discussion between the two sides is in itself, to a degree, an arms control measure.

NOTES AND REFERENCES

1.   Richard Hill, *Arms Control at Sea* (London: Routledge, 1989).
2.   Ibid., p. 115.
3.   This statement was made before the US Navy's announcement of a unilateral reduction in nuclear weapons holdings in April 1989.
4.   The problem of submarine notification is discussed in Hill, op. cit., pp. 198–9.

Maritime arms control could certainly be a major influence on the the future naval balance between East and West if it had a significant effect either on the strength of the two sides' forces or on the manner of their deployment. But the majority view at the Conference and, it appears, in the West generally, was that it was unlikely to do either. It is even possible to argue, moreover, that maritime arms control is not of fundamental importance, and that the increasing attention devoted to it may, in fact, be a distraction likely to complicate and retard progress in areas of real concern.

LEVELS OF TENSION AND LEVELS OF NEED

Politics and presentation
One reason for believing that maritime arms control really does not matter very much and that its pursuit is essentially a distraction from the real issues, is the fact that at the moment there is little tension at sea anyway. This owes a good deal to the Incidents at Sea agreement of 1972. This agreement is particularly interesting in that in the first place it regulates superpower behaviour at sea in a way that considerably reduces prospects of inadvertent clashes between the two navies. Secondly, it provides for annual meetings between professional sailors on both sides to discuss the workings of the agreement in an atmosphere free from publicity and political consequence. As a result the participants have evolved a *modus operandi* that facilitates understanding. Of course, this would not prevent deliberate incidents occurring where the two sides were knowingly in contention, as they were for example during the two US Navy 'freedom of navigation' exercises in the Black Sea in 1986 and 1988. But, even here, the agreement tends to act as a useful form of constraint. The idea that such agreements are the best way of improving maritime agreement between East and West gains credence from the fact that Britain and West Germany have also negotiated such agreements with the Soviet Union and France is currently doing so.

Nevertheless, there is little doubt that, for its part, the Soviet Union is not so relaxed about present levels of tension at sea. The Soviet line on this is assiduously advanced at every opportunity and its broad outlines are well known. They were usefully summarized in an interview given by Fleet Admiral I. M. Kapitanets, Deputy Commander-in-Chief of the Navy in *Krasnaya Zvezda* in April 1989.[1] The Soviets argue that the main aim of the Vienna talks is to eliminate the potential for surprise attack and large-scale offensive operations on land, and that the natural logic is that that this should also be extended to the sea. In itself, the fact that the West consistently fails to concede this point, and even refuses to discuss the issue in any serious way, creates difficulties and at least the potential for tension.

From the Soviet perspective, the problem is aggravated by what they call the all-too-apparent offensive nature of Western naval forces. This is demonstrated by NATO's superiorities over the Warsaw Pact which are, again according to Soviet calculations, quite considerable. NATO has more personnel (by a factor of 4.5) more ocean-going warships (by a factor of 7.6) and more naval combat aircraft (by a factor of 2.4). The Warsaw Pact's essential defensiveness is alleged to be illustrated by the fact that its only superiority lies in 'coastal zone forces' where it has an advantage by a factor of 1.6. The argument that the West needs these superior forces, and that they have to be deployed assertively forward in order to protect its sea lines of communication, does not convince the Soviets. The Soviets make the point that their sea lines of communication from one end of the country to the other are in fact longer and given the deficiencies and vulnerabilities of their railway system more important than is often conceded in the West. The Soviet Union moreover, they argue, has neither the intention nor the capability of attacking NATO SLOCs in any case. As far as a wider world is concerned, 'experience in the Persian Gulf has shown that protection of SLOCs is in the interests of all nations and is best achieved under United Nations auspices by coordinated action by all interested parties on the basis of International Law.'[2]

From Moscow's standpoint, the conclusion is clear. The current naval balance *is* unacceptable both in the composition of Western forces and in the manner in which they are deployed. There is, consequently, a real risk of armed confrontation at sea, which can only be averted by compromise and negotiation.

Whatever Western naval experts might think of the validity of the Soviet case as a whole, there is sympathy in some Western quarters with at least parts of it.[3] Analysts often seem to distinguish between the actual likely consequence of a maritime arms control deal, and the desirability of engaging in an East–West dialogue on the subject. There are those who believe, for instance, that maritime arms control in itself is unlikely to yield substantive improvements in the state of international relations because progress in arms control is much more a consequence of political change and detente than a cause. Nevertheless, it is still worth talking about it both internally, and with the other side.

In particular, the notion that the West could go on demanding a sizeable reduction in Soviet superiority on land, while refusing even to discuss possible reductions in the alleged Western superiority at sea, is probably not politically sustainable, even in the West, for long. Public opinion might be seduced into expecting it, in consequence of the momentous events taking place in the East and of Mr Gorbachev's successful charm offensive in the West. The economies that might result from structural maritime arms reductions would also have their appeal to national treasuries. While it is true that the West continued to hold the line on maritime arms control for the remainder of the year and specifically made it clear in the run up to the Malta summit at the end of November 1989 that it would reject any such naval initiatives,[4] there had to be an element of doubt about how long such steadfastness could survive.

Given this, there were those who argued that it would be wise for Western navies at least to consider the issues so that when they were finally obliged to confront them, they would not need to do so unprepared and in a hurry. Moreover, it is not inconceivable that Western navies might have something to gain and therefore something to aim at in the maritime arms control field. After all, Western sailors have often said how worried they are about the improving quality of the Soviet submarine force and a deal which reduced the strength of that force, in return for compensating reductions on the Western side (say in aircraft carrier strengths) might have something to recommend it.

There were thought to be three fundamental problems for Western navies publicly addressing the maritime arms control issue. The first was maintaining a common line across the alliance, for it was undeniable that there were at least the differences of emphasis between the various navies to be expected from the diversity of their form and strategic circumstance. The second problem was the simple one that appearing to consider maritime arms control initiatives might further fuel the public's thirst for it. But the third problem was the more fundamental and that was how to persuade Western publics, and even Soviet decision-makers, that demonstrable Western superiorities at sea did *not* imply any desire on the part of Western navies to engage in confrontation at sea, to maintain and still less to increase tension; nor were they even 'offensive' in any real sense of the word.

This fundamental presentational problem derived from the strategic asymmetry of the two alliances. The Western alliance was maritime in a sense that the Warsaw Pact was not and that meant it was vulnerable in ways that its putative adversary would not be, especially given the technological advantages that offensive forces have at sea.[5] The only solution to the problem was for the West to maintain a level of force that on paper *looked* superior and, therefore, potentially offensive, but which was, in reality, essentially defensive when viewed from the perspective of a maritime alliance. This was not an easy message to put across and it was not surprising that Western sailors might be wary of entering into a public debate with so many presentational disadvantages. But sometimes bullets have to be bitten.

Do navies really matter?
There was, however, a second reason for doubting the seriousness of the issue of maritime arms control, and therefore whether the effort devoted to it would be worthwhile. This derived from a set of arguments not usually associated with sailors, namely the view that navies do not really matter very much anyway, because their ability to influence events ashore is

limited. Lawrence Freedman touched on the point in his chapter by arguing how infrequently naval activity was decisive to the outcome of conflicts on land.[6]

Because such a view tended to undermine the importance of the role played by navies in peace and therefore in war, it could not be expected to appeal to the sailors of either side. After all, the essential justification of the US Navy's Maritime Strategy is that its promise of projecting power ashore will alter the Soviet Union's strategic calculus quite significantly. Should that prospect be thought infeasible for operational reasons, or through arms control arrangements which for example limited the US Navy's deployment areas or the range of its weapons, then the whole strategy and the US Navy's present claim on US defence resources would atrophy.

Interestingly this also appears to be the conclusion of most Soviet analysts. They seem to take the strategic threat posed by the US Navy very seriously indeed. As we have seen, Soviet sailors have made it clear that, so far as they are concerned, there are 'lines' on the world ocean which cause concern when they are crossed by Western naval forces able to attack the Soviet Union directly, especially with SLCMs. These 'lines of concern' have been defined as being 1,000 km off the Kuriles, an equal distance off the Norwegian coast south to Trondheim, north of a line from Muscat to Karachi and east of a line a little west of Crete.[7] In the general Soviet view, Western naval forces crossing those lines could have a significant ability to damage the Soviet Union and are therefore regarded as provocative and potentially destabilizing.

However, it should be said that not all Soviet analysts appear to think like this. In a recent article in the Moscow journal *International Affairs* Alexei Arbatov argued that Soviet defensive superiorities were such that 'We are capable of sinking all NATO aircraft carriers operating off our coast . . . [and that t]he forces we have are plainly sufficient for defending our littoral and protecting our sea-based strategic forces equipped with long-range missiles in coastal seas.'[8] The, paradoxical, conclusion to be drawn from this is that the US Navy should not be regarded as particularly threatening by the Soviet Union, and that maritime arms control need not have top priority. How important the Soviets really think maritime arms control is, remains a matter of controversy in the West. Clearly the debate about the strategic effectiveness of navies and the consequent importance of maritime arms control is as yet far from resolved.

Reductions will happen in any case
The last suggested reason for taking a fairly relaxed attitude towards maritime arms control was that reductions were likely to take place and, indeed, already had, in consequence of a number of quite independent factors, such as demographic problems and the ceaseless search for economies in an era of constrained defence budgets. Both sides had already announced unilateral cut-backs in present and projected force levels, and the US Navy's arsenal of nuclear weapons had dropped very sharply as the operational disadvantages of current nuclear ASW weapons

and nuclear SAMs had become ever more manifest and as effective non-nuclear alternatives became more available.

The US Navy is now quietly retiring its old ASROC and SUBROC anti-submarine missiles and its *Terrier* surface-to-air missiles. Some 1,100 nuclear weapons are to be taken off American vessels. Among the reasons advanced for this policy were increasing maintenance costs, and doubts about the operational value of such weapons. Indeed, there appears to be in the US Navy some doubt about the value of nuclear weapons at sea as a whole. Vice-Admiral Henry Mustin retired in April 1989 as Deputy CNO and shortly afterwards told Congress that 'There is a recognition that if there is a nuclear war at sea, we have got more to lose than the Russians . . . The concept of a nuclear war at sea is a concept whose time has passed.'[9] It is widely believed that the Soviet Navy is following the same path. These cuts in force levels and in some capabilities were not the contrived product of any formal arms control arrangement, but instead the largely uncontroversial and tacit recognition of shared economic/technological pressures and congruent interests.

If there was an emerging pattern of, to quote Sir James Eberle, 'Mutual Unilateral Decline' or MUD, perhaps there was no need for an urgent programme of maritime arms control. Indeed, such a programme might have the reverse effect, by actually dissuading countries from such unilateral reductions and so doing more harm than good. Better perhaps to let the trends work their own way through. For instance, attempting to come to a formal agreement on tactical nuclear weapon holdings would be a complex affair. There were two obvious reasons for this. First, professional opinion on the utility of tactical nuclear weapons at sea was divided on both sides. Some thought them a necessary response to hard targets and difficult situations (such as the destruction of aircraft carriers or large, modern twin-hulled deep-diving submarines); others believed they had little operational utility and their use would in any case escalate the conflict; still others thought of them as necessary 'weapons of desperation', to use Richard Hill's phrase. Secondly, on top of this there was the problem of linkages with the corresponding situation ashore. NATO, for example, might not feel able to sign up to a No First Use agreement at sea, if it was not prepared to do so on land. For such reasons, it might be best to let market forces have their way, rather than seek to impose premature and artificial conclusions to the debate.

Needless to say, not everyone would agree with this relaxed position on maritime arms control. Would it not perhaps be better for the process of reduction to be ordered and considered rather than improvised from one financial or technological crisis to another? At the least, why not seek to make a virtue out of necessity and claim arms control credit for reductions that would have probably taken place anyway? Again, talking about such issues (if not negotiating about them) would improve understanding between the two sides. One of the current problems in the Soviet response to the US Navy's Maritime Strategy, for example, derived from the fact that both sides had different concepts of maritime strategy in general. This led to misperceptions about what the opposition was actually doing; the better their knowledge of the other side's operating procedures, the less the chance of such misunderstanding both in peacetime and in crisis.

WAYS AND MEANS

If it is to be concluded that probably later rather than sooner both sides will enter into dialogue about possible approaches to maritime arms control, what are most likely to be the best avenues of approach? Almost certainly, attention would focus on confidence and security-building measures rather than issues of structural disarmament. Indeed, this was already the focus of Soviet proposals made to date. In February and March 1989 the Soviets made their proposals for this clear.[10] They suggested that there be notification of all exercises in which twenty vessels over 1,500 tons participate, or five over 5,000 tons armed with SLCM or aircraft, or over eighty naval aircraft. Observers were to be invited to naval exercises in which twenty-five or more ships over 1,500 tons or one hundred or more naval aircraft participate. Naval exercises were to be limited in scale to fifty ships and ten to fourteen days. There were many other more detailed proposals, all as controversial from the Western standpoint. For the remainder of 1989 issues such as these were the focus of considerable interest in the Western maritime arms control community.[11] None the less it seemed highly unlikely that either side would agree CSBMs that would seriously detract from its ability to do those things at sea that it thought it needed to do.

The other issue that attracted interest at the Conference and subsequently was the possibility of *negotiated* reductions in nuclear weapons at sea. Aside from tactical nuclear weapons and nuclear-capable carrier aircraft, this also focused on SLCMs and, of course, the maritime component of START. The broad outlines of START were well known and it was likely to reduce the number of SSBNs. If so, this could well have significant implications for other naval forces. It was thought, though, that there might be an interest in sending out submarines that were only partially filled with SLBMs because this would reduce the vulnerability of the force as a whole. Monitoring such an arrangement was likely to create verification problems, however.[12] Such reductions in SSBN warhead numbers might also raise difficult questions about the cost-effectiveness of SSBN versus other strategic delivery systems.

START was also complicated by the debate over SLCMs. Here, the issues were to do with producing a regime equitable to both sides. This was a difficult problem, given the fact that their SLCM arsenals were quite dissimilar in size, composition and likely role. Even if it were possible to come to an agreement about SLCM levels and capacity, verification problems would be severe. Indeed, there is every indication that the US Navy believes itself to be ahead in SLCMs, thinks them important to its future tasks and is deeply sceptical about the ability to monitor any agreement adequately. According to Admiral Huntingdon Hardisty, Commander-in-Chief Pacific Command, cruise missiles for our navy represent the most important achievement in modern warfare since the invention of the gun. They give us the combat capability and the combat power we need. We feel we are ahead of the Soviets in cruise missile technology and feel we still have an edge.[13]

If one side continues to think SLCMs are essential to the maintenance of the balance at sea, it is hard to imagine any very substantive arms control agreement on them for the time being.

A final issue worth remembering is that, in some ways, arms control might actually increase levels of naval threat. For instance, a START-induced reduction in the numbers of SSBNs would make them relatively more vulnerable to an opponent's anti-SSBN forces and therefore increase the possibility of destabilization. Conversely, a reduction in the Soviet SSBN level might release large numbers of modern Soviet SSNs for other activities, many of which would be regarded as threatening by the West. Further, any negotiated reduction of force levels in Central Europe, from the Western perspective at least, would be likely to increase the requirement for reinforcements and resupplies across the Atlantic, the Soviet interest in attacking them and the Western need to protect them.

On top of this, the fact that the Soviet naval construction programme, as yet, showed little sign of significant reduction or slowdown, five years into the Soviet Union's discovery of defensive sufficiency, was a powerful reminder of the momentum that naval programmes generated. But as we have seen,[14] it is possible for Soviet admirals to argue that, given continuing Western maritime superiorities, the Soviet Navy was already barely adequate for its task of homeland defence and could not be safely cut any further unless the US Navy was too. For its part, the US Navy would argue that its force levels are based on an objective appraisal of Western maritime vulnerabilities to threats from all quarters. In addition, navies had less potential for expansion in war than armies did because it took so much longer to build submarines than tanks. For all these reasons, professionals on both sides would be especially reluctant to envisage reductions on the scale apparently envisaged by their colleagues in the ground forces. In comparison, navies were already 'lean and mean' and had extensive commitments over and above their involvement in the East–West security relationship, particularly in a wider world. Arguably, they, therefore, had less capacity for large-scale reduction.

If these two points are added to the scepticism about early and dramatic outcomes to an East–West dialogue on maritime arms control, it would seem unlikely that the naval balance between the two in the 1990s would be substantially affected by maritime arms control measures that are foreseeable at the moment. Improved relations at sea, in short, may be more likely to derive from improved general relations than the consequence of any formal agreements between the two sides about naval forces, their composition and deployment.

NOTES AND REFERENCES

1. 'How to avert the threat from the ocean', Fleet Admiral I. M. Kapitanets, *Krasnaya Zvezda*, 18 April 1989.
2. Ibid.
3. For example, see Michael L. Ross, 'Disarmament at sea', *Foreign Policy*, Fall 1989.
4. 'Bush rejects naval cuts,' *The Guardian*, 29 November 1989.
5. These advantages, and the whole issue of maritime asymmetry is discussed in the Introduction.
6. See Chapter 14, pages 234–5.
7. This was the burden of an informal presentation by Vice-Admiral N. Markov of the Soviet Navy and General Staff at a Foundation for International Security Seminar at Adderbury, Oxfordshire, 17–20 November 1989.
8. Alexei Arbatov, 'How much defence is sufficient?', *International Affairs*, Moscow, April 1989, p. 42. Alexei Arbatov is Head of Department at the Institute of World Economics and International Relations of the USSR Academy of Sciences.
9. Quoted in Ross, op. cit., pp. 102–3.
10. They were tabled by Bulgaria for the WTO at the Vienna talks on CSBMs in March 1989 but not discussed.
11. E. J. Grove, *Maritime Strategy and European Security*, Foundation for International Security, June 1989, esp. chapters 8 and 9 and appendices I and II. See also the records of a Council for Arms Control conference on maritime arms control held in London in June 1989 and 'Superpowers moving towards maritime unilateralism', *JDW* 3 (June 1989).
12. 'DOD may allow intrusive verification of Trident subs', *Defense News*, 11 December 1989.
13. Quoted in *Jane's Defence Weekly*, 8 December 1989. See also David S. Yost, 'The most difficult question' in *Proceedings* of the USNI, September 1989.
14. This is discussed in Chapter 10.

Part III

The European Dimension

16 The INF Treaty and the future of NATO: lessons from the 1960s

Lawrence S. Kaplan

As the North Atlantic Treaty approached its fortieth anniversary the United States and the Soviet Union signed an Intermediate-Range Nuclear Arms Reduction treaty in December 1987. On one level this action represented a striking triumph for the West, and a vindication of the promise inherent in the North Atlantic Council's dual-track decision of 1979. America's firmness over deploying the cruise and Pershing II missiles in Western Europe led initially to a confrontation with the Soviet adversary in 1983 when its delegates walked out of the arms talks in Geneva. But it ultimately led to an agreement that would remove both the newly deployed American missiles and the Soviet SS-4 and SS-5 as well as the SS-20 missiles. An elaborate system of verification would follow over the following thirteen years. The signing of this treaty, with its Memorandum of Understanding and Protocols, and its subsequent ratification in 1988, seemed to testify to the validity of a major NATO assumption: namely, that a strong defensive posture was a prerequisite to genuine detente with the Eastern bloc.

On another level, however, the INF treaty raised doubts about the future of the alliance which could lead to its dissolution if its members could not respond to new challenges. Among the challenges is the aura surrounding Mikhail Gorbachev, the principal partner in the framing of the INF treaty.

President Gorbachev seems to herald a new foreign policy, in which the Soviet Union would face inward, reduce its military establishment, and become a regular if still powerful member of the nation states of the world without the revolutionary engine of communist expansion to threaten its neighbors. Since it was Soviet aggressiveness that brought the Western European states together in alliance, a reversal of that behavior, as symbolized in the INF treaty, could make the alliance unnecessary in the future.

The INF treaty between the United States and the Soviet Union in 1987 gave credence to European concern that the United States was turning away from its allies. Like the abortive Reykjavik plans of 1986, the INF arrangements might be a Soviet–American trade-off at the expense of Europeans. Despite the demands which the NATO allies had made for a Western counteraction against the SS-20s, and despite the obvious success of the dual-track initiative of 1979 in effecting their removal – and, moreover, forcing the Soviets into serious negotiations for reductions in nuclear weapons – there was fear that disengagement of American forces from Europe would be the end product of de-escalation efforts. Inconsistent though this sentiment may be with the new confidence Europeans have in living alongside a restructured Soviet Union, it was none the less a factor in straining the Western alliance. After more than thirty-five years of an American military presence in Europe, many wondered if the removal of intermediate nuclear weapons would lead to the removal, of American troops as well. If so, what effect would this action have on the security of the West?

As a result of Europe's re-examination of both the American ally and the Soviet foe, there is a new sense of European unity abroad. For half a generation, since the *Wirtschaftswunder* of the 1960s, Europe has had the potential of equalling both America and the Soviet Union in economic power. In 1992 the remnants of economic nationalism are expected to fall. And with their passing the idea of a United States of Europe could become a reality. Political and military integration could be built on the infrastructure of the Western European Union, enlarged to serve the European Community as a whole. Two of its members – the United Kingdom and France – are already nuclear powers. There is reason to anticipate the flowering of a genuine 'third force' in Western Europe in the 1990s.

In light of the challenges of 1989, critics have a right to suspect that the alliance is on the threshold of dissolution. As one acute observer has written:[1]

The Atlantic Alliance, which has been the keystone of American foreign policy during three administrations, has begun to founder under the impact of Europe's new nationalism and the apparent decline of the Russian military threat. There is no longer any agreement on how NATO shall be organized, where it is going, or even what its purposes are . . .

This disarray within the alliance is more than simply a dispute among allies as to the proper means toward a commonly desired end. It is the ends themselves which are now in question. The problem facing the Atlantic Alliance today is not so much how it shall protect Europe from Russian invasion – an invasion no one now believes in – but what kind of political settlement will be made between Russia and the West in Europe. The collapse of Atlantic unity is merely the result of the transformation of the old military impasse into a period of diplomatic fluidity where Europe's political future is at stake.

The extended quotation above encapsulates most of the issues that would account for the 'end of the alliance', the title of the book from which the quotations were taken. They include: Europe's new nationalism, decline of the Soviet threat, lack of agreement over the purpose of the alliance and the consequent irrationality of stationing of American troops in Europe. These are lively issues in 1989. But they were equally valid in 1964 when Ronald Steel published this book. In the foregoing paragraphs only the reference to 'three administrations' instead of 'eight' anchor this passage in time. In other words, all the generalizations made in 1964 about the impending termination of the alliance were as pertinent in the early 1960s as they are in the late 1980s.

Given these constants why did NATO survive its twenty-fifth anniversary and live on to commemorate its fortieth anniversary? From the American side in the 1960s, a major issue was burden-sharing, particularly in the form of the six US divisions in Europe. These divisions had been the fruits of the Great Debate of 1951, when General Eisenhower used his influence to win over a restless Senate to accept the Administration's decision to send four divisions to the support of the newly established SHAPE. The Truman Administration succeeded, but not without dissenting voices over the limits of executive right to send troops without the explicit permission of Congress.

The defense of Europe in 1951 demanded the American contribution, as plans were made to build up allied forces to provide a deterrence that had been absent in Korea the year before. Even when nuclear weaponry reduced the numbers of ground forces necessary to maintain the deterrent, the American forces remained in Europe, now more as a tripwire than a conventional force. The Eisenhower Administration continued the policies of the Truman Administration.

But with the amazing economic recovery in the West, questions arose over the ability of Europeans to provide a greater share of the economic burden of maintaining troops in Europe. These questions were made all the sharper because the older fears of invasion had lessened in the Khrushchev years. While such questions could be deflected by observing the continued threats from the East, given Soviet behavior in Berlin or in Cuba, another question was not so easily answered. In 1960 there was a danger of an excessive outflow of the American gold reserve, blamed – fairly or not – on the drain on the US dollar. If that drain was caused in good measure by the enormous cost of maintaining the divisions abroad – 250,000 to 300,000 men – then why should not the Europeans pick up those costs?

This was a concern that the Kennedy Administration had to cope with. It was a legacy of the Eisenhower Administration, and one that the new Secretary of Defense, Robert S. McNamara, was more than willing to manage. There was a potential $3 billion-drain that he intended to bring down to no more than $1 billion as quickly as he could. If the Eisenhower solution – bring home American dependants in Europe – aroused too much opposition, other answers would have to be found. McNamara had them, and they disturbed the European partners.

The Kennedy Administration was looking as much – or more – to Asia and Latin America in 1961 as it was to Europe. The crises points in 1961 were as much in Laos and Vietnam as in Berlin; and the Kennedy Administration undertook a sweeping revision of both the strategic thinking and the strategic emphasis of the Eisenhower Administration. In the course of its evaluations the heavy expenses of maintaining forces in Europe came under review.

High on McNamara's list of priorities was an emphasis on the need for highly mobile task forces to engage in low-intensity warfare, to strike out through counterinsurgency at the kinds of forces threatening American interest in south-east Asia. It is noteworthy that the budgets for FY 1962 and 1963 placed a premium upon aircraft capable of lifting troops to areas of conflict with dispatch and with limited costs. The dangers of conflict with the Soviet Union were to be encountered in areas where wars of national liberation were sponsored or supported by the Soviet Union, rather than in Europe where NATO and the Warsaw Pact were in a static confrontation.

The consequences for the European partners were quickly apparent. If US troops could be airlifted in a crisis, why should the United States maintain such a large standing army in Europe? If the allies wanted US forces to remain in place, they should be prepared to pay a larger share of their expenses. They could afford the costs after a decade of rising prosperity. Although it is unlikely that there was a machiavellian design in the Defense Department's development of a new strike force with a fleet of aircraft and ships to undergird it, it was equally unlikely that once conceived and implemented the designers of foreign military policy would not be reluctant to press their advantage.

All these actions helped to account for German and Italian willingness – and even French acquiescence – to enlarge their contributions to NATO in 1961. An *aide-mémoire* of 17 February 1961, less than a month after the Kennedy Administration was in office, prepared the way. While directed at all the allies, it pointedly was delivered to the West German delegation in the course of bilateral talks on the balance of payments. The document made clear, though, that the issue was not bilateral: 'The deficit of the United States arises wholly from the common defense of the free world', it stated. 'Without these freely assumed obligations the United States would now be running a heavy surplus in its commitments and action in balance of payments.'[2] Hence it was reasonable to expect a better balance to the partnership that would ease the balance-of-payments problem.

While the Europeans could resist the logic of this American assumption – including long-term reality of the gold drain – they could not resist the tide of events. The Berlin Wall crisis of the summer of 1961 undercut German objections. It led to a rapid buildup of US troops in Europe that forced the German hand as the projected US dollar deficit rose to almost $3 billion. America insisted and received compensation from the Federal Republic. Germany could hardly do otherwise, since the United States was sending 40,000 additional troops to bolster NATO's defenses in Germany.

To soften the blunt edges of its demands, the United States avoided direct payment for US troops. Instead, it accepted the purchase of American goods and equipment to offset US expenditures in Europe. Direct sale of US equipment was probably the least objectionable way of achieving results without offending German dignity.

Similar negotiations followed with other NATO allies, and although the results were more modest there was some easing of the problem. It took some time, however, before the extent of European cooperation entered into the congressional psyche. As late as February 1963, at hearings on military procurement authorizations for fiscal year 1964, Senator Richard Russell, chairman of the Armed Services Committee, was still asserting that the NATO allies had all been riding free and that the $50 billion establishment that you preside over, over there, has been the shield not only for Great Britain but for France and Germany. They got years behind in furnishing their troops.

McNamara was able to respond that,

We have signed agreements with the West Germans under which they are buying $650 million of equipment from us. We have signed an agreement in the last 90 days with the Italians under which they are buying initially $125 million of equipment from us.[3]

While Europe's assumption of some of America's economic burden displayed a continuing dependence upon America's military power, there was a concomitant impatience with American dominance of the alliance as well as growing doubts about America's reliability as an ally. Many of the fissures in the alliance in the early 1960s grew out of the confluence of two elements of change: 1. the successful launching of the first earth satellite, *Sputnik*, in 1957, and 2. the dramatic economic recovery of most European powers, reflected in the signing of the Treaty of Rome in the same year. *Sputnik* aroused alarm in the United States over Soviet advances in missile technology, which in turn stimulated the development of its ICBM. Yet *Sputnik* raised fears that the United States soon would be vulnerable for the first time to direct Soviet attacks. Would the United States come to the aid of a missile attack on Paris or Bonn if their own cities were at stake?

This question was answered negatively by France, particularly after General de Gaulle assumed the presidency in the Fifth Republic. France assumed that it was unnatural for any nation to place another's security ahead of its own, and it was equally unnatural to expect that the United States would remain indefinitely in Europe. When the United States rejected a reorganization of NATO that would have made France part of a triumvirate that would control the organization, de Gaulle's course of subversion and separation was set. As tokens of what would come to pass, the French fleet in the Mediterranean in 1959 and in the Atlantic in 1963 were removed from SHAPE and SACLANT authority.

It was obvious that de Gaulle's stand appealed to many Europeans. They might not necessarily agree to French leadership, but most Europeans could respond favorably to complaints about charges of American hegemony. Certainly the American pressures to assume more financial burdens bred irritation over the pre-eminent position of the United States. But the availability of intercontinental ballistic missiles coinciding with the conception of a more flexible nuclear response raised a variety of suspicions among Europeans. A less rigid reliance on nuclear defense could mean that America's new vulnerability to the nuclear weapons dictated the Kennedy Administration's new emphasis on conventional forces. Part of the reason for this pressure rested on the need for forces to cope with outbreaks where nuclear weapons might be counterproductive. To ask, as Secretary of Defense McNamara did at the North Atlantic Council meeting in Athens in May 1962 and then more publicly at a commencement address at Ann Arbor, Michigan, a month later, that Europeans prepare defenses on the basis of more troops on the ground was unsettling.

While McNamara actually spoke of a variety of weapons, and a flexible response to the problem at hand, Europeans heard the implication of raising the nuclear threshold and the prospects of a conventional war on the ground. The allies, with the obvious exception of Germany, considered the Berlin Wall crisis to be an aberration, a problem primarily for the Warsaw bloc, and not a reason to abandon the successful deterrent system of the past decade. To Americans the Berlin crisis of 1961 reinforced views that NATO required conventional forces to meet any level of non-nuclear aggression.

The result of these divergent views was European resistance to both the building of conventional defenses and to the principle of flexible response. Europeans were unimpressed with McNamara's claim that the West had exaggerated the extent of Soviet military power. The new team of systems analysts at the Department of Defense was convinced that the figure of 150 divisions was unrealistic. The size of a Soviet division was smaller than those of the West, and the equipment was inferior. There should be no reason why a modest conventional buildup of NATO forces should not be sufficient to hold off aggression from the Warsaw Pact bloc, at least long enough for other means of coping to come into play.[4]

The allies did not accept this judgement. What they saw was a rationalization for American willingness to subvert the security of the West which had been constructed under a nuclear umbrella. European discontent centered on the illogicality of conventional defense. It could invite conflict by raising the nuclear threshold to excessive heights. If the Soviets knew that American nuclear power would not be employed immediately, they might be tempted to employ tactics that could lead to protracted land warfare in Europe. No matter how vigorously the United States asserted that a flexible response would increase, not decrease, the deterrent capacity of the West, Europeans could not erase from their memories images of the First and Second World Wars. Nor could they ignore the prospect of a war that would destroy Europe but leave the superpowers intact. On the other hand, they were much less vocal about their unwillingness to bear the financial burdens that raising conventional armies would incur.

The allies had forums outside NATO where their discontent with American leadership could be expressed. The European Economic Community developing from the Treaty of Rome in 1957 was a reality even if its accomplishments were more in the future than in the present. It contained a potential for a 'third force' between America and the Soviet Union, which would be independent of both. This was President de Gaulle's vision of the future, when Europeans would not be second-class citizens with their fate decided by superpower politics. If there were tactical and intermediate nuclear weapons in Europe, they were controlled by the United States not by Europe. The result was pressure for development of national *forces de frappe*, particularly in France. It is noteworthy that Europeans were successful in resisting American pressure to raise their troop strengths. It was the United States that gave way. By the late 1960s Secretary of Defense McNamara had accepted these constraints on conventional forces. In fact, he converted the withdrawal of France from the organization in 1966 into an asset, or at least into a circumstance 'in no way disabling' to the military posture of the alliance.[5]

The Secretary of Defense used Europe's reluctance to increase its forces to justify the thinning of American troops in Europe during the Vietnam War. He was convinced that the combination of the NATO forces in place and the declining of a Soviet threat would still permit a flexible response to any Soviet challenge.

Just as Europeans had to make repeated financial concessions to keep American troops in Europe, so American leaders had to make serious efforts to appease Europe's increasing insistence on equality within the alliance, particularly with respect to the control of nuclear weapons. De Gaulle's challenge had to be met; Germany's unhappiness with its inferior status in NATO could not be left unheeded; and the smaller powers' sense of isolation from policy-making required attention as well.

The major effort was a multilateral force (MLF) which originated in the State Department's Policy Planning Staff under Robert R. Bowie, in the Eisenhower Administration and terminated in disarray under Johnson in 1964. Supreme Allied Commander, Europe, General Lauris Norstad seized on the concept to make NATO a fourth nuclear power in a way that would appease German if not French demands for equality and would dissolve doubts about America's dedication to the defense of Europe. The MLF took the form eventually of twenty-five surface vessels carrying eight Polaris A-3 missiles, each with mixed manned crews and nuclear warheads under joint ownership and custody. Each participating nation could veto the use of the nuclear weapon, although the United States would retain final control of the weapons.

It won some enthusiasm among dedicated American supporters of European unification. Bowie, in fact, urged the United States 'to concede to a European or NATO force the same degree of ultimate autonomy as it has already accepted in assisting the British force.'[6]

The MLF never materialized; it was always an illusion. If the United States kept its veto intact, the nuclear sharing was a charade. If it did not, there would be the prospect of fifteen fingers – or at least thirteen if France and Iceland were discounted – on the nuclear button. France was going its way with its *force de frappe*; Britain was smarting over the Skybolt debacle. This left Germany as the major enthusiast for the MLF, and Germany's enthusiasm had a dampening effect on the other allies. The multilateral force disappeared from the NATO communiques by the end of 1964.

Like offset agreements, the MLF was an action on the part of Americans and Europeans to take into account the other side's concerns. The MLF at least bought time for the alliance to sort out paths for survival. Both the burden-sharing agreements and the multilateral force represented a spirit of accommodation, even if the results were mixed or negative.

Admittedly, the MLF has gone down in NATO's history as a fiasco, while the offset agreements have been identified as a species of American blackmail. Neither served its intended purposes for very long. The American monopoly on the control of nuclear warheads led to the departure of France from the organization in 1966 and the demand for detente on the part of the other allies, as demonstrated in the Harmel initiative in 1967. And the need for further offset measures became more urgent as the Vietnam War diverted American troops and American attention from its NATO obligations. Pressures for more burden-sharing increased by the end of the decade. Yet each concession in its way postponed the dissolution foreseen by pundits at the beginning of the decade. And each represented a continuing importance that NATO represented for the allies. After all, in 1969 under the terms of Article 13 of the treaty any member state could have issued a 'notice of denunciation' and left the alliance. None of the members, not even France, followed this pattern.

There was a centripetal force at work in the 1960s. On the surface the organization was essentially unchanged; SACEUR and SACLANT and the Secretary-General remained in place. But with France's departure there was a subtle increase in the influence of the smaller nations of the alliance. NATO's Defense Planning Committee, created in 1963, assumed greater authority, with consequent lessening of American influence over military affairs. Similarly, the Nuclear Planning Group, founded in 1967 after France's withdrawal from the organization, brought nuclear questions more closely into the purview of the Secretary-General. If the nuclear warhead remained exclusively an American monopoly, nuclear planning became more oligopolistic after the Secretary-General moved from Paris to Brussels.

An unintended and perhaps unexpected by-product of that move was a diminution of the powers of the SACEUR. The old Standing Group, composed of the three major NATO powers in Washington was replaced by a military representative system with a wider NATO membership and with its center in Brussels. With the Standing Group dissolved, the smaller nations had a greater voice in military planning at the expense of the Supreme Allied Commander, Europe. Even the locus of his headquarters, thirty miles away from Brussels, helped to reduce the stature and influence that the SACEUR had enjoyed in Paris. While none of these changes was advertised as American responses to complaints against its dominance over NATO, they helped to elevate the role of the junior partners in the organization.

None the less, these alterations in the NATO structure may be labelled as cosmetic. America's commitment in 1969 remained as important as the American 'pledge' had been in 1949. The unifying factor through much of the decade was the continuing fear of a powerful and still dangerous Soviet Union.

The Berlin Wall crisis of 1961, the Cuban missile crisis of 1962, and the Czech crisis of 1968 reminded Europeans of the reasons for the founding of NATO, even as they noted with ambivalence American reactions to those crises. Contradictions continued to abound. The strength of the Soviet superpower – and its willingness on selected occasions in the 1960s to display it – generated pressures to keep American forces in Europe where they served as a guarantor of NATO's stability. At the same time there was a sense of a new era dawning in which the Soviets had moderated their ideological drive and were ready to coexist with the Western democracies.

This manifested itself in the Harmel Report of 1967 calling for steps towards detente to accompany military preparedness and a subsequent declaration – the 'Reykjavik Signal' on mutual and balanced force reductions at the Reykjavik meeting of the North Atlantic Council in 1968.[7]

The Reykjavik declaration was announced in June 1968 before Soviet intervention in Czechoslovakia. While the Council at Brussels in the fall of that year determined that Soviet action 'has seriously set back hopes of settling the outstanding problems which still divide the European continent', it also supported 'continuing consultations with the Warsaw Pact bloc' preparing for a time when the atmosphere for fruitful discussions was more favorable.[8] In this tense situation even Europeans most optimistic about detente and most hostile to the American role in NATO would be reluctant to risk destabilizing NATO through altering the force structure in NATO, let alone through a major reduction in the American presence in Europe. NATO itself remained vital both for defense and detente.

Is NATO still a vital force in 1990? The parallels of the 1980s and the 1960s have considerable validity, but how compelling are they? There are obvious differences over the twenty-year span, if only in emphasis. European unity in the 1960s was still undeveloped; the United Kingdom's effort to join the European Community had failed in 1963. De Gaulle, the dominant personality in Western Europe, was also a disruptive force. In 1989 the United Kingdom is a full member of a considerably enlarged European Community. Europe appears closer to an integrated whole than it has ever been before. Given this evolution, Europe could develop into a third force as readily as it could become a genuine second pillar of the Atlantic alliance. Is NATO needed any longer, as it obviously was two decades before? Cannot Europe stand alone at last?

These questions take on a special relevance in light of the new spirit animating the Soviet Union under Mikhail Gorbachev. His challenge to the Soviet past appears far more credible than Khrushchev's. The latter may have demonized Stalin's image and opened the way to detente, but his own volatile personality stood in the way of full confidence in the West's relations with the Soviet Union. His aggressiveness in supporting 'wars of national liberation' in the Third World and the risks he took in installing missiles in Cuba diminished expectations among the European allies. The Brezhnev succession did little to support a belief in a fundamental change in Soviet foreign relations, even though Brezhnev's conservative style encouraged hopes for detente.

Gorbachev has made *glasnost* and *perestroika* concepts that inspire much more than simple relaxation of tensions. He has recognized fundamental flaws in communism as an economic system, and has moved to make the Soviet Union a partner rather than enemy of a peaceful world order. Wherever one looks in 1989 – the United Nations, Afghanistan, southern Africa, the Middle East – and notably US–USSR relations – Gorbachev appears to have changed the face of the Soviet Union. A new order has arrived. The projections of George Kennan about the future of communism forty years before appear to have been realized. Containment has worked.

NATO in this case may be an anachronism, an alliance that has fulfilled its functions of protecting the West against communist ambitions.

After forty years of confrontation the alliance might be dismantled on the prospect of a new Soviet leader infused with what the North Atlantic Assembly has accepted as 'benign' intentions.[9] But undermining this acceptance are doubts of at least two varieties. One is over the question of the Soviet Union's new foreign policy objectives. With all the openness and reconstruction that has been exhibited, the Soviet Union remains a superpower whose military strength plays a role independent of its ideological bent. Gorbachev's objectives in many respects resemble those of his predecessors, namely, the removal of the United States from Europe. Gorbachev's posture could achieve this goal through the dissolution of the alliance. Are the members of NATO certain that destabilization would not result, leaving Europe exposed, as it has not been since the 1940s, to the influence of the strongest nation on the continent? Denuclearization of Europe increases the imbalance in conventional weapons between East and West.

There is, however, another consideration. What if Gorbachev fails to maintain control of the Soviet Union? The pull of conservative forces is strong, and resistance to his reforms could result in his departure, even without a failed policy that marked Khrushchev's removal. NATO remains an insurance against such a turn of events.

If uncertainty about Soviet goals and about the Soviet political system remains alive, even though less intense than in the 1960s, the condition of Western Europe as a political entity remains equally uncertain. European unity does not rest on the number of members in a community, nor even in the promises of an economic union in 1992. The major question centers on its willingness to compromise national sovereignty in favor of a united Europe. Despite periodic expressions of common purpose, in the Western European Union as well as in the European Community, centrifugal forces remain strong. Nationalism still survives. The community could come apart over economic issues alone. As long as there is no United States of Europe in place, the termination of the alliance risks not only a political and military imbalance with the Warsaw bloc but also new divisions within the West that could set back accomplishments of the past generation.

These cautionary notes are on one level of concern about the future of Europe. There is another that is rarely aired. This involves a post-NATO Germany. Where will it fit into a united Europe, or a divided Europe? What role would it have in East–West relations? Would Germany unfettered by NATO ties move out of a European Community toward reunification? Or would it stay inside to dominate the West and shape its foreign policy toward an *Ostpolitik* that neither its fellow members nor the Soviet bloc welcome? These considerations are alive even though usually unspoken. They bring to mind the assumption, going back to the 1950s, that a West Germany inside NATO was more acceptable to the Soviet Union than Germany armed and outside. Could conflict break out in Europe, not from the Soviets moving in on a weakened West after the departure of the United States, but from ambitions real or imagined, of German irredentism?

Do any of these considerations affect the United States? If the anger over unfair burden-sharing is fueled by an economic recession, or if the anti-American sentiment in Europe reaches a new volume, it would be understandable if a new administration should wish to leave the organization. Even if there are sufficient brakes against such a crisis, America in the 1990s – for all the reasons that surfaced in the 1980s, or in the 1960s – could lead NATO into dissolution. The Pacific emphasis, the troops issue, the relative decline of American power could all work toward a devolution into irrelevance, even if there is no violent crisis to mark its end. Yet, it is unlikely that any administration will take this path.

Scenarios of this sort have never been a part of any administration's agenda, for the obvious reason that NATO figures as a fixture in the late twentieth century with as much force as isolationism did a century ago. Disengagement from Europe into a fortress America poses too many disruptive prospects for any political figure or political party to take seriously. It would mean, among other things, leaving Europe to a Soviet influence of an order that the Soviet Union itself would not have dreamed possible in the past two generations. Secondly, a breakdown of Europe's will to survive as an entity could follow from the loss of American presence. As Colin Gray has put it, 'the geopolitical realities of European security are such that the security-producing potential of NATO-Europe is far less than is the sum of its several columns of national assets.'[10] America's own vital interests would be endangered by a recrudescence of the nationalist passions of the past, not least of which would be the revival of a German problem. Thirdly, does the technology of the twentieth century permit a withdrawal of the United States into its hemisphere in the fashion of the Monroe Doctrine? If it does not, in the interrelated world of interlocked economies and politics of the 1990s America's own security would be affected by a breakdown in an important part of the world.

Europeans recognize the dangers of destabilization even as they chafe against American controls, or against American bases, training exercises, or mistakes in statecraft. They show this by responding to charges of unequal burden sharing with evidences of their contributions. They urge the United States to look beyond superficial statistics. Colin Howgill of the British embassy in Washington observed that the overall contribution of Atlantic security defensive capability should be identified not merely by the amount of money spent; toleration of noise pollution caused by thousands of low level jet fighters flying in manuevers over Europe's countryside was itself a sharing of the defense burden not to be measured in dollars and cents. A report from the non-partisan Center on Budget and Policy Priorities in Washington made the same point by noting that 'the European states are carrying a substantial share of the alliance's military burden'.[11]

What is significant about these reports and Europe's efforts to rebut American criticism is not the number of governmental and private bodies and individuals criticizing Europe but the need Europe still feels to satisfy the United States about its activities . Equally significant, the repetitive American complaints always stop short of genuine action. There have been no formal withdrawals of troops although division-size has varied over the years, particularly in the Vietnam period. In 1987 when the question once again arose in the Congress, the Senate passed an amendment to keep American forces intact in Europe.[12]

The most eloquent evidence of American response to the need for stability in Europe derives from the silence in the presidential campaigns themselves. In 1984 Europeans were aroused by Senator Nunn's variation on troop withdrawal in June of that year – phased withdrawal would follow from failure of Europeans to increase their share. But even then the resolution was watered down to a pious hope for change.

Just as Europe fears that American exasperation over military costs could lead to American withdrawal of forces, so the Unites States fears the exclusionary potential of a United States of Europe. A United Europe was a goal of the founding fathers of NATO, but if achieved it could damage America's economy. Even more than this, a genuinely united Europe could challenge the United States politically as well. Is this then a reason for cutting loose? The consensus among American leaders has always been that European unification was in the long-term interest of the United States if only because a united Europe would block Soviet expansionism. There is little prospect for change in 1989, no matter how high the level of frustration over policies, political and economic, that a united Europe might take.

Looking ahead to the 1990s, a bipartisan panel of former policy-makers that included former Secretaries of Defense Republican Melvin Laird and Democrat Harold Brown as well as former SACEURs Alexander Haig and Bernard Rogers concluded that after forty years the original vision of the wise, skillful and determined founders who understood mutual benefits that would result from such a coupling of both sides of the Atlantic has been confirmed again and again. Such changes as greater efforts to reduce duplication through specialization, or greater increase in defense expenditures on the part of smaller members, or the 'progressive takeover of Europe's defense requirements by Europeans should be gradual and progressive'.[13] Whatever changes take place over the next generation should be made through a multilateral, not unilateral, action.

Such was the advice of veteran American 'wise men'. It is likely that their European counterparts' advice would be much the same. Even if the more extravagant hopes of 1989 should come to pass and the Cold War between East and West would be permanently terminated, NATO still will have functions to perform. The alliance always has been more than a military organization, and West–West relations more often than not have figured more prominently than East–West confrontations. Removal of American troops could follow the reduction in arms and in tension in Europe without necessarily ending the alliance. Even if the machinery of SHAPE were dismantled, wholly or partly, the transatlantic ties could keep the treaty if not the organization intact, not as an empty shell but as a bond of reassurance to both sides of the Atlantic. But until this happier climate among nations becomes a reality, there is no serious alternative to the infrastructure in the West that NATO has built over the past forty years.[14]

Changing NATO in a changing context
William Park

To be invited to contemplate NATO is to be invited to identify problems. Problem-articulation is inherent in the activity because problems are inherent in the alliance – indeed, are inherent in politics. After all, NATO began life as a political at least as much as a military alliance. For Europeans, it served as a vehicle to entangle the United States in the security arrangements of a destroyed and divided European continent. Established in the aftermath of the Second World War as well as at the onset of the Cold War, it met a need felt by many in Europe to prohibit or contain a resurgence of the German menace in addition to the more transatlantic appreciation of the requirement to 'do something' in the face of a strengthening manifestation of Soviet malignancy. By and large, Americans were more single-minded in their perception of the Soviet menace as the *raison d'être* of the alliance, but even in Washington there was either an opaqueness about what it was NATO was supposed to do in the face of the Soviet threat, or a belief that what it was chiefly supposed to do was to encourage and enable the Europeans to provide for their own defence. The Korean scare, combined with the debate over German rearmament and the further unfolding of the Cold War in the 1950s, afford a better explanation of the subsequent 'militarization' of NATO's profile than can be uncovered by an enquiry into the events preceding and prompting the 1949 treaty.

Not only in its origins but also in its evolution since 1949, NATO's existence has never been underpinned by any very profound, all-embracing or far-reaching consensus on the purpose or ends of the alliance. In one sense or another, NATO has always been 'in crisis'. It is surely in the nature of a free voluntary alliance of sovereign states of varying size, geography, history and culture, to be characterized by conflict. The scope for disagreement, whether it be over specific events such as the 1973 oil crisis or the US bombing of Libya, or over structural and therefore perennial or semi-perennial issues such as burden-sharing or extended deterrence, is intrinsic to such an organization. Compromise as an outcome may be less predictable than the existence of those differences which prompt the search for it, but throughout the history of NATO compromises have been sought and, generally, found. That some of these compromises – perhaps even including the 'strategy' of flexible response – may represent the lowest common denominator should not be regarded as an excuse for sneering. In politics, the alternative to the lowest common denominator is rarely the highest common denominator, but fragmentation and failure. No one in NATO has wanted that, all have ultimately sought to stave it off. No one has left the alliance, but new members have joined it. NATO has reached forty; even for those to whom the word 'success' might not come easily in the context of NATO's achievements, it has survived.

Why has NATO survived? The very existence of NATO as bureaucratic entity and a political talisman is a necessary though not sufficient part of the answer. The enormous investment in NATO and the reality of its existence serve to generate positive outcomes and the desire for them. Machinery is important in politics, and not only because – as with NATO – it is so often useful. Political machinery is also important because it is visible, it is there. This leads to two further observations. First, it is more difficult to dismantle an organization such as NATO than it is to create it in the first place. This is a reference not simply to the force of inertia, but also to the general absence of a negative political will so powerful as to provide pressure for NATO's destruction. Second, there is every reason to suppose that NATO shares with so many other pieces of political machinery the attribute of flexibility. Political machines can have an enormous capacity to undergo creative change, to metamorphose, to transform. The British political system throws up many such examples – the monarchy, the House of Lords, the Empire/Commonwealth. So does the international system. The United Nations has shown this capacity, and built into the European Community is an expectation that it should evolve and develop into something greater and deeper and different.

In other words, the relationship between NATO's capacity to survive and its capacity to change is symbiotic. It can survive and therefore change, and it can change and therefore survive. All this is highly germane in the context of a consideration of NATO's future. NATO is not now what many of its founders intended it to be, or envisaged it becoming. It has evolved to arrive at 1989, and it can evolve to arrive at – who knows when, or what? But how far can this argument be stretched? Is there no prerequisite for NATO's continued existence other than its current existence? Is NATO's flexibility such that any conceivable shape and format is within its capabilities?

It is perhaps at this juncture that we need to return to the Soviet threat, and to explore its nature more closely, for it is the Soviet threat that most observers would identify as the ultimate *raison d'être* of NATO. The seemingly remarkably single-minded determination of successive Soviet leaders to upset and worry NATO has clearly contributed massively to NATO's durability. Soviet behaviour has been the major contributor to the frozen situation in Europe. Although NATO leaders have disagreed on the seriousness and nature of the Soviet threat, and on how best to respond or react to it, there has been substantial agreement that in some form or another a threat has existed. However, whereas in 1949 we had the clarity of Stalin's menace, in 1989 we have the uncertain but potential enormity of Gorbachev's promise. Yet there is more than a little truth in the now legendary maxim that NATO's prime functions – initially at least – were to keep the Americans in, the Russians out, and the Germans down. We need to bear this multiple function in mind when considering the Soviet threat, for it is interrelated with other objectives of the Western alliance. The ramifications of 'the Gorbachev era' are that although the precise content of these concerns might be altering quite fundamentally, they persist. In particular, the Soviet Union will not cease to be a major player, Germany will continue to have a question attached, and the United States will not lose all interest in what happens in Europe. However, in each case there are large areas of imponderability. So, let us indeed take the Soviet threat first, but only against this background of multiple alliance objectives.

If it is no longer completely unrealistic to envisage a future Soviet Union posing almost no threat, then it would seem to follow that much of the glue which holds NATO together might simultaneously dissolve. The Soviet Union has embarked on the road to a much more open society, albeit one beset and increasingly preoccupied by enormous economic and political difficulties. Through a combination of unilateral and negotiated measures, Moscow's military capacity could conceivably contract to a level and structure consistent with little more than territorial homeland defence and strategic deterrence. The Soviet grip on Eastern Europe could slacken or even disappear. Even this most benign of futures – or rather, the transition to it, and that could take some time – would not be without its risks. A Soviet polity undergoing such violent change in its domestic arrangements and international status would surely create severe political strains which could take a form unsympathetic to Western interests and security. In Eastern Europe too, sweetness and light need not be the inevitable consequence of an increase in Moscow's toleration of self-determination. Historically speaking, empires in turmoil have not been an unalloyed blessing. Those states which currently constitute NATO are likely to want to face such instabilities together.

In any case, the Soviet future might not be so benign. Anything less than the complete elimination of the threat, or the full democratization of Soviet political life, or any realistic prospect of the failure or fall of Moscow's reformers, would in effect leave residual characteristics of the 'Cold War' in place. There is also the rather distant and perhaps implausible possibility of a revitalized Soviet Union reviving its threat to Western Europe. Certainly the Soviet Union has a lot of contracting and even collapsing to do before it can be deemed even regionally harmless. At a more global and geostrategic level, there are good reasons to suppose that the Soviet Union will continue to provide, even unintentionally, sufficient menace to legitimize some sort of response, as did its internally weak tsarist predecessor. In fact, it is worth bearing in mind this distinction between intended and unintended 'threats'. A Soviet empire in turmoil, even one headed by a government exhibiting no desire to harm the West, could produce a whole range of potential outcomes, crises and opportunities threatening to the broader objective of stability. The point here is that a range of uncertainties will serve to counterbalance any emerging sense of NATO's obsolescence. A forum for Western consultation will be required, and the NATO machinery is in place to provide it.

The German question is hardly less imponderable than the Soviet one. It too contains within it so many different possibilities and so many conceivable ramifications. The French in particular have come to fear German neutralization, a turning to the East, a 'Finlandization', perhaps as the flip side to the coin of a reduced Soviet threat and some kind of resolution of the German division. The French fear is not simply that they would lose their forward defensive barrier, but also that their own status and position would much reduce in the absence of the Franco-German axis they have cultivated so assiduously. All this is in addition to the more traditional unease in the face of a powerful Germany, simultaneously overbearing and mistrusted, geographically anchored in the centre of Europe but politically unattached or at least semi-detached. On the other hand, the activism of French diplomacy will ensure that Paris will not give up the fight easily, and the preferred French option would be to tie a future Germany of whatever shape or form even more securely into the Western orbit and more particularly into a more close-knit European Community. In any case this largely coincides with Bonn's preferences too, which would be to encourage the East into some relationship with the European Community rather than to allow Eastern temptations to loosen Bonn's ties with its Western friends and neighbours.

From this angle it can be seen that in the modern context the German question has in large measure become the European question. Does Europe have a future as a coherent, integrated, single entity? From the British perspective – and mine is a British perspective – scepticism remains the order of the day. Part of this scepticism has, paradoxically, a European root, for it is sharpened up against what has so often and for so long been an unwarranted American optimism regarding the ease with which a new Europe could be achieved. Confronted with such high and unrealistic expectations, it has been tempting to highlight Europe's internal differences, jealousies and complexities. There is also a sceptism which has a more purely British sustenance, and reflects Britain's insularity and perhaps the deep British mistrust of grandiose political projects. This would appear to be the scepticism of Prime Minister Margaret Thatcher, and she is not alone. The European adventure is still regarded by the bulk of the British people and across the political spectrum with a mixture of hostility, suspicion and indifference. Unity is seen as not only distant and difficult, but unwelcome too. If the British and others do not wish the adventure well, its achievement will be more problematic and much of its purpose lost. In any case, 'it' will not happen overnight. The creation of a united Europe is a process rather than an event, and as such is incrementalist. 1992 is best seen as just a larger increment rather than a giant step forward for mankind.

In the security arena too, Europe looks likely to persist in being something less than the sum of its parts. There may well be more cooperation, collaboration and consultation – although none of this is a foregone conclusion – but Europe is unlikely ever to achieve the economies of scale available to the United States, and in the political sphere it will never achieve the unitary quality which Washington is able to represent. Furthermore, American leadership – even if it is less stark and more qualified in the future than it has been hitherto – will continue to be more tolerable and more credible to Europeans than that which any single European state could ever hope to offer. Thus, from the European perspective, American involvement in the security issues of the European continent will continue to be desirable, if only because there is no obvious alternative at hand. As a superpower, the United States will have a unique capacity to counter the other superpower, to galvanize NATO, and to extend strategic deterrence – even if extended deterrence takes on a more existentialist quality.

In the context of the German question, the American connection would appear to be even more crucial. A Germany firmly anchored in the Western community will not want to be forced to make an unambiguous choice between Paris and Washington. And, paradoxically, as Eastern Europe enters a state of flux, there is every likelihood that Paris – and Moscow too – might become more wary of forcing that choice on the Germans. Precisely as the German question returns explicitly to the international political agenda, so American involvement will be all the more necessary to monitor, stabilize and legitimize such changes as do occur. More narrowly and concretely, the formal participation of the United States would be required for any negotiations on the future of Berlin and of Germany as a whole, on arms control, and on wider European security issues. Those NATO-European states in Europe's outer circle, and some of those in its inner circle too, will continue to look to Washington where security issues are concerned. And were Germany to move towards neutrality, or towards some private accommodation with the East, or towards re-unification, it is hard to envisage any West European state deliberately burning its transatlantic bridges.

What, though, if we are to assume that '1992 and all that' leads to an internally strengthened and more cohesive entity incorporating all the European Community's current members and perhaps others besides? What kind of threat to NATO would the emergence of a fully-fledged second pillar pose? The European idea contains two contradictory, even conflicting, impulses. First, there is the view that economic, technological and cultural developments are so transnational as to create an informally networked European reality. In this sense, the European Community is simply institutionalizing what is already becoming a reality; it is following in the rear of organic, historical developments. The other impulse is that, if it is to survive in an economically and politically competitive world, Europe must unite. Alone, each European state and each European economy is too small to count for much, to protect sovereignty, to enhance material well-being. In this variant, the European Community is an attempt to weld a unity out of what would otherwise remain discrete and vulnerable entities. These two impulses are at odds because, whereas the second leads, however gently, towards a Fortress Europe, the processes underpinning the first impulse do not stop at Europe's borders. A too tightly bound European entity would represent in its internal relations a response to a shrinking world, and in its external relations a denial of its logic and momentum.

This is not to say that Europe will not endeavour to take a protectionist, self-contained, path. It might. But there seems little reason to assume that such a direction would endure. It would increase tension both within Europe and across the Atlantic because the underlying processes of transnational intercourse and of a shrinking world would chip away at the foundations of exclusivity and protectionism. Open societies, by their very nature, do this anyway. An attempt to create two – or more – free worlds where there is one would be irrational, illogical and temporary. Europeans and Americans would continue to invest in each other's economies, consume each other's products, partake of each other's cultures, share each other's values. The infrastructure of transatlantic relationships is massive, deep, and unlikely to be permanently diminished by outbursts of political negativism. For NATO, the consequence of further European integration need not be worse than the oft-discussed dumb-bell structure of an alliance between two entities, Europe and the United States.

Similar arguments apply to the United States. Clearly, the degree and nature of Washington's participation in Europe's affairs will hinge on American as well as European desires and realities. A surprising number of Americans – including many who really ought to know better – have frightened themselves inordinately with tales of their own national decline. Certainly the budget deficit is worrying, and the massive transatlantic gap in material well-being and economic productivity which pertained forty years ago has inevitably – and desirably – largely disappeared. This shift in relative economic power has understandably underlined American burden-sharing concerns, but East–West relaxation is likely to address these issues from the unanticipated angle of arms control and unilateral defence sector contraction. It is without doubt easier to envisage the Americans doing less in defence terms than it is the Europeans doing more. Any such cuts should also help to undercut that part of Paul Kennedy's argument which says that high defence spending – overstretch – chokes off economic growth. The 'peace dividend', by undermining excessive fears of an American collapse under the weight of the obligations of alliance, could paradoxically serve to limit the appeal of isolationist sirens.

It seems necessary to restore some sense of perspective on the American future. The population of the United States is around four times that of its nearest West European rival, twice that of Japan, and three times that of a reunified Germany. The United States possesses almost unequalled physical resources, one of the world's very highest levels of economic productivity, and its society is characterized by pace-setting technological dynamism and entrepreneurial spirit. The post-war history of Western Europe has revealed the remarkably regenerative strengths of Western societies, and in the United States one finds the Western, and regenerative, society *par excellence*. A more interesting question than the economic one has to do with the American political will to be an active, global superpower. It was war, followed by the emergence of the Soviet, communist threat, which drew the American giant out of its isolationism. Peace, and Soviet self-absorption, would seem to imply the reappearance of isolationism as a real option. Even the suggestion that a less fraught Europe would release the United States to emphasize a more global, maritime role seems intellectually questionable. The world is now more interdependent, and along with some increase in vulnerabilty comes an increase in the number of states with a stake in this system of interdependence. Such issues as might call forth a military solution could – would – be dealt with by the growing number of capable and willing regional powers. Does an interdependent world need a world policeman? Is there much for a world policeman to do?

However, the intellectual appeal of such arguments – should they have any – must be distinguished from their political appeal. There are opposing arguments which are hardly less compelling and which are likely to find fertile soil in the United States. There is no necessary coincidence between the interests of the industrialized world, or more narrowly the United States, and those of any given regional power on any given issue. Some regional powers are not, or may become less, benign. There are interests which are peculiar to the United States and perhaps to its European allies too. There are conceivable scenarios in which only a superpower could be expected to muster the requisite coercive power. In any case, such emphasis on the military aspects of global policy is too crude and too restricted. Interdependence is fragile and requires management, and Washington is both well placed and needs, in its own interest, to take a leading role. It has also come to expect to play this role. To posit that the United States will continue to be the world's – and even Europe's – major actor is not to presuppose American force levels at anything like those to which we have become accustomed. It is to indicate that a retreat into some isolationist Fortress America is both unlikely to occur and, if it did, would constitute an act of political irresponsibility and self-delusion; and would therefore be temporary. There could, though, be fewer Americans in Europe, and Europeans might find themselves proportionally more responsible for their own defence. This need not spell NATO's demise, and in any case would simpy approximate to what NATO's American founders originally envisaged.

In short, there is a Western community, and it is transatlantic, and it will continue to exist. Its members are rich, free democracies who trade extensively with each other and with the outside world. NATO might not incorporate all the members of this community, but it remains the primary institution through which its security concerns are addressed. These security concerns might well take on a more political and less military dimension, and they might adjust their primary focus, but they are unlikely to evaporate. Furthermore, Washington remains the political hub of this community, linking together Turkey and Norway, and even – adopting a broader definition of the community – Tokyo and Seoul. And this brings us to one final set of observations – or, rather, an alternative way of articulating what has been a major underlying theme of this chapter. NATO also represents a deeper reality, which has far more substance than the alliance structure itself. Even if NATO were to cease to exist, many of the relationships that are subsumed within it would persist. A crumbling or dismantling of the formal alliance would not mean the collapse of shared perspectives, concerns and interests. Nor should we too automatically assume that any fissure which appeared would lie somewhere in mid-Atlantic. For example, contained within the current emphasis on the northern flank of NATO, and on the maritime dimension of the security of a number of NATO's allies, is the germ of a more purely – albeit looser – 'Atlantic' alliance, one to which the British at least seem as likely to sign up as they are to a more purely 'Continental' bloc. This would resemble a return to the 'stepping stones' concept of the alliance which inspired many of NATO's Anglo-American and Scandinavian founders. A France which felt it had lost or was losing its battle for the soul of Germany could well recover that enthusiasm for the transatlantic connection which was so characteristic of its diplomats in the immediate post-war period.

Above all, the wisest position for analysts and statesmen to adopt, particularly in the face of the twists and turns of the Gorbachev era, is one of 'wait and see'. Even so, it would appear far more likely that NATO will dissolve simultaneously, and by agreement, with the Warsaw Pact, than that it crumble as a result of its own internal tensions. And nothing would serve as a better testimony. It might also be that NATO's continued existence comes to be welcomed in the East too as a means of keeping the Americans in and – not to be repeated too loudly – the Germans 'down'. The last thing a weakened, defensive and unstable Soviet leadership would want is an untethered German bull in an unattended European china shop.

NOTES AND REFERENCES

1. Ronald Steel, *The End of the Alliance: America and the future of Europe* (New York: Viking Press, 1964), pp. 15–16.
2. 'Aide-mémoire, 17 February 1961', in *New York*, 21 February 1961.
3. Military Procurement Authorization 1964. *Hearings* before the Committee on Armed Services, US Senate, 21 February 1963, 88 Cong., 1st sess., pp. 342–3.
4. Alain C. Enthoven and K. Wayne Smith, *How Much Is Enough? Shaping the Defense Program, 1961–1969* (New York: Harper & Row, 1971), pp. 147ff.
5. McNamara testimony, 'The Atlantic alliance', *Hearings* before the Sub-committee on National Security and International Operations of the Committee on Government Operations, US Senate, 89 Cong., 2nd sess., pt 6, 21 June 1966, p. 187.
6. Robert Bowie, 'Tensions within the alliance', *Foreign Affairs*, 42 (October 1963), p. 68.
7. 'The Future Task of the Alliance' (Harmel Report), 13–14 December 1967, Brussels, North Atlantic Council, *Final Communiques*, pp. 198–202. Ibid., 24–8 June 1968, Reykjavik, North Atlantic Council, *Final Communiques*, p. 216.
8. 15–16 November 1988, Brussels, ibid., p. 214.
9. 'NATO in the 1990s', Special report of the North Atlantic Assembly, 1988, p. 26.
10. Colin S. Gray, 'NATO: time to call it a day?', *The National Interest* (Winter 1987/8): 24.
11. Quoted in Bernard E. Trainor, 'Sharing the defense burden: allies are listening', *New York Times*, 6 September 1988.

12. *Congressional Record*, 100 Cong., 1st sess., 8 May 1987, pp. 3329–31. The amendment to a military authorization bill in support of maintaining US troops in Europe was sponsored by Bill Richardson, and was accepted by voice vote.
13. 'The Future of NATO', Policy Consensus Reports, The Johns Hopkins Foreign Policy Institute (August 1988).
14. A somewhat different version of this paper was presented for the Core Seminar Series on NATO at Forty, sponsored by the International Security Studies Program of the Woodrow Wilson International Center for Scholars, Washington, DC, 31 January 1989.

17 The future of NATO: further discussion

Clearly, the future of NATO and Warsaw Pact alliance systems is dependent on the outcome of events in the Soviet Union and Eastern Europe. At the Conference, and subsequently, at least two schools seem to have emerged. First, there were those who argued that it would take a long time for the situation in the East to clarify. We in the West have always been uncertain about the Russian enigma, and never more so than now. Until the time came when we could be clear, it would be prudent for the West to keep NATO in as good order as circumstances make possible. NATO represents a vague sense of cultural and economic community and it seems to have worked as a mechanism for deterrence. The onus was on the advocates of change to prove the wisdom of their alternative choices.

This caution was, and is, challenged by a second school, those who dispute the essential need for NATO and who would emphasize, instead, Mr Gorbachev's likely preoccupation with internal matters and the consequently declining Soviet threat. NATO's future existence may be like a pantomime Tinkerbell, something absolutely dependent on people's willingness to believe in it and their preparedness to do something in support. It was hard to imagine in an age of *glasnost* and *perestroika* that public support could continue at the level it had maintained in the past. Therefore NATO's previous ability to survive one, allegedly terminal, crisis after another might not provide much of a guide to its future prospects.

But there is a second level of debate as well and this concerns the effect of increasing economic constraint on the future health of the Atlantic alliance. Some expressed the fear that with the decline of the unifying threat, nationalism would be even more likely to defeat a sense of commonality of purpose than it had in the past. Far from pulling the NATO countries together, economic constraint might instead aggravate their differences and rivalries. Moreover, the extent to which it is possible for enhanced military togetherness to help solve the resources-commitments gap is debatable. Role specialization has its technical and operational limits as well as its political ones. Some would doubt whether, in fact, it is possible for medium powers actually to design forces so that they only make sense as part of a wider whole.

On the other hand, another school of thought is more sanguine about the effects of economic constraint on the future well-being of the alliance. According to this view, there is now a much stronger pressure than before to share costs, to get acts together and to demonstrate evident solidarity in a more uncertain world. Indeed, the economic and industrial face of Europe is changing quite fundamentally and may provide even greater incentives for cooperative effort. The difficulty was that, to the extent that this development was not confined to Europe, the more likely it was to disrupt transatlantic harmony.

A third possibility has been canvassed in the light of events in the Soviet Union and Eastern Europe and that is that NATO may change, rather than fade away. Some commentators distinguish between NATO as a political alliance and NATO as an integrated military organization. It is quite possible to argue that, in the future, the emphasis might shift from the latter to the former.

Indeed, to many observers this seemed increasingly likely to be a problem common to both sides of the East–West divide. The Warsaw Treaty organization is similarly confronting the need for wholesale change in a manner which might very well much reduce its capacity to act as a unitary military organization. It is beginning to look more like an alliance between sovereign states rather than a defence mechanism imposed by one on many. But an evident intention on the part of the East European states to reduce defence expenditure and in many cases to work for the reduction of Soviet force levels in their countries and a generally heightened sense of their own differences and divisions are all likely to increase a drift towards disintegration. Perhaps we are seeing the beginning of a long process of reciprocal deterioration in the basic fabric of the two alliance systems, with incalculable consequences for the future of European security.

Nor should Europeans forget that their superpower allies both have major concerns elsewhere.[1] Although there is not much doubt that the Soviet Union continues to be preoccupied with its Western concerns, it is also a Pacific power with major interests east of the Urals, interests which have very little to do with its East European allies. It is far from inconceivable that this could lead to clashes with the Americans, for the United States is also a Pacific power as well as an Atlantic one. It has global preoccupations that are not always shared by its European partners. This could obviously cause tensions within NATO as an organization were it to lead to political dispute between the United States and all or some of its West European allies. Europeans often betray anxiety that there might, one day, be a return to the kind of Asia-lationism (a blend of isolationism and the Pacific First school of the Second World War years) that characterized some American policy-making circles in the 1940s and early 1950s. Such apprehensions could be seen in the European response to the 'Discriminate deterrence' document of January 1988.[2] US conduct in Central America or the Caribbean was construed, by some Europeans, as a kind of global unilateralism which was often an inappropriate over-reaction to the local circumstances and, moreover, one that was profoundly dangerous to the political cohesion of the alliance. Quite possibly, it would result in American forces being sucked out of Europe, or the Europeans being sucked into their main ally's distant quarrels.[3]

It is only fair to point out that some Americans responded with stereotypes of their own, complaining that Europeans were deeply parochial and quite neglectful of their broader global interests. 'West Europeans', remarked Lawrence Eagleburger 'are increasingly less interested in dealing with the stability of the world, and far more interested in dealing with stability in and around their own area.'[4] Such differences are hardly conducive to alliance cohesion or to the future health of NATO.

In some European quarters, moreover, there was and is considerable scepticism about the extent to which it was possible to use military forces to defend Western interests in a turbulent outside world anyway. The limits of naval power to control events ashore was made painfully obvious during the Lebanon and Gulf crises. Certainly there were growing economic and other interdependencies, but it was not at all evident that a new kind of maritime globalism could do much to defend them. In the past the clearest rationale for the West to maintain a capacity for intervention had been the apparent extension of Soviet influence into the Third World. However, Gorbachev has now clearly signalled his distaste for such involvements

Such questions were at the heart of the issue about whether, in face of the declining threat in Europe, NATO, or some other agency of Western military cooperation, should assume more responsibility for out-of-area concerns. Such possibilities have certainly been considered from time to time but, in truth, this does not seem to be a serious proposition. Given the diversity of view within the alliance about both the need and the form of a military role out of area, extending NATO's boundary would be highly controversial in political terms. As Dr Luns used to warn, it might lead to some members of the alliance feeling more equal than others and prejudice a record of success based on a concentration on affairs within the current boundary constraints.

The prospects of a formal European force operating under the auspices of the WEU were much encouraged by the success of the mine-sweeping endeavour of 1987. However, even in the Gulf, there were significant limits to European togetherness. The national forces operated with differing degrees of independence (with the French taking the most distinctive line and the British/Dutch/Belgians taking the most integrated). The various national contingents observed differently nuanced rules of engagement and the development of the force was always attended with political sensitivities[5]. It would be unwise to assume that either a European or a NATO naval force could too readily be built on such foundations.

In the meantime, Americans and some Europeans will doubtless continue to act individually in defence of their own interests out of area. Where more general Western interests seem to be at stake, NATO members with the means, willingness and experience to defend them will probably represent the alliance informally, as they do already. The advantages of close coordination between the Europeans, and between them and the Americans, seem obvious. Uncoordinated activities increase the prospects of inconsistency and the wasteful duplication of effort that some observers detected in the Beirut operation.[6] Moreover, the success of the Red Sea/Gulf of Suez mine-clearance effort (the organization of which depended on a series of bilateral arrangements between the individual European countries and Egypt and/or Saudi Arabia) shows that force integration is not necessarily a condition for success. It may well be that the Europeans are more acceptable to the locals if they come singly, rather than in whole battalions.

Appropriately tailored naval forces do not seem to have lost their utility for the management of containable threats to Western interests in an increasingly turbulent Third World, but it is not at all clear that NATO was an appropriate mechanism for their use. The essential utility of the NATO alliance in the future would be decided by the same criteria as it had in the past, namely its value in assuring the security of the members within the area defined by the original treaty. It stood or fell by that criteria. If it became evident that current changes in the Soviet Union or Eastern Europe were likely to render the organization obsolete (and it was as yet far from clear that this would be so) then it would fade away, whatever the situation out of area. This was not to say, however, that as a treaty, NATO might not continue to act as an agency for the coordination of American and European efforts in a wider and perhaps less secure world.

NOTES AND REFERENCES

1. For a good, early, survey see Gregory F. Treverton, 'Defence beyond Europe' *Survival*, September/October 1983.
2. '*Discriminate deterrence*' produced by the Commission on Integrated Longterm Strategy, 12 January 1988. For a European response see Sir Michael Howard, Karl Kaiser and François de Rose in *International Herald Tribune*, 4 February 1984.
3. For example, see European worries about US policy towards Central America in the spring of 1985: 'US Latin role upsets Europeans', *Los Angeles Times* 17 March 1985 and 'Why Europe worries and why Washington cares', *New York Times* 17 March 1985.
4. Laurence Eagleburger, remarks at John Davis Lodge International Center, Conference on the State of the Union, 31 January 1984.
5. For example, see *The Guardian* 23 September 1987. Mrs Thatcher was particularly clear that, while 'coordinated' naval operations were necessary, a joint force commander was not. *The Guardian*, 6 November 1987 reports a British government spokesman: 'This is a purely British operation. It is not being carried out at the request of any other party.' See also 'TN task force cool to switch', *The Guardian*, 22 January 1988.
6. 'Obituary: the MNF in Beirut', *Defence Attache*, no 1/1984.

18 European navies: problems and prospects

James Eberle

INTRODUCTION

From time to time there comes a widespread feeling, which transcends national boundaries, that we stand at a period of fundamental change in the affairs of the world. I have no doubt that we stand today at just such a period. In the Soviet Union we are witnessing the death throes of communism, as it has been practised since the revolution. Russia has dug itself into a seventy-year deep Marxist 'hole', from which Mr Gorbachev is trying to find a socialist way out. It is an immensely difficult and challenging task. In the developed, capitalist world a revolution in technology, and in the balance of the elements of production, have drastically changed the pattern of economic activity. The fostering of competition and individual enterprise has been shown to be the most powerful engine of economic growth. Advances in communication between countries have led to such high levels of interdependence that traditional concepts of 'nationhood' and the role of the state are being called into question. Man's insatiable appetite for 'more' threatens the very environment in which he lives.

Such times of fundamental change provide great opportunities for progress towards a world order which is more stable, more equitable and which provides more individual freedom. However, if change proceeds too slowly, then such opportunities may be missed. But change also involves risk. There can be no certainty of a new safe haven. And if change proceeds too fast, then we may cause storms which can prevent us from following the track we have chosen. Our political and diplomatic skills must be directed at identifying where it is that we wish to get to, and setting a course and speed that will allow us to get there in good order and without disaster *en route*. Clarity as to our long-term goal is important; without it, short-term adjustments of course, in the mood of pragmatism in the face of immediate problems, may lead us into dangerous waters from which it is difficult to extricate ourselves without damage.

A FUTURE EUROPE

For us in Europe this means having some vision of what sort of Europe we wish to see in the next century. What are its boundaries? For they are surely beyond those of the present European Community. What is its political and economic structure? And do defence and security arrangements need to be fully aligned with this political and economic structure? We at present accommodate one 'neutral' country, Ireland, within the EC. Could we accommodate another? – Austria for instance. Can Britain maintain close and special security relationships with the United States, without calling into question its full political and economic integration within the EC. The German Democratic Republic already has very strong economic ties to the Federal Republic of Germany (more than 50 per cent of the GDR's imports come from the FRG and some 60 per cent of its exports go there). In 1993 such access will be to all Community countries. Can we foresee a Europe in which other East European countries, such as Hungary perhaps, have close economic and political ties to Western Europe, whilst maintaining their security relationships with the Soviet Union and their place in the Warsaw Pact? These are some of the political questions that now demand our attention. They are not entirely new questions. The Harmel Report which provided the basis for NATO's policy of 'defence and detente' also called for the alliance to

examine and review suitable policies designed to achieve a just and stable order in Europe, to overcome the division of Germany and to foster European security. This will be part of the process of active and constant preparation for the time when fruitful discussions of these complex questions may be possible bilaterally or multilaterally between Eastern and Western nations.

That time for fruitful discussion is, I believe, almost upon us, if indeed it has not already arrived. Western Europe clearly needs to have its own conception of a 'wider Europe' and how this would fit in to a pattern of Atlantic and global security. But that conception does not exist.

We in Western Europe are at present principally involved in a process of integrating the national economies of the countries of the European Community to form a single internal market. This is what '1992' is all about. However '1992' is not only an economic process. It is also a political process. The creation of the single market requires agreement about the rules, and how these rules should be enforced. As in every other activity, with no rules we should soon descend into anarchy. But the political process of European integration goes way beyond the vision of a single market. Article 1 of the Single European Act states the objective of the European Communities as 'to contribute together to making concrete progress towards European Unity' – although European Unity is not defined. In Section III, dealing with Foreign Affairs, the Act requires that 'common principles and objectives [be] gradually developed and defined'. It also declares that 'closer co-operation on questions of European security would contribute in an essential way to the development of a European identity in external policy matters.' The nations of the Community go on to confirm that 'they are ready to co-ordinate their positions more closely on the political and economic aspects of security'.

How far beyond the requirements of economic integration the process of political union should be carried is, however, a matter of hot debate. It is argued by some that the consequences of further economic integration, such as European Monetary Union, would, in the words of a recent speech by a senior member of the British government at Chatham House, 'be nothing less than European government – albeit a Federal one – and political union: the United States of Europe. This is simply not on the agenda now, nor will it be for the foreseeable future.' There are calls by others for a 'social Europe' which raises fears in some countries of the imposition of legislation from Brussels which would impede the free operation of business and market forces. These are some of the challenges of the economic, political and social spheres. In them also lie the opportunities for the future.

THE SECURITY OF EUROPE

But what about integration in the European security field that lies outside the scope of the 'political and economic aspects' of defence policy? Defence policy is not concerned with opportunities. It is aimed at minimizing risk – the risk of violent conflict. And in Europe the defence policy of the Atlantic alliance has been very successful in maintaining the peace and security of its member nations. There is thus understandably a great resistance to change and a reluctance to grasp opportunities that involve risk. 'Why change a winning hand?' is a question which requires a clear response. However, defence is an expensive call upon national resources – and people do not want to pay for what they feel they do not need. Thus when so much else is changing, we need to examine very carefully the factors of change that are at work, and the direction of the main thrust of change. We can, of course, in the field of security policy, choose to stem the tide of change, in the belief that the tide will in due course turn – or to use the cross-currents to place ourselves in a better position to take advantage of future changes. But if we are in a powerful and non-tidal stream, as some would regard the concept of European Union, then in the longer term we have little alternative to going with the stream and taking advantage of it.

We have long heard calls for a stronger European pillar of the Atlantic alliance. It has not always been clear what the fundamental rationale for this was. Was it a burden-sharing argument – that the Europeans should do more so that the Americans might not do less? Or was it a European insurance policy against a certain inevitability that the United States would do less? Was it that a common European external policy only made sense if it were backed by a coherent element of 'European armed force'? Or was it that the vision of a United States of Europe required integration in the economic, political and security field – that a real 'Europe' had to stand on three legs, not two? We may individually accept or reject the idea of a United States of Europe, but we cannot safely ignore the rhetoric. For today's rhetoric may become tomorrow's reality. Chancellor Kohl, in a speech in Berlin in October of last year spoke of a European army. 'We cannot,' he said 'talk all the time about "European identity" or "the European pillar in the Alliance" without taking concrete steps. We must aim to bring about gradually a common European defence, possibly – if only at the end of the path – through a European army.' He also called for a Europe-wide force of police to deal with terrorism, drugs trafficking and internationally organized crime.

NAVAL ROLES AND TASKS

What does all this mean for navies today and what might we in Europe wish to do in naval affairs between now and the turn of the century that is significantly different from what we have been doing for the last decade? Let me first identify what I believe to be the principal thrusts of change in the world which affect the maritime scene.

First, I believe that the acquisition of territory is no longer a driving force in man's affairs. We are already seeing the breakup of the last of the great empires, the Soviet Empire. There was a time when the possession of territory provided wealth and power. Today it is the possession of information and knowledge that is the principal source of power. This cannot be acquired by military force. Dominant military power is therefore no longer a necessary condition for a nation to have wealth and influence. We need look no further than Japan for an example.

Secondly, I believe that the relationship between the costs of using military force in relation to the potential gains from its use no longer make large-scale military action an attractive option for the settlement of international disputes. By 'costs', I do not refer to just the high monetary cost of acquiring and maintaining modern weapon systems. I refer also to the potential destructive capacity of even conventional weapons in the increasingly complex and international infrastructure of our modern societies, and to the natural environment in which they exist.

Thirdly, I believe that the nature and interdependence of our global economic activity no longer provides the vulnerability to military action that was the case when seaborne trade was the lifeblood of the international trading system. Exchange rates, which now play such an important part in the international economy, are not driven up or down by military action. There are more cost-effective barriers to trade than the processes of war at sea. And there is increasing understanding that market forces, not military forces, are the key to prosperity.

Finally, I believe that there is a growing world-wide moral repugnance to the indiscriminate killing that is inevitably involved in war. War is no longer an activity whose effects can be confined to the armed forces of a state. War is no longer between governments. War is between peoples. There has, in effect been a 'democratization' of war. This does not, of course, mean the rejection of individual violence; indeed, sadly we see the reverse. It does not even involve the rejection of violence by the state; as many examples of 'state-sponsored terrorism' demonstrate. But it does increasingly mean that war, as an organized activity by the state, is neither an effective nor 'acceptable' form of political action. The outcome of the Iran/Iraq conflict is perhaps the latest example of a long list of the failure of wars to achieve political objectives.

What then does this imply for naval roles and tasks? I set this brief discussion against the background proposition that we shall not, in the timescale of the 1990s, construct a new framework for European security; and that NATO and the Warsaw Pact will continue to exist in broadly their present forms. However, I shall assume that the present momentum for arms reductions is maintained; and that a stable balance at significantly lower levels of forces is achieved in Europe. The Soviet Union would thus be seen as a reducing military threat, both for reasons of its changed intentions and because of unilateral or negotiated reductions in its force levels, including those at sea. In this situation, the task of countering the Soviet Navy is likely to become a much less dominant task for NATO navies; although, within the NATO area, the degree of attention that will need to be paid to the protection of the seaborne reinforcement routes will depend on the extent of the reduction of the Soviet maritime threat to them. Outside the NATO area, the task of the projection of power ashore, against armed and organized resistance, would carry a much lesser priority than it has held since the Second World War. There would be a strong case for organizing long-range intervention capability in small, highly integrated units of ground, air and naval forces.

The dominant naval role would remain the deterrence of war, with its principal tasks being the secure deployment of ballistic missile-firing submarines and the defence of coastal waters. At the other end of the scale of naval capability, the 'preservation of law and order' on the high seas, perhaps in the longer-term future under some form of United Nations direction, and within the limits of exclusive economic zones by national authorities, would become of increasing importance relative to other 'blue-water' tasks.

Against this background, and in the absence of full political integration within Western Europe, it is clear that a 'European Navy' would necessarily be the result of 'cohabitation' rather than 'marriage'. Each individual national navy would retain its own basic character and traditions which would remain the focus for national pride and patriotism that is essential to maintain efficiency as a fighting force. But there is clearly room for varying degrees of coordination in the functions of naval policy and planning, in operational control, in logistic support, including ship upkeep, in manpower, training and administration.

POLICY AND PLANNING

Final decisions on the allocation of national resources to their navy and on the shape and size of the individual fleets must remain a responsibility of the national political authorities. Increasingly, advice to defence ministers is provided through a Central Defence Staff to which a Naval Staff presents the 'naval case'. It is in the area of the presentation of the 'naval case' that coordinated European naval policy could have significant impact.

Before attempting to answer the obvious questions, 'How can coordination of European naval policies be achieved?', it is necessary to enquire why it is not achieved now. Regular bilateral talks do already take place between the naval staffs of several West European countries. The NATO naval authorities are themselves, at least in theory, in a position to guide such naval coordination. Indeed, in the Channel Command, the Chiefs of Naval Staff (CNS) of Belgium, Britain, France and the Netherlands, together with the CINCHAN, meet regularly as the 'Channel Committee', although this is often more of a social gathering than an effective business meeting. There is no easy answer to this lack of common policies, but it probably lies in the lack of multilateralism. Effective cooperation depends both on bilateral and multilateral discussion. It is the latter which is at present missing, except perhaps in the 'Channel Committee'; and this is too constrained to be of much practical European value.

Thus an essential element of a European navy would need to be a 'Naval Board' consisting of the CNS of each of the member countries. If the Board's deliberations were to be effective, it would need to be supported by a small international staff responsible for initiating thought on matters of long-term joint naval planning, for preparing the agenda for the Board's meetings, and for following through the implementation of the Board's actions.

OPERATIONAL CONTROL

Under present agreements, the majority of naval ships continue to operate under their own national operational control (OPCON) during peace, whatever their whereabouts. The major exceptions are the NATO naval standing forces, which do operate under NATO OPCON. Since in war the vast majority of warships from NATO countries would operate under international commanders, there is at least a prima facie case for more ships to be under international OPCON in time of peace. A European operational command arrangement, coincident with the NATO organization for operational commands, would be a way of achieving this. Thus, for instance, ships of all European navies deployed in the Mediterranean outside their own local sea area boundaries, might be placed under the operational control of COMNAVSOUTH, acting in a 'European' capacity. COMNAVBALTAP might act in a similar way for the Northern area; whilst CINCEASTLANT would so act for the Atlantic.

Detailed study would be necessary to assess the advantages and dis-advantages of such an arrangement. At first sight, it appears to contradict one of the first principles of any successful command structure, which is that it should be simple, but still of some utility. However, if the result contributes to the aim of increasing the sense of European identity within the navies of Europe, then the idea should not be lightly dismissed.

LOGISTICS AND UPKEEP

That logistics remains a national responsibility has long been a complicating factor in NATO planning. Much progress has been made in standardization and rationalization. But the basic fact remains that each of the NATO countries runs its own national naval logistics system. The NATO stores-referencing system ensures that a common format exists in all the countries, and this provides administration advantages; but the same stores reference number may still provide you with a bucket in one country and a part for a radar set in another!

It should be possible, with significant advantages in cost, flexibility and availability to set up a European naval supply system. For common user-items, a central purchasing agency would be able to exploit the advantages of bulk purchase and common insurance stocks. Such items could be readily available from any naval supply point, ashore or afloat and regardless of nationality, the appropriate charge being made by computer to the 'customer' navy. For items of national purchase, a central computer system would provide ready access through data channels to other national systems, without the usual clogging of naval operational communications.

For afloat support, a European logistics planning staff at designated operational command centres would be able to ensure that there was full coordination of the various naval tankers' programmes and would be in a position to recommend appropriate loading for stores supply ships to support task units of different navies. This would be to the advantage of both peacetime deployments and wartime plans.

The need for preventive equipment maintenance, and for periods of defect rectification are a significant constraint in the peacetime operational planning of operational ships. Because of continuing pressures for the reductions of ships crews, it is becoming increasingly necessary to employ extra shore-based maintenance staff to assist in shipboard maintenance. Although mobile maintenance units exist in some countries, it is more usual for ships to return to their own national base ports in order to allow this work to be carried out. Much greater operational flexibility would be achieved if facilities were available, Europe-wide, to allow ships satisfactorily to carry out their planned upkeep at the nearest base, irrespective of its nationality. However, it needs to be remembered that such facilities do not provide the necessary 'man-maintenance' requirements for the married man whose families reside in their ship's real 'home port'. Nevertheless, the benefit of a wider knowledge and experience of the upkeep requirements of the various ships and equipments of the European navies during peace, would also be a considerable operational benefit in war.

MANPOWER AND TRAINING

One of the more difficult tasks of naval management is to maintain a balanced manpower structure matched to the continuing needs of the Fleet. The difficulties arise from the long time-factor which is involved in making changes to manpower structure, in a situation in which there is a wide range of uncertainty in recruiting, in training requirements and in retention. The uncertainties of future political and economic circumstances add a further element of chance. The practical result is that there seldom seems to be a time in manpower planning when there is not either a surplus or a shortage of men in one category or another. It is sometimes possible to make trade-offs between such surpluses and shortages. But the smaller the navy, the less easy this is to achieve. If a degree of interchangeability of trained officers and men between European navies were practicable, then significant advantages in the flexibility of manning would accrue. Exchanges of personnel have been tried with success; for example, between the British and Netherlands navies when the latter were able to offer sea billets for seaman ratings that were not available in the British fleet. Again, in war, such flexibilities could be valuable.

To achieve the maximum degree of such manpower flexibility would involve a review of the manpower structures of the various navies with the intention of moving towards their alignment in the long term. It is perhaps of interest to speculate on what might be the moral, and indeed the legal, implications of EC regulations for the free flow of labour within the Community, and of the recognition of equivalent professional status in relation to the personnel of the European armed services, if a policy of manpower structural alignment was deliberately rejected; even though such speculation might have little practical impact.

A shorter-term measure to provide flexibility of manpower would be to work towards common levels of training. Much naval training is, of course, specific to certain types of equipment. Commonality in such training can only be achieved if the equipment itself is common. At present, such equipment commonality between the European navies is the exception rather than the rule, although efforts to achieve greater standardization (such as the NFR 90, NATO replacement frigate project) have high priority.

There are, however, more basic elements of skill training for which the training performance standards could with advantage be brought into line. Indeed, with such common elements of training it might be possible not only to produce men trained to agreed, common standards, but also to economize in the overall cost of training. Of course, there are practical problems of language and culture to be overcome. Would it ever be easy to teach British naval cooks to produce pasta, or Italian cooks to produce Yorkshire pudding? But perhaps this would be no more difficult than having to teach army and navy cooks to the same syllabus!

ADMINISTRATION

If there were to be the normal possibility of officers and men from one navy serving in the ships of another, there would clearly be a need for the alignment of some administrative, and perhaps also disciplinary, procedures. The potential field for such alignment, is of course, very large. However, the size of this field might look less daunting if viewed against the alignments which will be necessary to achieve the full internal market for the European Community by 1992. But it would be very important to avoid change for change's sake. A pragmatic way of tackling this subject would be to review what has already been achieved; and then to see where the major practical difficulties had occurred, with a view to proposing solutions which might be given formal status in some form of agreed 'Code of European Naval Administrative Practice'.

SYMBOLISM AND PRACTICE

What does all this add up to? Would results along the lines discussed add up to a vision of a 'European navy'? The answer in substantive terms is probably 'no'. But the concept of European Union is concerned with symbolism as well as substance. European Union is not about to produce a new supranational federated 'United States of Europe'. The countries of Western Europe are embarked on an enterprise which has never been tried before, involving a pooling of sovereignty to achieve mutual benefit. Seen against this background, then the sort of path down which this brief examination has taken us could be worthwhile as a means of contributing to a sense of shared European destiny and the common good. But a European navy would also need its own symbolism, if it were to have any tangible existence. For its ships a standard hull colour scheme and funnel markings would be sensible; and perhaps all ships could, in harbour, fly at the jackstaff a new 'Euro-jack'. For the men it would not, in the first instance at least, be practical to look to a common uniform, although a standard pattern of action working dress is a possibility. But similar badges of rank, the same cap badge and a 'Europe' shoulder flash are ideas which might reasonably be considered.

The final, and most important, questions which we must ask are: Would a 'European navy' as outlined here enhance European Security? and Would it be compatible with the need to strengthen the European pillar of NATO? In both cases the answer seems to be a clear 'yes'. Better coordination of European naval policy and practice cannot do other than strengthen both the deterrent and warfighting capabilities of the European navies; and a 'European navy' would surely be an example of Europe 'getting its maritime act together'. This is exactly what Europe is trying to do in the wider field of Atlantic security.

Thus there do appear to be practical steps that would lead us in the direction of a 'European navy'. And who knows where this might lead? With political and economic advance towards European Union, and with real progress in European defence equipment collaboration, is it too much to hope that it could eventually lead to a European navy that was more substance than symbol? Here is a path which can be trodden without the need for surrendering national sovereignty. A modest declaration of political will would be enough to start a proper enquiry into what might be achievable.

EUROPEAN MARITIME STUDIES

But where are we to study what might be achieved? What might be the future roles and tasks of European naval forces and how far might we progress towards the concept of a European navy? A 'revolution at sea' may well be occurring, perhaps in the field of military technology, but also in the field of international politics. We are faced with the possibility of fundamental change in the international system which will require major changes in all our navies. We have not started seriously to study in depth the implications of this, nor are we in Europe organized to do so. I suggest we should seek to set up a European Centre for Maritime Studies. Such a centre would be staffed appropriately with both uniformed and non-uniformed professional and academic staff, drawn from the principal maritime nations of Western Europe. Its task would be to carry out research, against the background of growing European economic and political integration, into the future maritime needs of Europe. Perhaps such a centre might appropriately be set up at Greenwich – a place that has in the past been the cradle of naval thought, innovation and development.

European maritime integration

J. J. J. A. van Rooyen

My intention is to describe the intensified level of cooperation between the European navies – and to speculate on its future, looking ahead, especially to the period 2000–10.[1] The first question is, why have those navies chosen the route of enhanced cooperation? In the first place, on the political level, a strong European pillar is needed in the longer term since it is in the interest of NATO itself. Sharing roles, risks and responsibilities, in short, burden-sharing, is vital to alliance understanding. Apart from noting the issue of burden-sharing, it is also necessary to make reference to the European Community Single European Act of 1986 and to the Platform on European Security Interests of the Western European Union of 1987. In both documents, it is stressed that closer cooperation on questions of European security is essential to a European identity, and that the construction of an integrated Europe will remain incomplete as long as it does not include matters of security and defence. The latest developments in the East–West context and the newest look-after-yourself attitude of the Soviet Union and the United States deepen this omission. For this reason, one of the assumptions that has been put forward in the Eurogroup is that, although NATO may continue in much of its present form, the relationship between members must allow scope for more than slight adjustments to defence arrangements. However, until now, and despite Gorbachev, Europe has lacked the political leadership and a political will to organize itself better.

In addition to these political issues, there are also economic considerations. Budgetary restrictions oblige the European nations to make better use of their resources. This concerns not only collaboration on the acquisition of military equipment but also coordinated long-term force planning. On top of this, the unexpectedly audacious disarmament proposals involving lower levels of non-naval and naval forces also reinforce the need for integrated European force planning. Last but not least, there are strong military reasons for closer integration: European maritime forces in the Eastern and especially Northern Atlantic form the bulk of in-place forces in peacetime. Especially because of this in-theatre presence, they form an important element of the maritime correlation of forces. It is therefore appropriate for them, in close cooperation with one another, to display surveillance and presence on behalf of the alliance, especially for crisis management.

So, what forces are we actually talking about when considering the navies of Europe? Limiting the figures to in-place Atlantic forces only, and not taking into account any future disarmament and budgetary restraints for maritime forces, European maritime forces in the year 2000 will consist of 10 SSBNs, 30 SSNs, 5 aircraft carriers, 130 major escorts, 70 SSK, 130 MPA and 140 MCM vessels. To these numbers, US in-place forces – about 40 SSN and 40 MPA – could be added. Those numbers, compared with the strength of the Soviet Northern Fleet, form a credible and substantial part of the initial force comparison.

The Soviet Northern Fleet forms an extension of the Soviet defence of the homeland, particularly the Kola peninsula, and also provides for the protection of the Soviet second-strike capacity. The Northern Fleet is partly hostage to those defences. Fear of horizontal escalation to the vital sea/land Kola peninsula area with its infrastructure and essential command/control facilities, would doubtless force the Soviets to regard the securing of the northern region as a vital pre-condition to crisis or war in the central region or elsewhere. Here lies an important link between the two areas. As a consequence of that pre-condition a Soviet maritime concept of defence in depth predominates. Furthermore, Soviet disarmament proposals aim first to reduce the platforms and weapons system that can reach the Soviet Union itself. Because the Soviet Union will undoubtedly always dispose of a maritime second strike capability – independent of any future disarmament measure – the northern region will always be vital to them and should not be compared to the central region. All these facts strengthen the need for a concept of a defence in depth.

Once the layered defence is secured, a certain number of Soviet SSNs could be freed from protective tasks and deployed also in the Atlantic. But the numbers of those SSNs depend on the credibility of crisis management and the success of the allied forward maritime defence. The allied aim is not to conquer lost territory either in Northern Norway or in Central Europe. The aim of the in-place forces is to maintain the present territorial integrity of the allied countries and to prevent their being undermined as a result of a deteriorating correlation of forces.

Whatever warning time these may be, and before the arrival of the US forces, the in-place European navies (and airforces) would form the main subject of a Soviet risk-assessment from the outset, and especially in the Northern Atlantic. Therefore, the conduct of operations has to be coordinated at a very early stage in order to make maximum use of the available forces of European countries in times of tension and crisis. Very early coordination of command and control, surveillance and precursor operations would be necessary. Those forces should prevent a military *fait accompli* by the Soviet Union. These aspects are not well covered in current NATO publications and procedures and therefore, for crisis management, special arrangements between European countries would be needed.

On the other hand, in war, there is no doubt that the conduct of operations will be executed within the NATO structure, and the European maritime forces should be able to facilitate the arrival and integration of US maritime forces. A major European concern is 'the significant capability of the Soviet submarine fleet to disrupt Allied shipping in the event of war' as indicated by a report on the threat by the Assembly of the Western European Union in 1987. Unless radical cuts in the Soviet submarine force occur, the submarine threat is considered the main one.

Because war must be prevented, the capability, presence and readiness of the in-place European navies, together with a forward maritime defence strategy, should be improved. Therefore, taking into account the need for a forward and flexible deployment in the Atlantic and the likely in-place contribution of US and Canadian forces, the required European maritime capability, in numbers and quality to counter the initial Soviet disposition, must form the ultimate European goal for planning. This goal should form the basis on which individual nations establish their priorities. As a first step, it is proposed that there should be an increased effort to harmonize long-term equipment planning in order to obtain *an integrated and balanced force structure*. As a consequence of budgetary constraints, this approach also creates room for role specialization. Those goals are strengthened by the lower level of eventual future maritime disarmament measures.

Furthermore, improved command and control arrangements between European countries, for early coordinated surveillance and precursor operations and in advance of a time-consuming DPC decision-making process, are needed. Command and control arrangements for crisis management need examination in order to decide how European maritime forces can first be coordinated to the best advantage and subsequently used to complement US forces. The proposal to harmonize national exercise calendars in order to create a fully coordinated exercise schedule is a step forward in this process (allied air forces have followed this practice for some years).

Such harmonization proposals are the first steps in overcoming the problems of the European allies, namely the inevitably changing character of NATO, the increasing constraints on their budgets and especially a very challenging disarmament process. Such proposals will not be easy to bring into effect but the regional context – between neighbouring countries – offers the best and most promising framework.

NOTE

1. The opinions expressed in this article are the author's own, and should not be thought necessarily to represent the official view in the Netherlands or elsewhere.

19 The navies of Europe: further discussion

The future of the navies of Western Europe will clearly be determined by the manner in which the Western alliance system develops over the next few years. Should 1992, in fact, be the start of a process of real political integration between the countries of Western Europe, then the establishment of a defence community of some sort would follow sooner or later. If it does, then at some future date there may emerge some kind of European navy. This is, of course, a distant prospect and the immediate question is whether it is worthwhile, or indeed desirable, for European sailors and their political masters consciously to work towards that goal?

Many European navalists believe that they should, for the reasons advanced by Commander van Rooyen. First, closer integration between the Europeans would provide a way of sharing burdens and ameliorating procurement problems. Defence inflation and demographic problems are going to make weapons acquisition more and more difficult anyhow. This problem is likely to be particularly acute in an atmosphere of detente and general arms reduction and when it is conceivable that the Soviet Navy might be significantly reduced, at least in numerical terms. The need to develop, discuss, analyse and effectively state the case for navies seems likely to become even more pressing in a period of change than it was in an age of cold war certainties. European navies, then, would need to work together in this common cause.

At the Conference it was argued that the NFR-90 NATO standard frigate programme was an indication of the need for collaboration in weapons procurement, of its difficulties and of its potential benefits. Eight Countries after all were collaborating in a programme designed to produce fifty-nine modern, and effective, frigates. It was seen as most exciting concept in the development of alliance commonality.

Subsequent events, though, have put the stress on its difficulties since during the course of the following year France, Italy, the United Kingdom, West Germany, the Netherlands and Spain all left the programme, effectively leaving the two non-Europeans, Canada and the United States, as the only remaining participants.[1] Among the problems associated with the NFR-90 programme were the inevitable ones of reconciling the different timings and different sizes of the various participating countries' individual construction programmes and different requirements for the ships and their weapons. For instance, the United States had always pushed for a frigate of some 5,500 tons, while most of the Europeans would originally have preferred a somewhat less capable ship 1,000 tons smaller. Some wanted a ship optimized for ASW operations, while others were more interested in AAW. Needless to say, there was also a good deal of industrial manoeuvring for a share of any resultant work and this too impeded effective collaboration.

The more sanguine pointed out that the likely failure of the NFR-90 project as a whole did not necessarily imply the same for the weapons system projects associated with it (like the NATO anti-air warfare system missile or the family of anti-air missile systems). Moreover, the mere fact that there had been effective discussion and collaboration between so many countries (at one stage ten, since both Belgium and Norway were originally involved in the scheme as well) in defining the project was in itself a real achievement in international cooperation. No part of the sixty-five strong project management team in Hamburg had been assigned to any single nation. Market forces were in any case rationalizing the European defence industry in a manner which would gradually reduce the disruptive effect of industrial competition. Finally, the undoubted success of the tripartite minehunter project demonstrated what could, and hopefully would, be done in the future, if not now.[2]

Other integration possibilities were and are discussed as well. It was pointed out, for instance, that while as yet the WEU had no real institutional structure and was really just a forum for the exchange and coordination of ideas established and put into effect at the national level, there was potential for development. The WEU might possibly develop a military dimension, perhaps building on its relative success in the Gulf. There were indications (such as the Franco-German Brigade) of growing collaboration at the operational level, and it was quite conceivable that this would take a naval form as well. Should it do so, then the command structure of NATO may have to be amended in the future. But this was some way off, since the process of integration was more likely to be messily organic than tidily imposed.

It was also worth emphasizing the point made by Commander van Rooyen that for all its faults and obvious deficiencies Western Europe did manage to produce a paper navy in the Atlantic of some considerable intrinsic strength. While of course it was true that the military effectiveness of this notional European fleet would be diminished by its multinational character and varying standards, it, none the less, compared quite well with that portion of the likely Soviet Fleet of the future that was likely to be encountered in European waters. This, of course, raised the issue of what the role of that 'European navy' should be. Discussion at the Conference, and subsequently, raised three points. First, and most familiarly, there was the prospect of enhanced European naval collaboration on the defence of Western interests in a wider world. The Gulf experience was frequently pointed out as an indication of the possibilities, but there were other less well-known examples as well, most obviously the Red Sea mine-clearance exercise of 1984.

Secondly, one consequence of the global preoccupations of the US Navy, and the United States' own concerns about stability in the rest of the world,

Table 19:1   The Navies of Europe (Extrapolated Military Balance 1989/90)

	European NATO states	European neutral states	Soviet Northern/Baltic/ Black Sea Fleets
Submarines			
SSBN	10	–	39
SSN	20	–	78
SS	113	18	106
Large surface combatants			
Carriers	7	–	2
Cruisers	5	–	26
Destroyers/Frigates	229	4	154
Smaller combatants			
Patrol Craft/MTB	225	130	❭ 275
Fast attack craft (missile)	125	54	
Minelayers	16	5	❭ 246
Minesweepers/Minehunters	254	48	
Amphibious ships			
Amphibious ships	42	–	50
Aircraft			
Combat aircraft	256	–	320
Combat helicopters	467	14	223
Maritime patrol aircraft	175	–	260

was likely to be a rather lower level of concentration on European waters than West Europeans have perhaps become accustomed to. Moreover, it was now clear that the US Navy's 600-ship programme was dead in the water and, in consequence, there might in the future be fewer US naval assets available anyway. This was not a particularly new development, and the Europeans had already demonstrated their acknowledgement of the possible need in a crisis or transition-to-war situation to hold the fort until the major units of the US Navy arrived. This requirement to contain the Soviet naval threat and to prevent it winning early positions of advantage is widely recognized among the European navies:

It must be assumed that only limited US Navy forces would be available in the Eastern Atlantic at the outbreak of hostilities. European Navies, and in particular the Royal Navy, must therefore be ready to play a leading role in initial operations.[3]

Most of the necessary initial surface and sub-surface assets would be provided by the Royal Navy, but the contribution of the other navies of North–West Europe, particularly the Dutch and Germans, would also be significant, especially in the localized waters off Northern Norway and the Baltic Approaches. Although, as an order of battle, these North European assets are by no means negligible either in quantity and quality, a comparison with the net forward air and submarine potential of the Soviet Northern and Baltic Fleets might make their containment appear an unrealistically ambitious aspiration for the Europeans to have. But the situation may not be so hopeless as might at first sight appear.

After all, it seems quite likely that the Soviet Navy may have to redefine its role to some degree in order the better to suit Moscow's new declaratory emphasis on defensive sufficiency. This could reinforce the traditional desire to emphasize the defence of the homeland above all other missions. This being so, a cautious Soviet Navy would, no doubt, be reluctant to hazard too high a proportion of its most important assets before its principal enemy, the US Navy appeared on the scene in strength. Although all Soviet military thought, the naval variety included, stresses the need for surprise attack and the gaining of positions of advantage as early in the conflict as possible, apprehension about what might happen immediately afterwards, if they lost too many assets in the process, might well deter them from taking more early risks than than they strictly need to.

Moreover, the modern technology of naval conflict is often said to be such that the navy concerned with sea denial has important advantages over the navy concerned with sea control. It is far from inconceivable that initial European efforts in defensive warfare around the Norwegian and Danish coastlines, and an active submarine campaign further to the east could prove surprisingly disruptive of any plans the Soviet Union might have. They would have most difficulty should it be necessary to reinforce Norway or Denmark, or both, against opposition, before the US Navy arrived, since this would obviously be the most demanding operational requirement the European navies might have to face.

This brings us to the third point raised by Commander van Rooyen, and that is the question of what contribution the Europeans should expect to make to NATO's concept of maritime operations, and how well the US Navy's Maritime Strategy suited their maritime interests.[4] It became clear at the Conference and afterwards that under British chairmanship, Eurolongterm, a working group of European NATO nations under the Eurogroup, is now busily elaborating a region-based study known as European Maritime Concept 2010. The idea behind this study is to produce a common baseline in maritime strategic thinking which will in turn act as a sound foundation for maritime cooperation. The studies are focused on the northern region, the Atlantic and the Mediterranean.[5]

One of the stresses of the northern region study, it seems is on the early commitment of European maritime forces (British, Dutch and West German) to the area in the event of tension and on enhanced maritime cooperation between them. In September 1989 the new Commander-in-Chief of the Royal Netherlands Navy, Admiral van Foreest, put it this way:

I expect diminishing tension in Europe which eventually will lead to the Soviets retreating behind the Urals and the Americans to the US. This means European navies will play a major role with in-place forces. The role they are best suited for is forward surveillance. That task, for which our ships are already well-equipped, would consist of keeping an eye on Soviet deployments at sea: Are there any changes in their normal behaviour which might indicate a change in their intentions? This would fit in well with the US Forward Maritime Strategy . . . In the event of a crisis, our main task would be to keep the Norwegian Sea clear for the US strike fleet.[6]

This would require the formation of a strong British–Dutch–German fleet, supplemented by French, Norwegian and Danish units together with aircraft, and quite possibly the Spanish 'Group Alfa' carrier task group as well.

This approach is said to have three advantages. First, it would make the most of constrained resources and, in political terms, cooperative efforts have considerable appeal at the moment. The issue here was the extent to which this level of cooperation was predicated on a degree of role specialization. According to some reports at least, the Dutch were said to have concluded that acceptance of a degree of role specialization was a prerequisite for the most cost-effective use of a, probably declining, number of assets, but they were encountering resistance on the part of allies reluctant to abandon individually balanced fleets. On the other hand, as Admiral van Foreest himself remarked,

I do not pursue task specialisation and I am not sounding out anyone on the matter . . . In the face of declining assets, you can do two different things: You can end up with a full-bodied man with a head and arms and legs, but who is a little smaller than he was before – one who is no longer six feet, but only five feet tall. Or you can end up with a creature with amputated limbs. I very definitely choose the first option. The main task of the Royal Netherlands Navy is ASW and you cannot fulfill this task if you have frigates, but no maritime patrol aircraft, no submarines, no helicopters. When people talk about 'task specialisation', they usually mean 'task disposal' and that is certainly of no use to the alliance.[7]

Evidently, this is an unresolved issue well worth watching.

Secondly, a more integrated and more active European naval force would provide the Europeans with an additional mechanism for exerting influence over the conduct of allied maritime forces in the event of a crisis. In this connection, it is sometimes argued that the Europeans and the Americans do not always see eye-to-eye on rules of engagement and crisis control and this could be a way of dealing with the problem.[8]

Finally, a greater European naval togetherness and political visibility would go some way to meet American sensitivities about the Europeans 'freeloading' at US expense. It would, in short, be good for the alliance, and good for NATO. For this reason alone enhanced European cooperation at sea could be thought essential for 'we in Europe must never believe [in a war] we can go it alone: without American help we would not survive'.[9]

NOTES AND REFERENCES

1. *Jane's Defence Weekly*, 23 December 1989 and 13 January 1990. See also presentation by Rear-Admiral G. Marsh on the NFR-90 programme at the Naval Futures Conference, London May 1989.

2. 'Tripartite – a model of international competition', *Naval Forces*, Special Supplement, no 1/1985.
3. *Statement on the Defence Estimates, 1985* Cmnd 8430, p. 53.
4. 'New Dutch naval chief sees "standing naval force Europe"', *Armed Forces Journal International*, September 1989.
5. See Cdr J.J.J.A. van Rooyen, 'A Dutch view of maritime strategy', *Proceedings* of the USNI, September 1988 and presentation by Jan S. Breemer, 'The Euro-Atlantic region' at a conference on The Undersea Dimension of Maritime Strategy at Dalhousie University, Halifax, NS, 23 June 1989.
6. 'New Dutch naval chief', op. cit.
7. Ibid., but see also Martijn Delaere, 'Dutch seek naval specialisation', *Jane's Defence Weekly*, 3 June 1989.
8. Delaere op. cit; New Dutch Naval Chief, op. cit.
9. 'New Dutch naval chief', op. cit.

20 Conclusions: navies in an uncertain future

There is a two-way connection between navies and the environment in which they operate. In some situations they may have an important influence on the development of that environment. On the other hand, the strategic, economic, political and social context determines the roles of navies and the resources with which they will need to be performed.

It has rarely been so difficult to predict the environment of the next decade, such is the pace of change. The scale of the problem becomes clear when the present is compared with the situation ten years ago. In 1979 people were talking about the end of detente, and the SALT process collapsed. President Carter discovered a Soviet combat brigade in Cuba. The Soviet Union invaded Afghanistan; Vietnam invaded Kampuchea; China invaded Vietnam. The Shah of Iran fell and the long hostage crisis began. Religious fanatics seized the Grand Mosque in Mecca. For the West, everything seemed to be falling apart and the future looked very dangerous.

The contrast between that situation and the present could not be greater, but the future could be different again. One of the most interesting visions of the future appeared in the summer of 1989, when the Director of the US State Department's policy planning division, Frank Fukuyama wrote an article in the journal *National Interest*. For a while it looked as though the article might have the same kind of impact as George Kennan's did four decades earlier.[1]

1989 has been a year which saw a good deal more than the fortieth anniversary of the founding of NATO. All the world's newspapers and TV channels have proclaimed that it will prove to be a momentous year in human history to an extent that few others have been. 1989 seems set to rival 1789 or perhaps 1914 as years which saw fundamental transformation in the international scene. But the essential difference was that while these two were portentous in that they ushered in long periods of catastrophic turmoil and conflict, 1989 would be different, or so Fukuyama thought. 1989 would see the beginning of the end of conflict. It would see, in effect, the final stopping place, the end of history.

His argument went like this. Just saying that the Cold War is now over is not enough. The Cold War has ended not because of a process of improved understanding or social convergence but because of the absolute triumph of the Western Idea, as exemplified by the concept of liberal democracy and the consumerist culture that this makes possible. The Western Idea is the product not just of economic efficiency but of the political and social values that underpin that efficiency. It represents the triumph of individualism (wealth, risk and capitalism) over collectivism (poverty, security and state socialism). The Western Idea is not just a passing phase but the real culmination of all human development; it is Hegel's absolute state, the ideal, the purpose and the ultimate achievement of human history.

Liberal democracy, he says, has defeated all its rivals. Fascism and communism have collapsed. Few believe in either anymore. Similarly, nationalism and religious fundamentalism are no more than the dying vestiges of an ancient past. Liberal democracy has no effective rivals and is sweeping across the globe, at different rates here and there perhaps, but with all the inevitability of the tide. But unlike the tide, it is not reversible, however much tragic events like those in China in the summer of 1989 might make us temporarily think so.

And what will be the effect of the triumph of truth, justice and the Western way? As more and more countries emerge from the mire of history, they will discover their commonality of culture and of political interest. They will be divided by less and less, united by more and more. Economic interdependence will take over from political and strategic antagonism. The world, says Frank Fukuyama in one of his less happy phrases, will be 'Common Marketized'. Power, conceptions of national interest and the military resolution of disputes will all prove obsolete. The end of history will see the end of conflict. It all might be, he says, rather boring.

Fukuyama is probably mainly right but partly wrong. There is no doubt that communism has proved a failure on a global and historic scale. No matter how hard the Soviets have tried and how much agony they have suffered since the Revolution, their economic and social progress has been much less than, say, the Italians over a comparable period. They have obviously been completely outclassed by the thrusting new states of the Pacific Rim. Gorbachev tells us in his book that what impelled him into his reforms was the sense that the Soviet Union was falling further and further behind its competitors.

Far from burying them, as the bombastic Mr Khrushchev used to promise in the 1950s, the Soviet Union was being buried by its Western rivals. Anyone visiting the Soviet Union will see its unkempt streets, parked cars with windscreen wipers safely locked inside, empty shops and a resentful population. All this is evidence that the regime is grotesquely inefficient and worse still, morally bankrupt. Interestingly, some of the military themselves were at the forefront of those who pressed for fundamental reform, because they realized how pressing the danger was that the Soviet Union might become a Third World country, or Upper Volta with rockets. Indeed, by some indicators (life expectancy, infant mortality, metalled roads per square mile) it already is![2] The Soviet Union will need, moreover, to catch up with where the West will be in fifteen or twenty years' time.

Although it is easy to focus on the failures of Soviet communism, the problem in the satellite countries of Eastern Europe was no less difficult to solve although it was different in form. On the one hand, in some countries – Hungary, Czechoslovakia, the GDR – economic inefficiency and economic deprivation were nothing like as bad as they were in the Soviet Union. The economic strains on the system were not quite so evident.

On the other hand, the Soviets at least had no one but themselves to blame; the Revolution may have gone wrong, but it was their revolution. Not so for the people of Eastern Europe, who have always thought it imposed on them in the wake of the advance of the Red Army at the end of the war. Marxism-Leninism in Eastern Europe was frailer, because it was associated with Soviet dominance. This was what brought hundreds of thousands of protesters out into the streets of the cities of Eastern Europe. In Eastern Europe the forces of change welled up from the bottom, but in the Soviet Union they were forced down from the top on a suspicious, conservative and hostile population.

Gorbachev realized that *perestroika* required *glasnost*, because the kind of economic reform the Soviet Union needed was information-led, transnational in approach and depended critically on the development of initiative in the local manager. No political reform – no economic reform; no economic reform – no future for the Soviet Union. The choice was as stark as that.

Perestroika also needed a massive, though possibly temporary, shift of state resources away from the military and into the civilian sector. Economic reconstruction depended on injection of capital, enhanced access to trained manpower and technological assistance from the West. For all these reasons, detente with the West and massive cuts in the Soviet Union's defence burden were necessary. This does much to explain Gorbachev's charm offensive, the unilateral military cut backs announced in December 1988 at the United Nations and his enthusiastic search for arms control arrangements with all his neighbours.

Of course, this is not to say that economic motives were or are the only ones driving Gorbachev's policy. Independently, Soviet leaders grew to the conclusion through the 1970s that it was by no means clear that communism would survive a nuclear holocaust any better than would capitalism. They had come to this conclusion well before Gorbachev's arrival on the scene as Mr Bhrezhnev's often ignored but seminal speech at Tula in 1977 quite clearly shows.

Over the past couple of years we have had ample opportunity to study Gorbachev's methods. They are fiendishly simple and fiendishly clever. He finds out what we want and then provides it. If we insist he leaves Afghanistan he leaves it. When we demand that he scraps his SS-20s and accepts intrusive on-sight inspection, he delivers what we asked for. We require asymmetrical cuts in conventional forces and ask that his armed forces be trained for more defensive operations, and he concedes the point. What can one do with such a man, but give in?

The results of all this were plain to see. Central Europe is no longer dominated by the military dispositions of the Cold War. Negotiations are under way that both reflect and produce a situation in Europe in which war between East and West will seem increasingly unthinkable. Indeed, it may even be that the process of fragmentation and realignment may go so far as to make talk of 'East' and 'West' essentially anachronistic. Instead, all the talk now is that both the major alliances, NATO and the Warsaw Pact, are facing either disintegration or at least fundamental change. If everything develops as expected, then both alliances will change character and become platforms for constructive dialogue with one another, for the continued management of change and, very likely, for West–West and East–East discord over who gets the benefit of what negotiated reductions.

As far as NATO is concerned, this is likely to mean a return to the original purposes of the organization. It will revert to what its architects always meant it to be before the Korean war, namely a political alliance between like-minded states rather than an integrated military system. But the process will be slow unless the pace of German reunification is much faster than most people now expect. NATO's track record in surviving previous crises, as shown by Professor Kaplan earlier, will also stand it in good stead.

Not so the Warsaw Pact, which has much less resilience because it was initially imposed upon most of its members and, therefore, lacks natural roots. Nevertheless, it is widely expected to develop in the same direction as NATO, with the countries of Eastern Europe becoming Finlandized in the manner once feared in Western Europe. The countries of Eastern Europe will probably become free, independent, doubtless of a social democratic persuasion but realistically appreciative of Soviet sensitivities and interests in their area.

As a result of this, both the superpowers are likely to pull their forces back, at least to some degree, and to reduce the extent to which they have dominated the affairs of Europe. What will this mean for the future of the American commitment to the security of Europe? We are already seeing a sense in the United States that wise statesmanship involves appreciating the limits as well as the possibilities of American power. A couple of years or so ago in Washington it was fashionable to talk at smart cocktail parties of the dangers of 'imperial overstretch' and it is certainly now a common view that the newly prosperous Europeans are not doing enough for their own defence. Put the two together, add a budgetary deficit and a determination to have 'no more taxes' especially in the age of detente, and the answer is clear: more downward pressure on defence spending, and a controlled withdrawal from Western Europe, if events make this possible. The caveat needs to be added since there are still dangers to be addressed, security interests common to both sides of the Atlantic, and a high degree of cultural, social and economic interdependence between Americans and Europeans. In a situation where there are still $125 billion American investments in Europe and $140 billion European investments in the United States how could it be otherwise? Nevertheless, we will almost certainly see the growing Europeanization of European defence.

This will also be partly a consequence and partly a cause of a chain of events proceeding independently of superpower relationships towards 1992 and the developing integration of Western Europe. Here, there are two contemporary and connected issues. The first is the extent to which the growth, or perhaps it should be the rebirth, of a European consciousness will result in a new kind of European superstate. The vision of some is that this will indeed slowly emerge and one consequence of this will be an increase in European cooperation at the military level. The emergence of European Maritime Concept 2010,[3] with its accent on Europeans thinking through common problems jointly, and the experience of cooperative European naval operations in the Gulf both suggest there may be substance in the dream.

On the other hand, there is the vision of the other sort of European who would prefer to see Europe develop into a closer association of free and independent states, where the motor for change is market forces, rather than political principle and where the accent is on improving mechanisms for the exchange of cabbages rather than developing a European identity just for the sake of it. Should this view prevail, then we should plainly not expect too much in the way of European naval integration. The recent tribulations of the NFR 90, NATO's standard frigate programme, suggests that this will be a slow rather than a fast process.

The other issue confronting an integrating Europe is who will be in and who will not. In the Western half of Europe (a cultural rather than a geographic term) countries like Austria, Norway and Sweden are likely to seek at least closer association if not full membership, and the same will apply to the struggling economies of the Eastern half, where Hungary has already signalled its intentions. The economic power of Western economies is hard to exaggerate; it attracts the citizens of the East, is vital to their economic reconstruction, but, in the last analysis, could always be resented by its recipients as a kind of Eurodollar imperialism. Nevertheless, the limits of their capacity to join in economic cooperation with the West, in some form, are much more likely to be set by our reluctance to pay the bill than theirs to present it.

Add all this together and it is clear that a shift in the global balance of force has started which will have profound consequences for the future of Europe. And this is, of course, to a considerable extent, if not exclusively, the product of the failure of the Soviet system, and the resultant decline of the Soviet threat. It is ironic that where Marx and Lenin used to prophesy that the internal contradictions of capitalism would cause its collapse, their successors have found that the prophecy has backfired. The lions have been eaten by the Christians.

So far so good. The future looks exciting, challenging and generally going our way. Conflict and the dangers of war will end just as history does. But it seems also that certain qualifications have to be entered against the argument. They do not invalidate it, but they do moderate the extent to which we should celebrate.

The first warning note was struck on NATO's fortieth birthday by Sir Geoffrey Howe when he was still Foreign Secretary. He pointed out that four months earlier Europe had in fact established a new record by beating the period of forty-three years and seven months, between January 1871 and August 1914, when it had been at peace with itself. Howe himself attributed this to the influence of NATO since the alliance had been instrumental in the creation of a new sense of stability in the affairs of Europe.

But how secure might that stability turn out to be? Is fundamental religion, for instance, really as dead as Fukuyama claims? It is hard to believe so when we see the role of fundamental Islam in worsening the situation in desperate countries like the Lebanon, Afghanistan or Iran. Religion and politics have, in their different ways, combined into a potent force in places as varied as Poland, the Ukraine and India. Even the strength of the debate about abortion in the United States attests to the residual capacity of religious and moral ideas to inflame passions and to cause conflict. No doubt it is natural that it should be so, because the religious, of all people, are aware of the imperfections of human nature. The recent history of Kampuchea shows that people still have their dark side.

Turning from the question of original sin, the survival of religious fervour might more charitably be seen as a reaction to the moral emptiness at the centre of communism and also the consumerism which Fukuyama links with liberal democracy. For such reasons, there will continue to exist competing sets of values, and radically different ways of viewing the world, quite possibly among the world's leaders. Some of them might be seen by Westerners as mischief-makers with a capacity to threaten regional or even world stability.

Nor should the continued possibility of error by policy-makers be forgotten. Mistakes will certainly be made not least because international affairs are not always conducted in an atmosphere of reason and calm. It is often far from clear what is the reasonable thing to do anyway. Given all this, it is easy to see why diplomats are often regarded as a set of people who make wise and statesmen-like decisions – but often only having tried all the alternatives first.

Much the same arguments also apply to the residual strength of nationalism, ethnic consciousness and even fascism, all of them potentially inimical to the basic concepts underpinning liberal democracy. We need only recall the fate of the Weimar Republic to appreciate that the advance towards democracy can be halted and reversed by the effect of such forces.

Nowhere are these dangers greater than they are in Eastern Europe and even inside the Soviet Union itself. In many ways, the Soviet Union is the last of the great nineteenth-century colonial empires and one that is slowly disintegrating through the evident failure of its rigorous programme of Russification and constant debilitating economic deficiencies. While it is not clear that losing the ability to exploit the unreliable geographic appendages around the edge of historic Russia is necessarily a source of weakness, the process of uncontrolled change and the revival of ancient antagonisms between subject peoples, as well as between them and their erstwhile controllers in Moscow, could so easily be a major source of instability and strife. Indeed, in the Baltic republics, Azerbaijan, Transylvania, Kosovo, Macedonia and Bessarabia, it already has. The case of the Turkish minority in newly liberalized Bulgaria is a particularly interesting case in point for it shows that giving the people more of what they want can be very unsettling if what they want is the suppression of ethnic minorities within their midst.

The results of all this could be severe. Put simply, Gorbachev could fail and perhaps fall. After all, Russia has always had a tradition of reforming Tsars who appear unexpectedly, sparkle fitfully for a few years and then fade into oblivion, leaving the basic fabric of the country essentially as it was before. Often they either go through a process of transformation themselves, or get replaced by an 'Iron Tsar' of some sort. Should Gorbachev turn out to be in this tradition, his failure could plunge us all into massive perturbations because it is hard to imagine that we could insulate ourselves against a massive breakdown of order a few hundred miles to the east. We tend to forget that Gorbachev has the limits as well as the strengths of a Soviet leader. He learnt the trade of politician in a very different situation from the one he finds himself in now and so his ideas will certainly have changed radically since 1985; by background and by definition he had little acquaintance with the genies he then started letting out of the bottle. His learning curve has been very steep. But all the talk in Moscow now is of the fact that windscreen wipers are now even more scarce than they were when he took over; the possibility that the *perestroika* process might fail can by no means be dismissed. It is because they feel that in trying to reform Leninism and reconcile it with economic efficiency President Gorbachev is attempting the impossible, that pessimists argue so strongly that trying to help him would be a waste of resources. Better to wait, perhaps until real reform on the Polish or Hungarian model is attempted in Moscow.[4]

In such a case, there is no shortage of scenarios about what would happen then. The Soviet Union might return to the *immobilisme* that characterized the Bhrezhnev years, though it is hard to see how that could be sustained for long. A glance at the curiously anachronistic pages of Slavophile journals like *Nash Sovremennik* or *Moldaya Gvardiya* will reveal the existence of a set of attitudes that make a right-wing backlash more than faintly conceivable. There has been speculation that the *Pamyat*, a bizarre organization, informed by an unholy set of autocratic, xenophobic, Slavophile and anti-Semitic values, might even take over in a coup and institute a desperate regime of Red fascism. These blood-curdling possibilities are not perhaps likely, but nor are they inconceivable for with the collapse of stability all kinds of ancient enmities and atavistic preoccupations may reappear like Dracula when the sun goes down.

But, we sometimes forget that there might also be dangers for the West if Gorbachev succeeds too much, if he turns the Soviet Union into an efficient, confident and thrusting superpower on the eastern edge of Europe. It may be unwise to assume that social and economic similarities necessarily imply good relations between converging states. The First World War, after all, was fought between countries that, while different, came from the same social, economic and political community. Imperial Germany was Britain's main trading partner in 1914; Admiral von Tirpitz, Commander-in-Chief of the Imperial German Navy spoke fluent English, read the novels of Jane Austen for relaxation, sent his children to English boarding schools and built a navy specifically designed to fight the British.

But there is a wider reason for qualifying the optimistic message of Frank Fukuyama too, namely the existence of important time differentials in the rate at which countries emerge from the mire of history. Europe may have come to the end of the road and, so far at least, without major bloodshed but other countries in different parts of the world have not. Although there have been settlements and improvements, for example in Southern Africa, concepts of liberal democracy are far from sweeping the world. The developed world may yet remain islands of relative tranquillity in a sea of troubles. The Third World is turbulent and dangerous and will certainly remain so for the next few years as major economic and social changes work their way through. Environmental degradation could also become a source of major political instability in the future.

So what conclusion should we come to about the optimism of the Fukuyama thesis?

Two competing models of evolution may perhaps have something to offer here. According to Charles Darwin, evolution was a long steady process of imperceptible adaptation to environmental change. But another view produces the interesting notion of 'punctuated equilibria'. This splits the process of change into shorter periods, each of which is a period of consolidation after some decisive environmental change or catastrophe.

Perhaps, then, we are not so much approaching the end of history as the end of a long and particularly important part of it. We may be moving into a new phase dominated by new concerns – environmental degradation, crack wars, Aids, irregular conflict. The most serious threat of the 1990s may be when the bomb or some other weapon of mass destruction falls into the hands of an agency like a terrorist group that is not geographically defined and so cannot be deterred by the prospect of catastrophic retaliation, or indeed pre-emption. The suspicion arises that after the end of history, there could be quite a lot more.

IMPLICATIONS FOR THE WORLD'S NAVIES

The implications of the present period of rapid change and an uncertain future for defence policy in general are many, varied and often obvious. Two in particular perhaps need to be picked out.

First, in the 1990s it is unlikely that we in the West will face a clear-cut adversary. Over the past forty years or so, the West has become accustomed to the relatively simple state of affairs where there was an obvious opponent, another side, and Western decision-makers tended to assume that this was normal. In fact it is not. It is really something of an aberration from the normal. Instead, the usual pattern is, as it was through most of the inter-war period and the nineteenth century where countries faced a multiplicity of vaguely defined threats. Getting used to this idea will be an uncomfortable process. The old certainties are gone or going. In the future it will be even more difficult to plan for a sensible defence and to know how much is enough.

Secondly, there is every indication, wherever one looks, of a downward pressure on defence spending, both in the East and the West, for a combination of reasons that are financial, demographic, political and environmental. Both sides are increasingly disposed to major surgery, both in the context of arms control agreements and of unilateral programmes of rationalization. In consequence, it may be that we are moving into a period where the discussion of *any* strategic or military issue will be dismissed as anachronistic, something so entirely out of keeping with the spirit of the times as to verge on special pleading by vested interests.

But what are the implications of this for navies in general, and the Royal Navy in particular? It is very early to come to any definite conclusions about this, but the auguries so far look surprisingly good from the institutional naval point of view. Both in the East and the West, there are clear indications that navies are going to be more important, mainly in relative terms admittedly, and there are a number of reasons why this might be so.

In the first place, open ocean navies are flexible, multipurpose instruments of state policy capable of catering for a wide range of contingencies. The result of this has been the adoption by naval policy-makers of the 'parametric' planning style noted earlier.[5] Sailors do not like to be tied down to one scenario since experience has shown them that this will often hinder them in others, and it is the 'others' that usually happen. Instead, they prefer to rely on the inherent flexibility of sea power to provide the necessary options.

The sailor's instinctive aversion to the specific, and its infuriating effects on the representatives of the other services is far from new. Thus Henry Stimson: 'The Navy Department . . . frequently seemed to retire from the realm of logic into a dim religious world in which Neptune was God, Mahan his prophet and the United States Navy the only true Church.'[6] Sailors therefore seem to make a virtue out of vagueness. Their point is that since navies need to be able respond to a very wide range of contingencies – wider than the other services would need to prepare for – they are interested in the creation of all round capabilities that are not specifically targeted. But this does not tend to cut much ice with those more used to, and happiest with, the relative precision that comes, for example from concentrating on the narrow requirements of defending against known forces along just 65 km of the inner German border. This has tended to make navies vulnerable in financial regimes where payment (or at least the allocation of resources) is by observable and measurable result, whether actual or anticipated.

However, in the present and future climate, the old certainties seem to be disappearing and what was a disadvantage for sailors may now be turning into a positive advantage. It is interesting to see, for example, that the US Army is endeavouring to diversify and to move away from its historic concentration on the requirements of heavy mechanized war in Central Europe. By 'going light' it can hope to cater for a wide range of low intensity conflicts around the world, which are in the nature of things impossible to predict or be specific about. In this situation, sailors – and marines – feel their inherent flexibility gives them the distinct advantage.[7]

Secondly, navies seem likely to have been strengthened *vis-à-vis* the other services in consequence of the arms control process. Unless there is a wholesale reversal of policy among the leading maritime states of the West and seemingly insoluble problems are resolved, there is unlikely to be much in the way of substantive or structural arms control at sea for the foreseeable future. There may well, of course, be some agreements in the margins of naval activity, such as constructive agreements to build a regime of confidence-building measures at sea. But these are unlikely to have a major impact on naval operations, and may indeed be regarded as essentially cosmetic by real arms controllers. Such agreements are unlikely to produce cut-backs in force levels over and above those that would have happened anyway through the increasing cost of weapons, platforms and manpower.

Moreover, it is, as we have seen, possible to argue that a CFE agreement in Central Europe may make navies more important in absolute as well as relative terms, since thinning out forces in Europe would tend to increase the need for transatlantic reinforcement and the strategic requirement to defend the shipping that would result. It is only fair to say again, however, that this argument does not impress Soviet analysts. They dismiss the Western view that they could more easily reinforce a thinned-out Central Front than the United States simply as a function of geographic proximity. On the contrary, the Soviet Union would not be able to do so, even if it wanted to, because the military equipment would not exist since CFE would require its destruction, because Soviet forces outside the CFE area have also been reduced and are needed for other commitments and because rail movement could be easily interdicted by the West. Since the Soviets cannot reinforce the Central Front, therefore, why should they be sympathetic to the Western concern for a level of naval force that would allow the United States to do so? Needless to say, these arguments are in turn rejected by Western analysts. The issue has every appearance of being a focus of much attention in the general field of maritime arms control in the future.

However, a caveat needs to be entered here, because the West can never exclude the possibility of there being in the Soviet Union some radical and dramatic unilateral cut-backs in their naval programmes. The Soviets have inflicted major surgery on their fleets before (say in the mid-1950s under Mr Khrushchev) and they may do so again. But as yet, the balance of contemporary evidence is that the Europeans will still have to contend with a significant Soviet Navy for the foreseeable future.

In some ways the situation in the last decade of the century will be analogous to what it was between Britain and Imperial Germany in the first. The seas that are essential to Soviet security are also essential to ours, simply as a function of living side by side. Moreover, given the growing global and Pacific preoccupations of the United States, the Europeans may have to be a little more self-reliant in their future naval response to this unavoidable situation than they have in the past. Detente notwithstanding, Europeans should therefore remain sensitive to the future prospects of the Soviet Navy

When considering the future for navies, there is, lastly, every indication that the concept of security will tend to widen, especially as concern spreads at the drift of events in a wider world through the 1990s. This is how NATO's Defence Planning Committee recently saw the problem:

As recent developments have underlined, improvements in East–West relations can have a positive impact on efforts to resolve regional conflicts. Notwithstanding these encouraging signs, there can be little doubt that the instability which has characterised the third world in recent years will continue to threaten local, regional and, therefore, global stability. The dynamics of underdevelopment and even the transition to more sophisticated economies and more democratic institutions on the part of developing countries will continue to be fraught with instability. Accordingly, individual Allies' contributions to global stability should become a relatively more important consideration in their share of responsibilities within the Alliance, and the Alliance as a whole will have to give greater emphasis to its role in global affairs . . . [G]rowing global interdependence suggests the impossibility of insulating North Atlantic security from events in other parts of the world.[8]

In the committee's view, the pluralistic West should deal with the general challenge of out-of-area situations by the adoption of 'differentiated approaches involving a broad gamut of policy instruments'. Navies will certainly come in handy here, and indeed have regularly done so since 1945. The flexibility and mobility of sea power suits it for such contingencies. Thus the US Navy's Under Secretary Lawrence Garrett III before Congress in March 1988:

Since 1955 the Navy has been called upon in 153 cases to respond to crises involving international conflict, tension or terrorist activity, or to protect US assets or citizens abroad . . . These actions represent roughly 80 per cent of the instances where American armed forces have been employed in this period. Sea based forces are often the *only forces available* to react *immediately* in defense of national interests.[9]

Nor has this been the exclusive preserve of the United States, for Western European navies have demonstrated their continued utility for the provision of a European response to Third World problems on many occasions through the 1980s. The Beirut operation of 1983, the Red Sea/Gulf of Suez mine-clearance operation of 1984, the Aden evacuation of 1986 and of course diverse operations in the Gulf through most of the decade are only the most obvious examples of the *genre*.

However, the Europeans will probably remain acutely sensitive to the potential political, military and economic costs of intervention in Third World contingencies. Accordingly, the use of force in such situations is most likely to be low-key and probably low-level. For that reason, fleet and ship designers will probably therefore become relatively more concerned about the requirements of low-level operations in distant places, even at the expense of hot-war tasks against a sophisticated adversary close at home. Stowage space, medical facilities, sustainability, will probably become rather more important in the future simply because they are among the characteristics that help navies to operate in such situations. In a sense, naval activity in the next decade may begin increasingly to resemble the operations of the Royal Navy in the nineteenth century. As one of its admirals said:

I don't think we ever thought very much about war with a big W. We looked on the Navy more as a World Police Force than a warlike institution. We considered that our job was to safeguard law and order throughout the world – safeguard civilisation, put out fires in shore, and act as guide, philosopher and friend to the merchant ships of all nations.

Already, there has been a growth of interest in the utility of sea power for these wider concerns.[10]

It may even be conceivable that, at some rather more distant date, Western and Soviet warships may specifically cooperate in some common purpose, wherein the naval balance is struck not by one against the other but between them and some other source of instability and threat. Should this happen, the naval dimension will help to determine, reflect and illustrate the changing political relationship between East and West in the last decade of the twentieth century.

NOTES AND REFERENCES

1. F. Fukuyama, 'The end of history', *The National Interest*, summer 1989. See also his rejoinder to criticism, 'The End of hysteria', *The Guardian*, 15 December 1989. Compare with George Kennan's (Mr X) celebrated article in *Foreign Affairs*, July 1947.
2. Sir Bryan Cartledge, 'The Soviet Union: prospects for change', *Journal* of the RUSI, Winter 1988.
3. For this see note 5 to Chapter 19.
4. See 'Z', 'The Soviets' terminal crisis: all roads lead to impasse', *International Herald Tribune*, 5 January 1990 and subsequent correspondence.
5. For this, see the criticisms of Robert Komer discussed briefly in the Introduction to this volume.
6. Quoted Kromer (1984), p. 52
7. See, for example, *JDW* interview with Major-General William Eshelmann, USMC, 27 January 1990.
8. Report by NATO's DPC, December 1988, 'Enhancing alliance collective security: shared roles, risks and responsibilities in the alliance'.
9. Quoted in Ross, cited in note 3 to Chapter 15. Emphasis in the original.
10. 'Navy chief sees terror and drugs as next targets', *Daily Telegraph*, 28 November 1989. But see also Ian Gambles, *Prospects for West European Security Co-operation*, London, IISS, Adelphi Paper 244, autumn 1989, pp 35–41. The nineteenth century Admiral in question was Vice-Admiral Humphrey Smith, quoted in A.J. Marder, *The Anatomy of British Seapower* (New York, 1940), p. 15.

Index